M & E ... for examination syllabuses all over the world. Because each Handbook covers its subject clearly and concisely books in the series form a vital part of many college, university, school and home study courses.

Handbooks contain detailed information stripped of unnecessary padding, making each title a comprehensive self-tuition course. They are amplified with numerous self-testing questions in the form of Progress Tests at the end of each chapter, each text-referenced for easy checking. Every Handbook closes with an appendix which advises on examination technique. For all these reasons, Handbooks are ideal for pre-examination revision.

The handy pocket-book size and competitive price make Handbooks the perfect choice for anyone who wants to grasp the essentials of a subject quickly and easily.

To EJS

THE M & E HANDBOOK SERIES

Practice of Banking

E P Doyle AIB AMBIM

Senior Lecturer in Banking at Liverpool Polytechnic and Principal of Liverpool School of Banking

Revised by

J E Kelly AIB ACIS

Manager, Recoveries Section, Securities and Recoveries Department, National Westminster Bank PLC

THIRD EDITION

Pitman Publishing Limited
128 Long Acre, London WC2E 9AN

A Longman Group Company

First published 1968
Reprinted 1969
Second edition 1972
Reprinted 1973, 1974, 1975, 1976, 1978, 1979
Third edition 1981
Reprinted 1981
Reprinted 1986

ISBN 0 7121 1755 5

Typeset, printed and bound in Great Britain

Preface to the First Edition

In my student days I often thought that there was a distinct need for a textbook which covered in full the Institute of Bankers' syllabus for Practice of Banking. Since taking up lecturing, I have found that this view is constantly shared by my students. I have written this HANDBOOK in order to meet this long-felt need. Additionally I hope that the HANDBOOK will also provide qualified persons in branch Security Departments with a handy reference as regards securities and general banking procedure.

Although the subject is aptly named "Practice of Banking", the actual practice has been evolved around an expansive legal framework. A knowledge of the points of law involved is essential before a banker can be in a proper position to make practical decisions.

The aim throughout the HANDBOOK has been, firstly, to outline the law concerning the subject matter and then to follow on with the practice which has resulted. I would stress that the questions in the examination are of a practical nature, but unless the law has been learned thoroughly first, it is unlikely that the question can be satisfactorily answered. An exception occurs with regard to balance sheet questions, where the law takes a more minor role.

Method of study. The student is advised to work quickly through the book in order to see the full extent of the subject matter. A second reading would require a more detailed study, and at the third reading memorisation of some of the important facts should be attempted. This examination is acknowledged as being the most comprehensive and difficult one in the Banking Diploma, and consequently it is only by working really hard and with purpose that the student can ensure success in this subject.

Progress tests. These have been included to provide the student with a continuing check as to whether he has taken in the main points of law and practice. The actual examination questions are much longer and of a practical nature, but unless the student can answer the progress tests he will be unable to apply himself to the examination questions.

Examination questions and technique. By kind permission of the Institute of Bankers actual past examination questions are detailed in Appendix V. It is suggested that the student should glance at these questions at the first reading of the book in order to familiarise himself with the type of question set. I regard Appendix IV on Examination Technique as particularly important. I suggest that this section should be studied comprehensively at the end of the first reading of the HANDBOOK.

Abbreviations. To save constant repetition in the text, the following Acts of Parliament have occasionally been quoted in abbreviated form:

BA 1914	Bankruptcy Act
BEA 1882	Bills of Exchange Act
CA 1957	Cheques Act
CA 1948	Companies Act
CA 1967	Companies Act
LCA 1925	Land Charges Act
LGA 1933	Local Government Act
LPA 1925	Law of Property Act
LP(A) A 1926	Law of Property (Amendment) Act
LRA 1925	Land Registration Act
MLA 1900	Moneylenders Act
SA 1957	Solicitors Act
TA 1925	Trustee Act

Where a section number of an Act has been quoted without actually stating the Act to which it relates, the section refers to either: (*a*) the main Act indicated in the chapter, or (*b*) the Act indicated in the appropriate section heading.
Example of (*a*). All section references in Chapters III and IV concern the Bills of Exchange Act 1882, unless otherwise indicated.
Example of (*b*). Chapter I section heading "Statute of Limitations"; section references thereunder refer to the Limitation Act 1980.

Other abbreviations used include the following:

C of A	Court of Appeal
C of P	Court of Protection
HC	High Court
H of L	House of Lords
J & S Liability	Joint and Several Liability

Acknowledgments. I should like to express my sincerest thanks to my friends, Mr H. A. S. Wilson, AIB, ACIS, of Midland Bank, and Mr M. McClay, AIB, of Martins Bank, both of whom gave me invaluable advice and help with the manuscript. To Mrs Margaret McClay I give especial thanks for typing the manuscript with exceptional efficiency. For the benefit of interested students, the address of the Liverpool school of banking is Orleans House, 45/47 Edmond street, Liverpool L3 9NG.

August 1968 EPD

Preface to the Third Edition

For many years this M & E HANDBOOK, prepared originally for the Institute of Bankers Part 2 Practice of Banking syllabus, has been a favourite textbook for students. Its size, method of approach and price have been found ideally suited to their needs for basic study and for revision purposes.

With the recent changes in the Institute of Bankers' examination structure, Practice of Banking in Stage II has become the subject of two papers. However, the syllabus for Practice of Banking Paper 1 is well covered by the HANDBOOK and much of the basic lending knowledge required by Practice of Banking Paper 2 can also be obtained from this HANDBOOK.

With its past proven success in mind, it was not incumbent on the person preparing a third edition to vary the original author's overall approach, and I have sought to maintain Mr Doyle's style. Over the last decade, however, banking practice has had to adapt to many changes imposed by Statute, case-law and an ever more complex environment. These changes are reflected throughout the text, and there is coverage of many new cases, and several pieces of legislation. Particular attention is drawn to the Companies Act 1980, the Consumer Credit Act 1974, and the decision in *Williams & Glyn's Bank* v. *Boland* (1979). These are areas where new banking procedures are still evolving, and the keen student will ensure that the knowledge obtained from this book is regularly updated and improved by what he learns in his branch.

I wish all students well, and trust that this work will go some way towards helping them obtain their qualification and a sound foundation for their future careers.

May 1981 JEK

Contents

PART FIVE: SECURITIES

PART SIX: ADVANCES TO CUSTOMERS

Table of Cases

(Where the facts are noted, the page number is in italics)

PART ONE

BANKER AND CUSTOMER RELATIONSHIP

CHAPTER I

Banker and Customer Relationship

WHAT IS A BANKER?

1. Meaning of a bank or banker. There is no specific statutory definition of a bank or banker, although from the use of the words in various old pieces of legislation and case law some help is found towards an understanding. The requirements necessitated by the Banking Act 1979, before The Bank of England will grant "recognition" and allow the word "bank" to be used, are informative.

2. Earlier partial definition by statute. The following definitions may be recalled:

(*a*) "Banking or discount company means any company which satisfies the Dept. of Trade and Industry that it ought to be so treated": Companies Act 1948, Eighth Schedule (for purposes of exemption from disclosing certain particulars regarding Profit and Loss Account and Balance Sheet). London Clearing Banks now *voluntarily* make these particulars available.

(*b*) "Any body of persons whether incorporated or not, who carry on the business of banking": Bills of Exchange Act 1882, s. 2.

(*c*) "... 'bank' means any firm, incorporated company or society, carrying on banking business and approved by the Minister": Agricultural Credits Act 1928, s. 5(7).

But what is the *business of banking*? This has required interpretation by the courts—*see* **3** below.

3. Earlier partial definition by the courts. The following dominant requirements have emerged:

(*a*) *Acceptance of money on current account and the collection of cheques* or other instruments for the customer.

(*b*) *Payment by the bank of cheques or orders drawn on them by the customer* (to the extent of moneys thereby deposited, or up to an agreed overdraft limit).

(*c*) *The business of banking* must be the *principal* activity undertaken: *Stafford* v. *Henry* (1850).

4. Avoidance of registration as moneylenders, under Moneylenders Act 1900, s. 6. Persons carrying on *bona fide* the business of banking are exempt from the requirement of registration.

In *United Dominions Trust Ltd.* v. *Kirkwood* (1966), the UDT (not having regarded themselves as moneylenders and therefore not having registered under the MLA, needed to establish their position as bankers. The Court of Appeal, by majority, decided that while not operating exactly like a conventional bank, the UDT established their position *by reputation*. The decision was reached by examining: (*a*) *Stability, soundness and probity*. (*b*) *General reputation and treatment as bankers by others*, e.g. by recognised joint-stock banks (who paid crossed cheques presented by UDT; answered their status enquiries; allowed them clearing house facilities); Inland Revenue (who allowed them to issue forms for claiming repayment of tax); etc.

5. Supervision of deposit taking institutions. Under the Banking Act 1979, supervision is exercised by the Bank of England, and three classes of such institutions are seen:

(*a*) Licensed deposit taking institutions.
(*b*) Recognised banks.
(*c*) Exempt bodies.

(*a*) *Licensed deposit taking institutions*. To obtain a licence, a deposit taking institution must satisfy the Bank of England that its business is conducted in a prudent manner and that the directors and management are fit and proper persons. Such a body must have an issued capital and reserves of at least £250,000, coupled with a good trading record. The Bank of England will take account of balance sheet ratios, liquidity, and the matching of liabilities and assets.

Upon obtaining its licence the institution may trade and accept deposits from the public, for whose protection this legislation was enacted following the secondary banking crises in the United Kingdom in the mid-1970s. A licensed deposit taking institution may not call itself a Bank.

(*b*) *Recognised banks.* A recognised bank must satisfy the Bank of England as to its standing and reputation in the financial community with special reference to the ability and competency of its management. It must have an issued capital and reserves of at least £5 million, and an adequate level of solvency for the extent of its operations.

The Bank of England will also take into account the extent of the banking service offered and the degree of specialisation. Amongst the basic services required are the acceptance of deposits, lendings, foreign exchange transactions and bill finance, investment management and corporate financial services, although the Bank of England has discretion not to insist upon the provision of all of the last named. The first two, however, are essential. Such a body is authorised to use the words "bank", "banking" and "banker".

(*c*) *Exempt bodies.* Exempted from the Banking Act are:
(*i*) The Bank of England itself.
(*ii*) National Savings Bank.
(*iii*) Trustee Savings Bank.
(*iv*) Building Societies.
(*v*) Insurance companies.
(*vi*) Local authorities.

BANKER AND CUSTOMER

6. Banker and customer. The relationship between a banker and his customers is essentially contractual. It is fundamentally the relationship of debtor (the banker) and creditor (the customer), with the roles sometimes reversed, but it also partakes of many aspects of the relationship of agent and principal. The working of the relationship is governed, therefore, by the following rules:

(*a*) *The general rules of contract,* e.g. the Rule in Clayton's Case (*see* **34** below).

(*b*) *The rules of agency*, where appropriate, e.g. where the banker acts as agent for his customer in collecting cheques on his behalf, or buying shares.

(*c*) *The rules of bailor and bailee*, where appropriate, e.g. where the banker retains his customer's deeds and documents for safe keeping.

(*d*) *Various rules of banking practice*, evolved over several centuries. These are largely recognised and enforced by the courts, and have something of the force of customary law.

7. What is a customer? There is no statutory definition of customer. The relationship arises when a person(s), society, firm or company, etc., makes an *offer* to become a customer, which the *bank* duly *accepts*. *Acceptance* may in fact be made subject to:

(*a*) *a condition precedent*, e.g. acceptance of the applicant's offer, conditionally, upon his providing satisfactory references, or

(*b*) *a condition subsequent*, e.g. agreement to open an account for the applicant immediately, but the right retained to close the account forthwith if satisfactory references are not ultimately received.

Note, however, that offer and acceptance will not always fit compactly into such well-defined limits.

8. Commencement of banker/customer relationship. The moment of time when the applicant becomes a customer is extremely important for two main reasons:

(*a*) *To claim the protection of* s. 4, Cheques Act 1957, the bank must collect cheques or other instruments ... for their *customer*: *see* **9** below.

(*b*) *The usual implied contractual obligations*, are incurred towards a customer from the moment he becomes established as such: *see* **10** below.

9. Commencement of customer relationship as regards Cheques Act 1957, s. 4 (which replaces Bills of Exchange Act 1882, s. 82):

(*a*) *Until 1914* it was generally believed that both *continuous dealings* and the *maintenance of an account* were essential factors to create a "customer" for the purpose of the section.

Thus in *G.W. Railway* v. *London & County Bank* (1901) it was held that the cashing of cheques over a long period for a person having no account deprived the defendants of the protection of the section.

(*b*) *From 1914* a change of emphasis occurred. In *Ladbroke* v. *Todd* (1914) and *Commissioners of Taxation* v. *English, Scottish & Australian Bank Ltd.* (1920) it was stipulated that "continuous dealing" was not of the essence, and that a "customer" relationship began immediately an account was opened and cheques paid in for collection.

10. Commencement of customer relationship as regards implied contractual duties. In respect of these duties it may be that the relationship is deemed to commence sooner than would be the case under **9** above.

In *Woods* v. *Martins Bank Ltd. & Anor* (1958) W was regarded as becoming a customer of the bank from the moment when, on the manager's advice, he made an investment in a private company. This occurred almost one month before W's current account was opened. It will be seen that the decision here throws some doubt on the future interpretation of "customer" for the purpose of CA 1957, s. 4.

11. Implied contract with customer. It has been said that the relationship between banker and customer is primarily that of debtor and creditor, with the roles reversed where the customer is relying on a loan from the banker: *Foley* v. *Hill* (1848). This case established the fact that the bank is not to be regarded as a trustee of the moneys deposited with it. It is not therefore accountable for the use of the moneys but only for the actual sums borrowed.

In addition to this simple relationship, there is a *complex implied contract* between a bank and its customers which imposes many duties on the bank similar to those of an ordinary agent. These duties—together with bankers' rights—are well established by banking practice and supported by many judicial decisions; the ain dutes being laid down succinctly in *oachimson* v. *Swiss Bank Corporation* (1921): *see* **12** and **13** below.

12. Duties of banker. These can be stated thus:

(*a*) *To receive his customer's money and cheques* and other instruments for collection.

(*b*) *To repay the whole or part of the money* upon presentation of the customer's written authority during banking hours at the branch where the account is held or at other banks or branches as agreed, e.g. under current cheque or credit card arrangements.

(*c*) *To give reasonable notice before closing a credit account.* This (*i*) gives the customer time to make other arrangements; and (*ii*) saves the bank from having to return cheques already issued by the customer, thereby preventing any action for damage to his reputation, *see* II, **15**.

(*d*) *To maintain secrecy in respect of his customer's account and affairs: see* **15** below.

13. Banker's right. The following rights are implied:

(*a*) *The bank has an implied right to charge a reasonable* commission for its services, and interest upon loans (either by express agreement or by banking custom). Interest is usually added to the debt half-yearly or quarterly and where definite times are agreed or fixed by custom, as, for example, when an account is being closed, or transferred to another bank. Interest should not be charged at other times without the consent of the customer.

(*b*) *When payment is required* the customer (creditor) must seek out the bank (debtor), *see* **12** above. This is a reversal of the normal common-law rule that a debtor must seek out his creditor.

(*c*) *The customer must make suitable provision* or have an agreed limit for any cheques he issues.

(*d*) *Unlike most agents, the bank has a general lien* over customers' securities in its possession, e.g. bills or cheques deposited for collection, promissory notes, coupons, etc. It appears that the lien arises over any securities deposited with the bank, unless there is an express or implied contract inconsistent with lien: *Brandao* v. *Barnett* (1846). The bank's lien differs from most others, in that it appears to confer an implied power of sale after reasonable notice. For this reason it has been described as a kind of "implied pledge": *per* Lord Campbell, *Brandao* v. *Barnett*.

NOTE: A lien does not arise in connection with articles or securities deposited: (1) by way of bailment, *i.e.* for safe custody: *see* II, **37**, or (2) for a specific purpose inconsistent with the banker's ordinary course of business, *e.g.* securities received from a customer for sale, or (3) where the item concerned does not belong to the customer; unless the bank is unaware of this and the item is negotiable.

14. Customer's duty. The customer owes a duty to the bank to exercise reasonable care in drawing his cheques, etc., so that: (*a*) fraud or forgery will not be facilitated, and (*b*) the bank will not be misled.

EXAMPLES: A fraudulent clerk made out a cheque for £2 for signature by his employer. He did not complete the amount in words and left a space between the "2" and the £ sign. After the cheque was signed, he raised the amount to £120, filled in the words and obtained payment from the employer's bank. The employer refused to be debited £120 and sued the bank for £118. HELD: The employer must suffer the loss because he had facilitated the *non-apparent* alteration: *London Joint Stock Bank* v. *MacMillan & Arthur* (1918). (2) The plaintiffs signed a cheque, drawn up by a solicitor, on which there was a gap left after the payee's name. The solicitor then fraudulently added to the payee's name "*per* Cumberbirch and Potts," and passed the cheque on after endorsement. When the fraud was discovered the plaintiffs objected to the debit in their account. HELD: The defendant (paying banker) could not debit the amount of this altered instrument to the plaintiff's account because it was avoided under the BEA 1882, s. 64; also, the plaintiffs had not been negligent in respect of the drawing up of the cheque: *Slingsby & Ors* v. *District Bank Ltd.* (1932). (NOTE: The judge added a rider that if this particular type of fraudulent alteration became prevalent, then the drawing of a line after the payee's name might well become a necessity. Some banks now intimate in their instruction booklets or cheque books issued to customers that after writing the payee's name the customer should rule through any remaining blank spaces and this *may* be helpful as a defence in any future action. In *Lumsden & Co.* v. *London Trustee Savings Bank* (1971) a plaintiff was held to be 10 per cent liable for contributory negligence where he signed a cheque as drawer on which the payee's surname was incomplete (with a blank space left in front) at the time of signing. The defence of contributory negligence available to a collecting banker was restored by the Banking Act 1979, s. 47, having been put in doubt by the provisions of s. 11(i) of the Torts (Interference with Goods) Act 1977.)

SECRECY

15. Confidential relationship. The relationship between banker and customer is confidential, and the banker must not divulge information concerning the accounts or affairs of customers without express consent. It was decided in the leading case *Tournier* v. *NP Bank Ltd.* (1924) that the duty of secrecy is not *absolute* but *qualified*, and that there are four instances when disclosure may be justified: these instances are outlined in **16–19** below.

T a customer of the NP Bank overdrew his account by a small amount without prior agreement. He contracted to repay at £1 per week but failed to keep to the arrangement whereupon the branch manager telephoned his workplace and, being unable to speak to T, discussed T's banking arrangement with his employer mentioning also that T was betting. At the end of his probationary period T lost his job. T claimed that the bank was liable for breach of secrecy and this was upheld by the C of A: *Tournier* v. *NP Bank Ltd.* (1924).

16. Disclosure under compulsion of law. This does not mean that disclosure may be made to police officers or tax inspectors, etc. *Compulsion* only exists where, for instance, a subpoena is served on the bank. Compulsory disclosure would also be necessary in the following instances:

(*a*) *Where inspectors are empowered by the Secretary of State for Trade* to investigate the affairs of a company, the company's bankers are under a duty to assist and if necessary produce any relevant books and documents: Companies Act 1948, s. 167, Companies Act 1967, s. 109.

(*b*) *Where the Director of Public Prosecutions* is investigating offences by members or officers of a company, bankers must assist: Companies Act 1948, s. 334.

(*c*) *In respect of interest credited to an account in any one tax year*, the bank, if called upon, must supply details of the customer's name, address and total interest received to the Inspector of Taxes: Income Tax Act 1952, s. 29; Taxes Management Act 1970, s. 17. Usually this is by way of an annual return covering relevant accounts in the branch. Returns from bankers may be called for under

(*i*) Income Tax Act 1952, ss. 22, 234; and

(*ii*) Finance Act 1962—in respect of capital gains.

(*d*) The provisions of the Bankers' Books Evidence Act 1879, enable the bank to produce certified copies of book entries in court instead of actual books of record. When served with a s. 7 inspection order the bank must comply. In *Barker* v. *Wilson* (1980) the Court allowed microfilm to be admissible evidence as a "banker's book", and it was said that this term included any form of permanent record made by modern technology.

17. Disclosure where there is a duty to the public, e.g. disclosure that a customer is trading with the enemy. Defence under this heading may provide greater protection to the bank against accusations of disclosure than is commonly appreciated.

EXAMPLE: A police sergeant calls at a branch investigating a local house theft, and requires to know the names and addresses of any customers who have paid in £200 in new £5 notes. There is no compulsion for disclosure in this instance but the bank would be at little risk in disclosing the information requested. (No prior consultation is necessary with, and no ultimate disclosure need be made to, the customers.) There would be no question of damaging customers' reputations, and the bank's action could be regarded as being in the interests of the public. It should be noted, however, that only the most necessary and the briefest details would be disclosed in any event and be confined strictly to police use. (NOTE: Some banks still refuse to co-operate without either (1) express authority from their customer or (2) issue of court order. The Institute of Bankers' Practice of Banking examiner (1970) supported this latter viewpoint.)

Circumstances could, however, arise where a customer should be *immediately* informed that disclosure of his name and address has been made to the police, e.g. where a police visit brings to light the fact that unauthorised use is being made of the customer's cheque book. Usually the bank would already be aware of any such unauthorised use, i.e. they would be returning cheques marked "no account" or "signature differs" as the case may be, and would have already requested the customer to whom the cheque book was issued to contact the police.

18. Disclosure in the interests of the bank, e.g. disclosing the balance of a customer's account when: (*a*) issuing a writ against him, or (*b*) calling up a guarantee for less than the full amount.

19. Disclosure with the customer's express or implied consent.

(*a*) Any *express* authority to disclose would usually be required in writing and signed, e.g. authority to divulge particulars of Z's securities to his accountant.

(*b*) *Implied* authority to disclose arises quite frequently in practice, in many cases without realisation. For instance, (*i*) where the partners of a firm expect the bank manager to contact their office manager to discuss any banking business of the firm, or (*ii*) where a bank answers another bank's enquiry concerning their customer without first obtaining authority to reply, *see* **21** below.

EXAMPLE: A bank returned a cheque for £2.75, drawn by S, for lack of funds (and also because S was issuing cheques to bookmakers). Consequently, S telephoned the bank to complain. In the course of conversation S's husband also recorded his displeasure, whereupon the manager disclosed the fact that S was betting. S ultimately sued the bank for breach of secrecy. The bank pleaded "implied consent." HELD: Disclosure was *in the interest of the bank*, and was justified here to explain the bank's attitude in respect of the returned cheque; the manager was supported in his presumption that S had voluntarily handed the telephone to her husband: *Sunderland* v. *Barclays Bank Ltd.* (1938). (NOTE: Too much reliance should not be placed upon this decision, as much would depend upon the particular circumstances involved.)

20. Practical considerations concerning disclosure.

(*a*) *Appreciation of risk involved.* The risk of inadvertent disclosure is always present, and due emphasis of the dangers involved should be impressed upon members of staff. For instance, a casual shout across the counter to X disclosing his debit balance might well coincide with the entrance into the banking hall of his chief creditor Y. Consequently, X's credit might be curtailed, whereupon an action would lie against the bank.

(*b*) *Elimination of risk:*

(*i*) *If doubt exists* as to whether disclosure would fall within the "exceptions" quoted under **16–19** above, then "express" authority to disclose should be obtained.

(*ii*) *Always check credentials* before divulging information, e.g. a customer may enquire what his balance is over the telephone. If his voice cannot be recognised, then he should be asked to confirm his address, approximate balance, last cheques issued, etc., before disclosure is made.

(*iii*) *Information handed out to an agent for delivery to a customer* should be under suitable cover. Information should be passed through agents only if: (1) the express consent of the customer has been submitted to the bank, or (2) it is obvious that implied authority exists, e.g. a company's account statement may, at the request of the secretary, be delivered to him, if no other arrangements exist.

BANKERS' OPINIONS

21. Giving of opinions concerning customers. Banks freely answer status enquiries directed to them by other banks and certain recognised trade-protection societies. This practice is extremely useful commercially. However, several interesting legal implications arise in consequence.

22. Authority to answer enquiries.

(*a*) *Express authority.* This occurs, for instance, where a customer: (*i*) gives a person his banker's name as a referee, or (*ii*) instructs his own banker to answer a specific enquiry to the enquirer's bank (or in some cases directly to the enquirer).

(*b*) *Implied authority.* Where the enquirer has not obtained the account-holder's authority to enquire, can the bank safely answer the enquiry? Most authorities regard the answer as being in the affirmative; they consider that by opening a bank account the customer impliedly accepts (*see* the Tournier Case above) the usual practice of answering all recognised enquiries.

NOTE: If the matter ever reaches the court for decision it may well be that the bank will rely on the fact that: (1) the customer knew of the usage when he opened his account and is therefore bound, or (2) there is a recognised usage which being reasonable binds the customer (almost certain to be a good defence in the case of a trading customer), or (3) a course of dealing regarding enquiries has been established between themselves and the customer.

23. Possible liability to own customer. This can arise as follows:

(*a*) *For breach of contract.* This would be for breach of duty of secrecy, i.e. either: (*i*) no authority to disclose, or (*ii*) excess disclosure.

(*b*) *For libel or slander*, i.e. if the customer considered the opinion defamatory. The probable defence would be either: (*i*) *justification* (if the opinion was true no liability could be incurred), or (*ii*) that the disclosure constituted *privileged communication*; this might be upheld provided the opinion was given honestly in good faith and without malice. (NOTE: In view of the recognised care taken by banks when framing their replies, there has been a paucity of cases under this head.)

24. Possible liability to enquirer. The enquirer may suffer loss when relying upon an opinion which has been given either fraudulently or negligently.

(*a*) *Liability for fraudulent misrepresentation.* A fraudulent representation (a most unlikely occurrence in a bank reply) is one made knowing it to be false, or recklessly, not caring whether it be true or false: *Derry* v. *Peek* (1889). It was decided in *Banbury* v. *Bank of Montreal* (1918) that liability under the Statute of Frauds Amendment Act 1828, does not attach where innocent misrepresentation occurs in giving a reply, but only where fraudulent misrepresentation occurs. Further, the Act lays down that no liability attaches in respect of a (fraudulent) representation unless it was made in writing and signed by the party to be charged. Consequently, the practice of not signing replies grew up and still prevails today, even though there is little protective benefit to be derived. In an Australian case, which could be persuasive on English courts in a similar future situation, despite a disclaimer of liability and the absence of a signature, the Court gave judgment against the bank, holding that the reply had been given fraudulently. (*Commercial Banking Co. of Sydney Ltd.* v. *R. H. Brown & Co.* (1972).)

(*b*) *Liability for negligence in tort.* Until the decision given in the Hedley Byrne Case (*see* below) it had long been established that no liability could attach where a careless or negligent reference was given, unless there was some *contractual* or *fiduciary relationship* with the enquirer.

In *Hedley Byrne & Co. Ltd.* v. *Heller & Ptners Ltd.* (1963), HB (advertising agents) enquired through their bankers, the NP Bank, as to the respectability, standing and trustworthiness in the way of business to the extent of £100,000 of Easipower Ltd. on whose behalf they were entering into advertising contracts. The following reply was sent by Heller—"For your private use and without responsibility on the part of the bank or its officials; respectably constituted company considered good for its ordinary business engagements. Your figures are larger than we are accustomed to see."

HB claimed that by relying on what they now regarded as a negligently prepared reply they had lost over £17,000 when E went into liquidation. The court decided that E's financial difficulties were known to Heller when they formulated their reply and this constituted negligence the reply being insufficiently qualified. Nevertheless Heller were under no duty imposed by law to exercise care in giving their replies the duty being only to act *honestly* in so doing. The C of A and the H of L upheld the decision. However, the latter did so on different ground: that the defendant bankers *disclaimed all responsibility at the time they gave the reference.* The H of L made it quite clear that any future claim would be upheld if no disclaimer was made and if it could be proved that a reply had been given negligently.

However, since the passing of the Unfair Contracts Act 1977, it is felt in cautious legal circles that the use of the disclaimer clause might not protect the bank unless it could meet the test of "reasonableness", i.e. the reply must have been appropriate in all the circumstances known to the bank. It must also be borne in mind that a reputable bank would not wish, in any event, to shelter behind a disclaimer where its reply, in an exceptional instance, had been given carelessly.

(*c*) *Liability for negligence in contract.* This can occur only if the bank is in contractual relationship with the enquirer, e.g. if the enquirer was a customer of the same bank.

25. Practical considerations. A banker must bear in mind the following:

(*a*) *The balance of the customer's account must never be divulged* (unless with permission).

(*b*) *The reply* must not only show up the bank's own customer in a true light but also provide the enquirer with a general answer from which he can draw his own conclusions by inference.

(*c*) *When formulating the reply the bank is under no duty to obtain information from outside sources: Parsons* v. *Barclay & Co.* (1910). Time being of the essence, the manager need only be concerned with fusing his own immediate knowledge of his customer's affairs with the current details of the account—a view confirmed in the Hedley Byrne Case (C of A) by Pearson L.J. (NOTE: The bank should never ignore relevant material facts which are in its possession at the moment of enquiry e.g. where an enquiry is received concerning an account holder who has only maintained a small private account but who is known to the bank chiefly in another capacity, say, as director and main shareholder of a limited company which is currently the subject of a petition for compulsory winding-up presented because of unpaid taxes, then the bank could not ignore this fact where it is *known to be pertinent to the situation of the enquiry*.)

(*d*) *A disclaimer should always accompany both telephoned and written replies*, e.g. "Given without responsibility on the part of the bank or its officials."

(*e*) *If there is a debenture* in favour of the bank this should always be mentioned.

(*f*) *The authenticity of all telephoned enquiries should be verified* and the reply given should be recorded carefully (including "disclaimer"). All telephoned enquiries should be confirmed in writing.

(*g*) *A direct enquiry received from a firm or member of the* public, etc., cannot be answered unless: (*i*) the bank's customer has given specific authority to make direct reply, or (*ii*) the bank is asked by the enquirer to make reply *to his bank*.

(*h*) *Records of all enquiries received should be maintained so that:* (*i*) a guide is available for the future; (*ii*) renewal enquiries are noticed; (*iii*) the extent of customers' obligations may be noted from the number and types of entries.

(*i*) *Relevance of Consumer Credit Act 1974*. The Office of Fair Trading has expressed the opinion that in answering status enquiries, banks are not subject to the provisions of s. 145(8) of the Consumer Credit Act 1974. (If they were, banks could be called upon to disclose their opinion.) Consequently all status replies now also include a mention of the fact that the bank is not a Credit Reference Agency pursuant to s. 145(8), Consumer Credit Act 1974.

STATUTE OF LIMITATIONS

26. The Limitation Act 1980. The effect of the provisions of this Act is of direct concern t the banker, particularly when an overdrawn account is allowed to remain dormant. However, most of the dangers in connection with the Act are rendered theoretical as far as bankers are concerned, because they do not allow overdrawn accounts to remain outstanding without obtaining either written acknowledgment, part payment or satisfaction through the court of the debt, within the limitation period.

27. Provisions of the Limitation Act. In relation to banking business, the main provisions of the Act are:

(*a*) *Simple contracts.* No action can be brought on a simple contract unless taken within *six years* from the date when the cause of action first arose: s. 5.

(*b*) *Specialty contracts.* As above for simple contracts, but the time limit is *twelve years*: s. 8(1). A specialty contract is one which is required to be made under seal.

(*c*) *Where a sum of money is secured by a mortgage or charge on real or personal property*, action can be brought to recover the principal sum within twelve years from the date when the cause of action first arose: s. 20(i).

NOTE: (1) Mortgages and charges on personal property include charges over stocks and shares and assignments of life policies, etc. (2) Actions on guarantees (not being personal property) extend only for six years, unless executed under seal, when the twelve-year period applies.

EXAMPLE: Where X gives an *equitable charge under hand* over land to secure the account of Y, then action against Y is barred after six years, but action on the security extends for twelve years.

28. Effect on banking accounts. *After the time limits* (quoted in **27** above) *have elapsed a debt becomes statute-barred* and the remedy of *action* is lost even though the debt still remains owing.

29. Commencement of limitation period.

(*a*) *Credit accounts.* The position is settled and the limitation period commences to run from the time when the customer has demanded repayment: *Joachimson* v. *Swiss Bank Corpn.* (1921). Thus an unclaimed balance is still reclaimable after any number of years.

(*b*) *Debit accounts.* An action to recover an overdraft or loan without a determinable repayment date is statute-barred six years after demand for repayment, although the period is extended by subsequent acknowledgment within the six years. (Limitation Act 1980, s. 6.) With a loan having a fixed repayment date, the period of six years commences from the promised date of a repayment instalment, and can be extended by acknowledgment within the six year period. Acknowledgment should be in writing or by way of payment of interest or capital. The inclusion of a debt in "sundry creditors" in a Balance Sheet was held to be sufficient acknowledgment to renew the time limit: *Jones* v. *Bellegrove Properties Ltd.* (1949).

If a debt is secured by direct security the form of charge will provide for repayment "on demand", and this puts the matter beyond doubt: *Lloyds Bank Ltd.* v. *Margolis & Ors.* (1954). Such a clause inserted in a *guarantee* is effective against the guarantor: *Bradford Old Bank* v. *Sutcliffe* (1918). (This would also apply against all depositors of collateral security.)

30. Non-recommencement of limitation period. Following the enactment of the Limitation Act 1980 a right of action, *once statute barred*, cannot be revived by subsequent acknowledgment or payment (s. 29(7)).

A payment of *part* of the interest due does not extend the period for claiming the balance then due, but a payment of interest is treated as a repayment of the principal debt, and as such will start the limitation period running again against that principal debt (s. 29(6)).

APPROPRIATION OF PAYMENTS

31. Appropriation of payments. Where there are several debts outstanding between creditor and debtor, and the debtor makes a payment which is not enough to discharge all the debts, it is important to ascertain which of the debts is to be discharged. In such cases the rules stated in **32–34** apply.

32. Appropriation by debtor.

(*a*) *The debtor has first choice, and can appropriate any payment to settle any debt*, providing he makes his appropriation at the time of payment. Appropriation may be *express or implied* from conduct. An example of the latter occurs where a debtor owes a creditor two debts, one for £*X* and the other for £*Y*, and pays the creditor £*Y*: *Marryatts* v. *White* (1817).

NOTE: (1) *It does not matter which debt is the longest outstanding*, nor that one debt is or will shortly be statute-barred; the debtor can still appropriate as he wishes. (2) *Mere undisclosed intention* to appropriate is not enough (e.g. entry in debtor's own books); there must be positive conduct indicating which debt is to be repaid.

(*b*) *Appropriation by the debtor rarely occurs when he only maintains one account*, but does occur where:

(*i*) A customer has both a loan account and a current account and pays a cheque specifically into the latter.

(*ii*) A customer pays in expressly to meet a particular cheque. If this occurs, then the banker must appropriate the payment as directed, irrespective of the state of accounts. A banker would not in practice agree to continuing appropriations of this nature, because the recording of, and compliance with, such orders would slow up the whole process of current-account operations. If a customer insisted on his right to appropriate in this manner, e.g. by sending in a credit to the bank by post to be appropriated against a particular cheque issued, then even if his account exceeded the limit the bank would be bound by the appropriation unless it could immediately contact the customer and exert pressure on him to pay the cheque in to reduce his overdraft by threatening to call up his account.

(*iii*) A customer pays in expressly to cover interest debited to his account so that he may be issued with a certificate of interest paid.

33. Appropriation by creditor. *If the debtor makes no appropriation the creditor may make any appropriation he chooses*, provided that the debtor has had a genuine opportunity of appropriating and failed to take it.

NOTE: (1) If the creditor accidentally, or in the course of mutual dealings, comes into possession of some of the debtor's money he cannot appropriate; he must give the debtor an opportunity to indicate his choice. However, in practice if a banker comes into possession of money received for a customer from a third party the banker would normally be able to claim express or implied appropriation (e.g. mandated dividends; account name and number on credit transfer; recognised usage, etc.) as a defence to any action. (2) Where a creditor is entitled to appropriate, his election is revocable until communicated to the debtor: *Simson* v. *Ingham* (1823). (3) The creditor does not have to appropriate at the instant of payment; he can make his appropriation at any time, even as late as after the commencement of proceedings by him against the debtor: *Seymour* v. *Pickett* (1905). (4) The creditor has complete freedom of choice as to what debt shall be discharged, e.g. he can make his appropriation in favour of either a simple or a specialty debt, where they compete. And he can apply the money in payment of a statute-barred debt, even though he could not have sued the debtor upon it: *Mills* v. *Fowkes* (1839).

34. The Rule in Clayton's Case (1816), i.e. Devaynes v. Noble. If neither debtor nor creditor appropriate and there is an unbroken current account, the law presumes (unless a contrary intention is shown) that (*a*) *where an account continues or goes into credit*, the first payments into the account are extinguished or reduced by the first payments out, and (*b*) *where an account continues or goes into debit*, the first payments out of the account are repaid or reduced by the first payments in. *The rule has extremely important practical usage, particularly where a debit account is concerned.*

NOTE: (1) The rule is only a presumption, and is rebuttable by clear evidence to the contrary, e.g. an express or implied appropriation (as previously outlined). (2) The rule does not apply between two accounts, but must be applied to each account separately; although an exception may occur where two accounts are treated as one: *Re E. J. Morel (1934) Ltd.* (1962). *See* XI, **62–3**. (3) If a personal-account balance consists of both trust and personal moneys, then the customer is always presumed to draw his own money first; the rule in Clayton's Case not applying. If, however, the customer draws in excess of his own money, then the rule applies between the various trusts involved. (In *Re Hallett's Estate* (1880).)

35. Example of operation of rule:

JOHN SMITH & WILLIAM BROWN—(J. & S. LIABILITY AGREED*)

Current Account Ledger

1981			*Dr.*	*Cr.*	*Balance*
Jan.	1	To balance			Dr. 500
	3	By cash		200 (A)	Dr. 300
	4	,,		300 (B)	Nil
	8	To cheque	400		Dr. 400
	10	,,	500		Dr. 900
	12	By cash		400 (C)	Dr. 500
	16	To cheque	600		Dr. 1,100

* *See* VIII, **17** for explanation.

(*a*) *The rule operates as follows.* Item A partly extinguishes the outstanding opening balance, while item B completes the extinguishment. Item C extinguishes the debit entry on the 8th. Thus the debit balance on the 12th is made up by the debit item on the 10th.

(*b*) *Using the same example*, it can be seen that if the bank receives notification of the death of Smith on the 11th and allows the account to continue, then credit entry C on the 12th extinguishes part of the liability of Smith's estate because of the operation of the rule. So although the debit balance on the 16th is £1,100, Smith's estate is only liable to the bank for £500.

(*c*) *The operation of the rule can be prevented by "stopping" the account* i.e. ruling it off, and this should always be done where it is required to preserve the bank's rights against any party to the account whose liability would otherwise be reduced or extinguished. A new account can then be opened, if necessary, for agreed future operations.

36. Rule operating to bank's detriment. Instances where the rule begins to operate to the bank's detriment if they fail to stop the account are numerous.

EXAMPLES: (1) On the death, bankruptcy or mental incapacity of a joint-account party (or partner), where the joint (or partnership) account is in debit and J. & S. liability has been agreed. *See, for instance, Royal Bank of Scotland* v. *Christie* (1841). (2) After notice has been received from a guarantor to determine his guarantee liability and the period of notice has run off. (3) On the guarantor's death or bankruptcy: *see* XII in respect of (2) and (3). (4) After notice has been received of the creation of a second mortgage where the bank are first mortgagees: *Deeley* v. *Lloyds Bank Ltd.* (1912) and *see* XIII, **28**.

37. Rule operating to bank's benefit. The rule may operate to the bank's benefit, e.g. in the following instances:

(*a*) Where a floating charge is executed by a company to secure an existing debt; providing the relevant provisions under CA, s. 322 (1), are complied with: *see* XI, **48**.

(*b*) Where a company is operating an overdrawn current account and also a separate account for wages advances then the application of Clayton's Case to the former account will have no detrimental effect on the latter account: *see* XI, **58**.

NOTE: Students must take particular note that the examples under **36** and **37** are given by way of illustration only, and the relevant sections of the HANDBOOK must be studied fully to obtain a complete picture.

SET-OFF

38. Definition. Set-off is a legal right which entitles a debtor to take into account the sum immediately owing to him by a creditor when determining the net sum due to the creditor. The debts must be: (*a*) ascertained sums, (*b*) due to and by the same parties, (*c*) in the same right, i.e. accruing due.

39. Automatic right of set-off. It is beyond doubt that a statutory or common-law right to set off all accounts arises immediately in the following instances:

(*a*) On the death, mental incapacity or bankruptcy (BA 1914, s. 31) of a customer.

(*b*) On the bankruptcy of a firm, or on the winding-up of a company. (CA 1948, s. 317.)

(*c*) On the receipt of a garnishee order.

(*d*) On receiving notice of assignment of a customer's credit balance.

(*e*) On receiving notice of a second mortgage over security charged to the bank: *Deeley* v. *Lloyds Bank Ltd.* (1912).

NOTE: In relation to (*c*), (*d*) and (*e*) the bank could not *normally* deduct a loan-account balance in arriving at the net position against their customer. Although a loan account is normally repayable "on demand", periodical repayments are usually agreed; consequently, many authorities consider that unless payment of the loan has first been demanded, or unless there is an implied agreement to the contrary—the loan account moneys are not accruing due and cannot therefore be deducted. The right to set off a loan account is usually undoubted in case (*a*) and (*b*) but note that even here where there has been an express or implied course of dealing between the parties the bank may, on the customer's bankruptcy or liquidation be required to set off accounts in certain order: *Re E. J. Morel (1934) Ltd.* (1962). *See* XI, **62–3**. The H of L decision below is very important.

EXAMPLE: The plaintiff company maintained an account with Westminster Bank which was overdrawn £11,338. The bank was displeased because the company had an account with Lloyds Bank to which they paid in all their trading credits. An agreement was reached whereby on April 4th the company transferred their Lloyds account to Westminster on the understanding that their existing £11,338 overdraft (now designated 1 account) was frozen and would in the absence of materially changed circumstances be unavailable for set-off for a period of four months. The transferred account was to be designated 2 account and was to remain in credit.

The company got into difficulties and on May 20th gave notice of a meeting of creditors to be held on June 12th to consider a resolution to wind up. On the morning of June 12th, before the meeting began, a cheque for £8,611 drawn in favour of the company was paid in for credit of their 2 account; the resolution to wind up was confirmed in the afternoon.

Thereafter the liquidator contended that the bank had no right of set-off and must relinquish the 2 account balance and prove for the 1 account balance. The High Court dismissed this plea but on appeal the C of A upheld it by majority because

(1) the May 20th notice constituted "materially changed circumstances" but the bank did not act on this by giving notice of determination, (2) the passing of the winding up resolution did not bring about the "automatic" determination of the agreement, (3) because the arrangement was so special the accounts could not be regarded as being "mutual" and therefore available for set-off in accordance with BA 1914, s. 31 as applied to companies' winding up by CA 1948, s. 317. However the H of L held in the bank's favour that (1) the dealings (even allowing for the "agreement") were mutual and (2) where *mutual dealings* take place s. 31 cannot be contracted out of by agreement or otherwise as it is *mandatory*. Thus set-off must be applied on bankruptcy or winding up: *National Westminster Bank Ltd.* v. *Halesowen Pressword and Assemblies Ltd.* (1972).

40. Right of set-off in relation to running current accounts. It appears that a banker can set off his customer's accounts (other than loan accounts) at any time, unless there is an express or implied agreement to the contrary, but great care is necessary, especially if cheques are to be dishonoured as a result.

NOTE: (1) *Where no overall overdraft limit has been agreed* a banker usually determines the net position on all his customer's accounts before deciding whether to pay or dishonour cheques. To this extent, therefore, reliance is made upon *Garnett* v. *McKewan* (1872), where the setting-off of a customer's credit balance held at one branch with a (dormant) debit balance held at another branch was considered justified, *there being no special contract or usage*: either to keep the accounts separate, or to give notice before combining accounts. This case has received further support in: *Barclays Bank* v. *Okenarhe* (1966).
(2) *Bankers do not feel bound by the statement made in Greenhalgh & Sons* v. *Union Bank of Manchester* (1924) (a case governed by its particular facts, concerning the appropriation by the bank of proceeds of certain matured bills). Here it was stipulated that when a bank agrees with its customer to open more than one account, then it cannot, without the customer's consent, move either assets or liabilities from one account to the other; the basis of the agreement being that the accounts will be kept separate.

41. Right of set-off in relation to loan accounts.

(*a*) If a customer has both a current account and a loan account these cannot be combined without giving reasonable notice, unless the customer has failed to make a loan repayment instalment on its due date.

EXAMPLE: B, a customer of long standing who maintained a secured loan account debit £600 and a current account credit £160, was suddenly informed that the balance on current account had been transferred in reduction of the loan account. As a result of this action, various cheques were subsequently dishonoured, and B succeeded in his claim for damages to the extent of £500: *Buckingham & Co.* v. *London & Midland Bank Ltd.* (1895).

(*b*) *Second mortgage created over security held for loan account.* Sir John Paget considered that even when a bank receives notice of a second mortgage created over its security a *loan account* should not, without reasonable notice, be combined with a current account.

EXAMPLE: X maintains: a loan account Dr. £3,600— secured by a mortgage over deeds of property valued at £4,600, and a current account Cr. £600. Subsequently, notice is received of the creation of a second mortgage for £1,000 over the same property. It seems that even though the mortgage may be drawn to cover the "ultimate balance owing on all accounts", the procedure to be adopted should be: (1) Stop the loan account (and in future allow only express repayments). (2) Pay all cheques presented up to £600, and thereafter see that the account is maintained in credit. (3) Apply debit interest to date (and future interest) on the loan account to the customer's current account or to a suspense account.

NOTE: Although there is no settled case law covering the above circumstance, the bank's action may in practice depend upon any pre-existing arrangements or upon any specific clauses incorporated in the security form giving them immediate rights. If the customer *knowingly* jeopardised the bank's position the bank might well attempt to rely on any protective clauses available.

42. Accounts which cannot be set off. Whether or not the accounts are "running" (as in **40**) or "determined" (as in **39**) *no* right of set-off can ever arise between the following accounts:

(*a*) *A private debit account and a trust credit account.* "Trust" includes: "Trustees of ..."; "J. Smith, Sports Club account", etc.

(*b*) *A deceased's credit account and an executor's debit account*, and vice versa.

(*c*) *A customer's credit account and a contingent liability on bills discounted*; unless a special agreement exists. (Set-off *is* allowed where bankruptcy or winding up intervenes.)

(*d*) *A solicitor's clients' account and a solicitor's overdrawn current account:* Solicitors Act 1957, s. 85(2).

43. Accounts which may be set off. These depend upon either reasonable notice, express agreement or usage—as the case demands.

(*a*) *Customer's credit account and debit account*, e.g. designated accounts; i.e. 1 a/c and 2 a/c; office account, value added tax account; deposit account, etc.

(*b*) A credit private account and a debit trust account, *where the private account holder is the sole trustee.*

(*c*) *A credit private account and a joint or partnership account where J. & S. liability has been established.*

(*d*) *A credit current account and a loan account.*

NOTE: (1) Where it is known (or should be known) that money in the customer's account is held on trust, then no right of set-off can arise; see, for example, *Barclays* v. *Quistclose Investments Ltd.* (1968). (2) Under (*b*), (*c*) and (*d*) the bank would usually only attempt to set off the accounts on the occurrence of death, bankruptcy (or winding up) or mental incapacity.

44. Express right of set-off. Subject to the conditions outlined in **38**, banker and customer are at liberty to agree an *express right of set-off*, unless the customer is holding money which to the banker's knowledge is held on trust.

(*a*) *Agreement may arise:* (*i*) *formally*, e.g. letter of set-off; clauses in security forms; written agreement, etc.; or (*ii*) *informally*, e.g. recording made in bank minutes, of agreement at interview—perhaps to charge interest on net debit position.

(*b*) *Letter of set-off.* If the bank wishes to establish its own formal position in respect of set-off, then a "letter of set-off" is obtained from the customer. This provides evidence that the bank is relying on the common-law right which already exists, and effectively protects the bank from any future objections which the customer might well raise if there was no such evidence. The letter of set-off is an agreement, under hand, signed by the customer and witnessed. *The important clauses are:*

(*i*) Continuing security covering ultimate balance(s).

(*ii*) Right to set-off (all) credit balance(s) against overdrawn account(s) at any time and without further notice.

(*iii*) Bank may return cheques drawn on appropriated account(s), even though the account(s) on which drawn is in credit.

(*c*) *If a limited company executes a letter of set-off* it should be drawn up so that it does not constitute a charge upon the credit balances of the company requiring registration under CA 1948, s. 95, as a "charge on the book debts of the company". The bank should be furnished with a copy of the board's resolution authorising the execution of the letter under the hand of a duly authorised official.

45. Present-day practice summarised. The bank usually sets off *all available accounts* (if necessary including deposit accounts) belonging to a customer to determine the net position before deciding whether or not to pay his cheques. The customer is normally informed of this practice *when he opens a second account. If no express or implied agreement has been made or created,* then if the customer draws a cheque on (say) his number 1 a/c in excess of his credit balance or agreed limit, then the bank will usually pay it, relying on a sufficient credit balance in (say) number 2 a/c. This may, however, present a problem for the future, in that the bank may have to pay all cheques drawn within the credit balance on number 2 a/c, *unless* the customer had been immediately informed of the irregular position on number 1 a/c, and had been told that the bank would pay no further cheques drawn on number 2 a/c unless covered by a net credit position or within an agreed net overdraft limit.

PROGRESS TEST 1

1. Why is the moment of commencement of the banker/customer relationship of importance? **(8–10)**

2. What implied duties does a banker owe to his customer, and vice versa? **(11–14)**

3. "The duty of secrecy is not absolute but qualified." Comment. **(15, 16–19)**

4. Outline the decision in the Hedley Byrne Case and show its effects on bankers. **(24)**

5. State why the Limitation Act rarely in practice proves detrimental to bankers. **(26)**

6. What do you understand by the Rule in Clayton's Case? Give instances where the rule can act to the bank's benefit and detriment. **(34–37)**

7. Has a banker a right of set-off without notice:

(*a*) over his customer's running current accounts? **(40)**

(*b*) over his customer's credit current account and loan account? **(41)**

8. What is the purpose of a letter of set-off? **(44)**

CHAPTER II

Banking Operations

OPENING AND CONDUCTING ACCOUNTS

1. Opening and conducting accounts. It has been mentioned previously that for the purposes of the Cheques Act 1957, s. 4. the banker/customer relationship commences as soon as the first cheque is paid in and accepted by the bank for collection. However, certain precautions must be taken by the bank both upon opening an account and during the running of it so that it can claim statutory protection against conversion and otherwise avoid actions for breach of contract, etc.

2. Opening a current account. It is unwise for a banker to open a current account until he is satisfied as to the character and standing of the applicant and knows the nature of the applicant's employment and the employer's name. These particulars are usually verified by either: (*a*) *obtaining personal introduction* from an existing customer or from another branch or bank. Such an oral introduction should be noted in the bank's records at the time, so that the bank can, if necessary, prove that it took a reference when opening the account and seek the protection of the Cheques Act 1957, s. 4 (*Marfani & Co. Ltd.* v. *Midland Bank Ltd.* (1968)), or (*b*) *taking references* (usually two—one of which should preferably be from the applicant's employer). *References are required* where personal introduction is not possible, because:

(*a*) *The general reputation of the customer can then be established.* This will help the bank to avoid opening an unsatisfactory account, thus saving any future embarrassment.

(*b*) *The protection of* CA 1957, *s.* 4 *will be more readily available*, in that the bank will have done everything necessary, when opening the account, to avoid any contention of negligence.

If the person acting as referee is unknown and unverified and the reference proves to have been a forgery the bank will usually lose the protection of the section by reason of its own negligence: *Guardians of St. John's Hampstead* v. *Barclays Bank Ltd.* (1923).

EXAMPLE: The *Savory Case* gives a perfect illustration of the high standard of care expected when a bank opens a current account. Two dishonest stockbroker's clerks in the employment of S stole bearer cheques belonging to their employers and drawn payable to third parties. These cheques were paid in at City Offices of L Bank for credit of accounts at country branches. In one case the account was in the clerk's own name and in the other in the name of the wife. As a result an action for conversion was brought against the bank. HELD: (1) *In the case of the clerk's account.* First, the bank had been negligent in not obtaining his employer's name when opening the account; the fact that it knew that the customer was a stockbroker's clerk was insufficient. Secondly, although the branch where the account was held only saw the credit notes, and did not know the name of the drawer of the cheques, all the information necessary for checking the fraud was in the hands of the *bank* and should have been made available to the *main branch.* (2) *In the case of the wife's account.* Her husband's occupation and employer's name should have been ascertained when opening the account: *Savory & Co.* v. *Lloyds Bank Ltd.* (1932). On this basis, and following the passing of the Sex Discrimination Act 1975, similar details should be obtained in respect of a wife's job and employers, when a man opens an account. Some banks, however, have decided on practical grounds not to do so and to discontinue the enquiries indicated by the Savory judgment, where a woman opens an account. Whilst there must be some risk in that decision, the approach can be justified overall, on cost grounds and for the sake of avoiding complaints and obtaining goodwill.

Since this judgment banks *always* obtain the fullest information concerning occupation when opening an account, and pass on details of third-party cheques paid in for credit of accounts at other branches. Banks are not expected to know the name of a customer's employer where changes of job occur: *Orbit Mining & Trading Co. Ltd.* v. *Westminster Bank Ltd.*, (1962). The bank's favourable decision in *Marfani & Co. Ltd.* v. *Midland Bank Ltd.* (1968) should be studied for the C of A's current exposition concerning references, opening formalities, etc.

A Pakistani named K introduced himself as E and made friends with a Pakistani restaurateur named A. Then K introduced himself to the Midland as E, stating that he was about to set up as a restaurateur and gave A's name as one of two referees. Pending receipt of the references the Midland permitted E to pay in £80 and next day a cheque for £3,000 (which K as office manager in M's employment had drawn in favour of one of M's creditors, E, and had got M to sign). Thereafter on receiving only A's reply (verbally) to the reference indicating "that he had known E *for some time* and believed that he was about to set up as a restaurateur", the Midland issued E with a cheque book and on the £3,000 cheque being specially cleared allowed E subsequently to pay away most of the balance.

Marfani sued the bank for *conversion* alleging that they had been *negligent* concerning the account opening and the cheque collection. The decision of the C of A upholding that of the H.C. was given in the bank's favour, but it was very fine.

The court accepted *normal banking practice* as the standard a prudent banker should adopt, and agreed that in the circumstances of this case *it was unnecessary, inter alia*, (1) to ask for the customer's passport to establish identity, (2) to ask for previous occupation—but compare *Savory* v. *Lloyds* above, (3) to pursue A's rather general reply or the failure to receive a second reference—as A was a good customer of the bank and had introduced several satisfactory customers, (4) to compare the handwriting on the cheque and paying-in slip as the amount was not overlarge nor was any fiduciary relationship suspected. Cairns J. added a warning that the court would be hesitant in future in supporting any standards for opening accounts which were too low. NOTE: Where a prospective customer and his referee were supposed to be professional men—recently arrived from Australia, the bank were held negligent in failing (1) to see the prospective customer's passport and (2) to enquire further where the referee failed to give his banker's name: *Lumsden & Co.* v. *London Trustee Savings Bank* (1971).

3. Opening a deposit account. References are not usually taken when a deposit account is opened, unless: (*a*) the account is opened with lodgment of a cheque, or (*b*) the lodgment of cheques is likely in the future.

If references are not obtained when opening a deposit account, are they then required if a current account is subsequently opened? This is debatable; much would depend upon the knowledge which the banker had gained of his customer during the period when the deposit account had been open; perhaps if the account had been opened recently and the bank had not had opportunity to assess the customer's integrity, references would be required. The decision is a practical one, and the likelihood of loss would need to be weighed against the risk of offending the customer and the possibility of losing his account.

4. Completing opening formalities.

(*a*) Where the account which is opened is not a sole account a *mandate covering all operations* is necessary.

(*b*) *Specimen signatures* of all parties to the account are required. (This applies as regards all the various types of account holder in the HANDBOOK.)

(*c*) It is preferable to reach agreement at the outset regarding *rates to be charged for commission and interest* rather than rely on the implied right to recover reasonable charges. (This may be difficult, e.g. where the use which is to be made of the account is not known at the outset.)

(*d*) *A cheque book should not normally be issued until any cheque paid in has been cleared* and until satisfactory replies to enquiries regarding the customer's integrity have been received. This requirement is not so much for the protection of the bank (who would always be in a position to return cheques wrongfully issued—"refer to drawer") but for the protection of the public who might be defrauded, thus perhaps lowering the image of the bank.

(*e*) *Cheque guarantee cards* should not normally be issued to a new customer until either (*i*) the bank have had time to establish that he conducts his account regularly and is a person of responsibility and integrity, or (*ii*) it can be established initially that he is undoubted, or (*iii*) he is willing to provide the bank with acceptable security beyond their total risk (i.e. on a 30-cheque book—£1,500). Regarding (*iii*) it must be noted that he may be able to gain access to further cheque books and care is necessary to prevent fraud.

5. Delegation of authority. *Where a customer wishes to authorise an agent to sign on his account*, it is preferable for the banker to obtain an express written mandate signed by his customer which precisely defines the limits of the authority. Banks have drawn up standard mandate forms with the express intention of protecting all parties, thus avoiding the need to rely on an agent's implied authority, or to require legal interpretation of a power of attorney.

The following must be noted regarding delegation of authority in connection with a bank account:

(*a*) *Delegation by the principal is not always permitted by law*, e.g. trustees may have power to delegate only in certain circumstances.

(*b*) *All parties to the account must authorise and agree before any delegation can be allowed,* e.g. where X and Y operate a joint account, both must give the authority for Z to sign cheques, etc., in place of Y.

(*c*) *An agent need not himself have contractual powers*, e.g. a minor can act as agent. (But note that it is inadvisable to allow a *bankrupt* person to act as agent, and that a *mentally incapacitated* person cannot be appointed as agent.)

(*d*) If power is given to an agent to sign on an account this does not include power to draw, accept, or endorse bills of exchange or to overdraw or charge the principal's property as security, *unless such power is fully outlined in the mandate.*

(*e*) *The mandate should stipulate that:*

(*i*) the within mentioned powers have already been given to the agent and that the mandate provides confirmation of this to the bank and *gives them authority to act on the agent's signature*;

(*ii*) the bank will continue to honour such instructions *until notice of revocation in writing is received from the principal* (or from his personal representatives).

(*f*) *A specimen of the agent's signature* is required.

(*g*) *No stamp duty is payable* on the mandate.

(*h*) *The agent must sign in such a way that he avoids personal liability*, e.g. per pro X—signed Y. The mere signature of Y without indication that he signs for a principal will not avoid his personal liability: BEA 1882, s. 26 (1).

6. Termination of banker's authority to pay. This occurs in the following circumstances:

(*a*) *Where the customer's balance or limit is insufficient* to cover the cheque.

(*b*) *Countermand of payment*. (Not permitted on cheques issued against a cheque guarantee card.)

(*c*) *Notice of customer's death/mental incapacity*. Observe that *notice* is necessary. A banker is not liable if he pays a cheque after the customer's death, provided he has no notice thereof.

(*d*) *Notice of an act of bankruptcy* committed by the customer.

Once such notice is received, the bank must not pay cheques drawn in *favour of third parties* (unless they wish to rely on the judgment in *Re Dalton* (1962), but can continue to pay cheques drawn by the customer on his credit balance in *favour of himself*; even this authority ceases on the making of a Receiving Order.

(*e*) *Notice of presentation of a Bankruptcy Petition* against the customer.

(*f*) *Making of a Receiving Order* against the customer (or of a Winding-up Order against a customer who is a company), whether the bank has notice or not.

(*g*) *Assignment* by the customer of the balance of the account.

(*h*) *Service on the bank of a Garnishee Order* attaching the balance of the customer's account; or of any injunction, etc., from the Court prohibiting transactions.

(*i*) *Notice of a defect in the presenter's title.*

(*j*) Notice that the customer or the payee is an *undischarged bankrupt*.

(*k*) *Notice of a breach of trust* by the customer in drawing cheques.

NOTE: (*b*) and (*c*) are discussed immediately below; students should refer to the relevant sections of this HANDBOOK for full discussion of the other situations.

7. Countermand of payment by the drawer. *Instructions to countermand payment* must be in writing and signed by the customer in clear and unambiguous terms. These matters are dealt with in paragraphs **8–13** below.

8. Notification of the stop must come directly into the bank's hands. Constructive notice is not sufficient:

EXAMPLE: A telegram from a drawer stopping payment of a cheque was delivered after hours into the bank's letter-box and was overlooked next morning when the box was cleared. An action ensued. HELD: The plaintiff's action failed; the cheque was not stopped. Nominal damages for negligence in failing to clear the box would probably have been awarded if claimed. *Curtice* v. *London City & Midland Bank Ltd.* (1908).

9. The correct number of the cheque must be given to the bank. Giving the wrong number will nullify the stop:

EXAMPLE: When placing a stop on a cheque which he had drawn, H inadvertently gave his banker the wrong number.

Later, being unable to contact H, the bank paid what they presumed was the duplicate; a cheque identical in all details but bearing a later number. H sued the bank for disobeying his instructions and for consequently returning other cheques for lack of funds. HELD: The bank had done everything possible to protect H and were justified in returning the cheque(s), because while two cheques can bear identical details, they cannot bear the same number: *Westminster Bank Ltd.* v. *Hilton* (1962).

10. Stops by telephone or telegraph. If the *authenticity of such a stop is undoubted*, then the cheque can be returned in the normal manner. Otherwise, if a cheque has to be returned before the authority can be verified care should be taken to avoid grounds for damage to the customer when framing the answer, e.g. "Payment countermanded by telephone/telegram, confirmation awaited", will usually suffice. In both cases written confirmation of the stop is required as soon as possible.

11. Time limits for stopping payment. The customer has the right to stop payment at any time until the banker has paid the cheque. If the banker has the right to return the cheque until the close of business, then the customer retains the right to stop it, even though it may have gone through the day's work.

NOTE: The following factors help determine the time limits for stopping payment: (1) *If a special presentation* received by post has been notified as paid the customer cannot then stop payment. (The banker must take care to pay *all* special presentations within normal banking hours.) (2) *Cheques received in local clearings* must be returned within the agreed time limits. (3) Where an open cheque is paid over the counter *it is deemed paid immediately the money is handed to the presenter*; but can be stopped until this moment: *Chambers* v. *Miller* (1862). (4) *Where a customer pays in a cheque drawn by another customer of the same branch*, the drawer can stop payment up to the close of business, unless the customer paying in the cheque has been specifically informed that the cheque is paid, e.g. if he asked when paying in whether the cheque was paid. If the drawee bank is not asked specifically and the cheque is simply taken over the counter with the credit slip for the payee's account, then the cheque is not "effectively paid" at that point and it could be stopped by the drawer later in the day. (5) *Cheques received in the general clearing are usually returned unpaid on the day of receipt.*

By agreement between the London Clearing Bankers, if a cheque has been paid inadvertently (e.g. the cancelling officer overlooked a "stop payment" authority, but the computer printout shows it on the next day) the cheque may be returned direct to the presenting bank on the next working day after receipt. Where the amount is more than £50, the presenting bank must be telephoned by not later than midday, and the details must be confirmed in writing. The written procedure alone is sufficient for cheques of a lesser amount. (6) *A bank is allowed a reasonable time after business hours to complete its business*. So that if a person who entered the bank *prior* to closing time receives payment of a cheque over the counter after closing time *the drawer cannot countermand payment before the bank's opening hour on the next business day*. *Baines* v. *National Provincial Bank Ltd.* (1927).

12. Authority to countermand payment. Persons having authority to countermand:

(*a*) Any one of several executors, trustees, partners or joint account holders *may countermand payment* of a cheque drawn by *any or all of them*. However, it is always preferable to obtain such authority signed in accordance with the account mandate.

(*b*) A *company cheque* can quite properly be countermanded under the sole authority of the secretary, but confirmation in accordance with the mandate would ultimately be required.

(*c*) A *payee* may attempt to countermand payment of the drawer's cheque if it has been lost or stolen; he should be advised to contact the drawer, who can then countermand payment himself. If it proves impossible to contact the drawer the bank are legally justified in disregarding instructions from the payee, but *depending upon the circumstances* (e.g. if the cheque is presented in the clearing bearing an endorsement then it can be returned "endorsement requires confirmation") *and standing of the payee*, they may well agree to postpone payment *in order to protect the interests of their own customer*. (As the bank are only *contractually* bound to their customer no liability can attach to the presenter for refusing payment.)

Removal of a stop must *always* be authorised by *all* the required signatories. If a bank pays a stopped cheque it has no authority to debit the customer's account, and it must reimburse him as soon as possible. There is, of course, a considerable risk to the bank should it have dishonoured other cheques because of lack of funds in the account occasioned by its own error in wrongly depleting the balance.

In *Barclays Bank Ltd.* v. *W. J. Simms Son & Cooke (Southern) and Another* (1979), the bank was allowed by the court to recover from the payee money paid away in error under mistake of fact, when they had overlooked a "stop" authority, as the payee had not changed his position in the meantime.

13. Countermand rules where the customer maintains two or more accounts.

(*a*) *If maintained at the same branch* it is well established that any stop must be noted against all accounts; otherwise loss will result if the cheque is paid: *Reade* v. *Royal Bank of Ireland Ltd.* (1922).

(*b*) *If maintained at different branches*, then the customer must notify any stop to the branch upon which drawn; if this is done and the cheque is paid at another branch, then the bank will usually have to bear the loss.

EXAMPLE: B maintained accounts at both Borough and Bromley branches of the W Bank. B was issued with a cheque book on Borough branch which was MICR encoded for computer usage. B issued a cheque, but altered Borough to Bromley, writing in the address. He did not alter the MICR coding. B then instructed Bromley to stop payment of the cheque. However, the cheque went through the *Borough* branch computer and was debited to B's account (the alteration being unnoticed).

B brought an action against the bank, and the latter contended that on the front of the cheque book was a notice "cheques in this book will be applied to the account for which they have been prepared"; B contended he had not read this notice having had many cheque books in the past. HELD: Because B had not either: (1) read the "amended" notice, or (2) signed any document indicating consent to altering the original contractual relationship—then he was not bound by the notice: *Burnett* v. *Westminster Bank Ltd.* (1965).

NOTE: (1) It had previously been the practice of banks to pay cheques with amended addresses providing the drawer's signature was undoubted. (2) *New* customers would be bound by the current notice on cheque books. (3) *Established* customers must agree to the change in procedure.

14. Death of customer.

(*a*) *Until notice of death is received* a banker is entitled to pay all cheques; cheques received after notice should be returned unpaid marked "Drawer deceased". (A note of cheques so returned should be kept.) Notice of death may be formal, e.g. production of death certificate, or *constructive*, e.g. obituary column in a newspaper.

(*b*) *Death cancels all mandates and authorities relating to the account*, e.g. those given in favour of agents. However, contracts *in the course of completion* should be completed, e.g. the bank can still debit the customer's account on an order to pay for shares, or cheque presented issued against a cheque guarantee card.

(*c*) *If the bank wish to retain the liability of the deceased in respect of a debit account* to which he is a party, then it is necessary to stop the account to prevent the operation of the Rule in Clayton's Case.

(*d*) If the deceased conducted a *sole* account no further debits (unless qualifying under (*b*) above) should be placed thereto.

(*e*) *If the deceased is one of several parties to a credit account*, then there will *usually* be no need to stop the account.

(*f*) Where notice of death is received in respect of a person who signs in a *representative capacity or as an agent*, then cheques drawn on the principal's account may still be paid, even after the agent's death, e.g. cheques drawn by a director on a company account or by a treasurer on a society's account. (The mandate should be examined to see whether any amendment is necessary.)

NOTE: For a fuller outline of the effect of death on the operation of accounts, students must refer to the sections on personal representatives, joint accounts, bailor/bailee, trustees, partnerships, companies, etc.

15. Closing an account.

(*a*) *Interpretation of reasonable notice.* Before a bank can close a *credit* account *reasonable notice* must be given to the customer to enable him to make other arrangements. What is reasonable notice is a question of fact, and may be a few days or a few months, depending upon the type of account and circumstances involved.

EXAMPLE: A bank gave a limited company customer one month's notice to close a credit account. The customer claimed that this was insufficient notice. HELD: As the customer had started a world-wide "snowball" insurance scheme which the bank had originally approved, the notice was insufficient: *Prosperity Ltd.* v. *Lloyds Bank Ltd.* (1923).

(*b*) *Closing an unsatisfactory credit account.* A customer may habitually fail to cover cheques drawn or cause the bank inconvenience in some other manner. The bank will usually request him to close his account by withdrawing the balance and returning his unused cheques.

If he refuses to co-operate formal notice in writing allowing him reasonable time to close will be sent; the notice will stipulate the final date on which lodgment of credits will be accepted, and he will be asked to withdraw the balance and return his unused cheques by this date. If the two latter conditions are not complied with the bank could send him the account balance, and any cheques drawn and dated after the notice had expired could fairly safely be returned. Similarly any monies paid in could be returned to the customer.

(*c*) *Closing an unsatisfactory debit account.* An overdraft is invariably granted on "usual banking terms", and is repayable on demand, in the absence of a specific commitment to extend the facility for a longer period: *Williams & Glyn's Bank Ltd.* v. *Barnes* (1980). The bank would have no difficulty therefore in closing an unsatisfactory account which had been operating *beyond any agreed limit*.

If the account was working within an agreed limit *which had not been reached* the bank would not arbitrarily withdraw facilities, but would certainly threaten to do so unless the unsatisfactory conduct was corrected.

Before being able to call in a loan account, it would be necessary for the bank to ensure that there has been a breach in the agreement or facility letter, e.g. default in meeting a repayment instalment or paying interest due on a certain date.

POWER OF ATTORNEY

16. Definition of power. A power of attorney is a formal authorisation in writing and signed and sealed, giving a person(s) called the *donee or attorney* power to act generally or in a manner specified on behalf of the person who gives the power, called the *donor*.

Powers of attorney are of two types: (*i*) *specific*, i.e. a power given for a specific purpose; or (*ii*) *general*, i.e. a general authority being intended to operate for a length of time.

A P/A requires stamping 50p (impressed).

17. Powers of Attorney Act 1971. This act makes new provisions in relation to powers of attorney as regards: (*a*) their execution; (*b*) proof of valid instrument; (*c*) protection of donee and third persons where the power is revoked but the fact is unknown; (*d*) delegation by trustees at any time, amending Trustee Act 1925, s. 25 (*see* VIII, **32**).

NOTE: (1) LPA 1925, ss. 123–129, formerly concerning P/As (with the exception of s. 125(2)–(3) concerning the right to receive free copy of the power), have now been repealed. (2) A P/A or copy *cannot* now be filed at the Central Office of the Supreme Court or with the Land Registry: s. 2.

18. Form of powers. A P/A is usually made out in the following form:

(*a*) *Preamble* (recitals), i.e. names, addresses, description of parties, together with brief outline of the reasons for giving the authority.
(*b*) *Various clauses* outlining the specific terms and limits.
(*c*) *Omnibus or general clause.*
(*d*) *Ratification clause.*
(*e*) *Time limits* (if any).
(*f*) *Signature and seal of donor* (and usually witnessed): s. 1 (1).
NOTE: Where the power is not executed by the donor or where the power is given by a body corporate certain other foralities apply: s. 1(2)–(3).

19. General P/A in specified form. Where a general power is set out in the form below (or in a form to a like effect) and is expressed to be made under the Act (s. 10), then it operates to confer on the donee(s) authority to do on behalf of the donor anything which he can lawfully do by an attorney.

FORM OF GENERAL POWER OF ATTORNEY FOR PURPOSES OF SECTION 10

THIS GENERAL POWER OF ATTORNEY is made this day of 19 by AB of .

I appoint CD of
[*or* CD of and
EF of jointly *or*
jointly and severally] to be my attorney[s] in accordance with section 10 of the Powers of Attorney Act 1971.

IN WITNESS etc.,

It remains to be seen whether the court would, in every case, interpret s. 10 to the benefit of a third party (e.g. the bank) where for example a donee acting under such general (unlimited) power had been allowed to overdraw the donor's banking account or charge the donor's assets as security, *see* **22** below.

NOTE: The section does *not* apply to functions which the donor has as a *trustee* or *personal representative*: s. 10(2).

20. General rules.

(*a*) *Generally, any person*(*s*) *having power to contract* may appoint an attorney.

(*b*) A *corporation* may appoint an attorney to complete *intra vires* acts, and the memorandum and articles should be consulted to ascertain any specific procedures or restrictions.

(*c*) The attorney, being an agent, *need not have contractual powers*, e.g. a minor can be appointed.

(*d*) *An attorney cannot delegate* his powers except under the clearest authority.

(*e*) A power given to two or more *trustees* jointly may be exercised by the survivor or survivors of them: Trustee Act 1925, s. 18(1); in respect of other joint appointments the death of one attorney will determine the power unless the survivor was severally appointed.

21. When used. A P/A is extremely useful when, for instance, the donor is (*a*) going abroad, or (*b*) ill or infirm, or (*c*) a trustee/personal representative wishing to delegate power for under one year.

22. Banking operations.

(*a*) *Examination of the power.* It is normal practice for the existing (or prospective) banking account of the donor to be mentioned in the power and authority given to the attorney to operate the account. Care must be exercised to see that: (*i*) the power is operated exactly within the specific objects laid down; (*ii*) the power is still in force; (*iii*) the identity of the attorney is verified; (*iv*) the power is under seal. The bank will require a certified copy of the power for its records.

(*b*) *Examination of specific clauses.* The bank must ascertain the exact nature and extent of the attorney's powers; *particularly as they will wish to be certain of binding the donor.*

A general power to collect and pay debts and transact business does not usually include authority to:

(*i*) *Collect, draw and endorse* bills of exchange.

(*ii*) *Borrow*. Specific authority to draw cheques does not imply power to overdraw the donor's account: *Jacobs* v. *Morris* (1902).

(*iii*) *Charge the donor's property* as security.

(*iv*) *Withdraw safe custody items*, ... etc.

NOTE: Before the bank would allow the attorney to proceed under (*i*) to (*iv*) above it would need to be satisfied that *specific authority exists, bearing in mind also the objects of the power.* An ambiguous power or clause would need legal interpretation.

(*c*) The probable effect of a general power under s. 10 has been mentioned in **19** above.

(*d*) *Omnibus or general clause*. A clause is usually found in every power stating that *"the attorney may do any act or deed which the donor could do"*. This does not mean literally that the donor can do anything he likes; it is only inserted to enable him to do any ancillary acts in connection with any aforementioned specific powers: *Attwood* v. *Munnings* (1827).

(*e*) *Ratification clause*. The donor may agree to ratify "whatsoever the attorney shall do or purport to do". However such a clause has been held not to extend the scope of the power: *Midland Bank Ltd.* v. *Reckitt & Ors.* (1933). The effective scope of a ratification clause must therefore be treated with reserve.

23. Revocation/determination. Revocation or determination may occur in the following ways:

(*a*) *By the donor or attorney expressly revoking the power.*

(*b*) *By operation of law*, e.g. upon the death, mental incapacity or bankruptcy of either the donor or attorney. (Bankruptcy of the attorney does *not* in fact determine the power, but makes it advisable for the donor to expressly revoke.)

(*c*) *Upon the expiry of the period* for which given.

(*d*) *Upon the completion of the purpose* for which given.

(*e*) *By implication*, e.g. (*i*) where the circumstances leading to the giving of the power are no longer applicable—"return from abroad"; (*ii*) where a new power is executed in favour of the same or another attorney; (*iii*) where, after a period of time, the donor recommences operating on his account. (Confirmation should always be obtained from the donor.)

24. Statutory protections on revocation or determination. Various protections against *revocation/determination* are available as under:

(*a*) *Protection of donee.*

(*i*) Where *unknown to the donee* the power has been revoked, e.g. by donor's death or revocation, he incurs no liability in connection with acts carried out in pursuance of the power: s. 5(1).

(*ii*) Where the power is *expressed to be irrevocable and is given to secure* either (1) a proprietary interest of the donee or (2) performance of an obligation owed to the donee, *then* if the interest or obligation remains undischarged the power is not revoked by death of donor, etc., or without the consent of the donee: s. 4. Thus, where in an equitable mortgage under seal a bank manager is appointed as attorney with power to execute a legal mortgage if the donor (i.e. borrowing customer) should default, neither the donor nor his personal representatives can revoke the power.

(*b*) *Protection of third party.*

(*i*) *In respect of all P/As*, where a third party (e.g. bank) deals with the donee not knowing that the power is revoked, e.g. by the death of the donor, the transaction remains valid: s. 5(2).

(*ii*) Where the power is *expressed to be irrevocable and given by way of security* then the third party shall be entitled when dealing to assume that the power cannot be revoked unless the donee confirms that he has already consented to the revocation: s. 5(3).

25. Misuse of power. A P/A is *strictly interpreted by the courts*, either from the express terms or by necessary implication. Even where a power is widely drawn loss can occur to a bank or other party.

EXAMPLE: (*Lord Terrington, attorney for Sir Harold Reckitt*). Lord T had an overdrawn account with M Bank, which became dissatisfied and pressed for repayment. Lord T repaid the overdraft with cheques drawn by himself as attorney, to his own favour. HELD: The bank had been negligent in not enquiring of the donor regarding the drawing of these cheques. Also, the fact that the power was widely drawn and contained a ratification clause did not excuse enquiry in these circumstances: *Midland Bank Ltd.* v. *Reckitt & Ors.* (1933).

PASSBOOKS AND STATEMENTS

26. Duty regarding passbooks and statements. There is an implied duty that when a customer opens an account the bank will furnish him with either: (*a*) a passbook in which account transactions are recorded, or (*b*) a statement of account which is delivered periodically (or as agreed) or within a reasonable time after demand. Great care is exercised when posting items to customers' accounts, but occasionally an item is posted to the wrong account, and an incorrect entry on statement/passbook may result. The liability of the banker must be discussed in this respect, as unfortunately it is well established that a customer is under *no obligation* to examine his statement/passbook.

27. Errors in customer's favour. A credit received for the account of X may inadvertently be credited to Y. Consequently, Y's statement/passbook may be dispatched before the error is discovered. In such a case the entry is *prima facie* evidence against the bank *but not conclusive*. The bank can endeavour to show that the entry was made in error. The bank cannot, however, recover its money if the customer can show that in *good faith* and relying upon *the accuracy of the entry* he had been induced to alter his position.

Over a number of years Lloyds Bank investment department credited Miss Brooks the sum of £1,108 in respect of dividends on certain second preference shares to which she was not entitled. (She was also being credited with dividends on first preference shares in the same company to which she was entitled under a trust.) On the matter coming to light the bank reclaimed the moneys as being payment under mistake of fact. However, Miss Brooks' claim that she had relied on the bank's representations and altered her position accordingly was upheld: *Lloyds Bank* v. *Brooks* (1950).

It would be difficult for a *businessman*, who would usually be expected to know his day-to-day position, to convince a court that he acted in good faith in altering his position; the same would not necessarily apply to a *private individual*, e.g. an old lady may well rely completely upon the accuracy of her bank statement/passbook. Much would depend upon the circumstances, e.g. the change in the amounts and type of entry shown on the statement/passbook.

EXAMPLE: An army officer received the wrong pay credits (overpayment) and adjusted his position accordingly. HELD: The adjustment being *bona fide*, the army paying agents could not recover: *Skyring* v. *Greenwood* (1825).

NOTE: (1) A customer cannot *knowingly* take advantage of an error: *Rhind* v. *Commercial Bank of Scotland* (1860). (2) If no *communication* of the error has been made to the customer, then he cannot plead that he was misled.

More recently, in *United Overseas Bank* v. *Jiwani* (1976), it was said that there are three conditions which must be satisfied if estoppel is to be made good:

(*a*) There must be a duty to give accurate information, which duty has failed, or there has been a misrepresentation of the balance in the account for which the bank is responsible.

(*b*) It must be proved that the inaccurate information misled the customer.

(*c*) It must be proved that because of his mistaken belief the customer changed his position in a way which now makes it inequitable for him to be called upon to repay.

28. Errors to the customer's disadvantage. These may arise in two main ways: (*a*) *mistake by the bank*, e.g. where the bank (*i*) wrongly debit a customer's account with another customer's cheque, or (*ii*) fail to credit a customer's account with an amount received for his credit, i.e. the wrong customer gets credited; or (*b*) *acting without authority*, e.g. where the bank debit a customer's account on a forged drawer's signature.

(*a*) *Possible defences available to the bank* in respect of actions arising under heading **28**(*a*)(*i*) and **28**(*b*) above—presuming that the errors have been entered on the statement/passbook and communicated to the customer.

(*i*) *If a stated or settled account could be established*, then the customer may well be estopped from denying the correctness of any entry. The courts have been reluctant to accept a stated or settled account in the absence of *express* approval by the customer.

EXAMPLE: Where a passbook was returned to the bank with *all items ticked* this was *not* held to imply agreement of the entries or an admission of settled account: *Chatterton* v. *London & County Bank* (1891). However, in *London Intercontinental Trust Ltd.* v. *Barclays Bank Ltd.* (1980), where the bank had paid cheques on one signature although two were required by the mandate, it was said that whilst the company owed no duty to the bank to examine its statements of account, since it had done so and had not advised the bank of the breach of mandate and authority, it had represented that the cheques were properly drawn. Thus it was estopped from reclaiming the funds later through its liquidator; the bank had been deprived of the opportunity of recovering the monies when it might still have been able to do so.

(*ii*) *If the bank could establish a duty by the customer to examine his statement/passbook*, then failure to spot an error or a forged cheque debited to the account *could* amount to *negligence*. But the courts have been unwilling to impose such a duty, and without a duty *negligence cannot* arise. (*See* IV, **19**, for situations where the customer is estopped from denying a forged drawer's signature, the bank being able to retain such debits to his account.)

(*b*) *Credits entered to the account of another*. If, for example, it is discovered that a credit for X has been placed to Y's account, then there is no protection available for the bank, and X must be credited immediately, irrespective of whether or not it proves possible to debit Y's account.

(*c*) *Debits wrongly entered to customer's account*. In view of the existing common-law positions expressed in **28**(*a*) above, the bank would feel obliged to credit the account of a customer who had been wrongly debited immediately the error was discovered. The correct account would then be debited (under advice and apology if the error had occurred some time ago).

29. Practical considerations.

(*a*) *Rectifying mistakes*. Where the bank makes a mistake when crediting/debiting accounts loss rarely results, because *most errors are discovered prior to communication to the customer*. In any case the customers concerned usually fail to query amending entries and quite reasonably accept the bank's apologies.

This does not lessen the need for care on the bank's part, because there is always the danger that:

(*i*) it might return cheques issued by a customer because of wrongly debiting or failing to credit him; or

(*ii*) a customer might rely on a credit balance and alter his position accordingly; or

(*iii*) it might prove impossible ultimately to debit the correct account because of the intervening death, bankruptcy or mental incapacity of the customer, etc.

NOTE: If (*i*) above occurs then an immediate apology admitting the bank's error should be made both to the customer and the payee and the latter should be asked to re-present the cheque previously dishonoured. Care must be taken to adjust any interest or commission affected by the wrong entries.

(*b*) *Adoption of further legal safeguards.* It may be mentioned that the laws of some foreign countries protect banks, in that customers *must* check their statements/passbooks and report discrepancies within a reasonable time, e.g. this applies in American law *see*, for instance, *Leather Manufacturers' National Bank* v. *Morgan* (1885).

It would possibly be of some benefit if English banks adopted a system requiring customers to confirm within a stipulated period after delivery that the statement/passbook is correct. This would raise a presumption that the account was in order, and the longer the period allowed to elapse after confirmation, the greater the chances of upholding entries on the account; unfortunately if the customer pleaded fraud (e.g. forgery of his signature) or misrepresentation (e.g. credit entries which he relied upon), then it appears that the bank's chances of success would still be slim: *Dickson* v. *Clydesdale Bank* (1937).

NOTE: In view of the foregoing, the *main safeguard* for the bank is to send out statements/passbooks *regularly* and to impress upon customers the need to check the details of account *carefully* and to notify the bank *immediately an error is discovered.*

GARNISHEE ORDERS

30. Definition and distinction of parties.

(*a*) *Definition.* A garnishee order (or summons) is an order from the court obtained by a *judgment creditor*, ordering that a debt owing or accruing due by a *third party* to the *judgment debtor* at *the time of service of the order* be paid to the judgment creditor (through the court).

(*b*) *Parties.* Where the order is *served on a bank in respect of money held in a customer's account*, then: (*i*) the bank is the third party (i.e. garnishee), (*ii*) the bank's customer is the judgment debtor, and (*iii*) the party having obtained the order (or summons) is the judgment creditor.

31. Types of order and summons issued.

(*a*) *An order will originate from either:* (*i*) the High Court (*order nisi*), or (*ii*) the County Court (*garnishee summons*). Under (*i*) the order may attach all sums owing by the bank to the customer, or may be for a limited amount plus costs. Under (*ii*) the summons will be for a limited amount plus costs.

(*b*) *Garnishee order nisi.* An order nisi is only an *interim order*, and although it attaches *immediately*, no funds should be paid over to the court until the order is made *absolute* (i.e. final), otherwise a good discharge is not obtained against the customer nor in the event of his intervening bankruptcy the trustee in bankruptcy.

(*c*) *Garnishee summons.* When a summons has been served, funds can safely be paid over to the Court in accordance with the instructions (these usually require payment within eight days of service, if further costs are to be avoided). In an exceptional case the bank could make an appearance with or without consultation with their customer.

32. Bank's procedure on receipt of order or summons. *Immediately* on receipt of an order or summons (for convenience now both called "orders") the bank should proceed as follows:

(*a*) *If the order is served on the bank's head office* (usually the case), then the branch where the account is held should be notified, a reasonable time being allowed for this.

(*b*) *If the account concerned is in debit* there is nothing to attach, and the order will usually be withdrawn by the judgment creditor's solicitor. No action need then be taken.

(*c*) *The customer should be advised of the order* and his admission to the debt should, if possible, be obtained in writing.

(*d*) *If the order is for a limited amount* (the modern practice), then the amount involved (or such amount available) plus charges can be transferred to a separate account pending payment into court. *There is no need to stop the customer's account.*

(*e*) *If the order attaches all debts owing or accruing due* to the customer *without limit*, then his account must be stopped. If the amount of the judgment debt and costs is ascertained, then the bank can *at its own discretion* allow the customer an overdraft on a new account against the surplus balance of the garnished account. It should be remembered that if the customer becomes bankrupt prior to the order nisi becoming absolute, then the whole of the balance of the garnisheed account vests in the Trustee.

NOTE: Cheques previously credited to the customer's account which have not been cleared should be transferred to a new account in the customer's name, as they are not attached.

33. Conditions for attachment of funds.

(*a*) Funds are not attachable unless *standing in the name of the stated party* (or in his trading or business name).

(*b*) *Funds must be immediately owing or accruing* due to the customer. For example, funds paid into the customer's account *subsequent* to receipt of the order are *not* attachable.

NOTE: Immediately an order is received the bank has an *automatic right of set-off* over all the customer's accounts except (it appears) over a loan account. However, a Mayor's Court has authorised a loan account to be set off against a current account. Nevertheless, to establish a firm precedent a High Court decision is necessary.

34. Funds not attached. The following are not attached:

(*a*) *Uncleared cheques previously paid into the customer's account* are *not* attached, *unless* the bank has treated them, impliedly or by agreement, as cash: *A. L. Underwood Ltd.* v. *Barclays Bank Ltd.* (1924), and *Fern* v. *Bishop Burns & Co. Ltd. and Lloyds Bank Ltd.* (1980).

(*b*) *Savings accounts*, if falling under: Administration of Justice Act 1956, s. 38(2).

(*c*) *Proceeds not yet in the bank's hands*, e.g. funds due in respect of sale of customer's stocks and shares.

(*d*) *Joint account moneys*, if the order is in a *sole* name: *Hirschorn* v. *Evans* (1938).

(*e*) *Partnership account moneys*; unless the order is made against all the partners or is in the name of the partnership.

35. Funds attached.

(*a*) *Current accounts.*

(*b*) *Deposit accounts*: Administration of Justice Act 1956, s. 38.

(*c*) *Trust accounts.*

(*d*) *Solicitors' clients' accounts*; unless specifically excluded: *Plunkett* v. *Barclays Bank Ltd.* (1936).

NOTE: Under (*c*) and (*d*) appearance would be made to have such funds released.

(*e*) *Cash* credits paid into the customer's account *prior to receipt of the order* at any branch of the bank.

(*f*) *An order in joint names* attaches a joint account in those names (and private accounts, if any).

36. Action on receipt of the order.

(*a*) *If on the day of receipt of an order:*

(*i*) *Cheques have been received in the clearing* drawn by the judgment debtor, then unless there are sufficient surplus funds (after deducting the amount of the order) the cheques should be returned unpaid, even though they may have passed through the day's work. (This would not apply if the presenting bank had already been informed that the cheques were paid.)

(*ii*) Cheques drawn by the judgment debtor *had been paid into the account of another customer*, then they should be returned unpaid unless the customer paying in the cheques was informed at that time that they were paid.

(*b*) The bank *cannot* retain funds against the contingent liability on bills discounted.

(*c*) If cheques *have to be dishonoured* in consequence of the service of an order, then the stated answer should be "refer to drawer".

BANKER AS BAILEE

37. Creation of bailor/bailee relationship. This arises where a person called the *bailee* is given control of the property of another person called the *bailor*, *for a specific purpose*, e.g. where a customer of a bank deposits valuables in safe custody with the intention that on request they will be returned to him or to his order.

38. Gratuitous bailee and bailee for reward.

(*a*) *Gratuitous bailee.* A gratuitous bailee is one who makes *no* charge and it was once said that he is "only bound to take the same care of the property entrusted to him as a reasonably prudent and careful man may fairly be expected to take of his own property of the like description": *Giblin* v. *McMullen* (1868). However, the correctness of this decision was doubted in *Port Swettenham Authority* v. *T. W. Wu & Co.* (1979), where it was said "the standard required of a gratuitous bailee, although high, may be less exacting than that required of a bailee for reward".

(*b*) *Bailee for reward*, i.e. a bailee who *makes a specific charge or receives some reward.* Consequently, he must take the highest degree of care possible and adopt all the precautions and devices that could be reasonably expected from a person in *that line of business*.

(*c*) *Category attaching to bankers*. It is controversial as to whether a banker who makes no *specific* charge for bailee services is a gratuitous bailee or bailee for reward. The question is mainly academic, and in any case banks today take the same good care of all custody items irrespective of whether they act gratuitously or not.

39. Liability attaching to bailee.

(*a*) *For conversion*, i.e. for carrying out "an unauthorised act which deprives another person of his property permanently or for an indefinite time": *Hiort* v. *Bott* (1874). Bankers may incur liability here if, for example, custody items are delivered to the wrong depositor. (*Innocence* is no defence, and it matters not whether the bailee is acting gratuitously or otherwise.)

(*b*) *For wrongful interference with goods*—formerly known as detinue. A banker would only refuse to return custody items where the identity of the person demanding delivery was doubted, or where the depositor's signature requesting delivery to a third party did not appear to be in order. (In these circumstances delay in delivery would be justified in the interests of the depositor.)

(*c*) *For theft*. If there is no negligence by the bailee, then no liability can attach. In a High Court case in 1969 the National Bank were sued for £17,000 jewellery stolen from custody. The plaintiff, Lady Moynihan, alleged negligence in the security arrangements. The National settled out of court.

(*d*) *For fraud by bailee's employees*. If caused by negligence on the bailee's part, then damages may result, e.g. if a bank allowed one employee to hold all keys to the custody safe, thereby facilitating fraud. If there is an absence of negligence no liability can attach.

> NOTE: Under both (*c*) and (*d*) above no reputable bank would attempt to avoid liability where it was obvious that their standard of care/safety fell below their usual general standards. Thus in the absence of any obvious negligence on their own part a bank would dispute liability.

40. Banker as bailee. It is the custom of bankers to receive and take care of certain items of value belonging to their customers, e.g. sealed envelopes, packets and parcels; locked boxes, documents of title, *wills* etc.

NOTE: (1) The safety of property is not guaranteed, and depositors are usually advised to insure valuable items. (2) Safe-custody procedures vary in every bank, and banking students should therefore consult their own manuals for exact details.

Certain formalities must be complied with, and these are detailed in **41–45** below.

41. Deposit of articles into custody. Where the property deposited is handed over the counter to the bank by a depositor or third party, then it is usual to require their signature to the safe-custody receipt counterfoil. In most other instances (e.g. custody received by post) there is no need for signature on the receipt counterfoil unless the article is not sufficiently identified in any covering letter.

42. Issue of receipts. Generally, a numbered receipt (signed by an authorised official) is issued for all items deposited in custody. The receipt should contain a concise description of each item deposited in order to facilitate identification.

EXAMPLES: (1) *Registered shares* ... if in favour of a holder other than the depositor, mention should be made of this fact. (2) *Loose bundles of title deeds* ... usually shown as "one bundle of deeds and documents relating to property known as ... as per signed schedule attached". (3) *Locked boxes and sealed parcels/packets* ... boxes should be securely locked and labelled (it is preferable for every box to have identification marks), and the key is retained by the customer; other parcels/packets must be securely sealed in accordance with the instructions of the accepting bank. It should be stated that the "contents are unknown to the bank" or "said to contain ...".

NOTE: If a customer complains of *damage* to property in his box, then presuming that the contents were *unknown to the bank* (or if known, required no extra-special care) they will normally *be able to refute any suggestions of negligence on their part*, provided they can show that their own valuables were carried and stored similarly. (The foregoing applies whether the bank are deemed to act gratuitously or otherwise.) In *exceptional circumstances* a bank might make a gratuitous payment to a depositor without admitting liability.

The receipt form invariably disclaims liability, although the efficacy of this practice is now in doubt, bearing in mind the possible need to satisfy the test of "reasonableness", should the Unfair Contracts Act 1977, apply.

The depositor is usually advised to insure the property himself, although insurance can be arranged for him through the bank's insurance service if one is operated and the customer so wishes.

43. Withdrawal of custody items.

(*a*) *Withdrawal of all items enumerated on one receipt.* Most banks require the custody receipt to be returned, duly discharged by the depositor in accordance with the mandate. The receipt is so worded that the depositor can request delivery to either himself or a named party.

(*b*) *Withdrawal of some items enumerated on one receipt.* The original receipt is sometimes *amended* and the depositor's discharge obtained on a separate receipt form.

(*c*) *Lost receipts.* It is normally the practice to obtain the depositor's discharge to another receipt and to ask him to return or destroy the original receipt if and when found.

44. Mandates authorising withdrawal.

(*a*) *Custody held for joint depositors.* If articles have been deposited under the names of two or more parties, then the signature of *all* is necessary to authorise release, *unless* a mandate *to deliver to less than all* has been taken.

(*b*) *Custody held for executors.* Signature of *all* executors is necessary to authorise release *unless* a mandate to deliver to less than all has been accepted: *see* VIII, **23**.

(*c*) *Custody held for trustees.* Signature of *all* trustees is necessary to authorise release, because they have limited powers of delegation *unless* the trust deed states otherwise: *see* VIII, **32**.

(*d*) *Custody held for a partnership.* May be delivered on the instructions of any one partner (in a trading partnership) or, where a mandate has been taken, in accordance therewith.

(*e*) *Custody held for a limited company.* A mandate (in conformity with the company's Articles) stipulating the parties authorised to withdraw custody is taken when the account is opened.

45. Mandate allowing agent access to articles in custody. An authority allowing *access* does *not* cover *withdrawals* by the agent; withdrawals must be permitted only if specific authority has been granted. An agent acting under authority who is permitted *access* to the depositor's custody must be kept under *surveillance* during each examination.

The agent's authority is determined on notification of death, bankruptcy or mental incapacity of the depositor.

46. Effect of death of depositor.

(*a*) *Custody held for sole depositor.* Any mandate is determined, and items should only be delivered to the deceased's representatives *after* production of probate or letters of administration. (Signatures of *all* executors/administrators are required.)

(*b*) *Custody held in joint names.* The mandate is determined, and although *joint* property vests in the survivor(s), it is the *usual practice* of banks to require the receipt of *both* the survivor(s) *and* executors/administrators (after production of probate or letters of administration). Legally the bank is permitted to release *joint* property to the survivor(s), e.g. bearer securities, stocks and shares in joint names, deeds of property conveyed jointly.

Property which is not held jointly (e.g. items held in common) should *not* be released to the survivor(s) alone, e.g. jewellery, locked boxes, sealed parcels and packets, chattels, etc.

(*c*) *Delivery of will in custody.* Under both (*a*) and (*b*) above, if a will belonging to the deceased is held in custody, it may be delivered to the named executors against their receipt, provided they can identify themselves satisfactorily, or it may more safely be sent upon their signed instructions to a solicitor against his receipt.

(*d*) *Locked boxes and sealed parcels/packets.* With the authority (and often in the presence) of the deceased's relatives (if any), these can be opened by the bank's officials in order to discover whether there is a will and to enable all the contents to be scheduled for preparation of the Inland Revenue affidavit for capital transfer tax purposes. (Sometimes for this latter purpose the contents are forwarded on loan to the acting solicitor against his receipt, or alternatively, he may inspect them at the branch.) If there are no known surviving relatives to give authority to open the box, then it is usual for it to be opened in the presence of two responsible bank officials. A signed schedule of the contents is then replaced in the box and it is relocked until further action is necessary.

47. Effect of bankruptcy of depositor.

(*a*) *Custody held for sole depositor.* After the making of a *receiving order* against the depositor the title to his custody vests in the trustee in bankruptcy.

If the bank delivers custody items to the depositor *after* notice of an act of bankruptcy but before the making of the receiving order *it is protected* by Bankruptcy Act 1914, s. 46. *No protection is available* if delivery occurs either: (*i*) after *notice* of the presentation of a petition, *or* (*ii*) after the making of a receiving order.

(*b*) *Custody held for joint depositors.* On the bankruptcy of *one party* the mandate is determined and *no* custody items must be released *except* on the instructions of both the solvent party *and* the trustee in bankruptcy (or Official Receiver).

(*c*) *Custody held for a partnership.* On the bankruptcy of one partner the mandate is determined, but the solvent partners can deal effectively with partnership custody, usually under new mandate.

48. Effect of mental incapacity of depositor.

(*a*) *Custody held for sole depositor.* No withdrawals should be allowed except on the instructions of the receiver (or other official) under authority of the Court of Protection.

(*b*) *Custody held for joint depositors.* On the incapacity of *one party* the mandate is determined and the custody items should only be released on the instructions of both the sane party *and* the receiver (or other official), under authority of the Court of Protection.

(*c*) *Custody held for a partnership.* On the mental incapacity of one partner the mandate is determined. The bank should proceed as in **47**(*c*) above. The sane partners will need to account to the receiver appointed for the incapacitated partner.

ADVICE ON INVESTMENTS

49. Specialist investment services. Many banks now advertise their "specialist investment services", whereby they manage customers' investments for a specified (scale) charge. The service arranged may include: (*a*) *periodically advising changes* in a customer's portfolio, or (*b*) *initiating portfolio changes* on a customer's behalf, and (*c*) dealing with all notices and dividends, etc. It is a particularly useful service for customers who have insufficient time or expert knowledge to attend to their investment affairs.

The bank are contractually bound for any breach of contract. This would include liability for negligence, e.g. failing to take the normal care in the selection of shares for purchase.

50. Liability for general investment advice. The practice of advising customers and others on the general merits of investing, e.g. in National Savings Certificates, gilt-edged securities and equities, etc., appears to be free from danger. However, it is the duty of bankers when providing such information to endeavour to supply the correct facts, e.g. in respect of prevailing interest rates and maximum permitted holdings of NSCs, etc.

51. Liability for specific investment advice. The general rule followed by bankers is to refrain from giving their own advice on specific investment problems, but to pass on advice provided by their stockbrokers. If specific advice is given by a bank official, then the bank may well incur liability if any negligence is proved (*see* (*b*) below).

(*a*) *Procedure to be adopted in cases where customer requires specific investment advice:*

(*i*) The customer will need to provide the bank with as much information as possible regarding his financial position and existing portfolio, etc. He will be asked to state his main aim, e.g. safety of capital; high income; capital appreciation; etc.

(*ii*) The bank will pass on the above *details* to one or more of their authorised stockbrokers (without disclosing the customer's name unless authorised) so that they can consider the customer's requirements and position, and advise.

(*iii*) The *recommendations* provided by the brokers are copied and forwarded to the customer, together with *an express disclaimer of liability on the bank's part*. (No charge is made for this service, by either brokers or bankers.)

NOTE: (1) If the foregoing procedure is followed it is likely that the only duty necessary on the bank's part is to *choose their stockbrokers with care*, and to pass on the recommendations in *clear and unambiguous terms*. (2) If the customer requires recommendation on a *specific shareholding* the procedure is still as outlined under (*a*) (*ii*)–(*iii*) above.

(*b*) *Danger of liability when a bank official provides specific advice.* It had long been laid down that it was not part of the ordinary business of a banker to give investment advice, but that occasions might arise when advice should be given by a banker as such: *Banbury* v. *Bank of Montreal* (1918).

However, this position has changed, and it has been established recently that where an authorised (or apparently authorised) official gives specific investment advice to a customer (and probably to a non-customer), then a duty of care is owed when giving it: *Woods* v. *Martins Bank Ltd. & Anor*. (1958).

A manager of M Bank advised a customer (W) to invest funds in a private company which maintained an account at the same branch. W did so and lost money. HELD: The bank were *vicariously liable* for the *negligent* advice which had been given by their manager. The bank's main plea, that it was no part of its business to give investment advice, was dismissed after examination had been made of its advertisements; one of which specifically stated, "if you want help or advice about investments our managers will gladly obtain for you advice from the best available sources": *Woods* v. *Martins Bank Ltd.* (1958).

52. Purchases and sales of investments. When a bank *buys or sells shares on its customers' behalf* it is acting as an agent. (A share of the commission charged by the broker is returned to the bank—so that in effect the bank receives payment.) The bank must use due skill and care in the execution of all such orders and is liable for its mistakes. (It is also probably liable for any mistakes made by the broker.)

The general procedure to be adopted on receipt of a purchase or sale order is as follows:

(*a*) *The customer must complete the printed sale/purchase form* which is used. *Full written instructions are required*, e.g. in respect of a purchase—details of stock; amount to be bought; price to be paid (or at "best"); name into which stock is to be placed; customer's signature.

(*b*) *Orders to sell* must be signed by all registered holders, or in the case of bearer securities by all those holding themselves out to be the owners. (Share certificates must usually be produced if available.)

(*c*) *Order to purchase*: check that the customer has or will have the funds to cover (speculating?) and take his cheque or more usually his authority to debit his account. (The latter is usually incorporated in the purchase order form which he must sign.)

(*d*) *Buying and selling limits* must be strictly adhered to. If it proves impossible to deal at these limits periodical confirmation of the order is usually required. (Unrealistic limits should be discouraged.)

(*e*) Brokers' contract notes and transfer forms on sale *should be delivered without delay*.

(*f*) If the bank *telephones the order directly to a broker* a foolproof system is necessary to prevent the same order being executed twice.

STANDING ORDERS

53. Definition. Standing instructions given by customers to their bankers to make regular periodic payments from their accounts to the accounts of customers of the same or other banks.

Each order must be signed by the customer in accordance with the account mandate.

54. Advantages of standing orders. They are particularly useful for payment of recurring items, e.g. insurance premiums, subscriptions, hire purchase and mortgage repayments, etc. The customer is provided with a record of payment and a cheap transmission service; also the onus of making payment at the correct time rests with the bank.

55. Practical considerations.

(*a*) *If the customer's account balance is insufficient to allow payment to be made on the correct date*, then the bank incur no liability for failing to obey the order.

NOTE: Although there is no duty upon the bank to do so, it is usual practice to hold out unpaid orders and to examine the customer's account periodically to see whether late payment can be effected.

(*b*) *If instruction is received direct from a payee to cancel an order it must be disregarded* unless confirmed by the customer. If immediate confirmation cannot be obtained, then the bank should continue to make payment to the payee in conformity with its customer's mandate. The payee should be advised to contact the customer direct so that cancellation of the order can be effected. (The order can only be cancelled on the written instructions of the customer.)

If the payee refuses to accept a payment (e.g. if the order requires the issue of a monthly cheque for rent) the bank should continue to endeavour to make each payment which falls due, notifying each refusal of acceptance to their customer.

(*c*) *If a bank receives an enquiry from a payee asking why a standing order has not been paid* he should be advised to contact the customer direct to ascertain the reason. By dealing in this manner the bank avoid any liability for breach of secrecy.

DIRECT DEBITS

56. Comparison. Similar in objective to the standing order system, the direct debit varies in that the beneficiary's bank originates the entries, and debits are received through the clearing system or by computer electronic entries. The payer must of course have given a written authority to his banker legally enabling him to debit the account. Before the beneficiary may operate this system he is required to enter into an indemnity addressed to all the clearing and Scottish banks, safeguarding them against all actions or claims which might arise.

57. Dishonour. If there are inadequate funds in the payer's account when the direct debit is received, it should be returned to the originating bank with the answer "refer to debtor". Other answers include: "no mandate", "debtor deceased", "mandate cancelled", "out of date", "amount not yet due", as appropriate.

PROGRESS TEST 2

1. Why are references required when opening a current account? **(2)**

2. List several circumstances where a banker must cease to continue to pay his customer's cheques. **(6, 7–14)**

3. How would you deal with an unsatisfactory customer who refuses to close his credit account? Would you proceed in a different manner if his account was debit? **(15)**

4. How should the bank proceed when asked to allow operations on an account under P/A? **(22)**

5. Distinguish between a garnishee order and a garnishee summons. **(31)** Does an order attach: (*a*) a deposit account; (*b*) a solicitor's clients' account; (*c*) a trust account; (*d*) proceeds of uncleared cheques? **(34–36)**

6. Distinguish between a gratuitous bailee and a bailee for reward. Into which category does a banker fall? **(38)**

7. On the death of a joint account party, can any safe-custody items (held in joint names) be released on the instructions of the survivor(s)? **(46)**

8. Discuss the decision in *Woods* v. *Martins Bank*. **(51)**

PART TWO
NEGOTIABLE INSTRUMENTS

CHAPTER III

Negotiability

Students should have studied negotiable instruments in some depth already. This chapter gives a brief outline of the more important aspects of negotiability which concern bills of exchange and cheques. (References to bills include cheques.)

NEGOTIABILITY GENERALLY

1. Meaning of negotiability. Certain choses in action have been recognised by either statute or mercantile usage as negotiable instruments, and as such are outside the common-law ruling: "nemo dat quod non habet" (no one can give that which he has not got). Thus where a thief passes on a negotiable instrument, e.g. a cheque, then a transferee will acquire a perfect title if he is a holder in due course.

Bills of exchange are the most important type of negotiable instrument which concern bankers, but other negotiable instruments include promissory notes, bearer bonds, debentures to bearer, Treasury Bills, etc.

2. Attributes of negotiable instruments. A negotiable instrument has the following attributes:

(*a*) *Title passes* by delivery only or by endorsement and delivery.

(*b*) A transferee taking such an instrument in good faith and for value: (*i*) can acquire *a better title* than that possessed by his transferor; (*ii*) is *not affected* by prior equities.

(*c*) The holder can *sue in his own name.*

(*d*) The holder *need not give notice* to prior parties to establish his title.

3. Meaning of negotiation. A bill is negotiated when it is transferred from one person to another in such a manner as to constitute the transferee the holder of the bill, i.e. by delivery of a bearer bill, or by delivery plus endorsement of an order bill: BEA 1882, s. 31.

A bill ceases to be *transferable* (and thus negotiable) when it contains words prohibiting transfer or indicating that it should not be transferred, e.g. a cheque marked "Pay B. Brown only" or "Not Transferable" ceases to be transferable. Cheques drawn in this manner create insuperable problems for bankers: *see* V, **8**.

A bill ceases to be *negotiable* where it bears evidence destroying negotiability, e.g. where a cheque is crossed "Not Negotiable".

4. Order and bearer bills.

(*a*) *Order bills* are those payable to or to the order of a specified person without words prohibiting further transfer, e.g. (*i*) pay B. Brown, or (*ii*) Pay B. Brown or order, or (*iii*) Pay B. Brown (or order) being endorsed Pay S. Smith (or order) signed B. Brown. (An *order* bill requires *valid endorsement* in order to complete transfer.)

(*b*) *Bearer bills* are those: (*i*) drawn payable to bearer, or (*ii*) on which the only or last endorsement is an endorsement in blank, or (*iii*) drawn payable to a fictitious or non-existing payee.

EXAMPLES: (1) Pay Bearer, (2) Pay B. Brown or bearer, (3) Pay B. Brown (or order) and endorsed by B. Brown in blank. (An endorsement *in blank* is the mere signature of the endorsee and on an order bill *converts the bill to one payable to bearer*.)

NOTE: A *bearer* bill is transferable by *mere delivery* without any necessity for endorsement.

5. No liability without signature. No person is liable as drawer, endorser or acceptor of a bill who has not signed it as such: s. 23. Note, however, the following exceptions in **6** and **7** below.

6. Transferor by delivery: s. 58. Where the holder of a bearer bill negotiates it by delivery without endorsing it he is called a transferor by delivery.

Although a transferor by delivery is not liable on the instrument, *he warrants to his immediate transferee being a holder for value* that: (*i*) the bill is what it purports to be; (*ii*) he has the right to transfer it; (*iii*) he is not, at the time of transfer, aware of any fact which renders it valueless. Consequently, a transferor by delivery remains liable where:

(*a*) *the bill is a forgery*, e.g. where the drawer's signature is forged; or

(*b*) *he is aware* at the time of transfer that the bill is *valueless*, e.g. where he knows that the drawer has stopped payment; or

(*c*) *he has no right to transfer it*, e.g. where he has a defective title.

NOTE: Where the holder of a bearer bill adds his signature (i.e. endorsement) to the bill, he becomes liable as an *endorser*.

7. Endorsement by a stranger. Where a person signs a bill otherwise than as drawer or acceptor, he thereby incurs the liabilities of an endorser to a holder in due course: s. 56.

FORGED SIGNATURES

8. Forged signatures: s. 24. "Subject to the provisions of this Act, where a signature on a bill is forged or placed thereon without the authority of the person whose signature it purports to be, the forged or unauthorised signature is wholly inoperative", and unless the party against whom it is sought to retain or enforce payment is precluded from setting up the forgery or want of authority *no rights can be acquired through the forged signature*. (An *unauthorised* signature *not amounting to a forgery* may be ratified.)

9. Forgery on cheques. S. 24 has important repercussions as regards cheques.

(*a*) *Drawer's signature forged.* The cheque never becomes a valid instrument as regards the drawer, but remains *actionable* as between all *other* parties. A banker could not usually debit a cheque bearing a forged drawer's signature to his customer's account, but *see* IV, **19**.

(*b*) *Forgery of an essential endorsement.* A correct and genuine endorsement is necessary to effect a legal transfer of an order cheque, therefore a forged endorsement nullifies transfer. A transferee who takes a cheque bearing a forged endorsement gets no title to it and cannot claim against any person who became a party thereto prior to the forgery. However, as every endorser guarantees (under s. 55) the genuineness of the cheque to his immediate or subsequent endorsee, then recovery can be effected from any endorser *who signed subsequent to the forgery*. Consequently, loss falls upon the victim of the forgery unless he can recover from the forger.

(*c*) *Forgery of an endorsement on a bearer cheque*. As a bearer cheque does not require an endorsement to effect a legal transfer, the addition of a forged signature has no consequence, and the signature can be completely ignored. Thus all parties remain liable on the cheque.

POSITION OF HOLDER

10. Holder and holder for value.

(*a*) A *holder* is the payee or endorsee of a bill who is in possession of it or the bearer of a bearer bill: s. 2. Thus a person who takes an *order* bill bearing a forged endorsement is *not* a holder, since he is neither the endorsee of it nor the bearer.

(*b*) A *holder for value* is the holder of a bill for which value has at *some time* been given. He can enforce the bill against all parties *prior to the giving of such value*: s. 27(2).

NOTE: (1) A holder is *presumed* to be a holder in due course until proved otherwise. (2) A holder who derives his title through a *holder in due course* obtains the rights of that holder in due course. (3) A holder or holder for value *cannot obtain a better title than his transferor possessed*. But if there is *no defect* in prior title he will be the *true owner* with full rights of recovery.

11. Holder in due course. Where a person is a *holder in due course*, he is in a *paramount position*. He holds the bill free from all defects and can enforce payment against *all* parties liable on the bill.

12. Meaning of holder in due course. He is a holder who has taken a bill: (*a*) complete and regular on the face of it; (*b*) before it was overdue; (*c*) without notice of previous dishonour; (*d*) in good faith and for value; (*e*) without notice of any defect in the transferor's title.

NOTE: (1) There can be *no* holder in due course where a bill (1) is marked "Not Transferable", or (2) "Pay B. Brown only", or (3) bears the forgery of an essential signature. (2) A *payee* cannot be a holder in due course because the bill is issued to him but not negotiated: *R. E. Jones* v. *Waring & Gillow Ltd.* (1926).

PROGRESS TEST 3

1. What is a bearer bill? **(4)**

2. How are order bills and bearer bills transferred? **(4)**

3. What is the effect of a forged endorsement? **(8–9)**

4. Distinguish between a holder, a holder for value and a holder in due course. **(10–11)**

5. Why can a holder in due course be said to be in a paramount position? **(11–12)**

CHAPTER IV

Cheques and Bankers

CHEQUES

1. Definition. A cheque is a bill of exchange drawn on a banker payable on demand: BEA 1882, s. 73. The rules relating to acceptance do not apply to cheques.

2. Stale cheques (as regards payment): one which has been in circulation for a considerable period of time without being presented for payment. Most bankers refuse to pay a cheque dated more than six months previously without the confirmation of the drawer.

NOTE: (1) The *drawer* remains liable on a cheque for six years from its date of issue, except in respect of any loss incurred by reason of delay in presentment for payment, e.g. where the drawee bank is unable to pay the cheque in full owing to its insolvency: s. 74. (2) *Endorsers* are completely discharged from liability if there is an unreasonable delay in presentment for payment: s. 45(2).

3. Overdue cheques (as regards negotiability): one which has been in circulation for an *unreasonable time*: s. 36. (A person who takes an overdue cheque cannot be a holder in due course.)

NOTE: What is an unreasonable time depends upon the circumstances, e.g. three days was held to be an unreasonable time where the drawer had intended that the cheque be presented for immediate payment: *Wheeler* v. *Young*. (1897).

4. Undated and post-dated cheques.

(*a*) *Undated cheques.* If an undated cheque is presented for payment the bank can either: (*i*) return it unpaid, or (*ii*) enter the estimated true date (being the person in possession of it) and pay it: s. 20(1); the latter procedure is more usual.

(*b*) *Post-dated cheques.* If a cheque is post-dated and the drawee bank pays it *before the due date* it is disobeying its customer's mandate and the customer may refuse to be debited with the cheque.

NOTE: A viewpoint is held that if a post-dated cheque was debited prematurely, but the payment ultimately became due, then in equity the customer would not be able to claim a refund of the amount debited, but only claim nominal damages. This might occur, for instance, where a post-dated cheque, for tax becoming due, was prematurely debited to a customer's account.

Also the following *further dangers* may arise in consequence of paying a post-dated cheque:

(*i*) The customer may *stop payment* of the cheque before it becomes due.

(*ii*) If the cheque is held *pending arrival of the due date* the customer may fail or die in the meantime.

(*iii*) The bank may incur damages if it returns cheques subsequently presented (which would otherwise have been paid) for lack of funds.

5. Measure of damages for wrongful dishonour. In deciding the measure of damages under **4**(*b*)(*iii*) above, or in any other case where the *drawee* bank *improperly refuses to honour a cheque*, the court applies the following rules:

(*a*) *Damage to a trading customer's credit, for breach of contract*, will be presumed without proof. Damages may be substantial or exemplary. *Any other account holder* would need to prove special damages, otherwise only *nominal* damages will be awarded: *Gibbons* v. *Westminster Bank Ltd.* (1939).

(*b*) An additional or alternative action *for the tort of libel* may be brought, e.g. if the customer contests the words "Refer to drawer".

EXAMPLE: Certain cheques were wrongly dishonoured by the drawee bank, being marked "Refer to drawer". HELD: The drawer of the cheque was entitled to damages of £1 for breach of contract, and £400 for libel; the words "Refer to drawer" being held libellous and meaning "no funds": *Pyke* v. *Hibernian Bank Ltd.* (1950).

NOTE: This, being an Irish Supreme Court decision, *is not binding but persuasive* on English courts; it would still be possible, but unlikely, for English courts to follow Scrutton J.'s opinion that the words meant, "We are not paying; go back to the drawer and ask why": *Flack* v. *London & SW Bank Ltd.* (1915). However, in *Jayson* v. *Midland Bank* (1968), the defendants returned J's cheque marked "refer to drawer", but were held *justified* in so doing. But the court held that the words would have been libellous if funds had been available.

CROSSINGS

6. Object of crossing cheques. The main object of crossing a cheque is to make it difficult and more unlikely for fraudulent activity to succeed; also to help provide certain safeguards for the drawer (and successive holders) of a cheque.

As crossed cheques should not be cashed over the counter (unless it is certain that the *true owner* is being paid: *see* **17** below), but collected for an account, *the drawer is protected in various ways*:

(*a*) It makes it more difficult for a fraudulent party to obtain the proceeds of a cheque.

(*b*) It increases the time available for discovering the fraudulent activity.

(*c*) The fraudulent party and/or his accomplice may possibly be traced back to the collecting banker.

(*d*) The drawer has more time to stop payment of any cheque he has issued.

(*e*) A "not negotiable" crossing and other special crossings provide the drawer with further protection: *see* **7** below.

NOTE: (1) The *drawer or any holder may cross a cheque* or add to an existing crossing, e.g. a holder of a cheque crossed generally can add the words "Midland Bank": *see* s. 77. (2) *A banker may cross a cheque specially to himself*, e.g. when he crosses a cheque prior to presentment for payment, or when passing the cheque to another bank for collection: s. 77(5) & (6). (3) *Crossings* are instructions to the *paying* banker, with the exception of an "account payee" crossing which is directed to the *collecting* banker: *see* **7** below. (4) *A crossing is a material part of a cheque*, and any unauthorised alteration thereto is unlawful (s. 78) and avoids the cheque: s. 64.

7. Types of crossing.

(*a*) *General crossing*, i.e. two parallel transverse lines drawn across the face of the cheque, with or without the words: (*i*) "and company" (or abbreviation thereof), and/or (*ii*) "not negotiable" . . . written between, or near, the lines: s. 76(1). *The effect of such a crossing* is to make it necessary (in normal circumstances) for the cheque to be paid *into an account*, and for the proceeds to be collected from the drawee bank: s. 79.

(*b*) *Special crossing*, i.e. a crossing bearing the name of a *particular bank* (with or without the words "not negotiable"): s. 76(2). *The effect of such a crossing* is that the cheque must only be paid by the drawee banker *to the banker named in the crossing* (or to another banker acting as its agent): s. 79.

8. "Not negotiable" crossing. This crossing deprives the cheque of its negotiability (but not its transferability). A person taking such a cheque shall not have, and shall not be capable of, giving a better title to the cheque than that which the transferor had: s. 81. *Examples of the effect* of this crossing are as follows:

(*a*) A cheque drawn (*i*) payable to bearer, or (*ii*) payable to order and bearing a genuine endorsement in blank would, if passed on by a thief, vest a good title in a holder in due course. If, however, the cheque was crossed "not negotiable" the hoder could only obtain as good a title as the thief had, i.e. no title at all.

(*b*) If P agrees to do some work for D, then D may issue a cheque in advance. If P fails to carry out the work and if the cheque has been crossed "not negotiable," any future holder cannot obtain the title of a holder in due course, and would therefore have no rights against D.

EXAMPLE: A clerk took a signed blank cheque from his employer which was already crossed "not negotiable" and fraudulently made it payable to P. HELD: The employer could recover the value from P (who had obtained cash), since the clerk had received no title to the cheque, and P could get no better title because of the crossing: *Wilson & Meeson* v. *Pickering* (1946).

9. "Account payee" crossing. This has no statutory authority, and does not concern the *paying banker*, nor affect the *negotiability* of the cheque. However, it is well recognised by the courts that the crossing *is directed to the collecting banker*, who may be deemed negligent if it collects such a cheque for a party other than the named payee; thus losing the protection of CA 1957, s. 4.

The collecting banker should not collect such a cheque for a third party unless the standing of this party (i.e. customer) is undoubted, and a satisfactory explanation is obtained as to why the cheque has been negotiated (to be regarded as *satisfactory* the explanation must be reviewed in the light of surrounding circumstances).

NOTE: Even if the collecting bank are held negligent, they will have a right of indemnity against their customer for any loss incurred; what this is worth depends upon the standing of the customer.

EXAMPLE: A solicitor called in a trust mortgage and then proceeded to pay in the resulting cheque (which was drawn payable to the named trustees or "bearer", and crossed "account payee") to his own account. When an action for conversion was brought against them the collecting bank pleaded that it had collected the cheque as directed, i.e. for the bearer. HELD: As the cheque bore the name "F. S. Hanson & others" across its face the bank were negligent in collecting the cheque without enquiry: *House Property Co. of London Ltd. and Ors.* v. *London County & Westminster Bank Ltd.* (1915).

ALTERATIONS AND ENDORSEMENTS

10. Alterations on a cheque. Where a cheque is materially altered, then all parties cease to be liable on it, with the exception that a party remains liable if he: (*a*) altered, assented to or authorised alteration of the cheque; or (*b*) became an endorser of the cheque *subsequent to the alteration*: s. 64.

NOTE: (1) *On a cheque*: alteration of date, amount, payee's name, words or figures, or any crossing, would be deemed material. (2) A bank would refuse to pay an altered cheque *unless the drawer's initials were appended thereto.* (3) Where (1) a crossing is opened (e.g. to enable cash to be paid to the drawer or his known agent), or (2) the words "or order" have been altered to "bearer", then the full signature of the drawer is normally required to the alteration.

11. Endorsements. The general rules about endorsements apply to cheques.

Note that the Cheques Act 1957, s. 1, protects a banker who pays an unendorsed or irregularly endorsed cheque drawn on him, provided payment is made in good faith and in the ordinary course of business. After the passing of this Act it was confirmed by the London Clearing Banks that the following instruments would still require proper endorsement before *payment* could be effected:

(*a*) Combined cheque and receipt forms marked with a large capital "R" before the amount in figures.

(*b*) Bills of exchange other than cheques.
(*c*) Promissory notes.
(*d*) Drafts drawn on HM Paymaster, etc.
(*e*) Cheques cashed over the counter.
(*f*) Travellers' cheques.

PAYMENT BY CHEQUE

12. Payment by cheque.

(*a*) *Conditional payment.* Payment by cheque is conditional, i.e. payment is not effective until the cheque is honoured. A creditor can refuse to accept payment by cheque.

(*b*) *Cheques through the post.* If a cheque is sent through the post and is lost the loss falls upon the sender, unless the creditor requested this method of payment. Such a request must be express and not implied.

(*c*) *Cheques as evidence of payment.* An unendorsed cheque which appears to have been paid by the banker on whom it is drawn is evidence of receipt by the payee of the sum payable by the cheque: Cheques Act 1957, s. 3.

(*d*) *Lost cheques.* Where a holder loses a cheque (or bill) before it is overdue, he may demand a duplicate from the drawer (but he cannot compel any former party to sign it): s. 69. In case the original cheque falls into the hands of a holder in due course (who could enforce payment against the drawer), the drawer may demand security before issuing a duplicate cheque.

NOTE: *If the lost cheque is either* (1) crossed "not negotiable", or (2) drawn payable to order, but unendorsed, then the drawer cannot be made to pay out on it.

13. Cheque not assignment of funds. In England a bill does not operate as an assignment of funds in the hands of the drawee available for payment thereof: s. 53. Consequently, if there is an insufficient balance to meet a customer's cheque it should be returned marked "refer to drawer" with or without "please re-present", as the situation demands. There need be no further worries regarding the remaining balance (if any) on the account, and this can be utilised in paying any further cheques which are presented.

Words such as "*not sufficient*" should be avoided when returning cheques, as the customer might later contend that this amounted to unnecessary disclosure. If a customer's balance is insufficient to cover all cheques drawn by him which are presented on the *one day* it is the practice (unless the customer intimates otherwise) to pay the cheques of smaller amount up to the available balance, the aim being to preserve as much as possible of the customer's credit.

PAYING BANKER

14. Banker as drawee. In relation to cheques, the paying banker is the drawee banker who pays the cheque. If a cheque is paid other than by the drawee banker (e.g. under open credit arrangement at *another bank*), then this banker is not the paying banker and cannot claim the statutory protections applicable to paying bankers.

15. Liability of paying banker. The main risks attaching to the paying banker are:

(*a*) Liability for conversion to the true owner: *see* **17** and **18** below.

(*b*) Liability for damages for cheques wrongly debited to a customer's account: *see* **19** below.

16. Obligation to pay cheques. It has already been mentioned that the drawee bank:

(*a*) *Is under an obligation to pay its customer's cheques unless either*: (*i*) there is an insufficient balance, or (*ii*) the cheque is not drawn in proper form, or (*iii*) there is a legal bar to payment—

(*i*) *Insufficient balance*, i.e. the balance of the customer's account or agreed limit is insufficient to allow payment of his cheque(s). In this respect it should be remembered that uncleared cheques credited to the customer's account can be ignored in computing his available balance, *unless there is an express or implied agreement* allowing the customer to draw against such items: *A. L. Underwood Ltd.* v. *Barclays Bank Ltd.* (1924).

(*ii*) *Cheques drawn in proper form.* When paying a cheque *received through the clearing house, or one specially presented*, a banker must be sure that: the customer's signature is genuine; words and figures agree; the payee's name is completed; the cheque has not been stopped; the cheque is drawn on that branch; alterations are initialled by the drawer; the cheque is not crossed by two bankers (unless one is the agent of the other); the cheque is not stale or post-dated. There is no need to check endorsements unless the cheque bears a capital "R" before the amount in figures.

The above considerations also apply to *open cheques paid out over the counter*, with the exception that endorsement is required.

(*iii*) *Legal bar to payment*. This is dealt with fully under the appropriate headings, e.g. bankruptcy.

(*b*) *Must pay or dishonour cheques within statutory or legally recognised time limits*, viz.—

(*i*) Where an *open* cheque is presented *over the counter* by a holder, for payment, it must be paid or dishonoured immediately (unless there is doubt as to the presenter's title, when payment can be postponed).

(*ii*) Where an *open or crossed* cheque is specially presented *over the counter* by another banker, it must be paid or dishonoured immediately.

(*iii*) Where a cheque is presented *through the clearing*, the rules of the *Clearing House* govern the position. (This also applies in respect of *local* clearings.)

(*iv*) Where a cheque is presented for payment by another bank *by post*, the drawee bank can (legally) return it unpaid the next day. (In practice, notification of payment or dishonour is sent off on the day of receipt; where immediate notification is desired by the presenting banker, fate is telephoned.)

17. Payment in due course: s. 59. To obtain a complete discharge when paying a cheque, the *drawee* bank must make payment at *maturity, to the holder, in good faith and without notice of any defect in his title*.

The *drawer's* account can then be debited provided payment is: (*i*) legally in order; (*ii*) made in accordance with the drawer's instructions; (*iii*) made in the ordinary course of business, e.g. in normal business hours.

(*a*) *Open cheques*. There are various ways in which an open cheque may be discharged by due payment, e.g. cash over the counter to the holder.

(*b*) *Crossed cheques*. To obtain a good discharge against the *true owner*, a crossed cheque must be paid only *through a banker and strictly in accordance with the crossing*: s. 79. (Thus s. 79 places an *additional* duty on the drawee bank in respect of payment of *crossed* cheques.) *See also* **18**(*b*) below.

NOTE: The drawee bank when paying a cheque cannot usually know whether or not it is paying the *holder*, e.g. if a bank paid a cheque presented through the clearing bearing a *forged endorsement* it would not then be paying the holder: s. 24. To overcome this difficulty the BEA 1882, s. 60, was drafted to provide the drawee bank with the necessary protection: *see* immediately below.

18. Protection of paying banker.

(*a*) BEA, s. 60: *Against payment of cheques with forged or unauthorised endorsements*. The drawee bank is regarded as having paid the *holder* in due course if it pays such a cheque (*whether open or crossed*): (*i*) *in good faith*; and (*ii*) *in the ordinary course of business*, e.g. to act within the ordinary course of business when paying an open cheque over the counter it would need to purport to be correctly endorsed.

(*b*) BEA, s. 80: *Against liability to the true owner*. Provided the drawee bank pays a *crossed* cheque: (*i*) *to a banker, in accordance with the crossing*; (*ii*) *in good faith*; (*iii*) *without negligence*.

(*c*) CA 1957, s. 1: *Against payment of cheques with no endorsements or with irregular endorsements*. The drawee bank is deemed to have paid in due course if it pays such a cheque (*whether open or crossed*): (*i*) *in good faith*; (*ii*) *in the ordinary course of business*.

Section 1, as well as covering cheques, also covers: (*i*) documents (other than bills of exchange) issued by a customer to enable a person to obtain payment of the sum mentioned, e.g. conditional orders; and (*ii*) bankers' drafts.

NOTE: (1) *"Good faith"*. "A thing is deemed to be done in good faith, within the meaning of this Act, where it is done *honestly*, whether it is done *negligently* or not": BEA 1882, s. 90. For example, where a Paris money-changer changed English notes without referring to his "stop" list, it was held that although he had acted negligently, he had still acted in good faith and so could recover the value of the notes from the defendant: *Raphael & Anor*. v. *Bank of England* (1855). (2) The importance of BEA 1882, s. 60, as a protection for the paying banker has diminished since the passing of the Cheques Act 1957, which while not abolishing endorsements protects a banker who pays a cheque which bears no endorsement or is irregularly endorsed. (3) BEA, s. 60, will still (presumably) be a necessary protection for the paying banker *where forged endorsements occur*, e.g. where an open cheque is presented over the counter for cash, against a forged endorsement. Presumably the CA 1957, s. 1, will not protect the paying banker, as in this instance it would only cover *irregular* and not *forged* endorsements. (4) *If an open cheque* (unless payable to cash or bearer) *is cashed without endorsement* for a person not entitled to payment, then presumably there will be no protection for the paying banker from CA 1957, s. 1; because the banker would not be deemed to be acting within the ordinary course of business of requiring endorsement as laid down and agreed by the clearing banks. (5) The protection of BEA 1882, s. 80, has rarely (if ever) been used as a defence by the paying banker to an action brought against it.

19. Liability in respect of payment: forged drawer's signature or altered cheque. No statutory protection is available to the paying banker where it pays either: (*a*) a cheque bearing a forged drawer's signature; or (*b*) a cheque bearing a non-apparent (or an unauthorised apparent) alteration.

(*a*) *Payment of cheque bearing a forged drawer's signature.* This is clearly contrary to the *customer's mandate*, and the amount of any such cheques debited to his account will normally have to be refunded.

Exceptionally the drawer may be *estopped from denying the forged signature*, e.g. where he has either: (*i*) led the bank to believe that the signature was his own; or (*ii*) learned of the forgery, but (1) failed to inform the bank in sufficient time for it to take action against the forger, or (2) failed to inform the bank and this has resulted in the forger continuing in his activities.

EXAMPLES: (1) A wife forged her husband's signature to cheques which the bank duly paid. On discovering the frauds, the customer did not inform the bank, but merely told his wife not to repeat this activity. Some time later the wife committed suicide, and thereupon the husband sought reimbursement for the forged cheques. HELD: Because of his delay, he was estopped from denying the forged signature as his own; the bank now being unable to take action against the forger: *Greenwood* v. *Martins Bank Ltd.* (1933). (2) Acting under his mother's power of attorney, an old lady's son claimed against the bank in respect of 329 cheques on which her signature was alleged to have been forged by her servants. The bank admitted that 100 cheques were forged, *but denied liability*, stating that she was estopped from denying the signature because she had repeatedly represented the cheques as her own when approached by the bank's officials. HELD: Estoppel applied to the cheques paid both *before and after* enquiry by the bank's officials: *Brown* v. *Westminster Bank Ltd.* (1964). (The forged cheques paid *before* the bank's enquiry were allowed to stand, because of the subsequent representation made by the old lady as to their being genuine. This obviously influenced the bank into making no further enquiry at that moment.)

NOTE: (1) *Bank's duty.* The bank are under a corresponding duty to inform their customer if they ascertain that *his* signature is being forged. (2) *Contributory negligence by the customer.* To date this defence has not been successful when pleaded by banks in actions concerning forged drawer's signature, e.g. where a company customer employed a known forger and allowed him to sign jointly on their account it was held that the company could deny liability in respect of cheques on which he had forged the other party's signature: *Lewes Sanitary Steam Laundry Co. Ltd.* v. *Barclay Bevan & Co. Ltd.* (1906). However, when a *collecting* banker was recently sued for *conversion* in respect of a cheque which the drawer had signed without ensuring that his clerk had completed the full name of the payee (a space having been left in front of the name "Brown") the bank claimed that the Law Reform (Contributory Negligence) Act 1945 should be applicable if they were held to be negligent and thus lost the protection of CA 1957, s. 4. The court upheld this argument and held the drawer 10 per cent responsible: *Lumsden & Co.* v. *London Trustee Savings Bank* (1971), *see* I, **14**(2).

(*b*) *Payment of cheque bearing a non-apparent aleration.* The bank cannot debit a cheque bearing a non-apparent alteration to its customer's account *unless the customer has facilitated the alteration by his carelessness*: *London Joint Stock Bank* v. *MacMillan & Arthur* (1918), *see* I, **14**.

NOTE: The *MacMillan & Arthur Rule* applies only: (1) Where the altered instrument is a *cheque*. (2) Where the alteration is *non-apparent*. (3) Where the alteration was facilitated by the customer's *negligence*.

COLLECTING BANKER

20. Liability attaching to collecting banker. There is an implied term in the banker/customer relationship that a banker will receive his customer's cheques and other instruments for collection in order to receive the proceeds from the drawee bank. There are certain risks attaching, and liability may be incurred in respect of the following:

(*a*) *Conversion*, e.g. where the customer has no title or a defective title to the cheques which he pays in for collection, then the bank may become liable to the true owner for the face value of the instruments.

(*b*) *Breach of contract*, e.g. where the banker (acting as agent) fails to carry out the statutory or legally recognised duties required of him, then he may incur liability to his customer.

EXAMPLES: (1) Where a customer's cheque is returned unpaid and he is not informed of the dishonour within the time limits stipulated in BEA 1882, s. 49. (2) Where delay or error occurs in presenting a customer's cheques for payment and as a result the customer suffers loss, e.g. a cheque drawn payable at alternative centres was sent in the country clearing instead of (as was usual) the town clearing, and consequently payment was delayed. The collecting banker refused to pay cheques drawn in reliance of this collection. HELD: As the cheque would have been regarded as paid if dispatched in the usual clearing, the customer was entitled to damages: *Forman* v. *Bank of England* (1902).

21. Conversion. This is the *main danger* to the collecting banker. If a customer pays in a cheque or other instrument to which he has no title or a defective title, then the banker would be liable for conversion if it were not for the protection afforded by the Cheques Act 1957, s. 4. However, an alternative claim of contributory negligence by the customer may be contended by the bank as in the case of *Lumsden & Co.* v. *London Trustee Savings Bank* (1971): *see* **19**(*a*) above. *Alternatively*, but more rarely, a bank may be able to set itself up as a holder in due course, in which case it will then become the true owner of the instrument, and conversion cannot apply.

22. Protection afforded by Cheques Act 1957, s. 4. (*see also* Table I at end of IV). This section reads as follows:

"(1) Where a banker, in good faith and without negligence,

"(*a*) receives payment for a customer of an instrument to which this section applies; or "(*b*) having credited a customer's account with the amount of such an instrument, receives payment thereof for himself; and the customer has no title or a defective title, to the instrument, the banker does not incur any liability to the true owner of the instrument by reason only of having received payment thereof ...

"(3) A banker is not to be treated for the purposes of this section as having been negligent by reason only of his failure to concern himself with absence of, or irregularity in, endorsement of an instrument."

NOTE: (1) *Section* 4 *replaces* BEA 1882, s. 82, which has been repealed. (2) *The bank must collect*: (1) for a *customer*; (2) in *good faith*; and (3) *without negligence*. (3) The protection extends to both *open and crossed* instruments. (4) *Instruments covered include*: cheques, conditional or other orders to a banker to pay; PMG and Queen's and Lord Treasurer's Remembrancer's warrants; bankers' drafts: s. 4(2). (Bills of exchange (other than cheques) are specifically *excluded*.) (5) *Where a cheque is credited to an account other than that of the named payee* (i.e. where it has been negotiated), endorsement by the payee is necessary, but the endorsement of the person paying the cheque into his account is not required. (But *see Westminster Bank Ltd.* v. *Zang* (1965).)

The most crucial points are that the banker must collect (*a*) for a *customer*: *see* I, **7**, and (*b*) *without negligence* ... the latter being the most difficult requirement to fulfil.

23. Negligence and the collecting banker. Many banks have lost the protection of s. 4 (formerly BEA 1882, s. 82) because they have acted negligently.

The test of negligence for a banker is: "whether the transaction of paying in any given cheque coupled with the circumstances antecedent and present was so out of the ordinary course that it ought to have aroused doubts in the bankers' mind and caused them to make enquiry": Lord Dunedin, *Commissioners of Taxation* v. *English, Scottish & Australian Bank Ltd.* (1920).

Not only must enquiry be made but an answer received which would satisfy a most reasonable businessman; otherwise the contention of negligence will not be avoided in court. Unfortunately, the bounds of negligence know no limits, but the banker can usefully look back at past decisions and base his future conduct with these in mind.

Acts of negligence attributed to banks can be classified under three main headings:

(*a*) Failure to attend to account-opening formalities, thereby enabling cheques to be more readily converted by the customer: *see* **24**(*a*)–(*d*) below.

(*b*) Failure to make enquiry where cheques are paid into an account when there exists a *fiduciary relationship* between the customer paying in and the drawer or payee: *see* **24**(*e*)–(*i*) below.

(*c*) Failure to enquire into the surrounding circumstances where the unusual nature of the collection is or should be obvious: *see* **24**(*j*)–(*n*) below.

24. Examples of negligence on the part of the collecting banker.

(*a*) *Failure to obtain the name of the customer's employers*, or, in the past, in the case of a married woman, her husband's employers: *Savory & Co.* v. *Lloyds Bank Ltd.* (1932). But compare *Marfani & Co. Ltd.* v. *Midland Bank* (1968).

(*b*) *Failure to obtain references* where the new customer is unknown to the bank:

EXAMPLE: Ladbroke, a bookmaker, issued a cheque to a client which was intercepted by a thief who forged the endorsement. The thief then paid in the cheque to the defendant bank, who obtained immediate clearance of the cheque for him. HELD: The bank lost their statutory protection because of failure to take references: *Ladbroke* v. *Todd* (1914).

(*c*) *Failure to follow up references where the referee is unknown:*

EXAMPLES: (1) A customer opened an account in a false name, and giving his true name as referee, produced a glowing introductory reference. HELD: The bank had been negligent in accepting the reference of a stranger: *Guardians of St. John's Hampstead* v. *Barclays Bank Ltd.* (1923). But in like circumstances where the bank made enquiry on the referee to his bankers who reported that he was a suitable person to introduce an account the bank was held not negligent on that score: *Nu-Stilo Footwear Ltd.* v. *Lloyds Bank Ltd.* (1956). (2) A new customer (respectably introduced by another customer) opened his account by paying in a third-party cheque. The bank queried this, whereupon the customer produced a forged letter, supposedly from his employer, giving him authority to deal with the cheque. HELD: Confirmation from the employer was necessary in these circumstances: *Harding* v. *London Joint Stock Bank* (1914).

(*d*) *Failure to see a certificate of registration* under the Business Names Act 1916, and search the register where the customer is trading under a name other than his true surname, and pays in cheques payable to the trade name: *see* X, **4–6**.

(*e*) *Collecting for the account of a company official* cheques payable to his company:

EXAMPLE: Over several years, cheques payable to a company were endorsed by the managing director and accepted by the bank for collection to his *private* account. Ultimately, the bank was sued in respect of company money wrongly converted to the director's account. HELD: The bank had acted negligently, enquiry being essential in this instance: *A. L. Underwood Ltd.* v. *Bank of Liverpool & Martins Ltd.* (1924).

(*f*) *Collecting for the private account of a partner* cheques drawn payable to the partnership.

(*g*) *Collecting for the private account of an employee or his wife*, cheques drawn by or payable to his employer: *Savory & Co.* v. *Lloyds Bank Ltd.* (1932).

(*h*) *Collecting for the private account of an agent*, cheques drawn by him on his principal's account:

EXAMPLE: A, in his capacity as manager, was authorised to draw cheques "per pro" his employer M. He drew cheques both to "selves" and to his own favour and paid them into his private account. HELD: The bank had been negligent in collecting these cheques (paid in during the years 1907–8) without enquiry, as there was clear indication that A was signing as agent of the firm: *Morison* v. *London County & Westminster Bank Ltd.* (1914).

(NOTE: Liability for misappropriated cheques collected during 1909–11 was avoided because the plaintiff knew of the frauds or at least had opportunity to discover them—however, banks should beware of being "lulled to sleep", as this latter ruling has not been followed in subsequent decisions.)

(*i*) *Collecting for an agent's private account* cheques drawn in his favour, when there is an indication that he is only to receive them as agent:

EXAMPLE: McGaw, the former manager of the plaintiff's farm, received warrants as agent for the plaintiff drawn, "Pay D. McGaw" with "for Marquess of Bute" printed immediately outside the payee's box. McGaw opened an account at B Bank, who collected the proceeds for his account. HELD: The bank was negligent in collecting these warrants without enquiry to the plaintiff: *Marquess of Bute* v. *Barclays Bank Ltd.* (1954). (An interesting point arose as to who was the *true owner* of the warrants: the Marquess was held to be, even though he was not the named payee, because at the time the conversion occurred he was the person entitled to possession.)

(*j*) *Collecting for a company's account cheques drawn payable to another company.* Enquiry is necessary here because transfer of company cheques rarely occurs: *see London & Montrose Shipbuilding and Repairing Co. Ltd.* v. *Barclays Bank Ltd.* (1926).

NOTE: Where a *solicitor* paid cheques belonging to a company into his clients' account, this was held to be in order, as the solicitor gave a satisfactory reply to the bank's enquiry: *Penmount Estates Ltd.* v. *National Provincial Bank Ltd.* (1945). In the case of customers other than solicitors, satisfactory answers would almost certainly be required from the *payee company*.

(*k*) *Collecting cheques for amounts which are inconsistent with the customer's station in life or business:*

EXAMPLE: The plaintiff's secretary opened an account at L Bank, giving a false name and stating that he was setting up business as a free-lance agent. He then paid in third-party cheques drawn by the plaintiff company. HELD: Since the cheques amounted to £4,855, enquiry should have been made, as the amounts were inconsistent with his new business activity: *Nu-Stilo Footwear Ltd.* v. *Lloyds Bank Ltd.* (1956).

(*l*) *Collecting third-party cheques where the circumstances warrant enquiry:*

EXAMPLE: Cheques payable to a partnership were collected for a third party who had no title to them. HELD: Although the bank made enquiries and received the answer that the customer was dealing with the partnership's financial affairs prior to joining it, this was an answer calling for further enquiries: *Baker* v. *Barclays Bank Ltd.* (1955).

(*m*) *Collecting cheques crossed "account payee"* for an account other than that of the payee without enquiry.

(*n*) *Failure to enquire fully into third-party cheques* when past operations on the customer's account have been unsatisfactory:

EXAMPLE: T, a motor dealer, induced the plaintiffs (a hire-purchase company) to issue a cheque payable to a firm of car dealers. T then forged the endorsement and the defendants collected the cheque for his account (the cashier receiving what he considered a satisfactory reply regarding the third-party cheque). HELD: Because of the account history (many of T's cheques having been dishonoured over the past six months), the bank had not made sufficient enquiry: *Motor Traders' Guarantee Corporation Ltd.* v. *Midland Bank Ltd.* (1937).

NOTE: The cashier did not refer the third-party collection to the manager as instructed. It was held, however, that merely disobeying internal instructions would not *necessarily imply* that a bank had been negligent.)

The everyday practice of bankers may help to establish absence of negligence on their part if future court decisions are based on the guide lines given in the following case:

E was one of two signatories on a company's account, and after his co-signatory signed some blank company cheques, E added his signature, drew three cheques payable to "cash or order" and after endorsing them (illegible writing) paid them into his own account. An action was brought by the company against the bank for conversion. HELD: The bank were protected by CA 1957, s. 4. In reaching the decision it was stated that: (1) the bank were not put on special enquiry where cheques had been drawn in this manner; (2) the amounts involved did not call for enquiry (one of the cheques was for £1,270); (3) the bank could not be expected to know the employer's name where a customer had changed his employment; (4) the bank were not expected to scrutinise all the signatures on an instrument in the absence of a known fiduciary relationship; (5) the instrument was not a cheque, but was covered for collection by CA 1957, s. 4(2)(*b*): *Orbit Mining & Trading Co. Ltd.* v. *Westminster Bank Ltd.* (1962).

25. Bank as holder for value. A banker has no need to rely on the provisions of CA 1957, s. 4 for protection, so long as he can set himself up as a holder for value/holder in due course. A banker who gives value for cheques ceases to be his customer's agent, i.e. he collects the proceeds of the cheques for himself.

A banker is deemed to be a holder for value in four main instances:

(*a*) *Where he has given value for a cheque*, e.g. where Y bank cashes a cheque drawn on Z bank for the convenience of the latter's customer where there is no open credit arrangement.

(*b*) *Where he takes a cheque in specific reduction of an overdraft*, e.g. where a £500 cheque, being proceeds of a matured endowment policy, is paid in in permanent reduction of a long-standing overdraft: *see M'Lean* v. *Clydesdale Banking Co.* (1883). (A banker would not be deemed a holder for value where cheques received in the normal course of business are credited to an overdrawn account.)

(*c*) *Where the bank has a lien on a cheque*, e.g. where a cheque which a customer has paid in for collection has been returned unpaid, then the banker has a lien on the customer's account to the extent of the cheque. A holder who has a lien on a cheque is deemed to be a holder for value to the extent of that lien: BEA 1882, s. 27(3).

Consider the following recent cases:

EXAMPLE 1:

Mrs K, a customer of Midland Bank, committed an act of bankruptcy on 5th October 1962. On 12th October a petition was presented. On 16th November a R/O was made. On 30th November she was adjudicated bankrupt.

A cheque for £3,000 was paid in by Mrs K on 15th November. This cheque was cleared on the day of the R/O.

The Trustee contended that Midland could not apply the cheque in reduction of Mrs K's £1,350 overdraft. HELD: Midland had a *lien* on the cheque and were protected by BA 1914, s. 45 as dealing "for value", without notice of an act of bankruptcy and before date of R/O—the lien being attached on 15th November. The judge pointed out ... under BEA 1882, s. 27 ... valuable consideration in relation to a bill of exchange may be constituted by an antecedent debt. Further: the bank would in view of s. 29 also have been protected as a holder in due course: *Re. Keever* (1966).

EXAMPLE 2:

B had allowed Mabons Garage Ltd., their customers, to run their overdraft to £4,673 on the assurance that they *would pay in two days later* cheques for £2,850 issued by A.I.T. The cheques were paid in as arranged. Next day B paid further cheques leaving the overdraft £1,853. When A.I.T. realised that they had issued the cheques against forged Hire Purchase agreements they immediately stopped payment.

As Mabons were insolvent, B sued A.I.T. claiming to be holders in due course, i.e. claiming the "value" to be the *overdraft and the lien.* In other words B obviously considered they had no claim as regards either (*a*) uncleared effects or (*b*) specific reduction of overdraft. HELD: B had no knowledge of fraud and were holders in due course for £2,850.

NOTE: (1) B held to have a *lien* and thus deemed by BEA 1882, s. 27(3) to have taken cheques for *value* in respect of antecedent debt. (2) Milmo J. stated that he saw no conflict in a bank being an agent for collection of a cheque and a holder of that cheque for value *at one and the same time*. This upset the defendants' argument that being agents for collection the bank could not also be holders for value. (3) If the defendants had crossed the cheque NOT NEGOTIABLE the bank as holder for value could not have had a good title because its customer had no title: *Barclays Bank Ltd.* v. *Astley Industrial Trust Ltd.* (1970).

(*d*) *Where a customer is impliedly or expressly permitted to draw* against the value of *uncleared cheques* paid in for the credit of his account.

NOTE: (1) Banks *unsuccessfully* tried to establish themselves as holders for value in respect of advances against uncleared cheques in: *A. L. Underwood Ltd.* v. *Barclays Bank Ltd.* (1924) and *Westminster Bank Ltd.* v. *Zang* (1965); in both instances the bank's paying-in slips gave them the right to defer payment of any cheques drawn against uncleared effects, and they failed to establish an alternative implied or express right. (2) Banks have *successfully* become holders for value—against uncleared cheques in: *Lloyds Bank Ltd.* v. *Hornby* (1933); *Midland Bank* v. *Charles Simpson Motors Ltd.* (1961); *Barclays Bank Ltd.* v. *Harding* (*1962*); *Midland Bank Ltd.* v. *R. V. Harris Ltd.* (1963). (3) The conclusion which must be reached is that it is extremely difficult and rare for a banker to set himself up as a holder for value against uncleared cheques; also the decided cases have not given a particularly clear guidance for the future.

26. Effect of Cheques Act 1957, s. 2. This section reads as follows:

"A banker who gives value for, or has a lien on, a cheque payable to order which the holder delivers to him for collection without endorsing it, has such (if any) rights as he would have had if, upon delivery, the holder had endorsed it in blank."

This section does not *increase* a banker's protection but *preserves his rights as a holder* when he collects a *cheque* which is *unendorsed.*

TABLE 1. COMPARISON OF REQUIREMENTS AND PROTECTION FOR BANKERS: COLLECTING, UNDER S. 4. CHEQUES ACT 1957. GIVING VALUE, AS HOLDER IN DUE COURSE.

Instruments covered	Cheques, conditional and other orders drawn on bankers: P.M.G. Warrants, etc.; bankers' drafts NOTE: Bills of exchange (other than cheques) and promissory notes are not covered	Bills of exchange (including cheques): promissory notes: dividend warrants.
Requirements to be fulfilled	(*i*) For a customer (*ii*) In good faith (*iii*) Without negligence	(*i*) In good faith (defined BEA 1882, s. 90) (*ii*) BEA 1882, s. 29, e.g. value must be given, i.e. bank must firstly be in the position of a holder who has given value NOTE: *Need not be:* (*i*) for a customer; *or* (*ii*) without negligence
Protection	Bank is protected from any liability to the true owner where it has received payment	Bank is protected from any liability to the true owner and is allowed to sue any party on the bill to recover the proceeds
Effect of: (*a*) "Not negotiable" crossing	Does not concern the collecting banker	No one can be a holder in due course; therefore banker can only gain as good a title as his transferor has: BEA 1882, s. 81
(*b*) General crossing	Does not concern the collecting banker	Does not concern a prospective holder in due course
(*c*) Special crossing	Should only be collected by bank named in the crossing	Does not concern a prospective holder in due course (Unless the words "Not negotiable" are added)
(*d*) "Account payee" crossing	Should only be collected for the named payee unless satisfactory explanation (good enough to avoid contention of negligence in court) is received	Does not concern a prospective holder in due course
(*e*) Forged endorsement	Does not concern collecting banker (probably) provided all *necessary* endorsements appear to be in order.	Banker cannot become a holder in due course under a forged endorsement: BEA 1882, s. 24

Thus the banker is then in a position to establish himself as a holder for value/holder in due course, providing he can comply with BEA 1882, s. 27/s. 29, respectively. Since the Cheques Act was passed there have been several instances where a bank has established its position as holder by utilising s. 2:

EXAMPLES: A cheque for £4,500 was drawn by H in favour of Geoffrey Roberts (which was the trading name of Waytrade Ltd.). The cheque was paid into Waytrade's account without endorsement. Payment was countermanded by H. HELD: The bank were placed in the position of holders (s. 2), and as they had given value against uncleared effects, they could recover from H as holders in due course: *Barclays Bank Ltd.* v. *Harding* (1962).

Other case examples: Midland Bank Ltd. v. *R. V. Harris Ltd.* (1963); *Westminster Bank Ltd.* v. *Zang* (1965).

27. Collecting bank also acting as paying bank. Where a banker collects for a customer a cheque drawn by another customer of that bank, then the banker acts in the dual capacity of collecting and paying bank. In this case, if it is necessary to plead the protection of BEA 1882, s. 60 or s. 80, then it is also necessary to comply with CA 1957, s. 4, in respect of the collection of the cheque.

This ruling was established in a case where a bank pleaded the protection of *either* s. 60 *or* s. 82 (repealed by CA 1957, s. 4), and it was held that although it had complied with the former section, it also had to comply with the latter one, and this it had failed to do, having acted negligently: *Carpenters' Company* v. *British Mutual Banking Co. Ltd.* (1938).

PROGRESS TEST 4

1. What damages are payable for wrongful dishonour of a customer's cheque? How are such damages assessed? **(5)**
2. Give examples showing the effect of "Not negotiable" and "Account payee" crossings. **(8–9)**
3. A cheque is not an assignment of funds. Comment. **(13)**
4. Would the paying banker obtain any statutory protection if he paid an uncrossed cheque over the counter under a forged endorsement? **(18)**
5. Is a bank always liable to refund the amount of the cheque to its customer if it pays a cheque on which the customer's signature as drawer is forged? **(19)**

6. What do you understand by conversion? Outline fully the protection to be derived from CA 1957, s. 4, stating the conditions which need to be fulfilled. **(20–23)**

7. List several instances where banks have been held negligent when collecting cheques. **(24)**

8. Why was CA 1957, s. 2 enacted? **(26)**

CHAPTER V

Miscellaneous Banking Instruments

BANKERS' DRAFTS

1. Bankers' drafts.

(*a*) *Definition*: A draft drawn by a bank as drawer, on the same bank as drawee, being payable on demand to the named payee or to his order. As the drawer and drawee are the same person, i.e. the same bank, a bankers' draft is not a cheque, and BEA 1882, s. 60, does not apply where payment is concerned. However, the Cheques Act 1957, specifically covers the collection and payment of such instruments. (Instruments drawn by *one bank on another bank* are cheques.)

(*b*) *Purpose of drafts*. They provide an almost one hundred per cent certainty of payment being drawn by a bank. They are therefore used extensively where this certainty is required, e.g. payment for completion of house-property purchases. A customer requiring issue of a draft has to sign a draft request form.

(*c*) *Crossed drafts*. The CA 1957, s. 5 states that the provisions of the BEA relating to *crossed* cheques (i.e. ss. 76–81) shall so far as is applicable extend to bankers' drafts.

2. Lost draft—stopping payment. A banker is not normally prepared to stop payment of his own draft unless it has been crossed "not negotiable" or there is positive evidence that the payee has not endorsed it; otherwise if the draft came into the hands of a holder in due course he could enforce the payment against the banker as drawer.

If a customer asks the banker to issue a duplicate draft on loss of the original, the above points should be borne in mind, together with the amount and standing of the parties involved. In any case the banker: (*a*) would ascertain whether the draft had been presented for payment; (*b*) would require his customer's indemnity.

3. Bankers' drafts; protection of bankers.

(*a*) *Protection for paying banker.*

(*i*) Section 19, Stamp Act 1853: gives a good discharge when paying *uncrossed* drafts cashed over the counter, upon which there is a *forged endorsement*, provided the draft *purports* to be endorsed by the payee.

(*ii*) Section 1, Cheques Act 1957: gives a good discharge when paying *crossed and uncrossed* drafts which are not endorsed or irregularly endorsed, provided payment is made in good faith and in the ordinary course of business.

Thus an unendorsed or irregularly endorsed draft *paid other than over the counter* is obviously protected. But it appears doubtful whether an *unendorsed or irregularly endorsed open draft paid over the counter* is protected, as such payment would hardly be within the ordinary course of business.

(*iii*) Section 80, BEA 1882: covers *crossed* drafts, and provided payment is made in good faith, without negligence and in accordance with the crossing, then the drawee bank is deemed to have paid the true owner.

(*b*) *Protection for collecting banker.* The CA 1957, s. 4(2)(*d*) specifically protects bankers who collect drafts for customers who have no title, provided collection is made in good faith and without negligence.

CONDITIONAL ORDERS

4. Conditional orders. This is an instrument, usually in cheque form, but embodying instructions to the paying banker regarding the completion of a receipt. (NOTE: If the instruction is addressed merely to the payee then the order remains unconditional, i.e. a cheque.)

5. Combined cheque and receipt forms. Bankers strongly discourage the use of conditional orders particularly as: (*a*) the CA 1957 has in general removed the need for the paying banker to examine endorsements; (*b*) the statutory protection available is relatively uncertain in its application. Consequently, a customer who wishes to obtain the receipt of the payee *must* arrange with his bankers for the prefix letter "R" to be printed before the figures on his cheques. (It would appear that as such an instrument is drawn in an unconditional manner it would still be regarded as a cheque in a court of law.)

Few customers should require to use such instruments, and in this respect it is useful to point out to sceptics that an unendorsed cheque paid by a banker is evidence of receipt of the money by the payee: CA 1957, s. 3. Those who do utilise this facility are required to furnish an indemnity to cover the paying banker's position in the event of a lack of statutory protection.

6. Protection for banker paying a combined cheque and receipt form. Payment of the instrument (whether regarded as a conditional order or cheque) is covered by CA 1957, s. 1. As the clearing banks have agreed to examine the receipts to see that they appea o be n order, it would seem that if the instrument was unendorsed or irregularly endorsed, then the protection of the section would be lost.

7. Protection for banker collecting combined cheque and receipt form. Collection is covered by CA 1957, s. 4, and if (as is usually the case) it is stipulated that the receipt of the payee embodied on the back of the instrument is also to be regarded as an endorsement, then there appears to be no restriction on transferability. As the clearing banks have agreed that receipts on these instruments will be checked at the time of collection, it seems that failure to comply with this regulation would result in the loss of the protection of s. 4.

NON-TRANSFERABLE CHEQUES

8. Non-transferable cheques. These are cheques on which there is clear indication that transfer is prohibited (thus they cease to be either negotiable or transferable), e.g. (*a*) Pay J. Jones only, or (*b*) Pay J. Jones, marked "not transferable" ... the words "or order" or "bearer" being deleted and initialled by the drawer: *see* BEA 1882, s. 8(1).

NOTE: In 1958 the London Clearing Banks strongly deprecated the use of such cheques, and barred them because: (1) The paying banker would have no statutory protection if the cheque was cashed over the counter, and therefore positive identification of the payee would be necessary. (2) The payee's endorsement upon the cheque would be evidence that it had been transferred and the paying banker could not be sure that he was obeying his customer's mandate. (3) The collecting banker could not become a holder for value. (4) If the payee has no banking account it would be difficult for him to obtain payment, as the collecting banker should only collect for the named payee. (5) It is important to maintain the principles of transferability and negotiability.

IMPERSONAL PAYEES

9. Cheques drawn in favour of impersonal payees. Many such cheques are drawn in an extremely ambiguous manner, e.g. (*a*) pay cash or order, or (*b*) pay wages or order. Whether they can then be still regarded as cheques is unlikely in view of the fact that the payee is not a specified person or bearer in conformity with BEA 1882, ss. 3 and 7(1). In practice, no real difficulty emerges, because in respect of open instruments banks will only pay out cash to the drawer or his known agent.

It is dangerous to regard such instruments as being payable to bearer, although if the person whom the drawer intended to receive payment does actually receive it, then the lack of the drawer's endorsement will probably not prejudice the paying (or collecting) banker: *North & South Insurance Corporation Ltd.* v. *National Provincial Bank Ltd.* (1936). Recently it was decided that an instrument drawn "pay cash or order" was not a cheque, but that it fell within CA 1957, s. 4(2)(*b*), as regards collection; being a document issued by a customer of a banker which was intended to enable a person to obtain payment from that banker of the sum mentioned: *Orbit Mining & Trading Co. Ltd.* v. *Westminster Bank Ltd.* (1962).

CARDS

10. Cheque cards.

(*a*) *Description.* Usually made of plastic, this small card bearing a number, unique to the holder, and signed by the customer upon receipt, *guarantees* to a payee that cheques drawn by the customer in accordance with the terms printed on the card, up to a stated maximum (£50) in one transaction, will be paid by the drawee bank upon presentation.

(*b*) *Advantages.* The card is a move towards the "cashless society". It facilitates purchases for the holder, without delay or embarrassment and assures the seller that he will get his money. The risk of dishonour is avoided, and the cheque cannot be stopped or returned for technical reasons. Also, the holder is enabled to cash cheques at other banks and branches without prior arrangement. The card is usable overseas under the Eurocheque scheme and in other countries.

(*c*) *Terms.* These are printed on the reverse of the card and by agreement at time of issue, and usually include:

(*i*) On *issue*: (1) The card is and remains the property of the bank. (2) The card does not entitle the customer to withdraw monies which are not in the account or to overdraw the account without prior agreement. (3) The card should be carried separately from the cheque book (to prevent fraud in case of loss).

(*ii*) On *use*: (1) The cheque must be signed in the presence of the payee and the signature must agree with that on the card. (2) The card is not out of date. (3) The cheque form bears the sorting-code number on the card. (4) The cheque card number is written by the payee on the reverse of the card. (5) The cheque does not exceed the stated guaranteed amount (£50).

NOTE: There has been little, if any, case law concerning the use of the cheque card and the position of the drawee bank. Consequently several technical situations remain unclear regarding the drawee's position, if, for example, bankruptcy or garnishee proceedings intervene. In view of the small amounts involved, any such problems are probably settled in a practical way.

(*d*) *Fraud.* Banks have suffered losses through the misuse of cheque cards either by their customer or persons into whose hands they have fallen upon loss or theft. Great care must be taken before a cheque card is issued, as with a book of 30 cheques, credit of up to £1,500 could be taken. Banks insist that customers should have been in account for several months and have proved satisfactory before they issue a card.

The misuse of a card by the holder to obtain an unauthorised overdraft is a criminal offence under the Theft Act 1968: *R.* v. *Kovacs* (1974) and *Metropolitan Police Commissioner* v. *Charles* (1976).

11. Cash-machine withdrawal cards.

(*a*) *Types.*

(*i*) A small plastic card which facilitates the withdrawal of a small fixed sum when inserted in a machine and when used with a personal code number; the card is captured by the machine, and is returned in due course to the holder via his branch.

(*ii*) A small plastic card which facilitates the withdrawal of a variable chosen sum when inserted in the machine and when used with a personal code number by the customer; the card is returned immediately after use.

In addition to cash (the amount chosen by tapping digits, up to a limit previously agreed between the account-holding branch and the customer), the balance of the account can be ascertained and items such as statements and cheque books can be requested.

(*b*) *Usual authorities*

(*i*) Upon being issued with his card the customer authorises the bank to debit his account with all withdrawals effected and agrees to be jointly and severally liable for any overdraft created.

(*ii*) He agrees to exercise care in the control of his card and to keep his code number secret.

(*iii*) The card remains the property of the bank.

(*iv*) The customer undertakes to inform the Police and the bank immediately upon losing the card.

(*c*) *Issue.* As with cheque cards, care must be taken before issuing a card to prevent misuse by an unscrupulous customer. In the case of the fixed limit card which is captured, the risk is much smaller than in the second case.

12. Credit Cards. Although these plastic cards operate differently to the Cheque Guarantee Card, sometimes they are incorporated in the same card.

(*a*) *Issuer.* Usually this party is a finance house owned by the customer's banker and the contract is with the bank and/or the finance house. The customer's securities may therefore be available for any liability outstanding at any one time.

(*b*) *Retailer.* By prior agreement a credit limit is fixed for the customer and he is enabled to purchase goods on production of his card to retailers who are members of the scheme. The retailer is charged a small percentage on the transaction by the credit card finance house, but has the satisfaction of knowing that payment is certain. In the case of large amounts (where his floor limit is exceeded), the retailer can telephone the finance house to obtain sanction for the guaranteed transaction.

The acceptance of the card attracts trade to a shop. The retailer raises a voucher on which the card details are imprinted and this is signed by the card-holder. The retailer pays the voucher into his bank account, as he would a cheque.

(*c*) *Customer.* The customer is supplied with a statement of his transactions regularly and, dependent on the agreement, must either pay in full at once, or settle in a minimum sum and pay interest on the amount outstanding. Interest rates are usually higher than on normal bank overdrafts. A charge is sometimes made annually when a card is issued or renewed.

The card-holder can withdraw cash over his bank counter or from certain other banks to the debit of his credit card account.

PROGRESS TEST 5

1. What conditions must be fulfilled before a bank will be willing to place a stop on its own draft? **(2)**
2. Why do banks dislike conditional orders? **(5)**
3. What duties attach to a bank when paying a cheque bearing a capital "R" before the amount in figures? **(5)**
4. What are the advantages of a cheque guarantee card? **(10)**
5. What are the usual terms of use of a cheque guarantee card? **(10)**
6. Differentiate between a cheque guarantee card and a cash withdrawal card? **(10, 11)**
7. What are credit cards? How do they operate? **(12)**

PART THREE

FAILURE OR INCAPACITY

CHAPTER VI

Bankruptcy

PROCEEDINGS IN BANKRUPTCY

1. Objects of bankruptcy. When a person is *insolvent* (i.e. unable to pay his debts as and when they fall due) either he or his creditors may *petition* for the court to take over the administration of his estate and its distribution among creditors. This procedure is called bankruptcy and is governed by the Bankruptcy Act 1914, as amended.

The objects of bankruptcy are:

(*a*) *To secure fair and equal distribution* of available property among creditors.

(*b*) *To free the debtor from his debts* so that he can make a fresh start as soon as he is discharged by the court.

(*c*) *To enquire into the reason for his insolvency*, and so to deter people from rashly incurring debts they cannot pay.

NOTE: Students studying Practice of Banking will have already learned bankruptcy law for their Law Relating to Banking examination. However, it has been thought necessary to include sections on procedure and law (in abridged form) to show the legal framework on which bankers base their practical actions. Students requiring a fuller treatment of the law as opposed to banking practice should consult *The Law of Banking*, by David Palfreman (M & E HANDBOOK Series).

2. Procedure in bankruptcy. Before the process of bankruptcy can begin the debtor must first have committed an *act of bankruptcy*: *see* **4** below. An act of bankruptcy immediately raises a presumption of insolvency and enables a creditor (or debtor himself) to *petition* for the debtor's bankruptcy.

The stages in bankruptcy are as follows:

(*a*) An *act of bankruptcy* is committed.

(*b*) A *petition* based on an *available act of bankruptcy* may then be presented by a creditor (or the debtor may present a petition against himself).

(*c*) A *receiving order* making the Official Receiver the receiver of the debtor's property will be made if the petition is proved to the satisfaction of the court. (NOTE: Notice of the receiving order is *gazetted* by the Department of Trade and Industry.)

(*d*) A *statement of affairs* must then be drawn up by the debtor.

(*e*) A *meeting of creditors* is held to discuss the statement and to decide *whether to proceed with the bankruptcy of the debtor* or whether to accept any composition or scheme which he may offer; the receiving order is discharged if the court agrees to accept an approved composition or scheme.

(*f*) *A public examination* of the debtor takes place in court, although this may be dispensed with in a small bankruptcy.

(*g*) An *adjudication order* is made declaring the debtor bankrupt. This order is *gazetted.*

(*h*) A *trustee in bankruptcy* is appointed (to realise and distribute the debtor's property), and possibly a *committee of inspection* to supervise the trustee's work. The trustee's appointment is *gazetted.*

(*i*) *After adjudication* the bankrupt is automatically *discharged* after five years, unless the Court has ordered otherwise. The bankrupt then may need to apply for his discharge: Insolvency Act 1976, s. 7.

NOTE: A person is not bankrupt until stage (*g*) has been reached, i.e. until he has been *adjudicated bankrupt.*

3. Special classes of debtors. As a general rule, any debtor of full age who commits an act of bankruptcy in England can be made bankrupt: see BA 1914, s. 1(2). However, certain debtors are subject to special rules:

(*a*) *Infants* can only be made bankrupt for debts enforceable against them, e.g. for necessaries and for taxes. If a *partnership* which contains an *infant member* becomes bankrupt the infant cannot be made bankrupt on his own separate estate. However, all the partnership assets (including the infant's share) are available for partnership creditors.

(*b*) *A married woman* can now be made bankrupt under the same conditions as those attaching to a feme-sole: L.R. (Married Women & Tortfeasors) Act 1935, s. 1.

(*c*) *Mentally disordered persons* can only be made bankrupt with the consent of the court (or, if the act of bankruptcy was committed prior to disorder, without consent of the court).

(*d*) The *estate of a deceased person*, being insufficient to pay off all the deceased's debts, may be administered in bankruptcy.

(*e*) The *bankruptcy of a partnership* is governed by special rules: *see* **34** and **35** below and X, **20**, **21** and **23**.

NOTE: An *insolvent company* cannot be made bankrupt, but is wound-up: *see* XI, **64**.

4. Acts of bankruptcy: BA 1914, s. 1. An act of bankruptcy is committed by a debtor in *any* of the following instances:

(*a*) *Conveyance or assignment of* (*all*) *his property to a trustee for the benefit of his creditors generally*, e.g. transfer of property to a trustee appointed under a deed of arrangement: *see* **42** below.

(*b*) *Fraudulent conveyance, gift, delivery or transfer of any of his property.*

NOTE: (1) The word "fraudulent" is a little misleading here and means *any conveyance whether dishonest or otherwise which has the effect of defeating or delaying creditors.* Thus, in order to expand his business a builder formed a new limited company to which he transferred his assets, the company undertaking to repay his outstanding debts. The company then obtained facilities from L Bank against a debenture. On discovering the transfer, the builder's creditors began to press for repayment, with disastrous effects on liquidity, finally resulting in the bankruptcy of the builder. The trustee then claimed the assets transferred to the company as a fraudulent conveyance. HELD: The transfer, although not made with dishonest intent, had defeated and delayed creditors and was fraudulent; thus the bank's debenture was worthless; *Re Simms* (1930). (The bank *can avoid this danger* by ensuring that: (1) all creditors are paid off prior to transfer of assets, or (2) the debtor has sufficient liquid resources available to avert any pressure, or (3) all the creditors have agreed to accept the company as their debtor.) (2) A fraudulent conveyance is void and the transferee must return the property to the trustee in bankruptcy: s. 42.

(*c*) *Fraudulent preference*, i.e. a transfer of property by the debtor with intention to prefer one creditor of many: s. 44.

(*d*) *Departure from England, keeping house, absenting oneself*; with intent to defeat or delay creditors.

(*e*) *Seizure of the debtor's goods by a sheriff under process of* execution under court order; provided the goods have either: (*i*) been sold, or (*ii*) remained in the sheriff's hands for 21 days (except where an interpleader summons has been taken out).

(*f*) *Debtor's declaration filed in court*: (*i*) of his inability to pay debts, or (*ii*) of presentment of a bankruptcy petition against himself.

(*g*) *Debtor's failure to comply with a bankruptcy notice* (served on him by a judgment creditor) *within ten days*, unless he either: (*i*) raises a sufficient set-off or counter-claim, or (*ii*) pays the debt, or (*iii*) fully secures the debt.

(*h*) *Notice by the debtor* (in writing or otherwise) *to his creditors of suspension of payment of debts.*

(*i*) *Where damage or loss* is assessed in *criminal proceedings* at *over £15,000*, the Crown Court may make a *Criminal Bankruptcy Order* against the party(ies) found guilty upon trial.

> EXAMPLE: A debtor issued a circular to his creditors inviting them to meet him at a tavern so that he could submit a statement of his financial position. HELD: This amounted to notice of suspension of payments: *Crook* v. *Morley* (1891). *C. F. Clough* v. *Samuel* (1904).

> NOTE: An application for an administration order is now to be treated as an act of bankruptcy: Administration of Justice Act 1965, s. 21, as also is an order from the court requiring a debtor to furnish a list of all creditors in connection with an application for an attachment of earnings order: Administration of Justice Act 1970, s. 29.

5. The Petition. This is presented by the *debtor* or more usually by a creditor.

A *creditor's petition* (verified by affidavit) may be presented if the following conditions are complied with:

(*a*) *The debt owing is* £200 *or more* (after deducting the value of direct security if any). A joint petition presented by several creditors is permissible if the aggregate unsecured debt is £200: Insolvency Act 1976, s. 1.

(*b*) *The debt is a liquidated sum*, payable immediately or at a certain future time.

(*c*) *The act of bankruptcy relied on occurred within the three months prior to the presentation of the petition.*

The petition is usually heard not less than eight days after presentation.

6. The receiving order (gazetted).

(*a*) *When made.* (*i*) If the debtor has presented his own petition, then the receiving order is usually made immediately, but (*ii*) where a creditor's petition is presented the petition must first be heard by the court.

(*b*) *Gazetting.* A receiving order, when made, must be advertised in the *London Gazette* (this is deemed to be notice to all persons) and in a local newspaper: BA 1914, s. 11. (Gazetting may sometimes be delayed pending an appeal by the debtor.)

(*c*) *Registration concerning land.* (*i*) *Unregistered land.* To be of notice to a *bona fide* purchaser for value without notice of an available act of bankruptcy, a receiving order (or the petition, LCA 1925, s. 3) must have been registered in the Land Charges Register: LCA 1925, s. 6. (Registration is effected by the Official Receiver.) (*ii*) *Registered land.* Once registration of a petition or a receiving order is made on the Land Charges Register (under (*i*) above), then registration in the Land Register occurs automatically, i.e. by the registrar as soon as is practicable: Land Registration Act 1925, s. 61.

(*d*) *Effect of receiving order.* The Official Receiver (a Department of Trade and Industry official) becomes receiver (i.e. *protector*) of all the debtor's property; thenceforward all unsecured creditors have no remedy except in the bankruptcy.

7. Debtor's statement of affairs. Within seven days of the receiving order (or three days where the debtor filed his own petition) the debtor must prepare for the Official Receiver a statement of assets, debts and liabilities, showing the names of his creditors, and securities (if any) held by them: s. 14. The statement can be inspected by any creditor of the debtor: s. 14(4).

8. First meeting of creditors. This is summoned by the Official Receiver to be held fourteen days of the making of the receiving order. The meeting is conducted as follows:

(*a*) *The Official Receiver* (or his nominee) *presides* at the meeting.

(*b*) *Proposals*—

(*i*) *Any proposals for a composition or scheme of arrangement* must be passed by a *majority in number and three-fourths in value* of all creditors who have proved their debts; the court must then approve or reject the debtor's proposals.

(*ii*) *Alternatively: A majority in number and value of creditors* may pass a resolution for the debtor to be adjudicated bankrupt by the court. *Further:* If there are no resolutions or if no meeting is held the court will ultimately adjudicate the debtor bankrupt: s. 18(1).

(*c*) *Appointment of a trustee in bankruptcy* will usually take place at the meeting if it is decided to proceed with bankruptcy of the debtor.

9. Public examination of debtor. Unless dispensed with in a small bankruptcy under the provisions of the Insolvency Act 1976, s. 6, this takes place in open court and refers to his conduct, dealings and property. The hearing is held as soon as possible after the date fixed for submission of the statement of affairs. Unless the receiving order is rescinded, an order adjudicating the debtor bankrupt is issued by the court after the conclusion of the examination. The examination cannot be concluded until after the first meeting of creditors (if held).

10. Adjudication order (gazetted).

(*a*) *When made.* An adjudication order *declaring the debtor bankrupt* will be made by the court after the conclusion of the public examination if: (*i*) *the creditors so resolved* at their first meeting (or if *no decision was reached*), or (*ii*) there was *no meeting*, or (*iii*) *no scheme has been approved* within fourteen days of the conclusion of the public examination: s. 18, or (*iv*) the debtor fails without reasonable excuse to furnish his statement of affairs: s. 14.

(*b*) *Effect.* The property of the debtor vests in his trustee in bankruptcy and becomes divisible among his creditors.

(*c*) *Annulment.* If an adjudication order is annulled this fact is gazetted.

11. Committee of inspection. The creditors may appoint such a committee from amongst themselves to help the trustee in his management of the bankruptcy. (Maximum number is five; minimum three.)

12. Discharge of bankrupt. Following the passing of the Insolvency Act 1976, s. 7, if the court has declared that the debtor's examination has been either concluded or dispensed with (and he has been adjudged bankrupt), the court may order that unless otherwise discharged in the interim, he shall be considered automatically discharged on the fifth anniversary of adjudication.

Persons adjudged bankrupt more than five years prior to the relevant section of the Insolvency Act coming into force are automatically discharged on the tenth anniversary of adjudication.

Whenever a branch is in doubt as to whether a person is an undischarged bankrupt or not, it is possible to search in the Bankruptcy Register to ascertain the true position. (Similarity of names can be confusing however, as can be the use of more than one name by the person in question.)

DISTRIBUTABLE PROPERTY

13. Distributable property. Upon the debtor being adjudicated bankrupt, the trustee can utilise (for the benefit of creditors) all property attaching under:

(*a*) The doctrine of *relation back*: s. 37.
(*b*) The doctrine of *reputed ownership*: s. 38.
(*c*) Transfers amounting to a *fraudulent preference*: s. 44.
(*d*) Certain transfers amounting to a *voluntary settlement*: s. 42.
(*e*) *Fraudulent conveyances*: *see* LPA 1925, s. 172.

Property *acquired by or devolving on* the bankrupt *after adjudication and before discharge* can also be *claimed* by the trustee: s. 47. These are dealt with separately below.

14. Non-distributable property. Various classes of property do not vest in the trustee and are not therefore available for distribution. The chief of these are:

(*a*) *Tools of the bankrupt's trade*, together with his own and his family's apparel and bedding to the value of £250.

(*b*) *The bankrupt's personal earnings*; provided these are only reasonable for his own and his family's upkeep.

(*c*) *Property held by the bankrupt as trustee*.

15. Relation back: s. 37. The title of the trustee to the debtor's property *relates back to the first available act of bankruptcy which occurred within the three months, prior to the presentation of the petition*. (The first available act of bankruptcy is not necessarily the one on which the petition is founded.)

The doctrine can be seen to be severe in its application, as in many cases creditors are unaware of the impending bankruptcy until the receiving order is made and gazetted. Consequently, if it were not for the protection afforded by BA 1914, ss. 45–6 (*see* **22** below), it would mean that any dealing or transfer of property occurring *after* the first available act of bankruptcy and *before* the date of the receiving order would be void against the trustee.

16. Reputed ownership: s. 38. Because of the debtor's *apparent* ownership of goods he may have been granted additional credit. With this in view, this section provides that goods which *at the commencement of the bankruptcy* were in the possession, order or disposition of the bankrupt vest in the trustee, *provided they were used*: (*a*) in the *bankrupt's trade or business*; (*b*) with the *consent* of the owner; (*c*) in such circumstances that the bankrupt appeared the "reputed owner". (The latter is a question of fact, which may in any case be defeated by trade usage.) An owner of goods attached under this section may prove in the debtor's *bankruptcy* for their value.

17. Voluntary settlements: s. 42. The trustee may recover property involved in any *gratuitous settlement* made by the debtor: (*a*) within the two years prior to the commencement of the bankruptcy, or (*b*) between two and ten years prior to the commencement of the bankruptcy if the debtor was *insolvent* at the time (without taking into account the property settled). *Settlement of property* made before and in consideration of marriage, or accruing to a husband through his wife, are excluded and cannot be recovered by the trustee.

18. Fraudulent preference: s. 44. The trustee may recover property used by an insolvent party to give fraudulent preference to any creditor over other creditors within the six months prior to the presentation of the petition.

No debtor would voluntarily attempt to prefer the bank, but unfortunately the bank may be *indirectly* preferred by the debtor, who may pay in moneys especially to obtain the release of collaterally deposited security, e.g. deeds deposited by a third party. (Liability for fraudulent preference of any *surety or guarantor*—which covers not only guarantees but also all types of security deposited by third parties (*Re Conley*, 1938)—attaches to the bank as a result of s. 44.)

There is thus a distinct danger that the bank might release collateral security and then be faced with refunding to the trustee fraudulently preferred credits paid in during the six months before the petition. This hardship is mitigated to some extent by subsequent enactments. However, the best protection for the bank is to be wary before releasing collateral security, especially where a long-standing "hard-core" overdraft has suddenly been reduced or repaid without pressure.

NOTE: *In order to be classed as property transferred under fraudulent preference the trustee must prove that:* (1) *there was an actual intention to prefer one creditor of many;* (2) *the transfer was voluntary*, i.e. not under pressure by the creditor, for instance under threat of legal proceedings; (3) *the transfer took place within the six months prior to the presentation of the petition* and at the time of transfer the *debtor was insolvent.*

At this point students should consult XII, **29–31**.

19. Disclaimable property: s. 54. The trustee may in writing, within twelve months of his appointment (or within twelve months of discovering property of the bankrupt), disclaim any property of the bankrupt which is burdened with onerous covenants. Examples of such property would be: (*a*) valueless partly-paid shares; (*b*) unsaleable property; (*c*) unprofitable partly completed contracts, etc. (The court's permission is usually required where the trustee wishes to disclaim a lease.)

NOTE: (1) *Any person who suffers injury* because of the effect of disclaimer can prove in the debtor's bankruptcy to the extent of such injury. (2) *Any interested party can serve a notice on the trustee* requiring him to disclaim property within twenty-eight days or to forfeit his right of disclaimer. (3) *Bankers are occasionally affected by disclaimer*, as, for example, where their security is a short-term lease in which no equity exists for the trustee, and on which rents are falling due.

20. Order of distribution of property. Debts must be paid by the trustee in the following order:

(*a*) *Official Receiver's expenses.*

(*b*) *Trustee's expenses and remuneration.*

(*c*) *Preferential debts.* The Companies Act 1947, s. 115, states that preferential debts in bankruptcy are to be the same as those in the winding up of a company as listed in Companies Act 1948, s. 319(1). Such debts rank equally and abate in equal proportions if there are insufficient assets to pay them all in full: s. 319(5).

These debts will rank ahead of the bank, which is never a preferential creditor in bankruptcy, and include:

(*i*) *Local rates* payable within the year prior to the receiving order.

(*ii*) *Income tax* and other assessed taxes assessed up to 5th April preceding the receiving order (but not exceeding *one* year's assessment, although *any* one year may be taken).

(*iii*) *Value Added Tax* payable within the year prior to the receiving order.

(*iv*) *Wages or salary* of clerks, workmen, etc., for the four months preceding the receiving order (not amounting to more than £800 per claimant): Insolvency Act 1976, s. 1.

(*v*) *Accrued holiday remuneration* to employees.

(*vi*) *National Insurance contributions* payable within the year prior to the receiving order.

(*vii*) PAYE *deductions* payable as in (*vi*) above: Finance Act 1952, s. 30.

(*viii*) *Capital gains tax*: Finance Act 1965, Sched. 10.

(*d*) *Ordinary unsecured debts* rank equally.

(*e*) *Deferred debts*, e.g. loans by a husband to his wife (or vice versa) for business purposes.

POSITION OF BANKER

21. Position of banker. In view of the effect of the doctrine of relation back (*see* **15** above) and the fact that the banker may be completely unaware of his customer's impending bankruptcy, the protections available to the banker must be fully explored and understood.

22. Legal protection against relation back.

(*a*) Section 45, BA 1914, validates any of the following bona fide transactions:

(*i*) any payment by the bankrupt to any of his creditors;

(*ii*) any payment or delivery to the bankrupt;

(*iii*) any conveyance or assignment by the bankrupt for valuable consideration;

(*iv*) any contract, dealing, or transaction by or with the bankrupt for valuable consideration.... *Always provided* that these transactions take place (*a*) *before notice* of an *available act of bankruptcy*, and (*b*) *before the date* of the *receiving order*.

(*b*) Section 46, BA 1914, validates *bona fide* payments or delivery of property in the ordinary course of business to the person subsequently adjudged bankrupt or to a person claiming by assignment from him.... *Always provided* that these transactions take place (*i*) *before notice* of presentation of a *petition*, and (*ii*) *before the date of the receiving order*. Note particularly that a receiving order takes effect from the first moment of the day on which it is made.

23. Banker's practical position concerning dealings prior to the date of a receiving order.

(*a*) *Before notice of an act of bankruptcy*: s. 45 (and s. 46) applies:

(*i*) *All transactions* in respect of the customer's property are protected, e.g. cheques paid drawn payable to self, or third parties.

(*ii*) *Credits* may be received by the banker and drawn on by the customer as usual.

(*b*) *After notice of an act of bankruptcy but before notice of presentation of a petition*: s. 46 applies:

(*i*) *Credit accounts*. (*a*) *All cheques drawn by the customer in his own favour* may be paid; also the bank may deal with a person claiming by *assignment* from the customer, e.g. a trustee under a deed of arrangement: but *see* **43** below. (*b*) *Third-party cheques should not be paid* unless the *obiter dicta* given in *Re Dalton* (1962) (a case concerning payment away by a solicitor of his bankrupt client's monies) is relied on. Here it was stated that it would be an anomalous situation if the bank could, after knowledge of an act of bankruptcy committed by his customer, pay moneys directly to him (relying on s. 46) so that he could pay cash to a creditor; but could not pay the cheque if drawn directly in favour of the creditor.

(*ii*) *Debit accounts*. Pay no cheques, because a debt contracted *after notice of an act of bankruptcy* cannot be recovered from the trustee: s. 30(2).

(*iii*) *Credit moneys paid in* should be retained to see whether a petition is presented within the following three months, as if this occurs, the title to the moneys vests in the trustee.

(*iv*) *Safe custody items* must only be delivered up to the *customer*.

Note that once notice is received of the *presentation of a petition* against a customer the bank must stop *all* operations relating to his accounts and property.

24. Banker's practical position concerning dealings after the date of a receiving order.

(*a*) *Protection afforded by* s. 4, Bankruptcy (Amendment) Act 1926. This section was enacted to overcome the following hardship:

Thus a bank being completely unaware that a *receiving order* had been made against its customer continued transactions with him. (The receiving order had *not* been gazetted pending an appeal.) HELD: There was no protection for the bank in dealing after the date of the receiving order: *Re Wigzell* (1921).

S. 4 *provides* that where a bank has *no knowledge of a receiving order* made against its customer, then it is protected *up to the moment of gazetting*, in that the trustee must attempt to recover any money or property from the person who received it. If this proves impossible, then the trustee can recover from the bank.

(*b*) *Protection in respect of after-acquired property*: s. 47(1). *Unknowingly*, a banker may take security from or have dealings with the property of an *undischarged bankrupt*. Unfortunately, it matters not what time element is involved, e.g. that the bankrupt's adjudication occurred several years previously and that the banker had no knowledge of this fact. (The original adjudication order having been gazetted was notice to all persons.) The position is covered by the Act as follows:

(*i*) If the transaction concerns property which *belonged to the bankrupt at the time of his adjudication*, then this automatically vests in the trustee and must be returned to him.

(*ii*) If the transaction concerns property which the bankrupt *acquired after his adjudication*, then the banker can retain such property (i.e. money, security, or negotiable instruments) or obtain a good discharge for delivery at the bankrupt's orders, provided he dealt: (*a*) *in good faith*; (*b*) *for value* (this is expressly deemed present in dealings between banker and bankrupt involving money, security or negotiable instruments); and (*c*) *completed the transaction before the trustee intervened*: s. 47(1). (*See* **30** below in respect of *accounts of undischarged bankrupts*.)

25. Banker's proof in bankruptcy. In order to vote at a meeting of creditors or to receive a dividend from the bankrupt's estate, a banker must prove his debt: see BA 1914, Scheds. I & II, as amended.

Under the provisions of the Insolvency Act 1976, s. 5, a simpler form of proof has been introduced, and it is no longer necessary for it to be sworn in the presence of a Commissioner of Oaths, unless the Trustee in Bankruptcy calls for a sworn proof.

As an unsecured creditor a banker may submit his proof to the Official Receiver or trustee (i.e. statement of debt supported by affidavit) immediately the receiving order is made.

As a secured creditor (i.e. a creditor who has a *mortgage*, *charge* or *lien* over the property of the *debtor*), a banker has the following rights in respect of his security:

(*a*) to rely on it and not prove at all;
(*b*) to realise it and prove for any deficiency;
(*c*) to surrender it to the trustee and prove for his whole debt. (Highly unlikely in practice);
(*d*) to value it and prove for any deficiency.

NOTE: (1) *Where the banker elects* (*d*) *above*, then the trustee may redeem the security at this value or require it to be sold (or as directed by the court); *provided* that the banker may at any time in writing require the trustee to exercise his rights within six months following receipt of such notice, and if he fails to do so he loses these rights, and the property then vests in the banker, who may prove for any remaining deficiency. (2) *Proving for dividend purposes*. Bankers rarely prove under BA 1914, Sched. 1, for the purpose of *voting at meetings of creditors*, but always *prove for dividend* under Sched. II *unless*: (1) the realisation value of the debtor's security will *undoubtedly* cover the whole of his outstanding debt, or (2) it is obvious from the Statement of Affairs that *no* dividend will be paid to unsecured creditors. In every case a banker *always* consults the trustee (or Official Receiver) before taking any action in respect of his security. For example, it will usually be necessary to demand repayment of the debt from the trustee or Official Receiver prior to realisation of the security.

26. Proof: further points for bankers.

(*a*) *Change in value of security*. Where a banker makes a *bona fide* mistake in the valuation of his security *or* where the security value has increased or diminished since the original valuation, *he may amend his proof* to the satisfaction of the trustee (or court). Any surplus dividend which has been received must be returned, or if the amount of the proof is increased the banker is entitled to make up his dividend out of any further distributable moneys which become available (but no past dividend may be disturbed).

The same ruling is also applied *where a banker proceeds to realise security which he has previously valued*, i.e. the net amount realised is substituted for the amount of the previous valuation.

(*b*) *Interest on all debts may be added to the date of the receiving order*. The maximum rate of interest provable is 5 per cent p.a. An agreed higher rate cannot be recovered unless surplus estate funds are available, after all provable debts have been paid in full: s. 66.

(*c*) *Debts not provable by the banker are*: (*i*) debts contracted after the banker has received notice of an act of bankruptcy by, or presentation of a petition against, his customer, or (*ii*) debts contracted after the date of the receiving order.

(*d*) *Set-off*. To arrive at the net amount due between themselves and the trustee, the bank must set-off all amounts which are due between themselves and their customer and which are in the same right, e.g. 1 a/c; 2 a/c; loan a/c; etc. If a *net credit* balance remains, then this is paid to the trustee; if a *net debit* balance remains, then the bank proceeds with proof as previously outlined.

27. Proof: as regards bills discounted.

(*a*) *Where customer becomes bankrupt*. A banker who has discounted a bill for a customer who becomes bankrupt can prove in his estate for the amount of the bill. If the bill is duly paid in full at maturity by the acceptor, then the banker must return to the trustee the dividend which he has received. In the event of the customer's bankruptcy a credit balance standing in his name may be set off against the contingent liability on bills discounted: BA 1914, s. 31.

(*b*) *Where acceptor becomes bankrupt*. If the acceptor of a bill, discounted for a customer, becomes bankrupt the banker may immediately prove in his bankruptcy for the full amount of the bill. (Notice should be given to all parties liable on the bill to retain their liability in respect of any shortfall.)

28. Proof: collateral security ignored. Under the rule in *re Sass* (1896), the value of collateral security is *completely ignored* when proving in the debtor's bankruptcy, e.g. where X gives a guarantee (or other security) for £500 to secure Y's account, and a receiving order is made against Y when he owes the bank £600, the procedure to be adopted is as follows:

Submit proof in Y's bankruptcy for £600 (plus interest), i.e. third-party security is ignored *and* call upon X to repay £500 (which will be placed to a suspense account when paid).

In rare instances the bank may either (*a*) release the collateral depositor from complete liability or (*b*) await receipt of the dividend from the trustee in respect of the bankrupt principal's estate and then call on the collateral depositor for any remaining shortfall.

29. Restrictions imposed on undischarged bankrupts. The following restrictions are of interest to bankers:

(*a*) *He must not obtain credit of more than* £50 either alone or jointly with any other person without disclosing that he is an undischarged bankrupt: s. 155, and Insolvency Act 1976, s. 1.

(*b*) *He must not conduct a business in a name* other than that under which he was adjudicated bankrupt without disclosing that fact: s. 155.

(*c*) *He is debarred from acting as a director of a limited company* unless the court by which he was adjudicated bankrupt decides otherwise: CA 1948, s. 187(1). (In any event the office of director is vacated if a director becomes bankrupt and the company has adopted Art. 88, TABLE A, CA 1948.)

NOTE: A banker should not pay out on an open cheque to a person known to be an undischarged bankrupt (unless with the authority of the trustee) because the money may later be reclaimed by the trustee, who could argue that the banker had not paid in due course under BEA 1882, s. 59.

30. Accounts of undischarged bankrupts. Where a banker has a suspicion that his customer is an undischarged bankrupt, a search should be made of the Central Registers of the Department of Official Receivers maintained in London.

If the search confirms the banker's suspicions the customer's account must be immediately stopped (unless it is a trust account) and either the trustee in bankruptcy (if known) or the Department of Trade and Industry must be informed, preferably by recorded delivery. Thereafter if the banker receives no instructions from either the court or the trustee *within one month*, then the customer's account can be continued: s. 47(2). The same procedure should be followed where operations by the bankrupt are being carried out through a nominee's account, e.g. his wife's account.

BANKRUPTCY OF SPECIAL TYPES OF ACCOUNT HOLDER

31. Bankruptcy of a joint account holder. Where one party to a joint account becomes bankrupt, then the account must be stopped irrespective of whether it is in *credit* or *debit*, as the mandate is determined. Where the bank receives notice of an act of bankruptcy by, or the presentation of a petition against, a joint account party, similar considerations apply as to a sole account. The following practical considerations should be noted:

(*a*) *Credit account.* Having stopped the account, instructions are required from both the *trustee* (or Official Receiver) *and the solvent party* as to the disbursement of the account balance and release of custody items.

NOTE: (1) The bank may well agree to open a new account for the *solvent* party, to be maintained in credit or as otherwise agreed. (2) In order to avoid damage to the *solvent* party's credit, cheques presented drawn by him should be returned "Joint account holder 'X' involved in bankruptcy proceedings". (3) Cheques presented drawn by the *insolvent* party should be returned "Refer to drawer".

(*b*) *Unsecured debit account.* Having stopped the account, the bank may by virtue of *J. & S. liability* admitted by the account holders: (*i*) set-off any personal credit balance standing in the name of either party against the whole debt which *that party* owes; (*ii*) prove against the estate of the bankrupt party for the whole debt owing, while at the same time calling upon the solvent party to pay off the whole debt owing (allowing for any credit balances as in (*i*)).

32. Bankruptcy of a joint account holder: secured debit account.

(*a*) *Security deposited by a party to the joint account either*: (*i*) to cover the joint overdraft, or (*ii*) to cover his own personal account borrowing and all other liabilities owed to the bank either alone or jointly. In such a case the value of the security or realisation proceeds must be deducted by the bank from the amount owed by the depositor, but need not be deducted in respect of the amount owed by each of the remaining parties to the joint account, i.e. the security may be treated as collateral.

EXAMPLE: X and Y operate a joint account. On X being adjudicated bankrupt, the balance of the joint account is *debit* £2,000; X's plain account is *debit* £200. X has deposited security for his own account and joint liabilities valued at £500. J. & S. liability has been admitted.

General outline of procedure to be adopted: (1) Stop all accounts. (2) Add interest to the date of the receiving order. (3) Demand repayment from the trustee (or Official Receiver) and on default prove against X's estate for £1,700 plus interest (i.e. 2,000 + 200 – 500). (4) Demand repayment from Y of £2,000. (Any repayment which is forthcoming would need to be held on suspense account until the final dividend in X's estate has been received.) (5) Any surplus received would be apportioned by the Court.

(*b*) *Security deposited by a party other than one of the joint account holders* (i.e. collateral security) may be completely ignored when proving against the bankrupt party or when demanding repayment from the solvent party.

33. Bankruptcy of a member of a partnership. The bankruptcy of one (or some) of several partners automatically brings about the dissolution of the partnership (unless the partnership deed stipulates otherwise), consequently a new mandate is required:

(*a*) *A credit partnership account may be continued*, as it is the responsibility of the *solvent* partners to account to the trustee in bankruptcy in respect of the bankrupt partner's share in the business. (The authority of the bankrupt partner is, of course, terminated.)

(*b*) *A debit partnership account must be stopped* where it is required to retain the right of proof against the estate of the bankrupt partner or against security deposited by him, otherwise the Rule in Clayton's Case will apply to the bank's detriment, in that any future credits which are paid in will go in reduction of the amount owed by the insolvent partner. It may be that the bank are willing to release the estate of the insolvent partner, and in this case the remaining partners (together with any new partners) can issue a new mandate to the bank and draw a cheque to repay the overdraft of the old partnership, thereby releasing the bankrupt partner from his liability to the bank and creating a new overdraft in respect of the new partnership.

34. Bankruptcy of a partnership. A *receiving order* made against a *partnership* operates against each of the general partners. Ultimately *every partner is adjudicated bankrupt* on his own estate, and *this also brings about the bankruptcy of the partnership.*

Where *notice* is received of an *act of bankruptcy* committed by the partnership, BA 1914, s. 46, governs operations of the *partnership account*, in that only a *credit* balance may be withdrawn by the partnership.

The partnership account, together with any personal account of the partners, *must be stopped* immediately notice is received of the presentation of a petition against the partnership (or in the absence of such notice when a receiving order is made). The authority of the partners ceases and ultimately vests in the trustee in bankruptcy.

35. Bankruptcy of a partnership: proof.

(*a*) *Joint and several liability* (referred to as J. & S. liability throughout the HANDBOOK). As the bank will have established J. & S. liability against the partners, they can prove *for a partnership overdraft* concurrently against the joint partnership estate and against each partner's separate estate.

(*b*) *Partnership security deposited to secure the partnership account.* If the security does not fully cover the partnership debt, then any proof submitted against the partnership estate must be adjusted to allow for this security. However, the security is *ignored* in respect of the proofs made against *each of the partners on their separate estates.* (Partnership security deposited to cover both the partnership debt and an individual partner's debt may be dealt with as in (*c*) below.)

(*c*) *Security deposited by a partner for both his own and the partnership account* (i.e. for all liabilities owed either alone or jointly) may be appropriated to whichever estate the bank desires, i.e. the amount realised or the security value may be allowed for in respect of *either* the partnership proof *or* the proof made against the partner depositing the security. The bank will usually wish to appropriate the security to the estate which is likely to yield the smallest dividend, so retaining its right to prove as an unsecured creditor in the estate yielding the largest dividend.

(*d*) *Any credit balance standing to a partner's private accont* is set off against either: (*i*) the amount which *he* owes the bank in respect of the partnership debt, or (*ii*) the amount owed by the partnership in respect of the partnership debt; i.e. the proof against the partner's personal estate *or* against the partnership estate is arrived at by allowing for the credit balance.

SPECIMEN QUESTION ON PROOF

Smith and Brown (trading as S & B) are in partnership. A receiving order is made against the firm, when the position at the bank is as follows:

S & B Current account	Dr	£2,000
Smith	Dr	£300
Brown Deposit	Cr	£400

Security (deeds valued at £1,000) has been deposited by Smith for his own account and for all other liabilities to the bank.

J. & S. liability has been admitted by both partners. What proofs may be submitted by the bank?

ANSWER

(*a*) *Three proofs may be submitted to the trustee*, i.e. in respect of: (*i*) the joint partnership estate, (*ii*) Smith's estate, (*iii*) Brown's estate. (It must be remembered that this concurrent right stems from the admittance of J. & S. liability.)

(*b*) *The bank may appropriate Smith's security*, to *either* his own estate *or* to the partnership estate.

(*c*) *Brown's credit balance may be set off* against either his own estate *or* against the partnership estate.

Obviously, therefore, a variety of proofs are possible. Two alternative specimen proofs are shown:

	PROOF A	PROOF B
Proof against S. & B.	= £600 (i.e. 2,000 – 1,000 – 400)	= £2,000
Proof against Smith	= £2,300 (i.e. 2,000 + 300)	= £1,300 (i.e. 2,000 + 300 – 1,000)
Proof against Brown	= £2,000	= £1,600 (i.e. 2,000 – 400)

NOTE: (1) *Before deciding on their proofs* the bank will consult the various statements of affairs and the trustee, in order to ascertain the likely dividends. They will endeavour to arrange their proofs so that the largest proof is submitted against the estate likely to yield the highest dividend. (2) The rights in relation to sale of security, etc., and debit interest *have been ignored in this answer*. (3) Note that the bank are owed a total of £2,300, against which they hold security and credit balances worth £1,400. The dividends will augment the latter.

36. Bankruptcy of one of several co-trustees. The bankruptcy of one or some of several trustees does not affect operations on the trust account, unless the trust deed states otherwise. However, the solvent trustees or beneficiaries may deem it advisable to approach the court under the powers conferred by the Trustee Act 1925, s. 41, in order to have a new trustee appointed in substitution for the bankrupt party.

37. Sole guarantor's bankruptcy. Notice received by the bank of an act of bankruptcy by, or presentation of a petition against, a bank guarantor or (in the absence of such notice) the making of a receiving order puts an end to the continuance of the security. If no other arrangements are possible and the bank wishes to rely on the guarantor and to prove in his bankruptcy, then the account of the principal debtor must be stopped (unless a clause restricting the operation of the *Rule in Clayton's Case* has been included in the guarantee). Formal demand for repayment is served on the trustee in bankruptcy and on default proof is submitted.

38. Bankruptcy of one J. & S. guarantor. If one of several guarantors is involved in bankruptcy proceedings the bank can either rely on the remaining guarantors or proceed as in **37** above. When adjudication ultimately takes place the bank may decide either: (*a*) to release the bankrupt and rely on the remaining guarantors, or (*b*) to prove in the bankrupt's estate and at the same time demand repayment from the remaining guarantors.

NOTE: In relation to **37** and **38** above: (1) There is no need for the bank to make formal demand for repayment from the *principal debtor* unless they so wish. (2) Any moneys (under a total of 100p in the £) received under the guarantee should be held on suspense account in order to preserve the bank's collateral position. (3) *See also* XII, **40** and **43**.

DEEDS OF ARRANGEMENT

39. Arrangements outside bankruptcy. In order to avoid the strict rules of bankruptcy and the costs involved, a debtor may reach agreement with his creditors regarding the arrangement of his affairs for their benefit.

The Deeds of Arrangement Act 1914, applies to such agreements (whether under seal or not) made: (*a*) for the benefit of creditors generally, or (*b*) by an insolvent trader for the benefit of three or more creditors. (The administration of the arrangement is entrusted to a trustee.)

Alternatively, such agreement may take the form of a *composition with creditors*, i.e. a contract by which the creditors agree to accept (in complete discharge of their debts) a proportion of their claims, e.g. 50p in each pound owed.

A deed of arrangement is only binding on creditors who assent to it.

40. The Deeds of Arrangement Act 1914. If an arrangement or composition is embodied in a document, then it is *void* unless:

(*a*) *It is registered* at the Department of Trade and Industry within seven days of execution and is properly stamped: s. 2.

(*b*) *It is assented to* by a *majority in number and value* of the creditors (if made for the benefit of creditors generally) within twenty-one days of registration. If the deed affects land it must also be registered at the Land Charges Registry, otherwise it will be void against a purchaser for value of the land: LCA 1925, s. 13. (The time limits for registration may be extended by the Court.)

41. The trustee under a deed. He must within twenty-eight days of registration file a statutory declaration that the necessary majority of creditors have assented to the arrangement: s. 3. (Once registered, the deed can be inspected by any person on payment of a small fee.)

42. Deed of arrangement as act of bankruptcy. A creditor who has (*a*) *failed to assent* to a deed or composition made for the benefit of creditors generally, or (*b*) *assented* to a deed which becomes *void*, can use the deed as an act of bankruptcy on which he may base a petition within the three months of its execution. (The trustee can reduce this time to one month by serving notice of the deed on non-assenting creditors.)

43. Practical position concerning accounts of trustees appointed under deeds of arrangement. Where the customer has executed a deed for his creditors generally, his account should be stopped until such time as the deed and the "assents" have been registered, when any credit balance may be transferred to the trustee, relying on BA 1914, s. 46.

The trustee may open an account in the name of the debtor's estate, into which he may pay moneys, but he should not be allowed to draw cheques on this account until three months have elapsed since the execution of the deed, as unless all of the creditors have assented to the deed a petition could be based on it. (The three-months period may be reduced to one month where non-assenting creditors have been served with notice of the deed.)

NOTE: (1) Before assenting to a deed or before allowing a trustee to withdraw a customer's credit balance, a banker *would need to peruse its terms most carefully*. (2) After taking into consideration all the prevailing circumstances, e.g. standing of the trustee;

names of non-assenting creditors; reasons for requiring to operate account, etc., a banker may *exceptionally* be willing to allow the trustee to operate the account before the three-months period expires.

PROGRESS TEST 6

1. What do you understand by a fraudulent conveyance? **(4)**

2. Distinguish between the following and indicate which are gazetted:

(*a*) an act of bankruptcy (**4**);
(*b*) a petition (**5**);
(*c*) a receiving order (**6**);
(*d*) an adjudication order (**10**);
(*e*) appointment of a trustee in bankruptcy. **(2, 8)**

3. State precisely what is meant by "relation back". How may this affect the bank? **(15)**

4. Distinguish between Bankruptcy Act 1914, ss. 45 and 46, and also Bankruptcy (Amendment) Act 1926, s. 4. **(22, 23, 24)**

5. How may a bank be fraudulently preferred? Is there any statutory protection against fraudulent preference? (**18** and XII, **29–31**)

6. What rights has a bank as a secured creditor where the depositor of the security becomes bankrupt? **(25–26)**

7. Outline a banker's rights where he holds collateral security for his customer's account and the latter becomes bankrupt. **(28)**

8. If a banker suspects that he has the account of an undischarged bankrupt what action should he take? **(30)**

9. What effect does bankruptcy of the following persons have on the respective banking accounts:

(*a*) a party to a joint account (**31, 32**);
(*b*) a partner (**33**);
(*c*) a partnership? **(34)**

Deal with the situations of debit and credit balances in each case.

10. Outline fully the procedure for proof in the bankruptcy of a partnership. **(35)**

11. What is a deed of arrangement? **(39)** What are the practical difficulties concerning deeds of arrangement? **(43)**

CHAPTER VII

Mental Incapacity

1. Notice of incapacity. Where a banker receives notice of a customer's mental disorder, his authority to pay cheques and to act upon the customer's mandates and authorities is terminated.

Where a receiver (*see* **3** below) has *not* been appointed, it may be difficult for the banker to decide whether a customer is so mentally disordered that he does not understand the nature of the transactions into which he enters. *The danger for the banker is that*: (*a*) if incapacity is wrongly presumed, then liability may attach for dishonouring cheques which would otherwise have been honoured, or (*b*) if incapacity is not presumed when it should be, then liability may attach for paying away the customer's money after his incapacity. (It may be safer to assume sanity unless the customer has been compulsorily detained or a receiver has been appointed.)

The action to be taken by the bank upon notice of incapacity, will depend upon: (*a*) the type of account in which the customer is concerned, or (*b*) whether the incapacitated party has undertaken any liability towards the bank, e.g. by guaranteeing one of the bank's accounts:

(*a*) *Procedure to be adopted where incapacitated party is a member of—*

(*i*) *Sole or joint account.* Stop the account whether in debit or credit—mandate terminated. Return cheques on sole account, "Drawer's mandate terminated" or "Insufficient mandate". (NOTE: Exercise care in respect of the answer when returning joint account cheques signed by sane party.)

(*ii*) *Partnership account.* No need to stop account—mandate terminated, but incapacity of a partner does not bring about dissolution of partnership (only grounds for dissolution). *Debit* account—stop if required to retain liability of incapacitated partner. *Credit* account—cheques drawn by incapacitated partner can be confirmed by other partners and paid.

(*b*) *Where guarantor becomes incapacitated*, then unless new arrangements are made with the principal debtor, the bank should call up the guarantee after stopping the principal's account.

(*c*) *All other mandates and authorities given by the incapacitated party are terminated*, e.g. authority given to an agent to sign on the principal's account: *Drew* v. *Nunn* (1879).

2. Mental Health Act 1959. This Act has attempted to throw new light on problems of mental disorder by setting down modern ideas, e.g. the word "lunatic" is no longer used. A patient is now said to suffer from *mental disorder*; this means mental illness, arrested or incomplete development of the mind, psychopathic disorder and any other disorder or disability of mind: s. 4(1). Thus such things as senility, nervous breakdown and loss of memory are covered. Formal certification has been abolished, but a patient may still be *compulsorily* detained if necessary.

(*a*) *Patients admitted into hospital.* This may occur either: (*i*) *informally*, i.e. on a voluntary basis; or (*ii*) *compulsorily*, e.g. upon application to the hospital managers by nearest relative or by a mental welfare officer, provided such application is supported by two medical practitioners.

(*b*) *Patients admitted into guardianship*. In suitable cases a patient may be placed under the guardianship of a local authority or of a person authorised by a local authority.

NOTE: (1) In neither (*a*) nor (*b*) can mental incapacity be *conclusively* presumed, although the bank would normally be justified in stopping the account of a customer who had been *compulsorily* detained. (2) In both (*a*) and (*b*) it is advisable to ask the hospital managers or attending medical officers to confirm whether the disordered patient is able to attend to his own financial affairs.

3. Appointment of receiver by Court of Protection. *Under Part VIII of the Act* the Court of Protection has jurisdiction to manage and administer the property and affairs of persons who are incapable of so doing by reason of *mental disorder*, *whether or not they are compulsorily detained* or under guardianship under the provision of the Act and whether they are residing in their own homes or elsewhere.

(*a*) *Appointment of receiver*. The Master of the Court will (usually on the application of a near relative) appoint a near relative to act as receiver for the disordered person. The receiver may then with the Master's authority carry out the powers outlined under s. 102/3 of the Act.

(*b*) *Where a banker is advised that a receiver has been appointed he should:*

(*i*) *Stop the customer's account.*

(*ii*) *Inspect the receiver's authority* (office copy—bearing official seal of C of P).

(*iii*) *Open a new account* in the name of the receiver or act as otherwise directed in the authority.

(*iv*) Immediately contact the receiver if the customer's account in in *debit*; the receiver must deal with all creditors: s. 102(2).

NOTE: A receiver's authority ceases, without formality, on the death of the patient, and any balance standing in the receiver's name vests in the patient's survivors: s. 105(2).

4. Welfare of dependants. In the event of a customer's incapacity the bank should encourage the dependants to apply to the Court of Protection for the appointment of a receiver.

Pending such appointment the bank may, *exceptionally*, allow: (*a*) a dependant to draw on a new account, or (*b*) a dependant authorised to sign on the customer's account prior to incapacity to continue to do so. (An indemnity would usually be taken and withdrawals limited to *necessaries.*) The bank would have no recourse against the customer in such circumstances, as all mandates are terminated on notice of incapacity. However, if there was any dispute the bank would normally be able to recover moneys paid away from either: (*a*) the receiver, on his appointment, who can confirm past outgoings; or (*b*) from the customer's estate if his death occurs before application for appointment of a receiver:

EXAMPLES: (1) A customer became insane, but his eldest son was allowed to continue to operate his account for the upkeep of the family. The account became overdrawn. On the death of the customer, several of the executors objected to repaying the overdraft from the estate. HELD: The bank could recover to the extent of all payments for *necessaries* . . . this included the upkeep of both the customer's property and family up to their usual standards . . . the right to recover stemmed from *subrogation.* Bank charges and interest could not therefore be recovered: *Re Beavan, Davis, Banks & Co.* v. *Beavan* (1912). (2) A customer became insane, but the bank *allowed the balance of account to be transferred into his wife's name.* Ultimately the customer recovered and claimed back the balance which had been transferred. HELD: He could not recover the moneys, as they had been used to settle his debts: *Scarth* v. *NP Bank Ltd.* (1930).

PROGRESS TEST 7

1. State briefly the aims of the Mental Health Act 1959. **(2)**

2. How should the bank proceed when approached by a receiver appointed for one of its customers by the Court of Protection? **(3)**

3. What exceptional steps may a bank take to provide for the welfare of dependants of a customer who is mentally incapacitated? **(4)**

PART FOUR

VARIOUS TYPES OF ACCOUNT HOLDER

CHAPTER VIII

Conduct of Various Accounts

MARRIED WOMEN

1. Position in law. A married woman is capable of acquiring, holding and disposing of any property, rendering herself liable in respect of any tort, contract, debt or obligation, and is subject to the law relating to bankruptcy, in all respects as if she were a single woman: LR (Married Women & Tortfeasors) Act 1935, s. 1.

A married woman can thus open and operate a banking account and charge her assets as security in the usual manner, with the exception that if she is still a minor the rules concerning minors (*see* **5–8** *below*) also govern the position.

In all its dealings with a married woman, or a femme sole, the bank must not discriminate on grounds of sex alone: Sex Discrimination Act 1975. (*See Quinn* v. *Williams Furniture Ltd.* (1980) concerning a hire-purchase transaction held to have been wrongly arranged by a retailer who required the woman applicant to be guaranteed by her husband.)

2. Opening a banking account. The usual introductions/references are required. If she is employed her employer's name should be noted. The name of her husband, together with his occupation and employer's name, is still required by some banks, because of the rule in *Savory* v. *Lloyds Bank Ltd.* (1933), *see* II, **2**, and despite the passing of the Sex Discrimination Act 1975. Some banks however, have, now decided to waive that requirement, and carry any possible risk, which is thought to be slight in modern times. Such an approach avoids the possibility of offending new women customers, when they open an account.

3. Restraint on anticipation. These have been rendered completely inoperative: Married Women (Restraint upon Anticipation) Act 1949. However, care is necessary to ensure that securities deposited by a married woman are in fact her own property and not settled property.

4. Independent advice. Banks usually require that a married woman be *independently advised by her own solicitor* when depositing security for the account of another person. As there is *no presumption* of undue influence in the case of husband and wife, the wife would have to prove such influence if she wished to avoid her obligations to the bank, e.g. where she has secured her husband's account. To eliminate the risk of a successful action being brought by the wife, the bank would require her to be independently advised: *see* XII, **17**.

MINORS

5. Position in law. A minor (formerly referred to as "infant") is a person under the age of eighteen years: Family Law Reform Act 1969, s. 1. Minors are protected in law: in respect of contracts they are liable only for necessaries and for certain transactions of a continuing nature.

6. Position as account holder.

(*a*) *Credit account.* A minor can operate a credit account in the usual manner, the banker obtaining a good discharge in respect of all disbursements from the account.

(*b*) *Unsecured overdraft.* A minor should *not* usually be permitted to overdraw his account, since any contract for repayment of money lent is void under the Infants Relief Act 1874, s. 1.

(*c*) *Secured overdraft.* As a minor's contract in respect of a loan or overdraft is *completely void*, then any security deposited by a third party to secure the minor's account is unenforceable *unless* taken in the form of an *indemnity: see* XII, **14** and **28**. Obviously the minor cannot secure his own account.

7. Minor member of a partnership. A minor can be a member of a partnership and can bind the partnership in the ordinary course of business. Where a partnership which contains a minor member operates a banking account, the following points should be borne in mind:

(*a*) *The minor may be permitted to draw cheques and to overdraw the partnership account* as agent for the partnership. (The usual account mandate will be taken.)

(*b*) *The minor will not be liable personally* for the partnership debt, even if the partnership becomes bankrupt. However, all partnership assets, including the minor's share, are available for partnership creditors.

(*c*) *The minor's personal security cannot be accepted* for the partnership debt.

(*d*) *Liability after majority*. If the minor does not repudiate his position as partner either before or within a reasonable time of his majority he will be personally liable for partnership debts *incurred after his majority*.

8. Minor party to a joint account. It is perfectly permissible for a minor to be a party to a joint account. (He would not, of course, be liable in respect of any overdraft incurred.) The bank will require their usual mandate to be completed, which incorporates an express clause (to show intention) that the balance of the account will vest in the survivor(s) in the event of death: *see* **12** below.

> NOTE: (1) A minor cannot be sued on a *bill or cheque*, even if given for *necessaries*, though he will remain liable to pay for the necessaries. (2) A bank could not recover from a minor for whom it had *exchanged* a cheque which was subsequently dishonoured. (3) *A minor may act as an agent* for a party with full contractual powers, e.g. he may be authorised to operate his father's account (specific authority being required if he is to be permitted to overdraw). (4) A minor can be named as *executor*, but cannot act personally during minority. A minor cannot act as *trustee*.

JOINT ACCOUNTS

9. Definition. Joint accounts can be classified as accounts opened in the names of two or more parties, being persons other than trading partners, personal representatives or trustees. The most common type of joint account is that of husband and wife.

10. Account mandate. A mandate is required, signed by all parties to the account, covering the following points:

(*a*) *Withdrawal of moneys*. The general rule that a debt owed to several parties jointly may be discharged by a payment to any one of them *does not apply between banker and customer*. Consequently, if a banker is required to release moneys against the signatures of less than all, then the mandate must authorise this. (This also applies in respect of delivery of custody items.)

(*b*) *Joint and several liability*. Where any overdraft is contemplated the mandate must contain an express admittance of J & S liability by the account holders.

(*c*) *Borrowing*. In respect of overdrafts the account holders must agree that where less than all parties are authorised to sign on the account, then any overdraft which is created becomes the responsibility of *all*.

NOTE: (1) *Death*, *bankruptcy* or *mental incapacity* of any *one party* cancels the mandate irrespective of whether the account is in *debit or credit*: *see* the various paragraphs below. (2) *One party can countermand payment* of any cheques, as this amounts to a *partial revocation* of the mandate. (3) *All parties must join in any authority* for an agent to sign on the account. (4) *If one party opens an account in the joint names of himself and another* without the latter's authority, then the authority of both parties is still necessary to authorise release of funds.

11. Death of one joint-account party.

(*a*) *Credit account*. The rule of survivorship applies (*see* **12** below), but as death cancels the mandate, a new one is required *if there is more than one survivor*. Cheques signed by the deceased *or* cheques signed by less than all the survivors should be returned unpaid; in practice, it is usually possible to get immediate instructions from all the survivors.

(*b*) *Debit account*. J & S liability having been admitted; to retain the liability of the deceased's estate the account must be stopped on notice of death. Otherwise the *Rule in Clayton's Case* will operate in releasing the deceased's estate.

12. Common-law rule of survivorship. In respect of a *credit balance owed jointly* the rule is that on the *death* of one party the bank obtains a *good discharge by delivering the balance to all the survivors* or by acting in accordance with instructions incorporated in a new mandate signed by *all* the survivors.

NOTE: The survivors must account to the deceased's estate for his share of the balance; they must also disclose this amount to the Inland Revenue, because duty may be payable. Banks have agreed to issue an Inland Revenue memorandum to the survivors, pointing this out. Any settlement due, however, is entirely the survivors' responsibility.

13. Rule of survivorship: examples of application. *The rule is not dependent on the bank mandate.* Although provision is made in the mandate for delivery of the account balance to the survivor(s), this is only to show the *intention* of the parties, as the mandate is cancelled on death.

(*a*) *Rule as applied to husband-and-wife joint accounts.* The rule still applies unless there is an express or implied intention to the contrary of which the bank have notice.

EXAMPLE: An ailing husband converted his personal account into a joint account with his wife so that she could withdraw funds for necessaries. HELD: On his death his estate took the balance; there being clear intention that the survivorship rule should not apply: *Marshal* v. *Crutwell* (1875).

(*b*) *Rule as applied to adult-and-infant joint accounts.* Where an infant is a party to a joint account, then even if the account was opened and moneys provided solely by the adult party, it appears beyond doubt that on the death of one party the survivorship rule normally applies.

EXAMPLE: A father opened an account in the joint names of himself and his infant son (the mandate providing for the survivor to take any balance). On his death, *the father's executors* withdrew the £10,000 balance, and held it in trust for the son, who was still an infant. When he was twenty-five years old the son sought to recover the £10,000 from his father's bankers, as he maintained that on his father's death the balance vested in him. HELD: The bank had acted *improperly* in delivering the balance to the father's executors, as it should have been held for the son. But the son's claim against the bank did not succeed, however, because he had had control of the moneys and used them in carrying on his deceased father's business after reaching maturity: *McEvoy* v. *Belfast Banking Co. Ltd.* (1935).

(*c*) *Dispute between survivor(s) and deceased's representatives.* Where the bank are positive that the *intention* of the parties was that on death the balance should vest in the survivor(s), then usually the claims of the representatives can be ignored. (In practice, survivorship "intention" is *always* incorporated in the account mandate.)

NOTE: Where there is any element of doubt concerning the bank's *legal position* in any dispute, it should either (*a*) obtain the discharge of both executors/administrators *and* the surviving parties (if *all* agree), or (*b*) interplead, i.e. pay the moneys into court so that the respective rights of the parties can be decided.

14. Delivery of safe custody items. The signatures of all parties are required unless a mandate to deliver to less than all has been taken.

(*a*) *On death of one party.* As it is difficult to interpret the survivorship rule in respect of custody items (only *joint property* vests in the survivor(s)), it is the usual practice to require the receipt of both the survivor(s) *and* the personal representatives: *see* II, **46**(b).

(*b*) *On bankruptcy of one party.* Custody items must only be released on the joint authority of the survivor(s) *and* the trustee in bankruptcy (or Official Receiver): *see* II, **47** and VI, **23**.

(*c*) *On mental incapacity of one party.* Custody items must only be released on the joint authority of the sane party(s) *and* the Receiver appointed by the Court of Protection: *see* II, **48**.

15. Bankruptcy of one joint-account party. This determines the mandate.

(*a*) *Credit account. The account must be stopped*, as the balance can only be released on the joint authority of the solvent party(s) *and* the trustee (or Official Receiver).

(*b*) *Debit account. The account must be stopped* unless the bank are willing to rely on the survivor(s) to repay the overdraft and thus release the bankrupt's security and estate: *see also* VI, **31**.

16. Mental incapacity of one joint-account party. This determines the mandate.

(*a*) *Credit account. The account must be stopped*, as the balance can only be released on the joint authority of the sane party(s) and the Court of Protection.

(*b*) *Debit account. The account must be stopped* unless the bank are willing to rely on the sane party(s) to repay the overdraft and thus release the incapacitated party's security and estate.

NOTE: (1) *A garnishee order:* (*a*) in the name of *one* party does not attach a joint account; (*b*) in the name of *all* parties attaches the joint account and their personal accounts. (2) *Securities jointly owned, and deposited to secure an account,* must be charged by all owners. (3) Where the joint-account mandate authorises *less than all to sign*, then in cases of *confirmed dispute* between the parties the bank can regard the mandate as terminated and thus require *all* to sign, e.g. this would apply where a letter is received from a husband stating that his wife (who is in joint account with him) has left him, and subsequently the wife presents a cheque to withdraw the balance.

17. Distinction between joint, and joint and several liability. Where an account involving several persons is opened and borrowing is contemplated, a banker *always* requires the admission of *joint and several liability* by the account holders, as there are many advantages compared with *joint liability*. The requirement applies for various account holders, e.g. partners, executors, trustees, joint, etc., and can be dealt with here appropriately.

(*a*) *Joint liability: disadvantages.*

(*i*) *Only one action used to be available*, and if judgment proved unsuccessful or if a party were omitted from the action, further actions were barred: *Kendall* v. *Hamilton* (1879). This rule has however been abolished by The Civil Liability (Contribution) Act 1978, s. 3. It is therefore now possible to sue a party or partner who was omitted from the writ.

(*ii*) *No right of set-off exists* against credit private accounts, even on determination of the joint mandate.

(*iii*) *Death of one joint-account party completely* releases his estate. (Securities deposited by the deceased to secure the joint account would also probably be released, *but* the bank expressly retains rights against the security by including a clause "moneys owing by survivors on joint account".)

(*iv*) *If a joint-account party becomes bankrupt* is is doubtful whether proof can be lodged against his estate without losing the right of recovery from the solvent parties.

(*b*) *Joint and several liability*. (Referred to as J & S liability throughout the handbook.) *Advantages:*

(*i*) *There is a right of action against all parties severally and successively* until the whole debt is recovered (but *see* **17**(*a*) (*i*) above).

(*ii*) *A right of set-off exists* between credit private accounts and the joint overdraft, on determination of the mandate (or as otherwise agreed or after giving sufficient notice).

(*iii*) *Death does not release the estate of the deceased* for debts owing on joint account.

(*iv*) Proof may be lodged against the estate of a bankrupt joint-account party and *rights retained against the solvent parties.*

NOTE: Under (*iii*) and (*iv*) the joint account must still be *stopped* to prevent the operation of the Rule in Clayton's Case.

See also X, **21**, concerning J & S liability and partners.

PERSONAL REPRESENTATIVES

18. Executors and administrators. The persons appointed to wind up and distribute a deceased's estate are called *personal representatives.* Personal representatives appointed by the deceased's *will* are called *executors.* Personal representatives appointed by the *court* are called *administrators*, e.g. this applies, for instance, where the deceased dies intestate.

NOTE: The authority of administrators stems from their appointment by the Court, whereas the authority of executors stems from the will. However, even in the case of executors, they cannot be allowed to deal with the *deceased's* account or securities until *probate has confirmed their appointment.*

19. Administrator cum testamento annexo. Where a will fails to appoint an executor or where the executors refuse or are incapable of acting, an administrator *cum testamento annexo* (i.e. with the will annexed) is appointed.

20. Probate and letters of administration.

(*a*) *Probate* confirms the executors' authority and is the official copy of the will together with the certificate stating that it has been proved.

(*b*) *Letters of administration* is the official document empowering a person(s) called the administrator(s) to administer the estate of the deceased.

Before probate or letters of administration are granted estate duty falling due must be paid to the Inland Revenue.

NOTE: (1) Duty levied on *personal property* must be paid upon delivery of the Inland Revenue affidavit or on the expiration of six months from the death, *whichever occurs first.* (2) Duty levied on *realty* (and on certain other property, e.g. leaseholds, some unquoted shares or debentures, shares in a partnership business: Finance Act 1971, ss. 61–2) may, optionally, be paid by eight equal yearly or sixteen equal half-yearly instalments (plus interest); the first instalment is due a year from the death. On the *sale* of any such property the duty becomes payable immediately.

21. The deceased's account.

(*a*) *Credit account.* The balance cannot be withdrawn *until probate or letters of administration have been exhibited to the bank* and recorded. (This also applies in respect of withdrawal of *securities* and *custody* deposited by the *deceased.*)

NOTE: In practice, the bank *may* agree to pay out (under indemnity) balances under £1,500 to the persons holding themselves to be entitled, *without production of grant of representation.* This brings the bank's procedure *into line* with the amended provisions of the Administration of Estates (Small Payments) Act 1965, which permits the disposal of certain property (under £1,500 in each case) to persons entitled without representation.

(*b*) *Debit account.* To effect a recovery from the deceased's estate (his account having been stopped on notice of death), the representatives will be informed of his liability. If the deceased's security is held to cover his liabilities the representatives may wish to pay off the overdraft *immediately* in order to obtain its release. Alternatively, they may wish the security to be sold to pay off the overdraft.

(*c*) *Credits received after death.* As long as the bank have no notice that the payments have ceased to be due to the deceased on his death (e.g. annuity payable during life), they can be credited to his account or held in suspense until the representatives have power to act.

22. Executors'/administrators' account.

(*a*) *An executors' account* can be opened immediately on the death of the testator. The account is usually styled to allow for continuity, e.g. "Executors of 'A' deceased, XYZ executors".

(*b*) *An administrators' account* is not usually opened until letters of administration are produced.

NOTE: If the executors or administrators are unknown the usual references/introductions are required. The solicitor dealing with the estate often introduces the account.

23. Personal representatives' account mandate.

(*a*) *General rules.* Any *one* representative can sign for all and bind the remainder jointly *in connection with estate affairs*, but the bank *always* requires an express mandate covering drawings and *J & S liability*, etc. Any *one* representative can countermand a cheque drawn on the representatives' account.

NOTE: *Delegation of powers to an outsider is permitted only:* (1) where the will authorises this, or (2) where professional agents are required to act, e.g. solicitors, stockbrokers, bankers, etc: Trustee Act 1925, s. 23. (The powers outlined in s. 23 are insufficient to permit the appointment of an outsider to sign on the representatives' account.) Or (3) to any other person (not being the only co-representative) by power of attorney for a period not exceeding twelve months: Powers of Attorney Act 1971, s. 9(8).

(*b*) *J & S Liability*. Personal representatives only incur *joint* liability, hence admittance of *J & S liability* is obtained. Consequently, the bank obtains power to set off credit balances standing in the representatives' personal names against the executors'/administrators' account.

NOTE: The *deceased's credit account* cannot be set off against an *overdrawn executors'/administrators' account*, and vice versa. In practice, set-off may be allowed *for interest purposes only*.

(*c*) *Death of executor or administrator*. The following general rule govern the position:

(*i*) The powers of the representatives *may continue to be exercised by the survivors or survivor of them* for the time being: TA 1925, s. 18(1). The executors'/administrators' account need only be stopped if it is wished to retain the right of recovery against the estate of the deceased executor/administrator and thereby prevent the operation of the Rule in Clayton's Case.

(*ii*) *A new mandate is necessary* if the original mandate empowered *less than all to act*.

(*iii*) On the death of the *sole or last surviving executor* his executors, on proving his will, take over his executorship role, but if he dies intestate (or where a sole remaining *administrator* dies) grant of administration *de bonis non administratis* (of the unadministered estate) must be applied for by a party entitled.

24. Representatives borrowing to pay capital transfer tax. A *credit balance* standing in the deceased's name cannot be dealt with by the representatives *until probate or letters of administration are* granted. Consequently, they may require to borrow for payment of duty.

Before agreeing to lend, the bank will require:

(*a*) *To peruse the Inland Revenue affidavit and will* (*if any*) to ascertain the exact nature of the estate and confirm the duty payable.

(*b*) *To check that sufficient liquid assets* (e.g. marketable securities, life policies, cash, etc.) *are available* to provide speedy repayment.

(*c*) *To verify the integrity of the representatives and their solicitors.*

(*d*) *To obtain the usual account mandate* incorporating an undertaking to take out grant of representation without delay and to repay the overdraft out of the first proceeds of the estate.

NOTE: (1) A charge given by *executors before probate* over specific assets belonging to the deceased becomes effective only if probate is ultimately granted. Charges can only be executed by *administrators*, *after* grant of representation. (2) Security deposited by the deceased for his own account cannot be held as security for an advance to the representatives, unless they recharge it.

25. Borrowing by representatives to facilitate administration of the estate, e.g. payment of debts pending realisation of assets. Such borrowing is permissible (unless prohibited by the will), and as in all instances of borrowing by representatives, they become personally liable *jointly*. (But *see* **23**(*b*) above.) Only *specific* estate assets can be charged to secure the debt.

NOTE: (1) Although the representatives are personally liable, they are entitled to be *indemnified* out of the *estate* and the bank are *subrogated* to their position (i.e. allowed to stand in their shoes) for moneys advanced. (2) The representatives can, of course, charge their *own personal security* to cover borrowing if they so wish and provided this is acceptable to the bank.

26. Borrowing to enable continuation of the deceased's personal business.

(*a*) If: (*i*) *the will contains no express authority* (*and no express prohibition*) *to continue the deceased's business*, or (*ii*) *there is no will*; then the powers of the personal representatives to borrow in order to continue the business are clearly limited to funds for enabling *a sale or winding up* to be effected.

The representatives will commit a breach of trust if they

continue the business beyond a reasonable time (a question of fact). If the bank were regarded as being a party to the breach, then the *creditors* and *beneficiaries* could obtain repayment from the deceased's estate in *priority to it*, and may also be able to take estate security which has been deposited.

(*b*) If: (*i*) *express authority is contained in the will authorising continuance*, e.g. during the lifetime of the deceased's widow, or (*ii*) *there is a discretionary power to postpone conversion of the estate*; then this binds the beneficiaries *but not* the creditors.

NOTE: (1) *Before agreeing to lend*, the bank may require that the deceased's creditors (*a*) be paid off, or (*b*) agree to grant it a prior right of recovery. (This also applies to the beneficiaries under **26**(*a*) above.) (2) *Security* can be taken only over *specific assets used in the business* unless the will provides otherwise.

27. Executors becoming trustees. When the *winding up* of an estate *is concluded*, i.e. after payment of funeral and testamentary expenses, debts and legacies, *an executor automatically becomes a trustee* in respect of any *residue* which the will directs must be held in trust for beneficiaries. (An administrator may also be placed in the same position by law.)

The *trusteeship position* is usually reached some *six to eighteen months* after the representatives begin acting, and the bank must endeavour to notice this from any evidence which is available, e.g. regular periodic payments made out of the account to beneficiaries. Confirmation of the position should be sought.

As *trustees* cannot delegate their authority even among themselves (unless so authorised in the will or trust instrument; or unless by power of attorney, but not to a sole co-trustee unless a trust corporation), the bank must obtain a new mandate *where previously less than all the executors signed.* The account should be restyled and *must be strictly conducted as a trust account: see* **28–35** below.

TRUSTEES

28. Nature of trust account. A trust account may be defined as an account opened by one or more persons, which to the bank's direct or indirect knowledge is being operated by trustees, or persons acting in some other fiduciary capacity. There need be no formal trust instrument. Whether the bank is deemed to have notice of the trust depends upon the circumstances. Such notice may arise:

(*a*) *Directly,* e.g. where an account is opened as "Trustees of . . ."

(*b*) *Indirectly.* For instance, where the account heading signifies a *fiduciary* capacity, e.g. "B. Brown, Badminton Club account".

(*c*) *By operation of law*, e.g. executors/administrators may become trustees *if a trust arises out of the deceased's estate.*

29. Opening the account. A mandate signed by the persons holding themselves out to be trustees is required: *see* **33** below for signing arrangements. There is *no* duty on the bank to call for sight of the trust instrument (if any), and unless the trustees require to borrow, it is often better to avoid seeing the instrument, because the general laws outlined for trustees can then be followed.

Once the instrument is sighted, however, the bank are then bound, and would need to record any clauses likely to affect them.

30. Breach of trust by a trustee. If a trustee innocently or otherwise misapplies trust property he commits a *breach of trust* for which he is liable to the beneficiaries. If a banker *intentionally* or *negligently* facilitates a breach he may also be held liable. *See*, for example, the case involving District Bank: *Selangor United Rubber Estates Ltd.* v. *Craddock & Ors.* (1968).

31. Liability for breach may attach to banker.

(*a*) *Before a banker can incur liability:* (*i*) there must have been a *breach of trust,* (*ii*) to which he was *privy*, i.e. he must actually have known (or perhaps should have noticed) that trust money or property was being wrongly converted. In the absence of privity by a banker he will avoid liability: *Gray* v. *Johnston* (1868).

(*b*) *Deciding whether a banker is privy is difficult* and must depend upon the particular facts of each case. However, it is well established that:

(*i*) *Before dishonouring a trust cheque on the grounds of breach* a banker must have *substantial* evidence that a breach is being effected (mere suspicion or accusation levied by a third party, e.g. a beneficiary, is insufficient evidence unless supported by *legal process*).

(*ii*) *If a personal benefit to the banker* is designed or stipulated for, then privity is virtually established, e.g. where the banker fails to enquire when a known trustee draws a cheque on the trust account to reduce a personal overdraft for which the bank have been pressing him for reduction.

NOTE: A banker's primary duty is to his customer, and having therefore received money on his behalf and become his debtor, the banker cannot *when approached by a third party* (1) entertain claims in respect of the account moneys, or (2) in consequence of such claims dishonour cheques drawn by the customer, *unless* such claims are supported by injunction or other court order: *Tassell* v. *Cooper* (1850).

32. Delegation of authority. Trustees (*unlike* personal representatives) cannot legally delegate their authority among themselves *except*: (*a*) under specific powers outlined in the trust instrument, or (*b*) to another person (not being the only co-trustee, unless a trust corporation) by *power of attorney* (attested by a witness) and for a period *not exceeding twelve months*. Such delegation can be made *at any time* and is no longer confined to trustees leaving the U.K.: TA 1925, s. 25 as amended by Powers of Attorney Act 1971, s. 9.

NOTE: (1) *Delegation to an agent*, e.g. solicitor, stockbroker, banker, etc., is allowed when this is necessary for administration of the trust: TA 1925, s. 23. (The section is *not* drawn widely enough to allow such an agent to be given authority to sign on the trustees' account.) (2) *If delegation is wrongly permitted by the bank* it may well be held liable if a breach of trust ensues.

33. Signing on the trust account. Because of the legal position stated above, *all* trustees are normally required to *sign* on the account unless the trust instrument or law permits delegation. Occasionally trustees require (e.g. for convenience or because delegation occurred on the *executors' account*) to delegate their signing authority to less than all. Such a move must usually be resisted.

NOTE: Trustees can, of course (1) be *replaced* (TA 1925, s. 36), or (2) in certain circumstances, *retire* provided at least two trustees remain (TA 1925, s. 39), and this can often be suggested as a solution, e.g. where they are too old or infirm to act.

Exceptionally the bank may allow *internal* delegation, provided some of the following conditions are present or can be arranged which eliminate (partly or wholly) the likelihood of loss through breach of trust:

(*a*) If the integrity and financial position of the trustees is undoubted the bank may be willing to accept their J & S indemnity to cover any losses incurred through allowing delegation.

(*b*) The adult beneficiaries may be prepared to do likewise as in (*a*) above.

(*c*) To provide a regular check, the account statement can be certified periodically by all trustees/beneficiaries.

(*d*) Where there are more than two trustees, two signatures could be required, thus lessening the risk of fraud by one trustee.

(*e*) Two accounts could be operated; an *Income* account (delegation allowed), and a *Capital* account (delegation *not* allowed). (No doubt the beneficiaries would soon inform the bank if their income was withheld.)

(*f*) In appropriate circumstances *standing orders* can be signed to cover periodic payments for Income.

NOTE: With public or charitable trusts certain delegation among trustees is permitted by law: Charities Act 1960, s. 34.

34. Borrowing by trustees. Trustees rarely require to borrow and in fact have *no implied* power to do so.

(*a*) *Authority to borrow and charge trust property.*

(*i*) *Specific authority to borrow may be outlined in the trust instrument*. Even if this is the case, such borrowing may be secured by trust property only if the trust instrument specifically authorises this.

(*ii*) *Alternatively, in the absence of specific borrowing powers*, then if the instrument (or the law) authorises *trust capital money* to be paid or applied for any purpose or in any manner, then the trustees can raise such money *on the security of all or any part of the trust property*: TA 1925, s. 16. (This does not apply to trustees of charities or settled land.)

As a *mortgagee* advancing money the banker is *not* under a duty to see *that the money is actually wanted or correctly applied*: s. 17. (A legal opinion is often necessary to determine whether or not the instrument covers bank borrowing.)

(*b*) *J & S Liability*. Trustees (*like* personal representatives) are only personally liable *jointly* for any borrowing, and the bank therefore require their admittance of *J & S liability*. This also enables *set-off* between a trustee's personal *credit* account and a *debit* trust account, but not vice versa.

(*c*) *Lending to undoubted trustees*. In suitable cases of *temporary* borrowing a bank may lend to *undoubted trustees* against their personal undertaking under J & S liability and perhaps additionally their personal security.

35. Death of a trustee.

(*a*) *Other trustees remaining*. The joint powers of the trustees may continue to be exercised by the *survivors* or *survivor* of them for the time being: TA 1925, s. 18(1). (The trust account need only be stopped if it is wished to retain the right of recovery against the deceased trustee's estate and prevent the operation of the *Rule in Clayton's Case*.)

(*b*) *No other trustee remaining*. On the death of a *sole* or *last surviving trustee* his personal representatives take over the trusteeship until such time as new trustees are appointed: TA 1925, s. 18(2).

CLUBS, SOCIETIES, ETC.

36. Unincorporated clubs, societies, etc. Many such *unincorporated* associations exist for carrying out non-commercial activities, e.g. cricket clubs, horticultural societies, etc. They have no separate entity, and cannot therefore be sued in their own name.

37. Liability of members. Members are not liable for borrowing incurred on an association's behalf by appointed officers *unless they have individually assented thereto*. It appears that all appointed officers would normally be liable for borrowing authorised by the committee of management: *Bradley Egg Farm Ltd.* v. *Clifford & Ors*. (1943), but the legal position is far from settled.

38. Opening the account. The account should be opened in the association's name.

(*a*) *Rules*. The bank requires a copy of the rules and constitution; the account mandate should be in conformity therewith.

(*b*) *Account mandate*. This should confirm that at a meeting of the association it was resolved that an account be opened and cheques signed by the parties authorised. (Often the authority will extend to overdrawing the account and withdrawing custody items.) The mandate usually requires certification by the chairman and secretary.

(*c*) *Borrowing*. *Should not be permitted unless rules are in existence* and these have been perused to ascertain any borrowing formalities and restrictions, e.g. the rules may provide that borrowing may be undertaken only if the members so resolve in *general meeting*.

A certified copy of any such resolution is required. *In the absence of rules* responsibility for any borrowing would only fall on the members who had authorised it.

(*d*) *Security.* It is always advisable to take security for any borrowing, as on default it may prove difficult or legally impossible to recover moneys from individual members.

(*i*) *A third party who secures an association's account* must undertake prime responsibility for the debt, e.g. by signing a guarantee, deed or other memorandum which incorporates an *indemnity* clause: *see* XII, **28**.

(*ii*) *Association property deposited as security.* Such property will be vested in the names of trustees. To obtain an effective security the bank must ascertain from the rules and the trust deed that the trustees have power to charge the property for borrowing taken in their own or the association's name (as required).

NOTE: If instead of opening the account in the association's name it is opened in an individual's name, e.g. F. Smith a/c Midtown Choral Society, the individual becomes personally liable, but the bank must regard the account as a trust account, and it may be necessary to confirm the individual's authority to act on the association's behalf, e.g. where he wishes to pay in cheques drawn in favour of the association to his own account.

FRIENDLY SOCIETIES

39. Friendly societies. These are mutual insurance societies in which the members subscribe to provide benefits during sickness, in old age, and to widows and orphans. A society may *voluntarily* register under the provisions of the Friendly Societies Act 1974. Registration involves approval by the Registrar of Friendly Societies of the society's *rules*. A registered friendly society is *not* a corporate body.

40. Banking account of registered society.

(*a*) *Rules and mandate.* On opening the account in the name of the society a copy of the *rules* is required together with a *mandate* incorporating a certified copy of the resolution appointing the bank as the society's bankers. The mandate must strictly conform with the rules. *Before allowing any borrowing or accepting security to cover borrowing* the society's *rules* must be studied to ascertain the powers in relation thereto.

(*b*) *Borrowing.* It would seem that a registered society can provide by its rules that it may *borrow* in order to conduct its business *to the extent necessary to achieve its objects*. It is safer to lend on loan account to prevent the operation of *Clayton's Case* working against the bank.

(*c*) *Security*. A society (acting through appointed trustees) may hold and *mortgage* land if its rules so provide; and a mortgagee need not enquire as to the trustees' authority for any such mortgage: Friendly Societies Act 1974.

41. Unregistered society. The account should be dealt with similarly to those of clubs and societies. (*See* **36–38** above.)

SOLICITORS

42. The Solicitors Acts. The position as regards banking accounts is governed by the Solicitors Act 1957, and the Rules made thereunder, and in part by the Solicitors Act 1965.

43. Solicitor's account. A solicitor may open an account for his private or office transactions in the usual manner. A designated account *does not necessarily imply a trust*, e.g. office account, and such an account may be set off against his other accounts.

44. Solicitor dealing with clients' or trust money. Moneys received by a solicitor *which do not belong to him*, i.e. clients' money or trust money, must be placed to a client(s') account, i.e. an account in which the word "client" appears: Solicitors' Accounts Rules 1945 (*see* **45** below).

Alternatively, where the solicitor is a sole trustee or a co-trustee with a partner, clerk or servant of his or with more than one of such persons, he may place moneys belonging to the trust to a trust account, i.e. an account in which the word "trustee or executor" appears: Solicitors' Trust Accounts Rules 1945: (*see* **34** above regarding overdrafts on such accounts).

45. Solicitor's clients' account.

(*a*) *Must not be overdrawn*, as the Rules do not permit it.

(*b*) *No right of set-off*. A *credit* balance on *clients'* account *cannot be set off* against the solicitor's *private* or *office* accounts: SA 1957, s. 85(2).

(*c*) *Delegation*. Although a clients' account is by its nature a trust account, *signing authority can be delegated to other partners*, being solicitors, or to a Fellow of the Institute of Legal Executives of at least five years' standing.

(*d*) *Transfer of amounts due from clients' account to a solicitor's private account.* A bank is not put on enquiry as to whether such payments are due to the solicitor, except, perhaps, where it has been pressing him for repayment of his overdraft.

46. Solicitors' accounts: relief to banks. A bank cannot, in respect of a transaction on any account kept by a solicitor (other than an account as trustee for a specified beneficiary) incur any liability (excepting any liability or obligation existing outside the Act) or be under any obligation to make any enquiry or be deemed to have any knowledge of any right of any person to money credited to such an account: SA 1957, s. 85(1).

47. Death or bankruptcy of a solicitor. In these cases the following rules apply:

(*a*) *Operating a clients' account alone.*

(*i*) *On death.* The balance vests in the Law Society and not the solicitor's personal representatives: SA 1965, s. 14.

(*ii*) *On bankruptcy.* The balance does *not* vest in his trustee in bankruptcy, who may not interfere with the account: *Re a Solicitor* (1951). Nevertheless the bankrupt solicitor (or court) would need to appoint nominees, e.g. of the Law Society to act in place of the bankrupt.

(*b*) *Operating a clients' account with other solicitor(s).*

(*i*) *On death.* The rule of survivorship applies, and the remaining solicitor(s) continues to act.

(*ii*) *On bankruptcy.* The surviving solicitor(s) continues to act.

CHURCHES

48. Church of England. The operation of banking accounts is governed by the Synodical Government Act 1970. A Parochial Church Council is a *body corporate* having an existence separate from its members.

(*a*) *Account mandate.* The account must be styled "Parochial Church Council of ... Parish". The bank requires a mandate incorporating a certified copy of the Council's resolution, signed by the chairman and two other members of the council, authorising the opening of the account and appointing the person(s) authorised to act as treasurer and to sign cheques.

(*b*) *Borrowing.* There are no restrictions on borrowing, but the liability of the Council only extends to funds received from the congregation. The bank requires a certified copy of the resolution passed by the Council authorising such borrowing.

(*c*) *Security*.

(*i*) *Guarantees* from leading church members are often accepted as security.

(*ii*) A Council may, with the permission of the Finance Committee of the Diocesan Synod, *acquire real or personal property for ecclesiastical purposes or for education*: s. 5(1). The bank requires confirmation from the Authority before accepting such property as security.

(*iii*) *Property held on permanent trusts must be vested in the Finance Committee of the Diocesan Synod*, and the Council must obtain the permission of the Committee before the property can be charged as security.

In addition there exist since 1970 Deanery Synods, Diocesan Synods and the General Synod of the Church of England.

49. Roman Catholic Churches. Accounts are opened on the authority of the Diocesan Bishop, normally in the names of three priests (sometimes two), with any one being authorised to sign. (If the bank are requested to open a Church account without the authority of the Diocesan Bishop application should be made to the Financial Secretary of the Diocese.)

(*a*) *Borrowing*. Approval for borrowing must be obtained from the Head of the Diocese or Order (who may be resident abroad).

(*b*) *Security*. Usually a guarantee is sufficient. Such guarantees may be signed by: (*i*) Bishop, Archbishop or Head of Order; (*ii*) Trustees of the Diocese or Order; (*iii*) Finance Board of a Limited Company. Property (which is sometimes vested in a corporation created for the purpose) may be charged as security for borrowing.

50. Other Churches. Accounts are usually conducted in the names of bodies such as "Trustees of ... Church" or "... Stewards". Sometimes the account is conducted in the name of a Circuit or a Fund. The usual mandate is taken under resolution of the issuing body, and in appropriate cases the trust deed is examined.

(*a*) *Borrowing*. The trustees of the local borrowing body must authorise any borrowing, which may need to be supported by a higher Church authority.

(*b*) *Security* usually includes a joint and several promissory note or guarantee signed by the trustees/stewards.

RECEIVERS OF LIMITED COMPANIES

51. Accounts of receivers. These are normally conducted in credit and present few problems. Evidence of the receiver's appointment should be seen and a specimen signature obtained. A receiver may only deal with a company's credit balance (after allowing for set-off) where the debenture or Court Order under which he derives his powers refers to such type of asset. The receiver's appointment must be registered at the companies registry within seven days: CA 1948, s. 102(1).

52. Receiver's duties. These depend upon the terms of his appointment and on the statutory provisions regarding application of proceeds. The receiver's actions will be influenced by the company's trading position and he will aim to:

(*a*) realise sufficient assets to repay the debenture holder and then depart, leaving the company in the hands of the directors or liquidator, *or*

(*b*) run the business in order to sell it as a going concern, *or*

(*c*) reconstitute the business and repay the debenture holder.

53. Lending to receivers. A request for a bank advance may be made by a receiver appointed by: (*a*) a bank under its debenture, or (*b*) an outside debenture holder(s), or (*c*) a Receiver appointed by the Court. A receiver is only appointed where a company is in difficulties, and consequently it may appear foolhardy to lend further moneys at such a stage, especially as a *petition for compulsory winding up* might be presented. Nevertheless, everything depends upon the nature of the proposition. Where a receiver requires to borrow, for example, to pay wages in order to help complete work in progress, then if the bank can be convinced that a considerable benefit will result without too many attendant risks over and above the actual borrowing it may be prepared to help. This is more commonly the case with large concerns.

54. Enquiries prior to lending. Before agreeing to lend the bank will need to be satisfied:

(*a*) That the receiver has power to *borrow in order to continue the business* and that he is a person of known ability and standing.

(*b*) That the proposition should provide *benefit* for the debenture holder and not further losses.

(*c*) That the advance will be *temporary*.

(*d*) That the "statement of affairs" produced by the company to a receiver under a floating charge within fourteen days of his appointment is not misleading. The receiver will be required to give his opinion as to the worth of the assets, on both a going concern and gone concern approach. Professional advisers will be used to value specialised assets.

55. Lending to bank's own receiver. Whether moneys will be made available to the bank's receiver depends upon his report as to the company's position. The bank will not wish to jeopardise further the position of other creditors, especially preferential creditors who are entitled to prior repayment out of floating asset realisations.

56. Lending to a receiver appointed by outside debenture holders. Before considering any proposition the bank will need to verify the receiver's powers from his *appointment* and the *debenture*. A copy of the "statement of affairs" will be required. Bearing in mind the points outlined in **54** above, the following must also be noted:

(*a*) *Unless* the receiver is appointed as agent for the company (which is usually the case), the debenture holder(s) will remain liable for any overdraft properly incurred.

(*b*) *Specific power may be found* in the debenture permitting the receiver to borrow and charge security to rank in front of the debenture holder(s). **Or**

(*c*) *In the absence of any specific power* an appointment as "Receiver and Manager" to carry on the business gives the receiver *implied* power to borrow and charge prior-ranking security as in (*b*) above. *Nevertheless*, written agreement to postponement by the debenture-holder(s) is advisable and is absolutely necessary where no implied power exists.

(*d*) *The receiver remains personally liable for any borrowing* unless he arranges otherwise, but he has a right of indemnity from the assets: CA 1948, s. 369(2).

(*e*) The receiver can make application to the *court* for directions: CA 1948, s. 369(1).

57. Lending to a Receiver appointed by the Court. A copy of the Court order should be seen and any instructions followed. The considerations in **54** above apply together with the following additional points:

(*a*) *The Receiver can apply to the court* for permission to borrow and charge security to rank in front of the debenture holders, *or alternatively*, (*b*) *the Receiver can borrow without permission of the court*, but he remains personally liable as in **56**(*d*) above.

LIQUIDATORS OF LIMITED COMPANIES

58. Opening the account. Where the liquidator has been appointed:

(*a*) *By the Court.* The court order showing his appointment should be seen, and also the Department of Trade and Industry's sanction for opening the account at a bank other than the Bank of England.

(*b*) *By the creditors or members in a voluntary winding up.* A certified copy of the resolution appointing the liquidator is required.

59. Borrowing by liquidators. Is rarely encountered in practice, but where it is the bank must be 100 per cent sure that the advance will be *temporary and its money recoverable from a known source.* Liquidators do not incur personal liability unless they agree otherwise.

60. Borrowing by a liquidator appointed by the Court. A liquidator may, without sanction, borrow money against the assets of the company, but where he wishes *to carry on the business* the sanction of the Court or committee of inspection is required for borrowing and giving of any security: CA 1948, s. 245.

61. Borrowing by a liquidator in a voluntary winding up. The CA 1948 gives the liquidator express power to borrow and charge security, even where the business is continued. However, the confirmation of the creditors or committee of inspection (or company members in a members' voluntary winding up) would normally be sought for any large borrowing.

SPECULATIVE HOUSE BUILDER

62. Speculative builders. Finance of a short-term nature is made available to speculative builders of factories, shops, offices, flats, houses, etc. One of the commonest propositions for borrowing comes from speculative house builders, who often find it impossible to finance a complete project from start to finish.

63 A typical house builder's proposition. Your customer, House Builders Ltd., own a building site which cost £90,000. They propose to build sixty houses thereon for sale at £21,000 each. They estimate that each house will cost £15,000 to build plus an additional outlay of £500 for each house to cover provision of roads and sewers, etc. The company has operated successfully in the past, and the directors are expert in their field, but only smaller developments have been undertaken previously. The company has £75,000 available towards financing the project, and approaches you for £600,000 in order to complete the sixty houses.

64. Nature of the proposition. The bank would view any such proposition from three main angles:

(*a*) Its nature: to which will be applied the usual principles of lending.

(*b*) The amount and control of the advance.

(*c*) The security available.

These are dealt with below.

65. Banker's requirements. The bank will need to be satisfied:

(*a*) *That the builders are competent* and capable of carrying through the proposed scheme.

(*b*) That up-to-date *balance sheets and accounts* show a healthy position. (At least past three years required.)

(*c*) That a *good proportion of past profits* have been *retained* in the business.

(*d*) That the company will *not be over-reaching* as regards resources and finance. (Extremely important points.)

(*e*) That the company has prepared a *correctly costed construction programme* and financial budget and have taken into account bank charges and interest and retention moneys.

(*f*) That answers to the following questions are satisfactory:

(*i*) Has the land been paid for?

(*ii*) Will all roads and sewers need to be laid before building commences?

(*iii*) Has planning permission been granted?

(*iv*) What is the cost price and selling price of each house?

(*v*) What proportion of total cost can the builder find? (The bank may be prepared to finance up to 75 per cent.)

(*vi*) Will the houses be readily saleable? Is the builder a member of the National House Builders Registration Council? Has a Building Society undertaken to give mortgages?

66. Dealing with our proposition. Answers to some of the above questions are given in the proposition. Nevertheless all the figures produced should be *checked and verified*. Presuming all the answers are satisfactory and it is considered that the customer is worth helping, the danger of over-reaching both as regards resources and finance requires examination:

(*a*) *As regards resources.*

(*i*) Has the company sufficient employees and/or can it hire a sufficient labour force to complete sixty houses at one time?

(*ii*) What other projects are on hand or envisaged?

(*iii*) What danger is there of finishing up with sixty partly completed houses?

(*iv*) Can suitable control over materials and labour be maintained for a project of the size to which the company is unaccustomed?

(*b*) *As regards finance.* The bank's commitment in the scheme should not be unreasonably high. In this respect its commitment will be reduced if the number of houses being built at any one time is restricted.

67. Schemes envisaged for our proposition.

	SCHEME I	SCHEME II	SCHEME III
Total Cost	20 *Plots*	30 *Plots*	60 *Plots*
Land	30,000	45,000	90,000
Roads and sewers	10,000	15,000	30,000
Building costs	300,000	450,000	900,000
	£340,000	£510,000	£1,020,000
Maximum Advance Required			
Roads and sewers	10,000	15,000	30,000
Building costs	300,000	450,000	900,000
	310,000	465,000	930,000
Less Available funds	75,000	75,000	75,000
	£235,000	£390,000	£855,000
i.e. per house	£11,750	£13,000	£14,250
Bank's percentage commitment	69	76	83
Initial value of security, i.e. before bank advances any money	£165,000	£165,000	£165,000

NOTE: (1) It is obvious that the £600,000 the customer has requested would be insufficient if the sixty houses were completed before a sale was made. In any case, the bank would have too great a stake in the proposition. (2) The maximum advance for each scheme is based on the assumption that no sales are effected until each group of houses is completed. (The maximum advance in Schemes I and II would need to be greater if the roads and sewers had all to be laid first.) (3) The initial value of the bank's security equals the land value, £90,000, plus the company's share of the finance, £75,000. The latter must be utilised before the bank advances any moneys. (4) Should Scheme I be agreed a *financial cushion* becomes available to cover unexpected difficulty in that 2/3 land valued at £60,000 could, if necessary and with bank's agreement, be sold to provide cash. Scheme I is the best and safest from the bank's viewpoint. Scheme III is out of the question, as the bank would be too heavily committed.

68. Control of the advance. Having agreed the maximum advance to be made on each house, the bank will allow this to be taken as the various stages are completed, e.g.

From foundations to first floor	25%
At roof level, roof tiled and chimneys fixed	50%
Plastering, plumbing and joinery complete	75%
House completed	100%

Periodical site inspections should be made to see that the development keeps pace with the advance. Architects' certificates may be required. To facilitate ease of control, the advance should be taken on loan account as the building proceeds. A site plan should be obtained showing the numbered plots. A progress chart will be maintained from which can be seen the total amount expended on the houses to date. Sale proceeds paid in to the loan account should be sufficient to cover each house advance together with interest charges and service fee.

69. Beneficial aspect of restricting the number of houses being built at one time. The profit made on each stage becomes available to help finance the next stage.

In our example:

	£
Sale proceeds of 20 Plots	420,000
Less Repayment of maximum bank advance	235,000
Available towards next stage	185,000

The maximum borrowing required to complete the next 20 houses is £125,000 (310,000–185,000), i.e. 36 per cent of the *total* second-stage cost. Thus the finance is made available *on a revolving and reducing basis*, being subject to re-negotiation as the circumstances require.

In practice, the only foolproof way to ensure that the builder's *profit* becomes available to finance the next development stage is to require him to pay into his loan account, at each sale, more than he borrowed to finance that sale, e.g. amount advanced per house £11,750 (*see* **67**, Scheme I, above); amount required in reduction per house sale, say £15,000—to cover interest, fees, and part profit.

70. Security required. The more usual security is a charge over the whole of the building land (*see* XIII for procedure). The security automatically increases in value as the houses are built.

(*a*) *Legal mortgage* may be required so as to obtain the remedies of a legal mortgagee. A disadvantage is that with unregistered title the bank must join in each conveyance under seal, the mortgage being finally reconveyed when the last plot has been sold or the advance repaid.

(*b*) *Equitable mortgage.* Only a simple letter of release is required in respect of each property, but the disadvantage lies in the fact that only equitable remedies are available should the customer default.

NOTE: (1) The *builder's solicitors will hold the deeds.* The bank will, of course, hold the solicitor's undertaking to account for the sale proceeds or to return the deeds. The bank should periodically check the endorsements of sales on the conveyance against its records. (2) *If the land is charged by a company* registration at the Companies Registry is necessary within twenty-one days. (3) *An adequate fire policy* should be in force, and the bank should give notice of its interest to the insurers. (4) *When dealing with registered land* a legal mortgage is usually taken. The registry will *hold the land certificate* and issue new ones as the plots are sold (on the bank's instructions).

BUILDING ON CONTRACT

71. Financing contract work. Lending to customers to help finance contract work involves similar considerations to those outlined for the speculative builder. However, several additional features arise which will be examined in the light of the undermentioned proposition.

72. A typical proposition from a contractor. Your customer, Contractors Ltd., are capable large-scale builders with substantial assets which are fully employed in their business, including several large contracts. They are offered a contract for building a factory for a well-known car-components firm to be completed in two years at a price of £480,000, and ask you to finance it by placing at their disposal a limit of £120,000. Monthly payments will be made against architects' certificates, subject to a retention of 10 per cent. What considerations would influence you in first examining the proposal? How would you deal with the advance if you agreed to make it, and what security would you take?

73. Considerations influencing the proposal. The bank's decision as regards the proposal would be influenced by the following:

(*a*) The integrity, capability and business ability of the management.

(*b*) The company's progress over the last three years as evidenced from its Balance Sheets and accounts.

(*c*) Details of all contracts on hand, showing amounts certified, payments received, retentions, etc. Has the company previously completed a contract approaching this size? Is a sufficient supply of skilled labour available and also sub-contractors of standing?

(*d*) The construction programme and finance budget showing receipts and payments and the estimated peak advance requirements. Have the costings been adequately checked, and have retentions, delay in measurement of work and delay in payment been allowed for?

(*e*) The favourable reply to a status enquiry on the employer for the contract amount.

If the bank are satisfied this far, then the terms of the contract and position regarding sub-contractors must be examined.

74. The contract. Often a standard contract of the Royal Institute of British Architects is used, but clauses may be added to or varied. A "rise and fall" clause should be included to cover variations in cost of materials and labour. Penalty and other onerous clauses must be assessed.

75. Nominated sub-contractors. Under the terms of the contract the employer may be empowered to pay nominated sub-contractors direct or to do this if the main contractor fails to make due payment to the sub-contractors. The bank should take care to see that all due payments have been made to nominated sub-contractors.

76. Amount of advance. In our proposition the amount asked is £120,000. This amount seems unduly high. The project is to take two years, and if one allows, say, a twelve weeks' maximum between the completion of work and receipt of payment and presuming costs are spread evenly over the period (which of course they will not be in practice), then after twelve weeks the amount owing would be £60,000. Retentions must not be forgotten, of course, as these gradually mount to a final figure of £48,000. However, the amount asked calls for further enquiry!

The bank will usually agree to lend up to two-thirds of the amount expended on the contract. After the agreed first month's advance has been taken subsequent monthly advances will be granted against sight of architects' certificates. These advances will be made on separate account and will be extinguished when payment is received from the employer. A limit for working-capital purposes may be agreed for use on current account.

77. Controlling the advance. The bank should require monthly statements from the company in such form as to enable it to confirm whether: (*a*) all contracts are on schedule, (*b*) all due payments are being received, (*c*) all work is being certified speedily.

78. Security required. Unless the bank is entirely happy to lend unsecured against the company's assets, it will require a debenture and/or a legal assignment over the contract moneys. The latter will be more usual, and the company will be required to execute the bank's form of assignment. Notice must be given to and acknowledged by the *employer*, and the assignment must be registered at the Companies Registry within twenty-one days (thus preventing a repetition of *in Re Kent & Sussex Sawmills Ltd.* (1946).)

Where the bank are lending to a *sub-contractor* against an assignment of contract moneys, notice of the assignment is given to his employer, i.e. the *main contractor*.

The directors' J. & S. guarantee may be required as additional support. (Students should refer to XV, which deals with the technical aspects of charges over book debts.)

PROGRESS TEST 8

1. What restrictions, if any, attach to married women and minors with regard to banking accounts? **(1, 2, 5–8)**

2. What do you understand by the Rule of Survivorship with regard to joint accounts? Does the rule apply between father-and-son joint accounts? **(11, 12, 13)**

3. What do you understand by Joint and Several liability? In what circumstances do banks require account holders to admit such liability? **(17)**

4. Can personal representatives:

(*a*) Withdraw the deceased's will from safe custody?

(*b*) Withdraw the deceased's credit balance; before production of letters of administration or probate? **(21)**

5. Outline the procedure to be adopted where representatives wish to borrow to pay capital transfer tax. **(24)**

6. Why is the changeover from executorship to trusteeship of vital importance to the banker? **(27, 33)**

7. What is a trust account? Do special precautions need to be taken with regard to such accounts? **(28, 29–31)**

8. When, if at all, can trustees be permitted to delegate their authority: (*a*) to outsiders; (*b*) to one of their co-trustees? **(32, 33)**

9. What legal difficulties arise where a club or society wishes to borrow money? How can such borrowing be secured? **(38)**

10. What is the position with regard to a solicitor's office and clients' account in the event of his death or bankruptcy? **(47)**

11. With what factors will a bank be concerned before agreeing to lend to:

(*a*) A receiver? **(53, 54–7)**
(*b*) A liquidator? **(59–61)**
(*c*) A speculative house builder? **(64, 65, 68–70)**
(*d*) A customer wishing to finance a building contract? **(73, 78)**

CHAPTER IX

Corporate Account Holders

BUILDING SOCIETIES

1. Kinds of societies. There are two kinds:

(*a*) *Unincorporated.* There are very few of these, and they must conduct banking accounts strictly in accordance with their rules. *Unincorporated* societies may not now be formed.

(*b*) *Incorporated* by the Registrar of Friendly Societies and regulated by the Building Societies Act 1962.

2. Incorporated societies. There are two types of incorporated societies:

(*a*) *Terminating*, i.e. a society which by its rules is to terminate at a fixed date or when a result specified in its rules is attained.

(*b*) *Permanent*, i.e. a society with a perpetual succession which does not lay down a time for termination.

Of the incorporated societies few are the terminating type. Consequently, *the remaining notes are concerned only with incorporated permanent societies.*

3. Opening the account. The bank requires the production of the following documents:

(*a*) *The society's certificate of incorporation* issued by the Registrar of Friendly Societies.

(*b*) *A copy of the society's rules.*

(*c*) *An account mandate* incorporating a certified copy of the resolution appointing the bank as the society's bankers and authorising certain officials to sign on the account. The mandate *must* be in conformity with the rules.

4. Borrowing powers. Statutory power to borrow is outlined in the 1962 Act. Prior to incorporation the society *must elect in its rules* whether it will adopt the statutory limit *or* whether it will restrict this limit. The statutory borrowing limit (*see* below) *cannot be extended by the rules.*

5. Statutory borrowing limit. The total amount borrowed by way of *loans or deposits* must not exceed *two-thirds* of the amount for the time being secured to the society by *mortgages* from its members (excluding amounts: (*a*) secured by mortgages more than twelve months in arrears, or (*b*) where the society has been in possession of the property for twelve months): s. 39.

NOTE: If a society receives loans or deposits in excess of the limits prescribed by the Act: (1) The *directors* of the society receiving the loans or deposits on its behalf shall be personally liable *for the excess*: s. 40: (2) *Under the doctrine of subrogation* the lender may be able to recover excess borrowings (and even retain security deposited with him) provided the moneys were used by the society in payment of its *lawful debts and obligations*: *Blackburn Building Society* v. *Cunliff Brooks & Co.* (1882). (3) *If the society uses the borrowed moneys to make advances to its members* for which the members give security the lender is entitled to these securities, as the money advanced was in fact his: *Blackburn & District Benefit Building Society* v. *Cunliff Brooks & Co.* (1885).

6. Statutory Borrowing limit: method of compilation (*figures by way of example only*).

QUESTION: An *incorporated permanent society* approaches the bank for a £20,000 loan and produces the following up-to-date statement.

Will the amount required take the total borrowing beyond the permitted two-thirds limit presuming this has been adopted?

Liabilities	£	*Assets*	£
Due to shareholders	56,000	Owing on mortgages	81,000
Due to depositors	40,000	Mortgages twelve months in arrears	3,000
General reserve	4,000	Other assets	16,000
	£100,000		£100,000

ANSWER

	£
Maximum permitted borrowing ($\frac{2}{3}$ of £81,000)	54,000
Amount already being borrowed (i.e. money on deposit)	40,000
Additional sum which may be borrowed	14,000

Therefore a £20,000 loan would be beyond the permitted limit, and *ultra vires* to the extent of £6,000.

However, it must be noted that if the moneys to be borrowed are to be used to grant *additional mortgages*, then the total permitted borrowing limit will be *increased*.

If then we imagine that the *whole* £20,000 is required to grant *additional mortgages*:

	£
Total mortgages outstanding	81,000
Additional mortgages (*after* utilising bank borrowing)	20,000
	101,000
Maximum permitted borrowing ($\frac{2}{3}$ of £101,000)	67,333
Amount already being borrowed	40,000
Additional sum which may be borrowed	27,333

Therefore a £20,000 loan would be permissible and wholly *intra vires*.

NOTE: *Members shareholdings* and *society investments* are ignored in computing both the borrowing limit and the amount borrowed.

7. Reasons for requiring to borrow. Normally a bank will only be prepared to lend to a society provided there is no long-term element about the lending. The following are some of the more acceptable reasons for requiring to borrow:

(*a*) *Pending sale of assets*, e.g. investments.

(*b*) *To cover a sudden withdrawal of moneys by members*. (Provided the underlying reasons for withdrawal justifies support; and a return to the normal depositing pattern can soon be expected.)

(*c*) *On a fluctuating basis*, e.g. during periods of steady expansion in anticipation of deposits and shareholdings.

8. Bank procedure when lending. The general procedure is as follows:

(*a*) *Examine the society's rules* to ascertain whether the statutory or a lower borrowing limit applies.

(*b*) *Ensure that the bank borrowing will not be ultra vires.* Where there is little margin between the amount to be borrowed and the total permitted, the bank may require that: (*i*) the borrowing be taken on loan account, *or* (*ii*) the society's secretary furnishes a monthly statement certifying that the total borrowing limit has not been exceeded.

(*c*) Ensure that the rules allow the society to *mortgage and pledge its assets.*

9. Security required from the society. If the bank requires security, then a charge over the society's investments is acceptable if available. More usually a building society "omnibus" charge (being in the nature of an equitable sub-mortgage) is executed in favour of the bank under the common seal of the society in accordance with its rules. The members' mortgage deeds are duly lodged with the bank together with the form of charge.

The charge form contains clauses, *inter alia*:

(*a*) *Providing for the withdrawal and substitution of securities* so long as the agreed margin is maintained.

(*b*) *Whereby the society agrees—*

(*i*) to deposit any further securities necessary to maintain a margin of 50 per cent over the amount borrowed;

(*ii*) to restrict the borrowing to two-thirds of the amount on mortgage;

(*iii*) to execute transfers of the mortgages to the bank upon default, if demand is made for repayment. (The charge may include an *irrevocable power of attorney* clause appointing a *bank official* to act on the society's behalf.)

NOTE: (1) Notice of the omnibus sub-mortgage is *not* given to the individual mortgagors. (2) Separate sub-mortgages over individual properties are not usually taken, as this would cause unnecessary work and expense. (3) *Before taking security a banker must recall* that—a society whose shares have been designated as *trustee investments* will (almost certainly) lose this privilege if it creates a charge over its assets. (*Trustee status* is only granted provided the society has assets totalling at least £1 million and complies with certain other conditions.)

LOCAL AUTHORITIES

10. Local Government Act 1972. Under this Act the country is divided into metropolitan counties or districts and non-metropolitan counties or districts which are represented by Local Authorities. Greater London is separately treated.

11. The Account.

(*a*) *County Council.* The account may be styled in the name of "The XYZ County Council", or "The Treasurer of the XYZ County Council".

(*b*) *District Council.* The account must be styled in the name of "The ABC District Council".

(*c*) *Parish Council.* The account must be styled in the name of "The DEF Parish Council".

(*d*) *Community Council.* The account must be styled in the name of "The GHK Community Council".

12. Opening the Account—Mandate. In each case a resolution is required from the Council appointing the bank as the Council's bankers and a mandate on the bank's standard form must be given. The resolution will refer to the style of the account. The mandate will authorise the necessary person(s) to sign; in the case of (*b*) (*c*) and (*d*) above at least two Council members must sign.

13. Borrowing. This is either temporary or permanent. Temporary borrowings require no approval, but permanent borrowings require authority from the Secretary of State for the Environment. Permanent borrowings by the Greater London Council fall to be authorised by Act of Parliament each year.

Any borrowing from a bank will usually be temporary and may be for the purpose of defraying expenses, pending revenue receipts, rates etc. or pending the raising of an authorised loan.

In all cases the bank will need the written confirmation from the Treasurer or Chief Executive Officer that the Council has authorised the taking of the borrowing.

14. Protection to bank in respect of local authority borrowing. Persons lending to a local authority are not bound to enquire into the *legality or regularity* of such borrowing or as to whether the money raised was properly applied.

PROGRESS TEST 9

1. What are the statutory borrowing limits imposed upon incorporated permanent Building Societies? **(4, 5)**

2. Describe a "Building Society omnibus charge" and state the usual clauses to be found therein. **(9)**

CHAPTER X

Partnerships

NATURE AND FORMATION OF PARTNERSHIPS

1. Definition of partnership. "Partnership is the relationship which subsists between *persons carrying on a business in common* with a view of *profit*": Partnership Act 1890, s. 1. It is beyond the scope of this book to give examples showing where a partnership does or does not exist. Suffice it to say that the profit motive is imperative and that s. 2 of the Act together with various case-law decisions add to the *interpretation* of the above definition.

NOTE: In England a partnership is *not a separate legal entity in law*, but can sue or be sued in its firm-name. (2) A partnership contract is one *uberrimae fidei.*

2. Formation.

(*a*) *No formality necessary*. A partnership may be formed by: (*i*) deed, (*ii*) written agreement, (*iii*) word of mouth, (*iv*) implication.

(*b*) *Written agreement desirable*. Deed or written agreement is preferable, being known as "Articles of partnership".

(*c*) *Articles of partnership*. Partners are bound by the Articles (if any), and should any matter not be covered therein, the Partnership Act 1890, applies.

(*d*) *Maximum number of partners*. Two or more persons up to a *maximum of twenty* may agree to carry on *any* business without registering as a company.

This maximum limit *no longer applies* to qualified persons practising as solicitors or accountants, nor to persons carrying on business as members of a recognised stock exchange: CA 1967, s. 120.

3. Types of partner.

(*a*) *General* (*or active*) *partner*. A partner who takes an active part in the business.

(*b*) *Sleeping* (*dormant*) *partner*. A partner who takes no active part in the business.

(*c*) *Quasi or nominal partner*. A person who by his conduct leads others to believe he is a partner when in fact he is not.

NOTE: Under (*a*)–(*c*) each partner is personally liable for the whole of the firm's debts to the full extent of his private resources.

(*d*) *Limited partner*. A partner whose liability is limited to the amount of capital he has agreed to invest and who cannot take any part in the firm's management. A limited partner can only be a member of a firm which is registered under the Limited Partnership Act 1907. Such a partnership is extremely rare.

4. Registration of Business Names Act 1916. A firm carrying on business under a name which does not consist of the *true surnames of all its partners* formerly had to register under this Act within fourteen days of commencing business. A *certificate of registration* was issued by the Registrar of Companies. However, the Registry was abolished in 1982 under the provisions of the Companies Act 1981, and so this requirement is obsolete.

Now, any individual or partnership using a trade name or a name not consisting solely of his or her/their surname(s) must disclose the name of the proprietor(s) and his/their business or another address located within the U.K. These facts must be shown on all business correspondence, orders, invoices and receipts and written demands for payment of monies due, and must be supplied on request to anyone with whom business is being transacted. Also the relevant information must be on display in all business premises. Partnerships of twenty or more persons (e.g. solicitors, accountants, stockbrokers) are exempted from scheduling all the names and addresses on documents, provided a list is kept at the main place of business.

5. Former importance of the Business Names Act to banks. A danger for a bank dealing with a partnership account being operated in a name not consisting of every partner's surname is that it may collect cheques, drawn in favour of the partnership, to which the persons holding themselves out as partners are not entitled. Formerly therefore unless the bank had seen the certificate of registration and searched the register to ascertain the names of all the partners it would have been unable to avoid liability for *conversion*. (NOTE: Where a certificate obtained fraudulently did not disclose the *true* partners, the bank having seen and relied on it escaped liability. *viz*: A bank manager noticed his customer Bray paying in cheques payable to Argus Press. Bray contended that he was the owner of this firm (although actually owned by Smith and Baldwin) and produced the certificate of registration showing himself to be the sole owner. After Bray paid in several stolen cheques payable to the firm, Smith and Baldwin sued the bank for *conversion*. HELD: The bank had not been negligent, because having seen and relied on the (fraudulently obtained) certificate it was protected by BEA 1882, s. 82: *Smith & Baldwin* v. *Barclays Bank Ltd.* (1944).) Now however, as the certificate of registration does not exist, that case is of no protection, and banks, when opening an account for a partnership may need to take other steps to satisfy themselves, such as by seeing partnership letter headings or visiting the premises, to ascertain who precisely purport to be partners.

6. Wider application of the publication of a business name. The amended rules in the Companies Act 1981 apply not only to partnerships *but also to any person* (*including* corporations) trading under a name other than *his own real name*. If, for example, a *new* customer states that he is a freelance author using a *nom-de-plume* to which cheques will be made payable it might be prudent for the banker to ask for sight of his business letter heading or to require confirmation from his publishers.

7. Persons who may become partners. Generally any person having legal capacity to contract may become a partner. *Note particularly* that *a minor* may become a partner, but will *not* incur *personal liability* for the firm's debts contracted during his *minority*. (*See* VIII, 7.)

AUTHORITY TO DEAL WITH THIRD PARTIES

8. General authority of partners. The Act stipulates that *every* partner is an *agent* of the firm (unless the Articles provide otherwise) and binds it in the ordinary course of its business unless the party dealing with the partner as such is aware of his lack of authority: s. 5. Third parties are not deemed to know the contents of the Articles, and are not therefore bound by any secret restrictions of which they are unaware.

9. Implied authority of partners. Common law has recognised certain implied powers of a partner to bind his firm, but there are important distinctions affecting bankers concerning *trading* and *non-trading* partnerships:

(*a*) *In a trading firm*, i.e. a business which depends upon the *buying* and *selling* of goods. Any partner when acting in the *ordinary course* of his firm's business binds it on—

(*i*) Bills of exchange (including cheques).

(*ii*) Promissory notes.

(*iii*) Contracts of borrowing.

(*iv*) A pledge or sale of the firm's assets. (Except on transactions under seal.)

(*b*) *In a non-trading firm*, e.g. solicitors, accountants, etc. A partner cannot in respect of (*a*) (*i*)–(*iv*) above bind his firm (except on *cheques*) unless the above acts are part of the firm's *usual* business.

10. Where authority not implied. A partner cannot without *express* authority:

(*a*) *Bind the firm by deed* (as he must be appointed by deed so to act). NOTE: An executed but unauthorised *legal* mortgage can be regarded as an *equitable* mortgage: *Marchant* v. *Morton Down & Co.* (1901).

(*b*) *Execute a guarantee in the firm's name* unless giving guarantees forms part of the firm's usual business. Consequently, *all* partners must sign or authorise the signing of a guarantee given by a firm.

LIABILITY OF PARTNERS DEALING WITH THIRD PARTIES

11. Liability on debts and contracts. Partners are *jointly* liable to the full extent of their private means for the firm's debts and obligations; however, in the event of a partner's *death* his separate estate becomes *severally* liable for partnership debts *after payment of his separate debts*: s. 9. Although liability is only *joint* (unless otherwise agreed), if a creditor proceeds against some of several partners and obtains judgment which remains unsatisfied he can now proceed against the remaining partners, under the Civil Liability (Contribution) Act 1978. This overcomes the problem seen in *Kendall* v. *Hamilton* (1879), where he had only one right of action.

12. Liability for torts. Torts committed by a partner within the scope of the firm's business or with authority of his co-partners bind *all* partners *jointly and severally*: s. 12.

13. Liability of incoming partners. An *incoming* partner is not liable for debts and contracts *arising before he joined the firm* unless he agrees otherwise: s. 17(1). In practice, where the bank requires the incoming partner's liability in respect of an existing overdraft, he will be asked to join with the remaining partners in drawing a cheque to pay off the old partnership debt. The cheque creates an overdraft on the new partnership account for which all signatories are liable. A new mandate is required.

If partnership property has been charged as security, then provided the bank's form of charge allows for changes in the firm's constitution, the incoming partner need only endorse the existing charge forms; otherwise new security forms must be executed by all.

14. Liability of retiring partners.

(*a*) *Liability for subsequent partnership debts* ceases on retirement, *except* where the firm's business is continued, when to avoid liability the retiring partner must notify all persons who have: (*i*) *not* had previous dealings with the firm, by advertising his retirement in the *London Gazette*; (*ii*) had previous dealings with the firm, by giving *express* notice of his retirement.

(*b*) *Liability for partnership debts incurred prior to retirement* can only be avoided when individual creditors and all the remaining partners concur. Such agreement may be express or implied from the conduct of these parties: s. 17(2)–(3).

15. Liability on death or bankruptcy. The estate of a deceased or bankrupt partner is not liable for partnership debts incurred after either event: s. 36(3). Consequently, if the bank wishes to retain the liability of a partner in these circumstances (J & S liability having been established) the partnership account should be stopped to prevent the operation of the *Rule in Clayton's Case*.

16. Liability on continuing guarantees. A continuing guarantee given to a firm or to another person in respect of the firm's transactions is terminated as to *future transactions* by any change in the *constitution* of the firm: s. 18. This section does not apply where: (*a*) there is an agreement to the contrary, e.g. as in bank security forms, or (*b*) the guarantee is given *by* the firm: *see* XII, **16**.

DISSOLUTION OF PARTNERSHIP

17. By operation of law. Dissolution of partnership applies (unless overruled by the partnership Articles or agreement) where:

(*a*) The *term* fixed for the partnership expires.
(*b*) The agreed *adventure* or *undertaking* is completed.

NOTE: Under (*a*) and (*b*), if the partnership business is continued thereafter the usual rights and liabilities attach.

(*c*) A partner *gives notice of dissolution* to the other partners where the partnership is "at will". (This is a partnership entered into for an undefined time.)

(*d*) A partner *dies*, becomes *bankrupt* or suffers his share of the partnership property to be charged for a private debt (in this latter event dissolution is optional, dependent upon the wishes of the remainder).

(*e*) The *partnership* becomes *bankrupt* or *illegal*. (Dissolution is compulsory here.)

(*f*) *All* the partners agree. (This would override any contrary agreement in the Articles.)

NOTE: Where (1) a partner retires, or (2) a new partner joins the firm, the old partnership is in effect *dissolved*.

18. By court order: compulsory. The Court may order such dissolution on the application of any partner where:

(*a*) *A partner becomes mentally incapacitated.* Mental incapacity does not automatically bring about compulsory dissolution unless the partners have agreed otherwise.

(*b*) A partner's *conduct* becomes *prejudicial* to the firm's business or its operations.

(*c*) The business can only be carried on *at a loss*.

(*d*) Any circumstance arises *which renders dissolution necessary*, e.g. dispute between the partners.

19. Death of a partner. *See* **11** above for the position where *joint* liability exists. If *J & S liability* was admitted, however, then recovery by the firm's creditors may be effected from the deceased's estate in *competition with private creditors*.

20. Bankruptcy of a partnership. As technically a firm cannot be made bankrupt, an adjudication order is made against *each* general partner. In the event of a firm's bankruptcy (or a partner's death): The joint estate shall be applicable in the first instance in payment of joint debts and the separate estate of each partner in payment of his separate debts. If there is a surplus of the separate estates it shall be dealt with as part of the joint estate, and if there is a surplus of the joint estate it shall be shared by the partners in accordance with their respective rights: BA 1914, s. 33(6).

21. Advantages to the bank of admittance of J & S liability.

(*a*) *Multiplicity of actions.* The bank can if required sue any individual partner for the firm's debt and can concurrently or successively take action against some or all of the remainder.

(*b*) *Death or bankruptcy of one partner.* The bank can obtain recovery from the estate of the deceased or bankrupt partner in competition with private creditors without losing the right of recovery against the firm or remaining partners.

(*c*) *Death or bankruptcy of one, several or all partners.*

(*i*) The bank can set-off credit balances standing to a partner's *private* account against the *partnership* debt.

(*ii*) *Security* deposited by a partner *for all personal liabilities* may be appropriated by the bank against *either* his personal debt or the partnership debt. (*See also* VIII, **17**.)

BANKING ACCOUNTS OF PARTNERSHIPS

22. Opening the account.

(*a*) *The bank requires to ascertain:*

(*i*) *Who the partners are and the name in which they transact business;* remember registration under the Business Names Act.

(*ii*) *The nature of the partnership business.* The Articles of partnership are *not* required, *but if produced to the bank* the relevant sections *must* be noted.

(*b*) *Account name.* The account should be opened in the firm's name, otherwise it will not be bound: *Alliance Bank* v. *Kearsley* (1871).

(*c*) *Account mandate.* Although partners have *implied powers* (*see* **9** above), a mandate signed by all partners is taken to cover drawing of cheques, borrowing, charging, etc., and incorporating admission of J & S liability. The partners may sign cheques, etc., either in the firm's name or on behalf of the firm.

23. Bankruptcy.

(*a*) *Of a partnership.*

(*i*) *Where account is credit.* It *must* be stopped and the balance made available to the trustee in bankruptcy.

(*ii*) *Where account is debit*. It *must* be stopped, because only debts incurred prior to the date of the receiving order and without notice of an act of bankruptcy or presentation of a petition can be recovered. (*See* VI, **34**.)

(*b*) *Of a partner*.

(*i*) *Where partnership account is credit*. The other partners may continue the business in order to wind it up: s. 38. Consequently, the partners may continue operating the account for this purpose, but of course have to account to the bankrupt partner's trustee in respect of the bankrupt's share. (Cheques presented drawn by the bankrupt partner may be confirmed by the remainder and paid.)

(*ii*) *Where partnership account is debit*. If it is desired to retain the liability of the bankrupt partner or rights against security deposited by him, the account must be stopped and proof made in his bankruptcy.

24. Death of a partner.

(*a*) *Where partnership account is credit*. The other partners may deal with the balance and may continue the business in order to wind it up: s. 38. Cheques presented drawn by the deceased partner may be confirmed by the remainder and paid.

(*b*) *Where partnership account is debit*. Similar considerations apply as in **23**(*b*)(*ii*) above. Any claim is made against the deceased's estate.

> NOTE: *Where the account is continued after the death or bankruptcy of a partner:* (1) A new *mandate* is required. (2) The *surviving partners* have the right to *mortgage* the firm's assets in order to continue the business for the purpose of winding up: *Re Bourne* (1906). But if the bank has *notice* that the survivors are continuing the business *for their own ends*, then any charge would be subject to the rights of the estate of the *deceased or bankrupt* partner. (3) *Security previously deposited by the firm* can continue to be utilised for its account.

25. Mental incapacity of a partner. Provides grounds for dissolution by court order: *see* **18** above. If the bank wishes to retain the liability of the incapacitated partner it must stop the partnership account immediately it receives notice of incapacity.

26. Cheques collected for a partner. A banker is *not* put on special enquiry when collecting cheques for a partner's private account *drawn on the partnership*: (*a*) by one of the other partners, or (*b*) by the partner paying in: *Backhouse* v. *Charlton* (1878). (An exception occurs in the latter case, where the bank have been pressing for repayment of the partner's overdraft.) Special circumstances would necessitate enquiry to the partnership:

(*a*) *These may arise where* the amount of such cheques (drawn as mentioned above) is *exceptionally* large or the partner's integrity is doubted.

(*b*) *These definitely arise where:* (*i*) the cheques paid in are payable to the *partnership*, (*ii*) the cheques are *drawn by the partnership* payable to third parties and endorsed.

PROGRESS TEST 10

1. Why is the Registration of Business Names Act 1916, of importance to bankers? **(5, 6)**
2. Distinguish between the liability of incoming and outgoing partners for partnership debts. How in practice is the liability of a new partner obtained for an existing partnership debt? **(13, 14)**
3. How does the admittance of J & S liability by partners help the bank in the event of the bankruptcy of the partnership? **(21)**
4. What action is required by the bank if a *partner* becomes bankrupt where the *partnership account*: (*a*) is in credit, (*b*) is in debit? **(23(*b*))**
5. Are the bank put on enquiry when collecting for a partner's private account a cheque drawn by that partner on behalf of the partnership? **(26)**

CHAPTER XI

Limited Companies

In this book space can only be devoted to *companies limited by shares* and not to the various other types of association which may also be incorporated under the Companies Act 1948. It is assumed that banking students have already covered the groundwork in respect of company law from such works as *Law of Banking*, by D. Palfreman, or *Company Law*, by M. C. Oliver, both in the M & E HANDBOOK Series.

The aim of this chapter is o: () refresh students' minnds egarding the sections of company law which affect bankers, and to outline the practical application of such law; (*b*) discuss practical banking situations, particularly those likely to give rise to examination questions. (All section numbers, unless otherwise stated, refer to the Companies Act 1948.)

THE COMPANY AS A SEPARATE ENTITY

1. Separate entity. A company is a *separate legal entity*, quite distinct from its members and having perpetual succession.

EXAMPLE: S the principal shareholder in S Ltd., (owning all bar six shares) was owner of £10,000 worth of secured debentures issued by the company. When the company became insolvent and entered into liquidation the unsecured creditors claimed the assets comprising S's security on the grounds that as he and the company were one person, he had no priority. HELD: The company was a separate legal entity quite distinct from its members, and as S had lawfully contracted with it he was entitled to priority in respect of his security: *Salomon* v. *Salomon & Co. Ltd.* (1897).

TYPES OF LIMITED COMPANY

2. Public Company. The Companies Act 1980, s. 1(i) requires a Public Company—

(*a*) to state in its Memorandum that it is a Public Company,
(*b*) to have registered or re-registered as a Public Company,
(*c*) to have at least two members,
(*d*) to have issued *shares* which can be transferred without restriction,
(*e*) to have a minimum issued share capital of not less than £50,000,
(*f*) to have a name ending with the words "public limited company", although the abbreviation "plc" is permitted, or its Welsh equivalent, "ccc", where the company's registered office is in Wales.

The Act also lays down more stringent requirements for a Public Company than for a Private Company in respect of the manner in which profits available for distribution are calculated, and the steps necessary should the directors become aware of a deficit of an amount being 50 per cent or more of the called up capital in respect of the net assets of the company (Companies Act 1980 s. 34).

3. Private Company. A Private Company is any other company not being a Public Company, and must include all unlimited companies. Most private companies are likely by their Articles to continue to limit the number of their members to not more than fifty and to restrict the transferability of their shares.

NOTE: *Re-Registration of Existing Public Companies* under the CA 1980. This must be effected by 22nd March 1982 by a Board Resolution and then by the filing of forms with the Registrar of Companies if the company wishes to remain a Public Company or become a Private Company. Fines will be imposed on the company and its officers if no action is taken. Failure to re-register will not make the company's actions void. N.B. No action is necessary for an existing private company wishing so to remain.

OPENING THE ACCOUNT OF A LIMITED COMPANY

4. Opening the account of a limited company.

(*a*) The bank requires the following documents for *examination and record purposes*:
(*i*) The company's *certificate of incorporation*. (This is con-

clusive evidence that all the requirements of the Act in respect of registration have been complied with.)

(*ii*) The company's *trading certificate*; if it is a *public* company.

(*b*) The bank requires for *retention and record purposes*:

(*i*) *Up-to-date copies of the company's memorandum and articles of association*, duly certified by the secretary.

NOTE: These must be perused carefully and a note made as to the provisions affecting: (1) *the company's powers* (found in the memorandum), e.g. borrowing power, power to give guarantees and other security, and (2) *the directors' powers* (found in the articles), e.g. restrictions on borrowing when acting as agents of the company.

(*ii*) *A certified copy* of the board of directors' resolution appointing the bank as the company's bankers.

(*iii*) *A mandate* covering all banking operations relating to the company's account incorporating the names, number and positions of persons authorised to (1) draw, endorse and accept bills of exchange, promissory notes and cheques, etc., Table A, Article 85 applies, i.e. resolution of board of directors' required. (2) deposit and withdraw security and custody items, (3) overdraw the account. Table A, Article 79 applies.

Specimen signatures of directors and all authorised signatories are required. The bank must ensure that the mandate is in conformity with the memorandum and articles.

5. Memorandum and Articles of Association of a company limited by shares. The nature and contents of these documents must be known and clearly distinguished by students for examination purposes.

(*a*) *The memorandum*. Sets out the powers of the company and must include: (*i*) the name of the company including "limited", (*ii*) situation of the company's registered office, i.e. in England or Scotland, (*iii*) the company's objects, (*iv*) a statement that the members' liability is limited, (*v*) details of the company's share capital, (*vi*) subscribers' declaration.

(*b*) *The articles*. Sets out the rules governing the internal management of the company.

(*c*) Table A is a *model set of articles* divided into two parts. Part I is for *public* companies limited by shares and Part II for *private* companies limited by shares. If a company does *not* register articles, then Table A of the Act under which the company was incorporated *automatically applies*. Moreover, even if it *does* register articles of its own, Table A still applies automatically as regards regulations which have *not been excluded or modified*.

6. Public company: account transactions before issue of trading certificate. A public company may wish to open an account upon incorporation but before the issue of its *trading certificate*. The trading certificate is not granted until the company's prospectus (or statement in lieu of prospectus) has been filed at the Companies Registry and in the former case the minimum subscription reached and allotments made: s. 109. *Further*, if application is being made for an official Stock Exchange quotation the trading certificate will not be issued until a quotation is granted: ss. 51 and 109.

Prior to the granting of the trading certificate:

(*a*) *A special account* may be opened for receipt of *share application moneys*, but no withdrawals other than for return of moneys should be permitted.

(*b*) *An account* may safely be opened for receipt of credits, but no cheques should be drawn thereon. (In practice, the bank may allow the issue of cheques for urgent payments, relying upon the integrity and/or indemnity of the directors and also upon the knowledge of the probability of the successful outcome of the share issue.)

NOTE: (1) A *public* company *shall not commence any business or exercise its borrowing powers* until it has complied with the provisions necessary for obtaining its *trading certificate*: s. 109.
(2) Contracts entered into by a *public* company *after* incorporation but *prior* to the issue of its trading certificate are *provisional*, and only become binding when the latter is issued: s. 109(4).

7. Partnership or sole business formed into a limited company. There is a danger for bankers when accepting security given by a new company formed to take over the assets and liabilities of a *partnership* or *sole trader*. In the event of the bankruptcy of the partnership or sole trader within three months of the transfer of the assets to the company, the trustee in bankruptcy may be able to claim these back as a "fraudulent" conveyance. Thus the bank's security may become worthless: *Re Simms* (1930). *See* VI, 4, for an outline of this case and for the protective methods to be adopted.

BORROWING AND CHARGING POWERS

8. General comments. Most limited companies require on occasions to borrow from the bank. It is most important therefore for bankers to be able to ascertain *precisely* the total amount of borrowing (if any) which the company may have outstanding at any one time. Note particularly that the power of the company to borrow is normally exercisable by the directors, and that while the company's power is usually unlimited, the authority of the directors to exercise that power is often limited.

The following questions must be satisfactorily resolved before the bank will permit the company to borrow:

(*a*) Is the borrowing required for purposes within the objects? *See* **12** below.

(*b*) Has the company power to borrow the amount asked after taking into consideration existing borrowing? *See* **9** below.

(*c*) (If the answer to both (*a*) and (*b*) is "yes".) May the directors exercise the company's power in full or are their powers restricted? *See* **11**, **13**, **14** and **15** below.

(*d*) Has the company power to secure the debt? *See* **10** below and Appendix V.

9. The company's capacity to borrow.

(*a*) *Implied power.*

(*i*) *A commercial or trading company* has, subject to its memorandum, *implied* power to borrow *without limit* for the purposes of its business: *General Auction Estate & Monetary Co.* v. *Smith* (1891).

(*ii*) *A non-trading company* has *no implied power to borrow*, *but* express power to borrow may and usually is contained in its objects.

(*b*) *Express power.* Is invariably contained in the objects of every company's memorandum. Any restriction on total outstanding borrowing should be noted. (Limitations may be removed, *for the future*, by special resolution: *see* **18** below.)

10. The company's capacity to charge security.

(*a*) *Implied power.* An *express power to borrow* provides the company with an *implied power to charge* any or all of its assets as security for such borrowing: *Re Patent File Co.* (1870).

(*b*) *Express power.* Is invariably contained in the objects clause.

(A company cannot execute a *guarantee* unless specific power to do so is contained in its objects: *see* XII, **18**.)

11. Manner of borrowing. Assuming the memorandum and articles contain no departure as to the normal manner of borrowing, then the directors can, under Table A, Article 80, exercise all the powers of the company in this respect (except those which the Act or the articles specifically state must be exercised by the company in general meeting):

(*a*) *Presuming Article* 80 *applies* (as is usually the case). The bank can permit the directors to overdraw the company's banking account when drawing in accordance with the mandate.

(*b*) Alternatively, in a minority of instances the *company's memorandum and/or articles may provide that borrowing shall not take place unless*: (*i*) sanctioned by the company in general meeting, or (*ii*) sanctioned by special resolution. In these circumstances the bank would require a certified copy of the relevant authority.

12. Borrowing for purposes outside the objects. Any act done outside the objects is *ultra vires* (i.e. beyond the powers of) the company and void, unless the act can be deemed incidental thereto: *Ashbury Railway Carriage & Iron Co.* v. *Riche* (1875). As the memorandum and articles are public documents, banks should not knowingly grant *advances* for purposes inconsistent with a company's objects as they are *void* and will usually prove irrecoverable (but *see* Appendix II).

EXAMPLE: A liquidator's contention that debentures securing a £29,500 loan from NP Bank to I was *ultra vires*, was upheld by the C. of A. The bank had *knowingly* lent moneys to I for a pig-breeding scheme beyond its "physical" objects relying on an "independent borrowing object". The court decided that such an object *cannot be isolated* but must be related to other objects; thus the loan and security were void: *Re Introductions Ltd.* (1969)

NOTE: (1) Had the purpose of the loan been unknown to the bank it appears it would have remained valid: *Re David Payne & Co. Ltd.* (1904). (2) Other ancillary objects must always be related to the company's main objects unless they are specified as independent objects. (3) *See* Appendix V.

13. Directors' borrowing limits. Any limits imposed on directors when exercising the company's borrowing powers will be found in the articles.

14. Directors' borrowing limits: Table A, 1948 Act. In respect of companies incorporated under the 1948 Act, Table A, Article 79, limits directors' borrowing powers. But this Article may be partially or wholly excluded. Consequently, the following *alternatives* will *normally be found to apply as regards directors' borrowing powers*:

(*a*) *Table A, Article* 79, *may apply in full*: This provides that the amount of outstanding borrowing by the directors shall not exceed the *nominal amount of the issued share capital* without the company's sanction in general meeting. (*See* **16** below.)

(*b*) *Table A, Article* 79, *may apply, but the proviso* contained therein excluded:* This enables the directors to exercise in full the borrowing powers of the company.

(*c*) *Table A, Article* 79, *may be completely excluded*, and either:

(*i*) *An express restriction included*, e.g. directors' borrowing powers limited to £10,000 outstanding at any one time. *Or*

(*ii*) *An express unlimited power included*, e.g. directors' borrowing powers unlimited, i.e. they can exercise in full the borrowing powers of the company. *Or*

(*iii*) *No amending article substituted.* Consequently, Article 80 will apply, and the directors can therefore exercise in full the borrowing powers of the company.

NOTE: A Stock Exchange official quotation will not be granted unless a company's articles limit the borrowing power of the directors to an ascertainable amount.

15. Directors' borrowing limits: pre-1948 Act. As regards directors' borrowing limits, companies incorporated under earlier Acts are governed by the appropriate Table A, unless excluded; e.g. Companies Act 1929, Table A, Article 69, limits the amount of outstanding borrowing by the directors to the *issued share capital* without the company's sanction in general meeting (but no mention is made of "temporary loans": *see* **16** below).

16. Interpretation of Table A, Article 79, Companies Act 1948. Article 79 states:

"The *directors* may exercise *all the powers of the company to borrow money, and to mortgage or charge its undertaking,*

* The proviso is outlined in **16** below.

property and uncalled capital, or any part thereof, and to issue debentures, debenture stock, and other securities whether *outright* or as *security* for any debt, liability or obligation *of the company or of any third party:*

"(PROVISO) *Provided* that the amount for the time being remain remaining *undischarged* of moneys *borrowed* or *secured* by the directors as aforesaid (apart from *temporary* loans obtained from the company's *bankers in the ordinary course of business*) *shall not at any time*, without the previous sanction of the company in general meeting, *exceed the nominal amount of the share capital* of the company for the time being issued, but *nevertheless* no lender or other person dealing with the company shall be concerned to see or enquire whether this limit is observed. *No* debt incurred or security given in excess of such limit shall be *invalid or ineffectual* except in the case of express notice to the lender or the recipient of the security at the time when the debt was incurred or security given that the limit hereby imposed had been or was thereby exceeded."

The important points in this Article should be noted:

(*a*) *The amount of directors' borrowing outstanding shall not exceed the nominal amount of the issued share capital*, unless: (*i*) the company sanctions the borrowing in general meeting, or (*ii*) the loan is temporary and from a banker.

(*b*) *"Temporary loans" have not been defined.* Consequently, bankers are unwilling to rely on the protection.

(*c*) *No lender shall be concerned to see or enquire whether the limit is observed*, and no debt (or security given) in excess of such limit shall be *invalid* unless the lender had *express* notice of the excess when the debt was incurred (or security given).

But what is *express* notice as regards a banker? No doubt he would often be deemed to have *express* notice, e.g. where he sees from the company's Balance Sheet that the limit is already exceeded.

(*d*) *"Borrowing" includes:* loans from directors, deposits, bank loans, debentures and security given to third parties; *but not*: share capital, proceeds of bills discounted or amounts due to creditors.

17. Practical example concerning borrowing powers.

QUESTION:

ABC Co. Ltd. was incorporated in 1966 adopting Table A as its articles. In January 1981 the company approaches the bank for a £40,000 overdraft and produces the undermentioned figures from the liabilities side of its balance sheet as at 31st December 1980.

Discuss solely in relation to borrowing powers.

Authorised Capital	£100,000
Issued Capital 60,000 £1 shares	£60,000

	£
Paid-up capital 60,000 £1 shares at 50p per share	30,000
Debentures	20,000
Loan by director	5,000
Trade creditors	15,000
Reserves	23,000
Profit and Loss Account	21,000
	£114,000

The company is subject to a contingent liability in respect of a guarantee for £2,000 to secure a loan to an associated company.

ANSWER (IN BRIEF)

(*a*) *The company's memorandum should be examined* for any specific borrowing powers or limits. If the memorandum is silent, then as ABC Co. Ltd. is a *trading* company, it has implied unlimited powers.

(*b*) Companies Act 1948, *Table A, Article* 79, *has been adopted.* Therefore the directors' total borrowing outstanding is limited to £60,000 (i.e. the *nominal* amount of the *issued* share capital) without the company's sanction in general meeting.

The company is presently borrowing or securing:

	£
Debentures	20,000
Loan by director	5,000
Security given by way of guarantee	2,000
	£27,000

Consequently, the amount asked (£40,000) is £7,000 over the permitted limit, and this excess can only be advanced if either: (*i*) it can be regarded as "temporary", or (*ii*) the company sanctions the borrowing in general meeting, i.e. by authorising the directors to borrow a specific additional amount *or* an amount without limit (the latter is preferable), or (*iii*) the company removes the limit by amending its articles by special resolution, or (*iv*) capitalise the reserves and/or profit and loss account (if sufficient is available) to rectify the position. (*See* also Appendix V.)

REMEDIES FOR ULTRA VIRES BORROWING

18. Removal of a company's existing borrowing limit. By s. 5 of the 1948 Act a company may alter its *objects* by special resolution. This enables a borrowing limit to be removed. However, such an alteration *cannot operate retrospectively*, and is of no avail therefore if the company has already taken the borrowing.

NOTE: If within twenty-one days of the *passing* of a special resolution altering the objects, 15 per cent in nominal value of the company's shareholders or debenture holders request the Court to cancel the alteration, then the alteration only becomes effective to the extent confirmed by the Court.

19. Remedies for borrowing ultra vires the company. If the amount advanced actually exceeds the company's borrowing powers (and European Communities Act 1972, s. 9(1) cannot be claimed), then the *chance of recovering the excess is only slight*, because the borrowing *cannot be ratified* by the company members. A bank's hopes of recovery must rest upon:

(*a*) *Voluntary repayment by the company*, e.g. in the ordinary course of business as credits are paid in. Too much reliance should not be attached to the *voluntary* aspect, as dispute may arise or liquidation may occur.

(*b*) *Right of subrogation*. The bank has the right to apply to the Court to be *subrogated* to the position of company creditors who have been lawfully paid out with its money: *Sinclair* v. *Brougham* (1914). Complications would obviously arise if numerous creditors were involved.

(*c*) *Tracing order*. If the bank's money remains in the company's possession or has been used to purchase specific assets, e.g. stocks and shares, then the bank may be able to obtain from the

Court a *tracing order* attaching the money or assets: see *Sinclair* v. *Brougham* (1914).

(*d*) *Sue the directors for breach of warranty of authority.* This remedy would be available where the bank have in good faith relied upon the word of the directors that the company's borrowing limit had not been exceeded: *Weeks* v. *Propert* (1873).

20. Borrowing intra vires the company but ultra vires the directors. If the directors borrow within the company's powers but beyond their own, then although such borrowing is void (but *see* Appendix II, **9**(1)), the chances of rectifying the position are good, especially as the company are legally able and normally willing to ratify the position.

21. Remedies for borrowing ultra vires the directors. The bank may seek any of the following remedies:

(*a*) *Request* the company *to ratify the borrowing by resolution in general meeting.*

(*b*) *Request* the company *to amend its articles retrospectively by special resolution to remove the previous limit:* permissible by CA 1948, s. 10.

(*c*) *Where Table A, Article* 79 applies. Ask the Court to confirm: (*i*) that the borrowing was "temporary", or (*ii*) that it was not put on enquiry that the borrowing limit was exceeded (presuming a lack of *express* notice).

(*d*) *To rely on the Rule in Turquand's Case* (i.e. *Royal British Bank* v. *Turquand* (1856)), where the company refuses to ratify the borrowing and Article 79 has been excluded.

(*e*) To rely on European Communities Act 1972, s. 9(1) (*see* Appendix V).

(*f*) *To rely on one of the four courses quoted in* **19**(*a*)–(*d*) above.

22. Rule in Turquand's Case. Any person having read the memorandum and articles of a company can assume that any necessary *internal* formalities have been completed, e.g. the passing of a borrowing resolution which requires sanction in general meeting.

But the rule can only be relied upon by a banker so as to *bind* the company if he:

(*a*) Inspected the memorandum and articles.

(*b*) Knew of the required authority and relied upon it when lending the money.

(*c*) Was not put on enquiry as regards the transaction.

For instance, a banker *is* put on enquiry and must verify the position where borrowing reaches the sanction of a *special* or *extraordinary* resolution, as such resolutions become notice to the world when registered at the Companies Registry.

In practice, bankers usually call for a certified copy of any necessary resolution.

INTERESTED DIRECTORS

23. Common-law position. There is a general *common-law* rule that a director when acting as agent for the company cannot without express authority contract with himself or enter into any arrangement whereby his personal interests conflict with those of the company. The various Companies Acts have supported this law. *For example*, CA 1948, s. 199, provides that an interested director must disclose the nature of his interest at a meeting of directors, *and further*, Table A, Article 84, provides (with an important exception for bankers—*see* **25** below) that a director shall *not vote* in respect of any contract or arrangement in which he is interested.

Consequently, before acting upon the resolution of the company's board of directors a banker *who knows* that a director is personally interested in the arrangement should check to see whether he voted, and if he did so, whether this was permissible. (Interested directors are also discussed in XII, **19**, where the Rule in *Victors Ltd.* (*In liquidation*) v. *Lingard* (1927) is outlined in detail.)

24. Interested directors and bankers. A common example where directors are said to be "interested" occurs when having charged their own security, by way of guarantee or otherwise, to the bank to secure the company's account, they then proceed to authorise the giving of additional or substituting security by the company to secure its own account. They are regarded as "interested" here because *they are reducing their own liability*.

25. Voting rights of interested directors. Interested directors are not permitted to vote at a meeting of directors *unless* the company's articles expressly permit this *or* unless the company was incorporated under the 1948 Act and the transaction concerns one of the exceptions quoted in Table A, Article 84(2), if this article has not been excluded.

Article 84(2) particularly concerns bankers because interested directors *may vote* ... (*inter alia*) "on any arrangement for the giving *by the company* of any security to a third party (e.g. a bank) in respect of a debt or obligation *of the company* for which the director himself has assumed responsibility in whole or in part under a guarantee or indemnity or by the deposit of a security". Consequently, if this article applies, then in the circumstances outlined in **24** above the directors can validly vote.

26. How the bankers' position may be jeopardised. If a director votes when he is debarred from doing so, then:

(*a*) His *vote* does not count.
(*b*) His *presence* does not count towards a quorum.
(*c*) The company's liquidator may later attempt to declare the resolution invalid: *see* XII.

27. How the danger may be avoided or resolved. If interested directors are not permitted to vote, then a quorum (*see* **83** below) of disinterested directors could authorise the resolution if there are sufficient in number. *Otherwise:*

(*a*) The *members* must authorise the charging of the company's security, in general meeting. *Or*
(*b*) *The articles must be amended* to permit interested directors to vote. (Retrospective remedy is available here.)

NOTE: *Under* (*a*) the directors are in no way restricted from exercising fully their voting rights as *shareholders*. Thus if the directors are the only (or main) shareholders, then although they may be debarred from voting on a resolution as interested *directors*, they can vote on the same resolution in general meeting as *shareholders*.

REGISTRATION OF CHARGES

This section is extremely important, and students should learn the charges created by a company which require registration and note carefully the position which arises if registration is not effected within the prescribed time limit.

28. Charges requiring registration. S. 95 of the CA 1948 provides that the undermentioned charges (which expression includes *mortgages*) created by a company *must be registered with the Registrar of Companies* (at Companies House) *within* twenty-one *days of creation*, otherwise the charge becomes *void* against the *liquidator and any creditor of the company*. When a charge becomes *void* because of failure to register within the prescribed time the *debt* secured thereby is not invalidated, but *becomes immediately payable.*

The following charges require registration.

(*a*) A *charge* to secure *debentures.*

(*b*) A *floating charge.*

(*c*) A charge on *land* or any interest therein.

(*d*) A charge on a *ship.*

(*e*) A charge on *book debts.*

(*f*) A charge on *goodwill, patents, trademarks* or *copyrights.*

(*g*) A charge created by an instrument which, if executed by an individual, would require registration as a bill of sale.

(*h*) A charge on *uncalled share capital.*

(*i*) A charge on *calls made but not paid.*

Of the above (*a*)–(*e*) most commonly concern bankers.

29. Procedure for registration. It is the duty of the company creating the charge to register it. *Alternatively*, any person interested therein may register, and *banks always do so in practice.* Registration is achieved by completing Form 47, and lodging this and the instrument of charge (if any) with the Registrar of Companies within twenty-one days of execution of the charge. No registration fee is payable.

30. Further points regarding registration. The following are important:

(*a*) *Commencement of time limit for registration.*

(*i*) *If there is an instrument of charge* the twenty-one days commences to run from the *date of its execution and delivery to the bank.* Consequently, if a charge form bearing *no* date is duly executed and delivered to the bank, and subsequently when the advance is actually taken *a later date is filled in and the charge then registered,* it will be *void* unless registration has occurred within twenty-one days of actual *execution and delivery*: *Esberger* v. *Capital and Counties Bank* (1913).

However, where a bank's solicitors noticed in June that a charge in the bank's favour had not been registered although completed but left undated in February, they filled in the date as 18th June and registered it at Companies House on 3rd July. Thereafter on N's liquidation, the liquidator claimed that the charge was *void* as being unregistered within twenty-one *days of* creation. The C of A reversing the HC decision held that the certificate once issued is "conclusive" per section 98(2): *Re C. L. Nye Ltd.* (1970). The decision only appears rational where the "bona fides" of the parties is undoubted and the failure to register is unintentional. Whether the *Esberger* case would now be decided differently is open to argument.

(*ii*) *If there is no instrument of charge* the twenty-one days commences to run from the time the security is *deposited.*

(*b*) *Form* 47 must contain: (*i*) the date and description of the charge, (*ii*) the amount secured by the charge (usually "all moneys owing" where a bank is concerned), (*iii*) brief particulars of the property charged, (*iv*) a description of persons entitled to the charge.

(*c*) *Certificate of registration.* This is issued by the Registrar of Companies and forwarded to the bank. If a charge form was lodged this is returned, bearing the stamp of the Companies Registration Office.

(*d*) *Notice of registration.* Duly appears in the *London Gazette* (and in other trade gazettes, e.g. *Stubbs'*).

(*e*) *Searching the register of charges.* A bank may make a *personal* search at Companies House on payment of a £1 fee.

31. Companies own register of charges. *All* charges created by a company on its *property* must be recorded in its *own* register of charges (s. 104). But failure to record a charge therein *does not invalidate the charge: Wright* v. *Horton* (1887). Although the bank can institute a search on this register, it rarely does so, because the register may not be up to date.

32. Late registration. Where because of *accident, inadvertence or other sufficient cause* a charge is not registered within the prescribed time limit, the Court has power to authorise late registration: s. 101. (But this would only be authorised subject to intervening entries or rights.)

33. Effect of registration. The registrar's *certificate of registration* is *conclusive* evidence that the requirements of the Act as to registration have been complied with: s. 98(2). (The bank preserves this certificate with the charge form.)

If an entry on the register does not reveal details of *all* the property comprising the charge, *nevertheless* all persons are affected by the *actual terms* contained in the charge form: *National Provincial & Union Bank of England* v. *Charnley* (1924). The same position arises if the *amount(s)* secured by the charge is not fully revealed on the register: *Re Mechanisations (Eaglescliffe) Ltd.* (1964). Consequently, occasions may arise where a banker taking charge *over property already charged elsewhere*, e.g. under a floating charge, would be advised to examine the prior charge form to ascertain its full terms rather than to rely implicitly on the register.

34. Charges not requiring registration. Note particularly that the following charges do *not* require registration with the registrar of companies:

(*a*) A charge on stocks and shares.

(*b*) A charge on produce.

(*c*) A charge on negotiable instruments.

(*d*) A charge on a life policy, e.g. on a director's life.

(*e*) A charge on an Export Credits Guarantee Department policy.

Also, guarantees and letters of set-off executed by a company do *not* require registration.

35. Registration of satisfaction.

(*a*) *Complete satisfaction.* The company completes Form 49 (memorandum of satisfaction) under seal, and this is lodged with the registrar. The memorandum is supported by a *statutory declaration* completed by the company secretary and a director.

(*b*) *Partial satisfaction.* Where *part* only of property comprised in the charge is released the above procedure is adopted, but Form 49A is used.

NOTE: (1) Notice of satisfaction is *gazetted.* (2) Although it is not usual practice, *some banks* have long-standing arrangements whereby the *registrar* informs them when a *company* lodges satisfaction.

36. Gazette entries. Examining the weekly gazette entries (e.g. in *Stubbs'*) is a tedious but *vital* task for the branch security clerk. Entries concerning customers and also depositors of collateral security must be noted, so that the requisite action can be taken, e.g. stopping the customer's account. The bank may anticipate the appearance of an entry, e.g. where it has recently registered a charge. Occasionally, however, an unexpected entry appears, e.g. creation of a second mortgage by a company over property already secured to the bank.

The following are some of the more important notices concerning *companies* found in *Stubbs' Gazette*:

(*a*) Creation of *mortgages and charges*;

(*b*) *Satisfactions*;

(*c*) *Petitions presented*;

(*d*) *Winding-up orders*, including *resolutions for voluntary winding-up*;

(*e*) Appointment and retirement of liquidators, receivers and managers.

The relevant dates are noted in each case.

NOTE: Notices not concerning companies are also included, e.g. County court judgments, bankruptcies, dissolution of partnerships, etc. (*See* also Appendix II.)

37. Taking security from a company. The following procedure is adopted:

(*a*) The *company's objects, borrowing and charging powers are verified in the Memorandum.*

(*b*) The *articles are studied to ascertain*: (*i*) whether any *special* authority is required for the giving of security (*and, if not*), (*ii*) what the directors' borrowing powers are, (*iii*) whether the charge need be executed under seal. If a charge under hand on the company's behalf is acceptable then a directors' resolution to borrow and give security is required while the bank is supplied with a copy of the resolution.

If the charge requires execution under seal, e.g. as does a legal mortgage of land, then the sealing will be witnessed by company officials.

(*c*) *Before the security is accepted and the advance taken a search* is made on the company at Companies House to ensure that the property is not charged elsewhere, e.g. under a floating charge.

(*d*) *The security* (if registrable) *is then registered at the Companies Registry* within twenty-one days of execution: *see* also XIII, **56–8.**

DEBENTURES

38. Nature of a debenture. A debenture is simply a written acknowledgment of indebtedness by a company, usually given under its seal and setting out the terms for interest and repayment. Nowadays debentures are usually secured on the undertaking and property of the company which issues them.

A company may issue a *single* debenture, e.g. to a bank, or a *series* of debentures, e.g. to debenture holders. The debentures may be issued in favour of a registered holder or bearer, being secured on the company's assets or unsecured. Debentures may be irredeemable or redeemable at a fixed date or on demand, etc.

39. Nature of a bank debenture. A *single* debenture is issued by the company in favour of the bank, usually incorporating, *inter alia*, a *fixed charge* over the company's existing permanent property as specified, e.g. land, buildings, etc., *and/or a floating charge* over the company's other assets and undertaking (the "changing" assets) both present and future, e.g. stock, work-in-progress, debtors, etc. (but *see* **40**(*c*) re debtors). The debenture is given to secure all moneys owing at any time by the company.

NOTE: *Fixed-amount* debentures are rarely accepted by banks because additional lodgments would be necessary to keep them fully secured should the company's borrowing exceed the amount of the existing security.

40. Fixed and floating charges. Students must understand clearly the distinction between these two types of charges found in debentures.

(*a*) A *fixed charge* is a charge over *definite* or *specific property* of a permanent nature, e.g. the company's land, factory, fixtures, etc. The bank takes a *fixed charge by way of legal mortgage* over all fixed property mentioned in the charge, and thereafter the company cannot deal with these assets, e.g. by sale, etc. without the bank's consent.

NOTE: (1) If the fixed charge was not expressed to be by way of legal mortgage it would remain equitable. (2) The title deeds relating to the properties are held by the bank to restrain the company from dealing with them. (Once the debenture is registered, no further registration is necessary as regards land *except* for registered land.)

(*b*) A *floating charge* is an equitable charge *on a class of assets for the time being of a going concern*, e.g. over stock, work-in-progress, debtors (but *see* **40**(*c*)), cash, etc. Such a charge enables the company to deal *freely* with these assets *until such time as the charge crystallises*. (The floating charge is usually stated as covering all the company's other assets not included in the fixed charge.)

(*c*) In recent years some banks have taken the charge over Book and Other Debts (debtors) expressed to be by way of a *fixed* charge. The company undertakes to pay all sums so collected into its bank account and not to charge such debts elsewhere without the bank's consent. This fixed security overcomes the disadvantages encountered with a floating charge (*see* **46** below *re* preferential creditors; *see* **47** below *re* s. 322). The charge and the covenants are referred to in Form 47 when the Debenture is registered at Companies Registration Office. This type of fixed charge over debtors was accepted by the Court in *Siebe Gorman & Co. Ltd.* v. *Barclays Bank Ltd.* (1979).

41. Defects of floating charges. Floating charges suffer from several defects, and these are outlined in **42–47** below. *Nevertheless*, if due allowance is made for these defects a floating charge can often provide worthwhile security, e.g. where no other security is available, or as support for a fixed charge.

42. Accurate valuation is difficult. Everything depends upon the value of the assets comprising the floating charge *when it crystallises*, i.e. when the company enters into liquidation or when a receiver is appointed. In valuing a floating charge, a banker should always: (*a*) value the assets on a gone-concern basis after making due allowance for the type of business involved; (*b*) allow for realisation charges, expenses and the prior claims of preferential creditors; (*c*) keep the valuation up to date from current balance sheets, etc.

A problem highlighted by recent case law is that whereby a supplier of goods to the company retains the title to the goods until they are paid for. Thus, whilst the items might be in the possession of the company customer, and indeed appear in his balance sheet, a Receiver appointed under a Debenture will be unable to deal with them, and unable to sell them for the benefit of the debenture-holder. (*Aluminium Industrie Vaasen BV* v. *Romalpa Aluminium Ltd.* (1976). ("*Romalpa*").)

Types of retention of title clauses and agreements vary in contracts and on invoices, and sometimes the purchasing company itself can be unaware of the existence of Romalpa. This is an area of danger for the lender, although by two later decisions he has gained some comfort because of the nature of the agreements.

In *Borden (UK) Ltd.* v. *Scottish Timber Products Ltd.* (1979) it was held that where the product supplied is "mixed" with another product, so that it loses its identity, it cannot be "traced" on Romalpa grounds, unless the clause extends to the new product.

In *re Bond Worth Ltd.* (1979) where the goods were expressed to be security for moneys due in payment in respect of themselves and/or other goods supplied, it was held that the clause created a charge which was void for want of registration under the CA 1948, s. 95.

This whole problem is under review by the Insolvency Law Review Committee due to report in 1981.

43. Running down of assets. A floating charge is by nature worth least when it crystallises. Obviously a company which is in difficulties will of necessity run down its floating assets, perhaps drastically. In order to prevent being faced with an *unexpected* depletion of assets, the bank may require certain margins to be maintained or periodical trading figures to be produced. Invariably the main safeguard is for the bank to keep abreast of the company's position and to act speedily in appointing a receiver should its floating security be endangered.

44. Subsequent specific legal or equitable charges rank before floating charges. This has always been regarded as the position *unless* the person taking the specific charge *knows* that *by the terms of the floating charge* priority is barred. *Further*, it has been held that knowledge of the terms of registration does not amount to knowledge of any actual restriction contained in the debenture which has not been shown on the register: *In re Valletort Sanitary Steam Laundry Co. Ltd.* (1903).

Recently in *Re Mechanisations* (*Eaglescliffe*) *Ltd* (1964) it was decided that where registration of a charge is effected under CA 1948, s. 95, the whole terms of the charge are binding on the world, whether or not *all* the terms appear on the register. This decision appears to reverse that of the *Valletort Case*, and if this is so, then the sub-heading is no longer true.

Presumably, however, until the matter is finally resolved the bank will still take the usual precaution of incorporating a clause in its debenture to the effect that "the company is precluded from creating any charge ranking in priority to or *pari-passu* with the bank's charge". This clause is distinctly outlined in Form 47, which when registered *undoubtedly* becomes notice to the world.

45. Danger of execution by creditors. This danger exists until the bank crystallises its floating charge. *Even then* execution by a creditor is deemed complete if: (*a*) a *garnishee order* served on a third party in respect of moneys owing to the company has become *absolute*; (*b*) a *landlord* has distrained for rent; (*c*) a sheriff has *sold* goods belonging to the company on a *judgment* creditor's behalf. Where there is a likelihood of execution by a creditor the bank should appoint a receiver to crystallise its charge.

46. Preferential creditors rank before a floating charge: s. 319(5). If in a *winding-up* the assets of the company available for payment of *general* creditors are insufficient to meet the prior claims of the *preferential* creditors any deficiency of the latter must be made good out of the assets covered by the floating charge: s. 319(5).

NOTE: the same preferential priority attaches on the *appointment of a receiver under a floating charge*: s. 94.

A bank always includes in its *floating charge* all assets belonging to the company which have not been tied under its fixed charge. Obviously, therefore, unpaid preferential creditors must be fully satisfied out of these assets *before the bank can recover any moneys under its floating charge*. The bank itself however might have a preferential claim in respect of wages advanced. If so, and if the floating asset realisations are insufficient to meet *all* preferential claims, then a dividend will be paid and the bank will participate on a pro-rata basis with the other preferential creditors.

NOTE: (1) This defect cannot be overcome, and becomes more severe in its effect as taxation increases and the list of preferential debts grows. (2) The bank's *fixed charge* is in no way affected by the above provisions.

47. Floating charge may be invalid: s. 322(1). A floating charge on the undertaking or property of the company created *within twelve months* of the commencement *of winding up* shall, unless it is proved that the company immediately after the creation of the charge was *solvent*, be *invalid, except* to the amount of any *cash* paid to the company *at the time of or subsequently to the creation of, and in consideration for, the charge*, together with interest at 5 per cent p.a.... s. 322(1).

Note carefully the following points concerning this section:

(*a*) If the company *does not* go into liquidation within twelve months of creating the *floating charge*, then the charge remains *completely valid.*

(*b*) If the company *does* go into liquidation within twelve months of creating the *floating charge*—

(*i*) If the company was *solvent* after creating the charge it still remains *completely valid.*

(*ii*) If the company was *insolvent* after creating the charge it still remains valid *in respect of new moneys advanced to the company at the time of or subsequent to its creation.* The operation of Clayton's Case can be helpful here if the *bank debt was already in existence* (see examples below). Note that the test of *solvency* is whether the company could pay its debts as and when they fell due.

(*c*) The section in no way affects the validity of a *fixed charge.*

48. Examples of operation of Clayton's Case under s. 322. In *each* of the following examples it is presumed that a *floating charge* has been taken from the company to secure its *existing debt* and that *liquidation occurs within twelve months* and the company was *insolvent* when the charge was created.

EXAMPLE 1

	A Co. Ltd.		£
Floating charge given when account			*Dr* 50,000
Transactions prior to liquidation			
	Debits 50,000	Credits 40,000	
Balance at liquidation			*Dr* 60,000

Floating charge valid for £50,000 i.e. all debits

EXAMPLE 2

	B Co. Ltd.		£
Floating charge given when account			*Dr* 50,000
Transactions prior to liquidation			
	Debits 50,000	Credits 50,000	
Balance at liquidation			*Dr* 50,000

Floating charge valid for £50,000 i.e. all debits

EXAMPLE 3

	C Co. Ltd.		£
Floating charge given when account			*Dr* 50,000
Transactions prior to liquidation			
	Debits Nil	Credits 20,000	
Balance at liquidation			*Dr* 30,000

Floating charge completely invalid.

It will be noted from these examples that any *new debits* still outstanding will *always be covered.* But the *whole outstanding debit balance* will only be covered if the *original debit balance* has been entirely eliminated by payments in, as in Example 2.

The benefits resulting from the application of Clayton's Case were first confirmed in *Re Thomas Mortimer Ltd.* (1925), which decision was recently strongly contested by the liquidator in *Re Yeovil Glove Co. Ltd.* (1964), but again confirmed.

49. Rights of debenture holders. The rights of a debenture holder whose debenture gives a charge on the company's property will depend upon the terms of his security. For example, the bank usually retains power to (*a*) sue, (*b*) apply for a foreclosure order, (*c*) petition for winding up, (*d*) appoint a receiver; this latter power is invariably the one utilised.

50. Bank debenture form clauses. Clauses are included covering, *inter alia*:

(*a*) "*All moneys* due or accruing due."

(*b*) "*Continuing security repayable on demand.*"

(*c*) "*Fixed charge by way of legal mortgage* on the company's property and fixed charge on goodwill, etc.... *together with* usual insurance covenants, etc."

(*d*) "*Floating charge* on all assets not specified in the fixed charge ... *together with* usual insurance covenants, e.g. concerning stock."

(*e*) *Restriction on powers to execute further charges.*

(*f*) *Various undertakings* by the company, e.g. to produce trading figures on request.

(*g*) *Repayment of debt* to fall due on happening of stated occurrences, e.g.—

(*i*) on demand in writing being made by the bank;
(*ii*) where payment of interest falls in arrears;
(*iii*) where the company ceases business;
(*iv*) where winding-up proceedings are commenced;
(*v*) where a third party appoints a receiver;
(*vi*) where the company breaks any covenant.

(*h*) Agreement by company to maintain adequate *Employer's Liability Insurance.*

(*i*) *Bank's powers on company's default*: (1) power of sale, (2) power to appoint a receiver and manager. *Included under* (2): (*a*) method of appointment and removal, (*b*) receiver to act as "company's agent", (*c*) receiver's authority, e.g. power of sale.

51. Receiver appointed by the bank. The receiver is the person appointed by the bank to get in the debts and other assets of the company and meanwhile (if necessary) to carry on the business with the object of enabling the bank as debenture holder to recover its advance. The receiver will usually be a chartered accountant specialising in this work.

If the bank's security is in jeopardy because one of the positions mentioned in **50**(*g*) has arisen, e.g. a petition has been presented by the Inland Revenue for unpaid taxes, then it can without delay make demand for repayment and immediately on default appoint a receiver. The receiver is appointed by instrument under hand or seal as required in the debenture. He must serve notice of his appointment on the company and also notify the Registrar of Companies of his appointment within seven days on Form 53 (no registration fee is payable).

52. Crystallisation of floating charge. The floating charge *does not crystallise until positive action is taken*, e.g. the appointment of a receiver. It cannot be overstressed that merely calling up the debt does not crystallise the charge. A floating charge does automatically crystallise when liquidation commences or when the company ceases business, but the bank would still normally appoint a receiver, in either circumstance, if it became necessary to protect its position.

53. Re-issue of debentures. Before taking security from a company the bank should ascertain whether it has any uncancelled redeemed debentures outstanding. In certain circumstances outlined in s. 90 a company can re-issue these debentures with the same priorities as if never redeemed. Particulars of uncancelled redeemed debentures must be disclosed in the company's balance sheet, and this provides due warning to the bank, who will normally need to require their cancellation.

54. Taking the debenture as security. The procedure is as outlined in 37 above. The debenture will, of course, require sealing by the company. A copy of the certificate of registration must be endorsed on the debenture. The company's deeds are deposited with the bank which gives notice of its interest in respect of the various insurances.

ADVANCES FOR WAGES AND SALARIES

55. Priority for wages and salaries on liquidation. The CA 1948, s. 319(1), provides that all *wages* or *salary* of any clerk, servant, workman or labourer in respect of services rendered *during the four months before liquidation* shall rank as *preferential* up to a maximum of £800 *per employee* (Insolvency Act 1976, s. 1). Holiday remuneration accruing due at the date of liquidation also ranks as preferential. Further, if the above payments have already been made *out of money advanced by some person for that purpose* (e.g. the bank), then the person who advanced the money is *subrogated* to the employee's position and *can rank as a preferential creditor in his place*: s. 319(4).

NOTE: The bank *cannot* claim preferentially for wages advances made to a *partnership or sole business* as there is no corresponding enactment giving third-parties rights of subrogation.

56. Priority also attaches where a receiver is appointed. S. 94 applies the same priorities as in 55 above, *on the appointment of a receiver* under a *debenture containing a floating charge*.

NOTE: (1) On the appointment of a receiver or upon liquidation, *preferential creditors* must always receive payment in full before the holders of debentures under a *floating charge* can receive any payment. For this reason a bank having a floating charge retains an advantage *if it also ha a preferential claim for advances for wages*. (2) A list of preferential debts is given in VI, **20**.

57. Bank advances for wages. Where a company is in temporary difficulties due to lack of working capital, the bank may be prepared to advance unsecured sums for the payment of wages (which word from here on includes "salary") relying upon its right of *subrogation* under the Act.

However, if the company's position is more serious, then the bank may only be willing to allow any existing limit to be utilised, for withdrawal of wages. Whichever circumstance applies, it is prudent to require the company *to open a eparate wages account* rather than to allow it to continue drawing these from its current account.

58. Where no separate wages account is opened. The main danger for a bank i failing to require the opening of a separate wages account is that the liquidator (or receiver) may contend that it did not make any advances for wages. This contention was made and successfully repudiated by the bank concerned in the following cases:

In case 1: The debenture holder and receiver contended that as the bank required sufficient credits to be paid in before it would pay the company's wages cheque, then this amounted to an appropriation of the credits against the wages cheque. HELD:

The bank were only reasonably requiring that the overdraft was not increasing; this was not an appropriation and the Rule in Clayton's Case applied to the account; advances were being made for wages: *National Provincial Bank Ltd.* v. *Freedman & Rubens* (1934).

In case 2: The liquidator contended that as the bank refused to pay the company's wages cheque until assured by the company that covering amounts were due to it, then this amounted to appropriation. A similar decision as above was given. *In Re Primrose (Builders) Ltd.* (1950).

NOTE: In the absence of *special* arrangements concerning *wages advances* the bank can still rank preferentially for wages withdrawn from an *overdrawn* account, *but the application of the Rule in Clayton's Case may reduce the bank's claim.*

59. Practical operations of a wages account.

(*a*) At the bank's request *the company authorises the opening of a wages account* to which weekly (and/or monthly) wages and salary cheques are debited.

(*b*) Standing instructions are given to the bank to commence operating *immediately on payment of the eighteenth week's wages cheque*. The instructions require the bank to make *weekly transfers* from the company's current account of an amount sufficient to eliminate the longest outstanding week's wages cheque. This procedure ensures that only the last seventeen weeks' (i.e. four months') wages cheques make up the balance of the wages account *and that the whole of this balance is preferential.*

Example of operation of wages account:

COMPANY CURRENT ACCOUNT

		Debits only	*Balance*
Dec. 1	Balance b/f		*Dr* £25,000
,,	Transfer to Wages a/c	£600	*Dr* 25,600

COMPANY WAGES ACCOUNT

		Debits	*Credits*	*Balance*
Week 1		600		*Dr* 600
Weeks 2–17		8,000		*Dr* 8,600
Dec. 1	Week 18	500		
,,	Transfer from C a/c		600	*Dr* 8,500

Therefore the last seventeen weeks' wages total £8,500, the whole being preferential.

60. Further considerations regarding advances for wages.

(*a*) *The bank will always bear in mind*: (*i*) the £800 maximum per employee, (*ii*) that amounts for national health and PAYE are often included in the wages cheque, (*iii*) that a director's fee or remuneration is not preferential unless he is also employed in another capacity, (*iv*) that the weekly wages cheque should reduce if the company's business contracts. *Consequently*, the bank may require various certificates concerning the wages.

(*b*) *Items ostensibly drawn as wages* might not be regarded as such by the court, e.g. if the wages are drawn to pay sub-contractors: *In Re C. W. & A. L. Hughes Ltd.* (1966).

(*c*) *If a bank advance is utilised by the company to pay wages*, then the preferential position arises irrespective of whether the bank knew of the intended application of the moneys at the time of the advance: *In Re Rampgill Mill Ltd.* (1967).

(*d*) Direct security realisations need not be appropriated first in reduction or repayment of the bank's preferential claim. As it is usually to the bank's advantage to appropriate them to the non-preferential debt, this step will be taken and is acceptable to the Courts: *In Re William Hall* (*Contractors*) *Ltd.* (1967).

61. Advantages of opening a wages account. *First*, the liquidator is unlikely to contend that no wages advances were made. *Secondly*, the Rule in Clayton's Case will not act to the bank's detriment where a wages account is opened (but *see* **62** below), but may well act to its detriment where no wages account is opened. This is clearly shown in the following examples, where in each case the transactions are identical and liquidation is presumed from 16th December.

EXAMPLE 1: No separate wages account, but undeniable intention to advance for wages.

COMPANY CURRENT ACCOUNT

		Debits	*Credits*	*Balance*
	Balance b/f			*Dr* £12,500
	Wages paid out (weeks 1–15)	£7,500		
Dec. 2	Third-party cheques	2,600*		
8	Wages (week 16)	500	say	
9	Third-party cheques	2,600*	£16,300	
14	,, ,, ,,	2,600*	paid in	
15	Wages (week 17)	500		*Dr* 12,500

Because of the application of the Rule in Clayton's Case, the indebtedness of £12,500 is made up of:

*Non-preferential debt	7,800
Preferential debt	4,700
	£12,500

EXAMPLE 2: Separate wages account opened for wages advances.

COMPANY CURRENT ACCOUNT

			Debits	*Credits*	*Balance*
		Balance b/f			*Dr* £12,500
Dec.	2	Third-party cheques	£2,600	say	
	9	" " "	2,600	£16,300	
	14	" " "	2,600	paid in	*Dr* 4,000

COMPANY WAGES ACCOUNT

			Debits	*Credits*	*Balance*
		Wages paid out (weeks 1–15)	£7,500		
Dec.	8	Wages (week 16)	500		
	15	Wages (week 17)	500		*Dr* £8,500

Because separate wages account has been maintained the indebtedness of £12,500 is made up of:

	£
Non-preferential debt	4,000
Preferential debt	8,500
	£12,500

62. Decision in Re E. J. Morel. The *Morel* decision, although special, appears to have raised some possible future problems for bankers:

A guarantor who was securing a company's account was called upon to pay up under his guarantee. On default, the comp account was stopped to preserve his liability. Thereafter account was opened together with a current account be conducted in credit). Upon the compan balances were as follows:

1 a/c Dr £1,839 (secured by gu
Wages a/c Dr £1,624

The bank sought to set off the 1 a/c and 2 a/c and to rank preferentially for the Wages a/c balance. *The liquidator* required the bank to set off the 2 a/c and Wages a/c and to rank preferentially for £79. *The Court* supported the liquidator, because the evidence showed that the 2 a/c and Wages a/c were interdependent in that the bank had regard to the net (credit) position before paying wages cheques. Also the 1 a/c was regarded as being "frozen" and therefore identical to a loan account: *In Re E. J. Morel (1934) Ltd.* (1961).

63. Overcoming the Morel decision. In similar circumstances to those of the *Morel Case* the bank's remedy might be to permit all future transactions (excepting those for wages withdrawals) to be continued on the 1 a/c and to rely upon the usual protective clause contained in collateral security forms (e.g. in a guarantee), whereby the application of Clayton's Case is precluded, as against the depositor of security, in respect of the debit balance existing at the time the security is determined. (Such a clause has been previously held to be effective: *Westminster Bank* v. *Cond* (1940).) If the clause was confirmed as being *legally effective in these circumstances*, then there appears to be every chance of ranking preferentially for wages advanced on separate account, as it is unlikely that the 1 a/c could be regarded as being "frozen". However, everything will depend upon the circumstances of the case, and it might be thought to be safer to ensure that the guarantor's liability is retained with certainty, especially where it is supported by a valuable security, rat[illegible] than to maximise an uncertain potential preferential cla[illegible]

[illegible]DING UP

[illegible]e are several methods for *dissolving* [illegible]nly one which normally concerns

[illegible]ding up a company:

[illegible]ompulsory liquidation.

[illegible]ay be either: (*i*) a *members'* [illegible]*s'* voluntary winding up.

[illegible]*pervision*. (Such a winding [illegible]oluntary liquidation the [illegible]e the winding up. The winding up is deemed to commence from the moment when the resolution to wind up voluntarily was passed.)

The CA 1948, and the Companies Winding up Rules 1949, apply in respect of winding up, but only those matters concerning bankers are dealt with below.

65. Grounds for compulsory winding up. S. 222 states that a company may be wound up by the Court if:

(*a*) The company has passed a special resolution to that effect.

(*b* Default is made in delivering the statutory report to the registrar or in holding the statutory meeting.

(*c*) The company does not commence business within a year from incorporation or suspends business for a year.

(*d*) The number of members is reduced below the statutory minimum.

(*e*) The company is unable to pay its debts (*see* **66** below).

(*f*) The Court decides that it is just and equitable that the company should be wound up, e.g. where there is deadlock in the management.

NOTE: In order to bring about *compulsory* dissolution, a *petition* based on one of the above grounds *must be presented to the Court*, usually by either the company, a creditor or a contributory.

66. Definition of inability to pay debts. S. 223 states that a company is deemed unable to pay its debts if:

(*a*) a creditor for more than £200 has demanded repayment from the company, and three weeks have elapsed without the debt being either paid, secured or compounded to the creditor's satisfaction, *or*

(*b*) execution or other process is returned by the company unsatisfied, *or*

(*c*) it is proved to the Court's satisfaction that the company is unable to pay its debts.

67. Voluntary winding up. S. 278(1) states that a company may be wound up voluntarily if:

(*a*) The *period*, if any, fixed for its duration by the articles expires, or the *event*, if any, occurs on the occurrence of which the articles provide that it is to be dissolved, and the company resolves by *ordinary resolution* to be wound up voluntarily.

(*b*) The company resolves by *special resolution* to be wound up voluntarily.

(*c*) The company resolves by *extraordinary resolution* that it cannot *by reason of its liabilities* continue its business, and that it is advisable to wind up.

Notice of the *passing* of the above resolutions must be duly advertised in the *London Gazette* within fourteen days: s. 279(1).

68. Declaration of solvency. It has been mentioned in **64** above that there are two types of *voluntary* winding up. The main distinction between a members' and a creditors' voluntary winding up is that in the former case the members appoint the liquidator (the company being *solvent*), whereas in the latter case the creditors appoint the liquidator and control the winding up (the company *usually* being *insolvent*).

A *members'* voluntary winding up can only occur if the *directors* make a *declaration of solvency*. If *no* such declaration is made, the winding up will be a *creditors'* voluntary winding up.

For a declaration of solvency *to be effective* it must:

(*a*) be made at a meeting of directors and include their statutory declaration that, having enquired into the company's affairs, they consider *that its debts can be paid in full within twelve months of the commencement of the winding up*;

(*b*) be made *within the five weeks preceding* the date of the passing of the resolution for winding up and delivered to the registrar before that date;

(*c*) include therein a *statement of assets and liabilities* at the latest practicable date.

69. Commencement of compulsory winding up. Where the court orders *compulsory* winding up, this is deemed to commence *from the time when the petition was presented to the Court* (unless a voluntary winding up was already in process at this time, when the winding up commences at the time of passing the resolution): s. 229.

Bankers should note that commencement of the winding up "relates back". Unfortunately, the bank's first intimation of the impending liquidation may well be when it sees notice of the *petition and hearing date* in the *Gazette*. (The *date of the hearing* must be gazetted at least seven days *before* the hearing takes place.)

70. Commencement of voluntary winding up. A voluntary winding up *commences from the passing of the resolution to wind up voluntarily*: s. 280. Fortunately, notice of such a resolution is invariably given by the company to its bankers either before or immediately after the event. Consequently, there will be no question of the banker unknowingly permitting account operations to continue.

Further, if the winding up is to be a *creditors' voluntary winding up*, then the company:

(*a*) must call a creditors' meeting either for the same day or the day following that on which the resolution for winding up is to be proposed, *and*

(*b*) must give fourteen days' notice of this meeting in the Gazette, *and*

(*c*) must notify individual creditors of the meeting. (The bank will thus receive direct notice if the company is indebted to it.) This notice is usually a Statutory Notice pursuant to s. 293 and gives twenty-one days' notice of the meeting of creditors, at which the resolution to go into Creditors Voluntary Liquidation will be put. The name of the intended liquidator is stated.

71. Curtailment of directors' powers. The powers of the directors to run the company cease as soon as a liquidator is appointed, irrespective of the method of winding up. In practice, this means:

(*a*) *In a compulsory winding up.* The directors' powers continue *until the winding-up order is* made. (The Official Receiver then becomes provisional liquidator until such time as the Court appoints a liquidator.) However, *after presentation of the petition* the bank must regard the directors' powers as *cancelled* as regards the company's banking account (*see* **72–74** below).

(*b*) *In a voluntary winding up.* The directors' powers effectively cease *on the passing of the resolution to wind up* because a liquidator will then be appointed by the members or creditors, depending upon the type of voluntary liquidation. A *continuance* of the directors' powers may be authorised by: (*i*) the company or liquidator, in a *members'* voluntary winding up; or (*ii*) the committee of inspection or creditors, in a *creditors'* voluntary winding up. (The bank would require a copy of the authority *before* permitting the directors to continue action on the company's account.)

72. Banking-account operations between the presentation of the petition and the hearing. Although the company retains control of its business and can continue operating until the winding-up order is made, it must be noted that *dispositions of its property are not permitted* after the date of the petition.

The company's account is stopped on receiving notice of the petition. (There is no *specific* protection for a bank paying cheques between the petition and the winding-up order, irrespective of whether or not it has notice of the petition.) The company may, however, request the bank to allow it to continue to draw cheques during this period. All such requests should be refused, unless or until the company has obtained the sanction of the Court under s. 227, which states:

> "In a winding up by the court any *disposition* of the property of the company ... *made after the commencement of the winding up*, shall, *unless the court otherwise orders*, be void." *See* **73** below.

73. Payment made relying on s. 227. A banker, who agreed to pay cheques in the position outlined in **72** above, without a Court Order, knowingly took a risk and relied upon the fact that the Court could uphold such payments should a liquidator later raise objection. The Court, however, did not exercise its discretion in the bank's favour in respect of all the transactions. *Re Gray's Inn Construction Co. Ltd.* (1979).

74. The bankers' unenviable position in having to predetermine s. 227. This no longer exists. Following the decision in *Re Gray's Inn Construction Co. Ltd.* (1979) there seems to be no good reason why banks should take it upon themselves to carry an unnecessary risk, which could be very extensive if turnover were high, by agreeing to continue the company's account after a Petition has been lodged. If, therefore, it wishes to withdraw any funds the company should be requested to seek a Court Order regarding the continued operation of its bank account, and this must be exhibited to the bank. Very careful note must then be taken of any conditions on which the Order is made and of the transactions which are to be allowed.

75. Preferential debts in winding up. S. 319(1) outlines the main preferential debts and these have already been listed in VI, **20**. However, where a *company* is concerned:

(*a*) "The commencement of the winding up" must be read in place of "the receiving order" in the list of preferential debts outlined in VI, **20**.

(*b*) *Corporation tax* ranks as a preferential debt: Finance Act 1965.

(*c*) *Preferential debts take preference over floating charges:* CA 1948, s. 319(5).

(*d*) The preferential positions which arise in winding up *also arise where a receiver is appointed under a floating charge:* s. 94.

> NOTE: Where the bank holds *direct* security *worth less* than the amount of the company's total indebtedness, then it can appropriate the security against the part of the debt which is non-preferential *so as to leave its preferential claim unaffected*: *In Re William Hall* (*Contractors*) *Ltd.* (*In liquidation*) (1967). This decision confirms the general principle of law that a *creditor* may apply his security in discharge of whatever liability of his *debtor* he might think fit.

76. Proofs and claims in winding up. The bankruptcy rules apply to the respective rights of secured and unsecured creditors (*see* VI, **25–28**), and the right of set-off exists as at the commencement of the winding up. In a compulsory winding up proof is necessary, but in a voluntary winding up the liquidator usually only requires a formal claim.

77. Distribution of assets in winding up. The liquidator applies the assets in the following order:

(*a*) *Secured creditors* obtain payment out of the proceeds of their securities.

(*b*) *Winding up costs and liquidator's expenses* and remuneration.

(*c*) *Preferential creditors.*

(*d*) Creditors with *floating charges.*

(*e*) *Unsecured creditors.*

(*f*) Return of *members' capital.* (Surplus assets are then distributed proportionately.)

MISCELLANEOUS MATTERS CONCERNING COMPANIES

78. Postponement of directors' loans. Occasionally a banker is requested to make advances to a company which has *borrowed unsecured moneys from one of its directors.* The banker may be unwilling to make the advance unless:

(*a*) *the director gives an undertaking:* (*i*) not to claim repayment of his moneys while the company's overdraft limit is in being, *and* (*ii*) to pay over to the bank any money which he receives in reduction of his debt from the company; *and/or*

(*b*) *the company gives an undertaking* not to repay the director's loan moneys until the bank advance is repaid.

An additional undertaking may be required from the director to pay over his dividend to the bank should the company enter liquidation.

79. Postponement of charges. Occasionally a company customer requires to borrow additional moneys from an outside source, e.g. an insurance company, to provide for long-term capital expenditure. If the bank has as its security a debenture incorporating a fixed and floating charge over the company's property, the new lender may require the bank to postpone its security. If the bank agrees to such a scheme the Priority Deed entered into by the company, Bank, and the other lender should specify:

(*a*) who ranks first, second, etc., and up to what amount,

(*b*) in respect of which specified assets (fixed and/or floating), *or*

(*c*) whether all lenders rank parri-passu, *or*

(*d*) whether all lenders rank pro-rata (and at what date).

The effect of any preferential claim at the time of liquidation or receivership should not be forgotten at the outset of the agreement, nor should the effect of interest accrued and accruing.

Before agreeing to an arrangement of this type the bank should have full discussions with the company and its financial advisers regarding the implications of a limitation on bank borrowing on the company's future expansion.

80. Financial assistance by a company for the purchase of its own shares. A company *is not allowed to give financial assistance*, whether *directly or indirectly, to enable any person to purchase or subscribe for its own or its holding company's shares* except under the provisions of ss. 42 and 43 of the Companies Act 1981, where the objective must be undertaken in good faith and in the interests of the company. Financial assistance includes gifts, loans, waivers, securities, indemnities and guarantees, and there are certain procedures on which the company and a bank, if involved, should take legal advice.

If a breach occurs it appears that any security given to the banker would be invalid: *Heald & Anor.* v. *O'Connor* (1971) reversing the decision in *Victor Battery Co. Ltd.* v. *Curry's Ltd.* (1946). The decision in *Selangor United Rubber Estates Ltd.* v. *Craddock and others* (1968) worryingly extended problems for banks in those situations where it could be deemed that they "should have known" that a breach was taking place.

81. Loans, Quasi-Loans to Directors. The CA 1980, ss. 49 and 50 repeals CA 1948, s. 190, and more stringent rules have been enacted restraining companies from financially assisting directors and those associated with them. No company or its holding company may make a loan to a director or give a guarantee or any security for the director's liabilities.

In the case of public companies this prohibition is extended to "connected" persons and in respect also of "quasi-loans", and "credit transactions", although the latter are allowed if on usual commercial terms. Moreover lendings between a holding company and its subsidiary are allowed, as are also legitimate short-term loans to cover expenses pending reimbursement.

Loans may be made in the ordinary course of business, as by a bank to its director.

A breach of the CA 1980, s. 49, makes the transaction voidable at the option of the company, the director must reimburse, and both the director and the company are open to criminal proceedings (s. 53).

82. Bankruptcy of a director. Where a director of a company which banks with you becomes bankrupt, this factor does not affect the continued existence of the company nor its operations with you as bankers. Nevertheless the following points require attention:

(*a*) *The bankrupt director cannot* without the consent of the court continue as a *director*: CA 1948, s. 187(1) and in any event the office of director is *automatically* vacated if the company has adopted Art. 88, Table A, CA 1948. Thus the bankrupt's name must be deleted from the list of directors.

(*b*) *The company's mandate* must be examined to see whether it remains in conformity with the Articles and whether any amendment is necessary, e.g. if previously the mandate required X and Y as directors to sign cheques, and X becomes bankrupt, then obviously a board of directors' resolution amending the mandate is necessary.

(*c*) *If the number of directors has fallen below that laid down* in the Articles (if stipulated) or the minimum laid down by the Act (public company, two; private company, one) then the appointment of a replacement director is necessary.

NOTE: If there are insufficient directors left to form the directors' quorum, those remaining are nevertheless permitted to appoint an additional director under Art. 100, Table A, CA 1948. However, if there are no directors remaining then application to the court is necessary under s. 135.

(*d*) *Where the bankrupt director had previously charged his personal security* to the bank to secure the company's overdrawn account, e.g. as party to a directors' J & S guarantee, then the bank must decide whether to prove in his bankruptcy or release him from liability:

(*i*) *If they decide to prove* then the company's account will be ruled off and a new account will invariably be opened for the company's future dealings, to be conducted and perhaps further secured, as agreed.

(*ii*) *If they decide to release the bankrupt's estate from liability* it is usually the practice to obtain the agreement of the remaining directors and their signature to a new J & S guarantee.

NOTE: Under the CA 1976, (s. 29), the Secretary of State must maintain a Register of Disqualification Orders of Directors.

These arise under the Insolvency Act, 1976, s. 9, whereby the Official Receiver may apply for an Order to be made prohibiting an unfit person who has been a director of two or more companies which have gone into an insolvent liquidation within five years of each other from being concerned in the future management of any other company.

83. Resolutions and meetings. Throughout the HANDBOOK reference is continually made to *resolutions of the company in general meeting* and *resolutions of the board of directors*. Appropriate resolutions are, of course, necessary to authorise the various acts relating to the company's dealings with the bank. The following rules concerning resolutions and meetings are of interest to bankers:

(*a*) *Resolutions at general meetings*. Only *ordinary* resolutions are required *unless the Act or articles expressly stipulate otherwise*—

(*i*) An *ordinary* resolution is required to be passed by a simple majority—fourteen days' notice of the resolution is required.

(*ii*) An *extraordinary* resolution is required to be passed by a 75 per cent majority—fourteen days' notice of the resolution is required.

(*iii*) A *special* resolution is required to be passed by a 75 per cent majority—twenty-one days' notice of the resolution is required unless holders of 95 per cent of voting shares agree to shorter notice.

NOTE: *Under* (*i*) *to* (*iii*) *above:* (1) a *quorum* of members for the meeting unless otherwise provided by the articles is two for a private company and three for a public company, (2) the required *majority is of those members present and voting.*

(*b*) *Board meetings.* Table A, Article 99, provides that the *quorum* necessary for the transaction of business may be fixed by the directors, and unless so fixed shall be *two* (excluding interested directors unless the articles permit them to vote). A *simple majority of votes* decides the directors' business.

PROGRESS TEST 11

1. What is the procedure when opening the account of a private limited company? **(4)**

2. What is Table A? **(5)**

3. Where are the borrowing powers of a company and its directors found? **(9, 13)**

4. Discuss the bank's position where it has lent: (*a*) *ultra vires* the company, (*b*) *ultra vires* the directors, but *intra vires* the company. **(19, 20, 21, 22)** (*See also* Appendix II.)

5. What are the directors' borrowing limits under Table A, 1948 Act? **(14)** Interpret the relevant Article in your own words. **(16)**

6. Can a company increase its borrowing limit? Retrospectively? **(18)**

Can directors' borrowing limits be increased? Retrospectively? **(21*b*)**

7. Outline the Rule in *Victors Ltd.* v. *Lingard* and discuss fully the position regarding interested directors. **(23–27** and XIII, **19, 20)**

8. What charges created by a company must be registered at the Companies Registry? **(28)** Within what period must registration be effected? **(29)** What is the effect of non-registration? **(28, 32)**

9. Why is there a need to peruse the *Gazette* weekly? **(36)**

10. Outline the general procedure when taking security from a company. **(37)**

11. Distinguish between a fixed and floating charge. **(40)**

12. State the disadvantages of a floating charge. **(41–47)**

13. Outline in your own words CA 1948, s. 322. **(47)**

14. With what was the case of *Re Thomas Mortimer Ltd.* concerned? **(48)**

15. What rights attach to preferential creditors? **(46, 75** and VI, **20)**

16. How does a floating charge become crystallised? **(52)**

17. What advantage does a bank gain by making advances for wages? **(55–56)** Outline briefly the main cases concerning wages advances. **(58, 60, 61, 62)**

18. What difficulties may be encountered by a banker where a petition is presented for compulsory winding up of one of its company customers? **(69, 71, 72, 73, 74)**

PART FIVE

SECURITIES

CHAPTER XII

Guarantees

NATURE OF GUARANTEE

1. Definition of guarantee. "A written promise made by one person to be collaterally answerable for the debt, default, or miscarriage of another", Statute of Frauds 1677, s. 4.

Guarantees may be either *specific* or *continuing*.

(*a*) A *specific guarantee* relates to one isolated debt only, e.g. where a bank accepts a guarantee to cover a *single* loan, made to a customer to enable him to buy a car, the loan being repayable in instalments, i.e. Personal Loan. To prevent the Rule in Clayton's Case applying to its detriment, the bank would open a separate loan account for the customer, and a *specific guarantee* would be drawn up covering only this account. A bank is rarely willing to accept a specific guarantee because of the inflexibility of future operations permissible on its customer's account. If it does agree to the security applying only to one lending, the bank must note its records carefully to ensure that the security is made obsolete upon repayment of the moneys borrowed.

(*b*) A *continuing guarantee* is one covering a series of transactions, and is therefore eminently suitable as banking security for a current account. In drawing up such a guarantee, care is taken to see that it covers the *ultimate balance*(*s*) owing at the date of determination. Some banks now write to guarantor(s) every few years reminding them that reliance is still placed upon the security they have given.

2. Parties to a guarantee.

(*a*) *Three parties:* principal creditor, principal debtor and guarantor (surety).

(*b*) *Primary liability to pay* must attach to the principal debtor.

The guarantor only becomes liable to pay if the debtor defaults.

(*c*) *The guarantor has no interest in the contract* between the principal debtor and the principal creditor, except in so far as he agrees to accept liability if the debtor fails to pay.

3. Consideration. *Guarantees under hand must be supported by consideration*, although the consideration need not be stated in the instrument itself: Mercantile Law Amendment Act 1856, s. 3 (*see* **21** below). Guarantees under seal do not require consideration.

4. Guarantees not uberrimae fidei. Neither the principal creditor nor the principal debtor are under any legal duty to disclose facts to the prospective guarantor which might influence him against entering into the contract. Thus a bank need not disclose to the prospective guarantor that its customer's account is already overdrawn: *Hamilton* v. *Watson* (1845). Further, there is no need to disclose information regarding the past running of the debtor's account so long as the events would quite normally fall within the banker/customer relationship.

EXAMPLE: In *Cooper* v. *National Provincial Bank Limited* (1946) C gave two guarantees to secure the account of R. C later contended that the bank should have disclosed that: (1) R's husband was an undischarged bankrupt, (2) the husband had authority to draw cheques on R's account, and (3) the account had been operated irregularly, many cheques having been countermanded by the drawer. HELD: A contract of guarantee not being one *uberrimae fidei*, consequently, the bank had no need to disclose to the guarantor *the perfectly normal and regular happenings which had occurred.*

But note that in the following instances the guarantor may be able to avoid his obligations, and the guarantee may then be treated as voidable at his option.

(1) *Mistake as to the nature of document signed.* In *Carlisle & Cumberland Banking Co.* v. *Bragg* (1911). B avoided liability on a guarantee because when he signed it he was told it was an insurance document. Recently, however, the H of L overruled the above decision and held that the plea *non est factum* could not be relied on if the party claiming has been careless or negligent: *Saunders* v. *Anglia Building Society* (1970). Nevertheless bankers will continue to have the form signed in their own or a banker/solicitor's presence.

(2) *Pressure or undue influence imposed on the guarantor* by either the principal debtor or principal creditor: In *Davies* v. *London and Provincial Marine Insurance Co.* (1877), Fry J., said, "a contract of suretyship is one in which I think that everything like pressure used by the intending creditor will have a very serious effect on the validity of the contract."

Undue influence arises where one party to a transaction cannot exercise *his own free will.* This is *presumed*, for instance, in contracts arranged by patients in favour of doctors, clients in favour of solicitors and wards in favour of guardians. Banks, therefore, ensure that *independent advice* is given to the prospective guarantor by his own solicitor if such circumstances prevail. A suitable clause attested by the solicitor is added to the guarantee to the effect that the nature and purport of the document was explained to the guarantor and it was signed under his free will. (NOTE: There is no presumption of undue influence when a wife guarantees her husband's account, or an account in which he is interested, but *see* **17** below.)

(3) *Innocent or fraudulent misrepresentation by the creditor* (or by the debtor with the creditor's knowledge), e.g. In *MacKenzie* v. *Royal Bank of Canada* (1934), Mrs M was able to avoid her liability on a guarantee given to the defendant bank, because at the time she executed the guarantee the bank inadvertently misrepresented the fact that she could not obtain the return of certain shares (which she had previously deposited as security) unless she completed this new guarantee.

(4) *Active concealment of material facts* may amount to misrepresentation, e.g. where a bank manager remains silent when it is obvious from the *factual statements* made by the prospective guarantor that he is under a misapprehension.

(5) *Where a special relationship of "confidentiality" exists* between the prospective guarantor and the bank, e.g. the prospective guarantor is a customer of the bank himself and is impaired by age or frailty, and is relying on his bank for advice as to whether it is in his interests to give the security or not.

There is a conflict of interests here for the banker, which can only be resolved by the guarantor being told to take independent advice from his own solicitor: (*Lloyds Bank* v. *Bundy* (1975)). The facts were special, and the need for independent advice does not always exist where the guarantor is also a customer. Independent advice is not necessary where, for example, the guarantor is an active company director (and private customer) giving his guarantee for the company's liabilities and fully understanding the implications of his action.

5. Capacity to contract. Capacity to guarantee is generally co-extensive with normal contractual capacity, but *see* **14–18** below.

6. Joint and several guarantees. Where several persons join in the giving of a guarantee, then their liabilities will depend upon whether they have agreed to be jointly, severally, or jointly and severally liable.

(*a*) *Joint guarantors:* Each guarantor is personally liable for the full amount, but the creditor formerly had only *one right of action* against the parties, and needed to sue all in one action: *Kendall* v. *Hamilton* (1879). However, he is not now debarred from suing the remainder, *see* VIII, **17**.

(*b*) *Several guarantors:* Each guarantor is personally liable for the full amount, and can be sued separately and successively. In addition, each estate remains liable for claims arising *before* death, bankruptcy or mental incapacity.

(*c*) *Joint and Several guarantors:* Rules as in (*b*) above, with the additional advantage that the creditor can either sue the guarantors jointly or separately and successively.

NOTE: (1) Because of the *superior remedies*, bank guarantees are *always* drafted on the basis of joint and several liability, if several persons are securing an account by way of guarantee. (2) The bank takes *all* signatures before advancing money, because if one party is prevented from signing all may be discharged: *National Provincial Bank of England* v. *Brackenbury* (1906). (3) One guarantor must not vary the terms when signing, or all will be discharged: *Ellesmere Brewery Company* v. *Cooper* (1896). (4) A clause is included in the guarantee enabling one or more of the parties to be released or any composition made, without releasing the remaining parties from liability; such a clause is effective, but was unfortunately omitted in: *Barclays Bank Ltd.* v. *Trevanion* (1933).

GUARANTOR'S NORMAL RIGHTS

The guarantor has various common-law and equitable rights available against the principal creditor, principal debtor, and co-guarantors.

7. Against creditor (i.e. Bank).

(*a*) *At any time*, to call upon the creditor to inform him of the *amount of his liability* under the guarantee. In such circumstances a bank must exercise due care, in that it should not act outside the rules laid down in *Tournier* v. *National Provincial Bank Ltd.* (1924) (*see* I, **14**). The bank will therefore only divulge *either* (*i*) that it is relying fully on the guarantee, *or* (*ii*) the balance of the account if this is *smaller* than the amount of the guarantee. It will not hand out statements or divulge information regarding its customer's account *unless* express permission is obtained. (The bank will also remind the guarantor of the *period of notice which must run* before it can establish his ultimate liability.)

(*b*) *At any time after the debt has become due* the guarantor has the right to apply to the creditor, pay him off and then sue the principal debtor in the creditor's name (or in his own name if he obtains an assignment of the debt).

(*c*) *Set-offs and counter-claims.* If sued by the creditor, the guarantor can avail himself of any set-offs or counter-claims which the debtor has against the creditor.

(*d*) *Delivery of securities held by the creditor.* If the guarantor pays off his debt he is entitled to subrogate to all the rights possessed by the creditor. A guarantor can therefore take over all securities deposited to secure the account of the debtor: (*i*) whether or not he knows of the securities, (*ii*) whether or not they have been deposited before or after the date of the guarantee, and (*iii*) whether or not they have been deposited by the debtor or third parties. If the debt is greater than the amount of the guarantee only a proportionate share of the securities may be taken over. But *see* **23** below.

8. Against principal debtor (i.e. customer). As soon as the guarantor pays up under the guarantee, he has an immediate right of action against the principal debtor. If the principal debtor is *bankrupt* the guarantor may prove in his estate for the amount which he has paid up under the guarantee; but *see* **23** below.

9. Against co-guarantors.

(*a*) *Hotchpot.* A co-guarantor who has received securities from the principal debtor (or creditor) must share the benefit of them with other co-guarantors, even though they may have been unaware of their existence when they became guarantors.

(*b*) *Contribution from co-guarantors.* If one guarantor pays the whole debt he is entitled to compensation from co-guarantors (in a joint, several, or joint and several guarantee), even if: (*i*) their guarantees are contained in different instruments, or (*ii*) he did not know of the existence of the co-guarantors when he signed his own guarantee.

10. Restriction of normal rights. It is legally permissible for a guarantor to contract out of the normal rights available to him (*see* **7** and **8** above), and he contracts out of several of these when he signs a bank guarantee form. (*See* **21–36** below for the usual restrictions imposed by banks.)

BANK GUARANTEES

11. Advantages as good security.

(*a*) *Maximum contractual protection available.* The standard bank guarantee is drawn up to give the bank the maximum protection available.

(*b*) *Fixed value.* Provided the guarantor remains good, the bank guarantee provides a security of fixed value.

(*c*) *Easy to complete.* Usually under hand or more rarely under seal: *see* **13** and **18** below.

(*d*) *Speed of action.* Under the *terms of a bank guarantee* the bank can take action against the guarantor as soon as "demand" has been made upon him and he remains in default. There need be no recourse to any other securities.

(*e*) *Collateral security.* A guarantee (*or any other third party security*), being collateral, has further advantages in relation to bankruptcy: *see* VI, **28**.

12. Disadvantages of bank guarantees.

(*a*) *Value is dependent upon financial stability of guarantor*, which may, of course, fluctuate.

(*b*) *Bad feeling may result* if the guarantor is called upon to pay up, and this may strain his relationship with the bank; an important consideration when deciding whether to call up a guarantee, should the guarantor be a valued customer.

(*c*) *Costly litigation may be necessary.* If a guarantor fails to pay up when called upon it may be necessary to sue, and however carefully the bank guarantee is drawn up, there is always the chance that the case may fail for some technical or other reason.

The guarantor can divest himself of his assets during the period up to the trial.

13. Procedure on taking a bank guarantee.

(*a*) *Initial enquiries. Before taking* the guarantee and allowing any advance, enquiries are made against each guarantor's name, through his bankers, for the *full amount* of the guarantee. This is necessary because at some time in the future the bank may require to recover fully from only *one* of several guarantors. (A *diary record* is maintained as a remainder to renew guarantor enquiries, say, annually). Once satisfied that the guarantor will be good for his obligation, the bank will then require:

(*b*) *Completion of the guarantee:*

(*i*) *Preferably*, takes place at *the branch where the customer's account is held.* If this is impossible the guarantee is sent to the bank where the guarantor's account is held, with a request and instructions for that bank to obtain an effective security and in the process to *confirm the validity of the guarantor's signature.*

(*ii*) The guarantor's signature is *witnessed* in order to save future dispute regarding validity.

NOTE: No amendment should be made to a bank form of guarantee without the approval of the bank's legal department.

SPECIAL TYPES OF GUARANTORS

14. Guarantees to secure borrowing by minors. Under the Infants Relief Act 1874, s. 1, a minor cannot be sued for money borrowed, as such a contract is void. Likewise if a guarantee has been given to secure a minor's overdrawn account it is unenforceable against the guarantor(s), because *there can be no guarantee* if there is no principal debtor: *Coutts and Co.* v. *Browne-Lecky & Ors.* (1947); but *see* **28** below.

15. Guarantees given by minors. Under the Infants Relief Act 1874, s. 1, a minor is legally incapable of giving a guarantee, and if such a contract is entered into it is void and cannot be ratified after attainment of his majority.

16. Guarantees by a firm.

(*a*) A *partner* as guarantor has no power to bind his firm unless: (*i*) so authorised by *all* his co-partners, or (*ii*) giving guarantees is part of the firm's normal business. Even where he has authority, he cannot bind the firm on a *guarantee under seal* unless: (*i*) he is so authorised by deed (Power of Attorney), or (*ii*) all the partners sign the guarantee deed.

(*b*) *In practice*, all partners will be called upon to sign the bank's joint and several guarantee form drawn up *specifically* to cover a firm's guarantee undertaking.

If an ordinary *individual's* joint and several guarantee form is used, then it is usual for each partner to sign *both individually and in the firm's name*.

(*c*) *Change in constitution of firm*. A continuing guarantee given to secure the dealings of a firm is revoked *as to future transactions* by any change in the constitution of the firm, e.g. on the death or retirement of a partner: Partnership Act 1890, s. 18. A bank guarantee contains an express clause to exclude the operation of this rule (*see* **35** below).

17. Lady guarantors.

(*a*) A *married woman of full age* may enter into a contract of guarantee, and this contract is enforceable only against her separate estate: Law Reform (Married Women and Tortfeasors) Act 1935.

(*b*) *Guarantee given to secure husband's account or an account in which he is interested*. Undue influence is *not* presumed in the relationship of husband and wife, but the Court is more likely to imply such influence if it is pleaded by the wife when she guarantees her husband's account or an account in which her husband is interested, e.g. limited company in which her husband is a director: *Bank of Montreal* v. *Stuart* (1911). To avoid the likelihood of the wife's success with such an appeal (which must be conclusively proved on her behalf), the bank normally requires that she be independently advised by her own solicitor (*see* **4** above).

(*c*) *A single woman of full age* may enter into a contract of guarantee which will be legally enforceable against her.

NOTE: It is still the general practice of most banks not to accept a guarantee executed by a lady guarantor unless she has received independent advice. However, where she is a *business woman* (e.g. an active director) securing a third-party's account (e.g. the company's) there is no danger of her proving undue influence.

18. Guarantees by a limited company. Care must be exercised before accepting the guarantee of a limited company, and the following points in this paragraph and in **19–20** below should be noted:

(*a*) The *Memorandum of Association* must contain a specific power to execute guarantees (this applies whether the company is a trading one or not). If no specific power exists, any guarantee executed will be *ultra vires* the company.

NOTE: (1) The power *"to guarantee contracts entered into by third parties"* would appear to include guaranteeing a bank advance, as there exists an implied contract between banker and customer. (2) The power *"to subsidise or otherwise assist"* was held to cover the giving of a guarantee: *Re Friary Holroyd and Healy's Breweries Ltd.* (1922). (3) The concluding objects clause *"the company shall have power to do all such other things as are incidental or conducive to the attainment of the above objects or any of them"* is thought to be insufficient to support the giving of a guarantee *unless* specifically covered in a prior clause. (4) If there is any doubt regarding the power of the company to execute an *intra vires* guarantee a legal opinion should be sought. If necessary the company can, under CA 1948, s. 5, *alter its Memorandum by special resolution to cover this point.*

(*b*) The *Articles of Association* stipulate the manner in which the guarantee may be executed, i.e. *either*: (*i*) under the *hand of a duly authorised official*(*s*) *by resolution of the board of directors*, or (*ii*) *under the seal of the company*.

NOTE: Most company guarantees may be completed *under hand*, and the bank obtains a *certified copy* of the resolution authorising the giving of such a guarantee under the hand of a duly authorised official. The copy resolution is usually typed and certified on the original guarantee to avoid any future assertion that the guarantee actually signed was not the one authorised at the meeting of the board.

19. Interested directors: Rule in Victors Ltd. (in liquidation) v. Lingard (1927).

A joint and several guarantee given by its directors to secure the account of V Ltd. preceded the issue of a debenture, authorised by the same directors, given on behalf of V Ltd., to secure its own account. HELD: (But for other extenuating circumstances) the debenture would have been void against the liquidator of V Ltd., because *interested* directors had resolved to create it, at a time when they were expressly excluded by the Articles from voting on matters in which they were personally interested, i.e. the directors were reducing their own liability to the bank by authorising the giving of further security by the company, as the bank would then have every right to realise the company's security first if so required.

NOTE: This ruling applies to *all subsequent securities* given by a company to secure its own account where one of its own directors has previously guaranteed (or secured) the same account.

20. Protection available against operation of rule. A bank may be protected from the operation of the rule in that:

(*a*) The Articles of Association may give the directors *specific* power to vote on matters in which they are interested, *or*

(*b*) CA 1948, TABLE A, Article 84(2), may apply, in that directors may vote in respect of contracts regarding security for bank advances. This latter protection is not available where TABLE A has been excluded or where the company concerned was not incorporated under the 1948 Act.

If neither (*a*) nor (*b*) are available, one of the four following protections would be adequate:

(*c*) (If possible) a disinterested quorum of directors may be able to authorise the giving of the company's security.

(*d*) If security has not yet been arranged it will be possible to date the guarantee given by the directors after the other security given by the company.

(*e*) Obtain authority for the giving of the company's security from the members of the company in general meeting.

(*f*) Alter the Articles by special resolution at a general meeting so that directors may vote on all contracts in which they are interested. (Retrospective remedy is available here if the bank has already mistakenly contravened the rule.)

BANK GUARANTEE CLAUSES

Bank guarantee form are drawn up to give the bank the greatest possible protection. As the clauses contained therein are extremely lengthy, only a brief outline and abbreviated heading is given for each one.

21. Consideration (*see* **3** above). Although it is not legally necessary to incorporate the consideration as a clause in the guarantee form, banks invariably do so, e.g. "In consideration of your giving time credit or banking facilites and accommodation". This would normally cover the bank in respect of a guarantee given to secure a *past* debt, i.e. a debt already in existence. If there is any doubt, however, the guarantee could be either: (*a*) executed under seal (a guarantee under seal does not require consideration), or (*b*) a specific letter could be taken from, and at the request of, the guarantor incorporating a suitable consideration clause, e.g. "forbearing to sue for past debt".

22. Continuing security. This clause is required so that *all further advances* are covered under the terms of the guarantee. If the clause was omitted the Rule in Clayton's Case would apply to the bank's detriment, in that all payments into the account would automatically extinguish the initial borrowing, while any subsequent borrowing would not be covered by the guarantee.

23. Whole debt guaranteed. The *whole debt* is guaranteed with a limitation on the maximum amount recoverable from the guarantor. As the *whole debt* has been guaranteed the guarantor is: (*a*) unable to claim alongside the bank if the debtor becomes bankrupt, (*b*) unable to take any securities deposited by the debtor or third parties, unless in either of the above instances he is willing to pay off *the whole debt remaining owing to the bank*: *see* **7** above.

A clause specifically stipulating the above terms is usually included to emphasise the bank's rights, although this is unnecessary where the whole debt is guaranteed: *Re Sass* (1896). A further clause is also included restricting the right of the guarantor to *sue* the debtor until the creditor has been paid in full, and this is a useful protection.

24. Guarantee payable on demand, in writing being made on the guarantor. This clause prevents the operation of the Statute of Limitations (*see* I, **26–30**) until six years after the bank has demanded repayment from the guarantor: *Bradford Old Bank* v. *Sutcliffe* (1918). If the clause was omitted the six-year period would begin to run immediately each advance was made to the principal debtor: *Parr's Banking Co.* v. *Yates* (1898).

25. Preclusion of operation of Clayton's Case, when the guarantee is determined and the bank fails to break the debtor's account.

The efficacy of such a clause was tested and upheld in *Westminster Bank Ltd.* v. *Cond* (1940), where on the death of the guarantor, the bank failed to break the account of the debtor, relying on a clause in the guarantee which stated that further operation of the account and receipt of credits was permissible, and such action was not to affect the bank detrimentally.

NOTE: It is the usual practice to open (where necessary) a separate account for the debtor when the guarantee has been determined. Nevertheless, a *preclusion clause* would be beneficial if the account was allowed to continue inadvertently.

26. Bank retains right to compound with or make any arrangement with the debtor or other party. It has been established that *unless otherwise agreed*: (*a*) if the principal creditor releases, or varies his relationship with the principal debtor, then the guarantor is discharged, e.g. agreeing to a composition by the debtor under a deed of arrangement, or granting time to the debtor, (*b*) if the principal creditor releases any co-guarantors or securities deposited by third parties the guarantor will be released in part or in whole from his liability. *To avoid these events* the bank expressly reserves the right to make any arrangements it wishes.

27. Determination clause in respect of due notice by guarantor. A clause requiring the guarantor (or his personal representative(s) if he is deceased) to give written notice of determination of his guarantee is stipulated by the bank; such notice to take effect on the expiration of (usually) three calendar months from the date of receipt.

This enables the bank to adjust its position *vis à vis* the guarantor and debtor, and also gives it time to decide how to deal with the debtor's account immediately after notice of determination has been received. If this clause was omitted the guarantor would have a right to know his liability at any time, and to immediately pay off the bank, even though the principal debtor had issued cheques in reliance of the continuance of the guarantee: *see* **7** above.

28. Indemnity clause. Necessary in respect of minors, unincorporated bodies and *ultra vires* borrowing, etc., in order to protect the bank in the event of the incapacity of the debtor, by making the guarantor *primarily liable* for the debt, e.g. the bank would gain protection if a limited company borrowed *ultra vires* against the security of a guarantee, provided a suitable indemnity clause was included. *See* also *Coutts & Co.* v. *Browne-Lecky*; **14** above.

29. Fraudulent preference. A suitable clause is necessary to protect the bank from risk of loss through the fraudulent preference of the depositor of collateral security by the principal debtor. The risk of preference attaches to the bank as a result of the application of 1914, s. 44, in the case of individuals and CA 1948, s. 320, in the case of companies. If no protective clause was included the danger would be as described below.

30. How fraudulent preference may operate in practice. For example, X has an overdrawn account of £200 secured by a guarantee (or any other collateral security) deposited by his father. X realises that he is in financial difficulties, and therefore diverts all receipts into his bank account. Upon the account reverting into credit the bank release X's father from his guarantee liability. X immediately files his own bankruptcy petition. Upon examination of the bank statement the trustee in bankruptcy may try to prove fraudulent preference, which, if upheld, means that the bank will have to repay him all receipts converted fraudulently, thus leaving the bank account of X unsecured.

NOTE: The trustee in bankruptcy (or liquidator) must prove that: (1) the *preference* occurred within the six months prior to the presentation of the bankruptcy petition or winding up of the company, *and* (2) the debtor was *insolvent at the time of preference*, i.e. he was unable to meet his debts as and when they fell due, *and* (3) there was a definite intention by the debtor *to prefer a particular creditor*. (Any pressure by the creditor on the debtor will usually defeat the contention of the fraudulent preference.) Point (3) is the most difficult one for the trustee to prove, and all will depend on the evidence brought out as to the running of the account during the period in question. If it has been conducted in the same manner as formerly, i.e. there has been no noticeable change as to the amounts and type of transactions on the account, then the trustee may well lose: *J. S. Lyons ex parte Barclays Bank Ltd.* v. *The Trustee* (1934). But if, for instance, a long-standing overdraft suddenly reduces or is repaid, then the trustee may well be successful: *Re M. Kushler Ltd.* (1943).

31. Bank's protection against fraudulent preference.

(*a*) *Pressure* can be brought to bear upon the debtor to repay if the bank realises the significance of events in sufficient time. They would therefore demand immediate repayment from the debtor, and refuse to release any collateral securities until the danger of bankruptcy (or liquidation) within six months was past.

(*b*) CA 1947, s. 92(4), in the case of bankruptcy, and CA 1948, s. 321, in the case of liquidation of companies, give some measure of indemnity whereby if the bank has released the collateral security or guarantor before the trustee (or liquidator) brings an action against the bank it has the right to be joined by the preferred party, who may therefore have to repay some or all of the amount preferred; alternatively, the bank can claim reimbursement from the preferred party, who is made personally liable under these sections.

(*c*) *A clause is usually added* in guarantees and collateral charge forms, whereby the guarantor or charger agrees that in the event of fraudulent preference the bank retains the right to recover from the preferred party, even though the security has been released.

32. Guarantor not to accept security from principal debtor. If a guarantor was allowed to accept such security, then any dividend received by the bank in the event of the bankruptcy of the debtor would be reduced.

33. Fresh account. "On receipt of notice of determination the bank is to be at liberty to open a fresh account for the debtor." Although invariably such a clause is included, it is not thought absolutely necessary in view of the decision in *Re Sherry, London and County Banking Co.* v. *Terry* (1884).

34. Guarantee additional to and not in substitution for any previous one. This clause covers the bank if at a future date the guarantor refutes the idea that the second guarantee was *an additional* one. To put the matter beyond doubt, some banks cancel the first guarantee and have the new guarantee drawn to cover the *total* amount.

35. Guarantor to continue liable despite change in name or constitution of firm, unincorporated body, committee, trustees, or joint account holders, or any amalgamation or change in the name of the bank. The bank would in any case take appropriate action if any of these events occurred.

36. Admissions by the debtor. The guarantor promises to accept as binding upon himself any admissions of liability to the bank (made by debtor or bank), e.g. by Recorded Delivery to last known address. Procedure is important here when envisaging court action.

PRACTICAL APPLICATION OF RELEASE

In relation to this section it must always be remembered that the remedies available to the bank are usually of a flexible nature, and therefore, in many instances, it would be neither prudent nor equitable for the bank to insist upon its full legal rights, unless all parties had been consulted, and no satisfactory alternative arrangements were possible.

37. Repayment by principal debtor.

(*a*) If it is intended *that the guarantor be released*, then the bank retains the guarantee so that reliance can still be placed on the protective clauses.

(*b*) A continuing guarantee will often be retained as security, even though the debtor's account has reverted to credit. In this case the guarantor will still be liable for any future advances. However, some banks feel it equitable to inform the guarantor of their continuing reliance on the guarantee, especially if the original purpose for which it was given has now changed. The guarantor is thus enabled to review the position and if necessary determine his liability.

38. Voluntary payment by guarantor.

(*a*) If debt *is greater than amount of guarantee* the bank can accept any payment made by the guarantor and place it to a guarantee security account to preserve its collateral position in the event of bankruptcy. (Retain guarantee.)

(*b*) If debt *is less than amount of guarantee* then:

(*i*) Remind the guarantor of *necessary written notice required*—it is thought that the bank could legally allow the debtor's account to reach the maximum liability under the guarantee during the running of such notice (but *see below*).

(*ii*) Any payments offered should be placed in a guarantee security account, and any receipt given for such money should *show clearly* that this is only to be regarded as part payment until the ultimate liability of the guarantor can be established on the date of determination. (Retain guarantee.)

(*iii*) *A meeting of guarantor, debtor and bank manager* should be arranged to enable a satisfactory compromise to be reached.

NOTE: The bank will try to protect their customer, by allowing him to pay off outstanding commitments entered in reliance of the guarantee, e.g. cheques issued but not yet presented. The bank is also under an obligation to protect the guarantor should the debtor try to take advantage of the position, and can, if necessary, *call up the debtor's account on demand*; a useful remedy where the debtor is unsatisfactory and the guarantor is an important customer.

39. Notice of determination received from guarantor. Proceed as in **38**(*b*)(*ii*)–(*iii*) above.

40. Death, bankruptcy or mental incapacity of principal debtor. *The bank should:*

(*a*) *Stop debtor's account on notice of such* happening and endeavour to recover from either his executors/administrators, trustee in bankruptcy or the Court of Protection as the case may be.

(*b*) (Usually) *Call up the guarantee immediately*. In any case the guarantor should be advised of the situation.

(*c*) *Place any payments received* from the guarantor to a separate guarantee security account to retain the bank's collateral position, and advise the guarantor that he cannot prove against the debtor or take action unless he pays off the *whole debt* owing to the bank. (If recovery of more than 100p in the £ is made the excess will be repaid to the guarantor(s).)

41. Death of guarantor

(*a*) *Sole guarantee*. Usually determined on notice of death, but clause prevents determination until executors/administrators have given the bank, say, three months' notice. The bank should therefore *either*:

(*i*) *continue to rely on guarantee*, informing executors/administrators of contingent liability and outlining procedure necessary for determination, *or*

(*ii*) *stop the account of the debtor and call up the guarantee*. The latter is more usual especially if the bank do not wish to rely on the determination clause, because for instance:

(1) the guarantor's estate is insubstantial, *or* (2) it is not wished to involve the deceased's estate in further liability.

(*b*) *Joint and several guarantee*. If no covering clause is included, the remaining guarantors (but not the deceased) would still be liable for *future advances*, and the bank could rely on their liability in this respect.

NOTE: Bank guarantee forms contain a clause (as outlined under (*a*) above) retaining the deceased's liability and also stipulating that *notice of determination must be given by all guarantors* (*or representatives*) *together*. Sometimes a new guarantee is taken, but this is thought unnecessary.

42. Mental incapacity of guarantor. On receipt of notice of incapacity of either a sole guarantor or joint and several guarantor, the bank should stop the debtor's account (if relying fully on guarantor) and call upon all parties to pay up under the guarantee. *No* protective clause *is included* in a bank guarantee to allow the bank to make further advances which would retain the liability of the mentally incapacitated party, *however*, the remaining guarantors would still be liable for further advances: *Bradford Old Bank* v. *Sutcliffe* (1918).

43. Bankruptcy of guarantor.

(*a*) *Sole guarantee*. On receiving notice of an *Act of bankruptcy* by the guarantor or on the *making of a Receiving Order* against the guarantor, no further advances should be made to the debtor because the guarantor's estate would not then be liable after either of these events: *see* VI, **37**–**38**. If it *proved necessary* to recover from the bankrupt's estate, then the bank would:

(*i*) *Stop the debtor's account and call it up*.

(*ii*) *Prove in the bankruptcy* of the guarantor for the amount of the guarantee or debt outstanding whichever is the smaller. (Interest at 5 per cent per annum running against the guarantee liability after demand upon the guarantor may be recovered up to the date of the Receiving Order.)

(*iii*) *Hold any payments* received from the *trustee in bankruptcy* on a separate account, to retain the bank's collateral position against the debtor.

NOTE: If recovery of more than 100p in the £ is made, then the trustee in bankruptcy will receive a return of dividend.

(*b*) *Joint and several guarantee*. If necessary, proceed as above (**43**(*a*)(*i*)–(*iii*)), and in addition call upon the remaining guarantors to repay the bank. If no proof is made against the bankrupt guarantor it is usual to take a new guarantee from the remaining guarantors, as the bankrupt guarantor is not then released by the bank, but by *process of law*.

44. Income Tax Certificate. The amount called up from the guarantor may include a sum in respect of unpaid interest owed by the debtor. However, the guarantor is not entitled to a certificate for such interest paid, as immediately the interest is added on to the debtor's account it becomes part of the *principal* sum: *Holder* v. *Inland Revenue* (1932).

A guarantor may request a Bank Interest Certificate in respect of interest paid by himself on the principal amount demanded upon call-up. A suitably amended certificate may then be supplied, but under current legislation it is unlikely to assist the guarantor in obtaining tax relief from the Inland Revenue.

PROGRESS TEST 12

1. Is a banker bound to disclose the position of his customer's account to a prospective guarantor? **(4)**
2. What do you understand by a joint and several guarantee? **(6)** What precautions are necessary when taking such guarantees as security? **(6)**
3. What disabilities have the following in relation to the execution of a valid guarantee: (*a*) minors (*b*) firms; (*c*) limited companies; (*d*) ladies? **(15, 16, 17, 18)**
4. Outline fully the procedure necessary when a limited company wishes to give a guarantee. **(18)**
5. What are the main clauses found in bank guarantee forms, and why are they necessary? **(21–36)**
6. How does the bank protect itself where a guarantor wishes to determine his position immediately? **(38)**

CHAPTER XIII

Land

GENERAL COMMENTS

1. Land law is complicated. Land law is covered in the main by the Law of Property Act 1925, Law of Property (Amendment) Act 1926, Land Charges Act 1925, Land Registration Acts 1925 and 1936, and Settled Land Act 1925. This chapter is only intended to give a review of the main factors concerning land as security for bankers' advances.

2. Land as security. Land suffers from several disadvantages as security, but nevertheless has become increasingly more acceptable (mainly due to steady inflation), particularly where the borrower cannot offer more worthwhile security. For example, a company may have no acceptable assets to charge other than its premises.

3. Procedure when taking security. The customer wishing to charge land as security will *usually* have a legal estate, being either a *freeholder* or *leaseholder*. The procedure to be adopted to perfect security over *freehold* or *leasehold* land will depend upon whether the title is: (*a*) registered, (*b*) unregistered. These procedures are dealt with separately below.

NOTE: Students must always remember that the term "land" denotes not only the ground but also *any building or fixture attached thereon*. Consequently, if a customer creates a mortgage of his land in the bank's favour and then proceeds to build a factory on that land the building automatically becomes part of the bank's security.

4. Disadvantages of land as security. There are several of these:

(*a*) *Valuation is extremely difficult.* Compare the difficulties involved in placing an accurate valuation on houses, flats, shops, offices, factories, investment properties, etc.

(*b*) *The depositor's title to the land must be verified*, and this is often involved, costly and time-consuming, particularly in the case of unregistered land.

(*c*) *Completing the security is costly*, especially where a registered legal mortgage of registered land is concerned.

(*d*) *Realisation of the security by way of sale may prove especially difficult* where there is only a small market demand, and consequently, the price realised may be less than anticipated. Adverse publicity might be caused by an eviction.

(*e*) *The effect of various statutes*, e.g. Rent Acts, Town & Country Planning Acts, etc., may reduce the desirability of taking the land as security.

(*f*) Any tenancy created by the mortgagor might mean that the property is only attractive to an investor, as vacant possession cannot be given. The asking price must be reduced substantially, therefore, as against the vacant possession basis. Usually the right to create a legal tenancy is restricted by the bank's mortgage form, under which the bank's prior permission will be required. In the event of the permission not having been sought, the bank will need to take Court proceedings against the tenant and may need to evict.

5. Valuation of security. Accurate valuation may prove exceedingly difficult, depending upon the type of property involved. Consider the following:

(*a*) *Houses.* Accurate valuation can usually be made by the branch manager by reference to sale prices of similar local properties. Valuation will be influenced by the type of title, i.e. freehold or leasehold, type and size of property, state of repair, amenities, etc.

(*b*) *Agricultural land.* Valued as in (*a*) above. Additional factors are taken into consideration, e.g. the acreage, quality of land, accessibility to markets, condition of buildings, etc.

(*c*) *Factories and other industrial buildings.* Extremely difficult to value accurately, *even by professional valuers.* As a general rule, the more specialised the building, the more conservative should be the valuation when making allowance for a *forced sale.*

Wherever possible the bank will require a *good margin* between the security valuation and the amount to be advanced.

6. Legal estates in land. The law concerning land was revolutionised by the passing of the Property Acts in 1925. S. 1 of the Law of Property Act 1925, provides that there are now only two *legal estates* in land:

(*a*) an estate in fee simple absolute in possession (known as *freehold*);

(*b*) a term of years absolute (known as *leasehold*).

A *freeholder* is to all intents and purposes the absolute owner of his land and is able to deal with it as he likes, subject only to the law.

A *leaseholder* (lessee) derives a legal estate for a term of years from the *freeholder* (lessor) or *sub-lessor* (leaseholder). The lessee is free to deal with the land when acting within the terms of the lease and within the law. When the lease expires *the land reverts back to the freeholder* or *sub-lessor*.

Usually *long leases* are offered as security to the bank, e.g. a lease for ninety-nine years, and these present few problems. *Short leases* are undesirable as security: *see* **37** below.

7. Legal interests in land. There are five *legal interests* in land which may be created. The most important to a banker being a *charge by way of legal mortgage*.

8. Legal mortgage always preferable to an equitable mortgage. The remedies of a legal mortgagee are so superior to those of an equitable mortgagee that a legal mortgage should always be required unless the mortgagor is of undoubted standing and the borrowing is of short-term nature and repayment is assured.

9. Creation of a legal mortgage.

(*a*) *Over freehold land.* S. 85 of the LPA provides *two* methods of creating a legal mortgage over *freehold land*:

(*i*) *By creation of a long-lease* for a term of years absolute, e.g. 3,000 years, with the provision for cesser on redemption.

(*ii*) *Creation of a charge by deed* expressed to be by way of *legal mortage* (giving the same effect as (*i*)).

(*b*) *Over leasehold land.* S. 86 of the LPA provides *two* methods of creating a legal mortgage over *leasehold land*:

(*i*) *Creation of a sub-lease* for a term shorter than the original lease. (Usually created ten days shorter so that further mortgages can be granted.)

(*ii*) *Creation of a legal mortgage*, as in (*a*)(*ii*) above (giving the same effect as in (*i*) above).

A charge by *deed* by way of *legal mortgage is* usually used in practice because one standard bank form can be made available to cover both freehold and leasehold land.

10. Creation of an equitable mortgage. An *equitable mortgage* may be created by a simple deposit of title deeds or land certificate with or without a memorandum. (A second or subsequent equitable mortgage can be created without deposit of the deeds or land certificate, but it is rarely met in practice.) The bank usually requires the customer to sign a memorandum of equitable mortgage under hand, as the terms of the memorandum give the bank added rights and powers.

11. Remedies of a legal mortgagee. As mortgagee the bank has the following concurrent remedies if the customer defaults. In practice, it will exercise either (*d*) or (*e*). Only in the case of (*b*) is the Court's consent necessary.

(*a*) *To sue for the debt* on the mortgagor's personal covenant to repay.

(*b*) *To foreclose*, i.e. to obtain a court order vesting the property in the mortgagee's name, thus extinguishing for ever the mortgagor's equity of redemption. Banks hardly ever institute foreclosure proceedings.

(*c*) *To enter into possession* of the land at any time. Banks rarely enter into possession, because of the liabilities they thereby assume, e.g. insurance, rates payable on empty property, repairs, etc.

(*d*) *To appoint a receiver*. Particularly appropriate for let property, e.g. a block of flats. The bank appoints a receiver, who takes possession of the property and collects rents and profits in order to reduce the mortgagor's debt. He is also responsible, however, for any outgoings and his position is akin to a landlord's. In addition, the receiver's remuneration (5 per cent) will be deductible before he accounts to the bank for net income.

The receiver is regarded as the *agent of the mortgagor*, who in law is therefore responsible for his defaults.

(*e*) *To sell the property*. This is the most commonly used remedy.

NOTE: *Under* LPA, ss. 103 and 109, power to sell or to appoint a receiver only becomes *exercisable* when either: (1) the mortgage money has been demanded and remains unpaid for three months, or (2) some interest is two months in arrear, or (3) there has been a breach of some provision in the mortgage deed or the Act, other than the covenant to repay. The bank *excludes these sections* and provides that it can exercise its powers *immediately the mortgagor defaults after demand for repayment*.

12. Remedies of an equitable mortgagee. As equitable mortgagee, the bank has the right to *sue* on the money debt, but if it wishes to exercise any rights against the property it must first apply to the Court, e.g. for an Order for Sale. This applies also if the mortgagor has undertaken to complete a legal mortgage if called upon to do so, but has refused to co-operate.

13. Equitable mortgage by deed. An equitable mortgage may be completed by *deed* and contain either: (*a*) an *irrevocable power of attorney clause*, appointing a bank official as attorney, or (*b*) an admittance that the mortgagor holds the property in *trust* for the bank, who are empowered to remove him at any time. In both instances the remedies available to the bank are the same as for a *legal mortgagee* (*see* **11** above).

The main advantage to be gained over taking a legal mortgage is that on release of the security the discharged deed does *not* form part of title. Equitable mortgages under deed *are rarely taken by banks*.

14. Nature of a second mortgage. If a person borrows against the security of his land he may later create a second mortgage by charging the same land as a security for further borrowing.

EXAMPLE: If B mortgages his property worth £5,000 to X for a loan of £1,000, then if he wishes to raise further money he may grant a second mortgage of £1,000 to Y and a third mortgage of £1,000 to Z. B will probably be able to find further lenders until such time as his *equity* in the property is exhausted, i.e. until he has borrowed up to the value of the property. (Lenders require margins, and therefore total borrowing will not usually reach the property value.) All three mortgages will, in practice, be charges by way of *legal* or *equitable mortgage*, although they could be created by long-lease. The procedure for completing a second mortgage is outlined in **33** and **54** below.

15. Nature of a sub-mortgage. A sub-mortgage is created when the original mortgagee (lender) borrows money against the security of his mortgage deed. The situation is commonly explained as "a mortgage of a mortgage". The original mortgagee becomes sub-mortgagor and the new lender becomes sub-mortgagee. The procedure for completing a sub-mortgage is outlined in **35** and **55** below.

UNREGISTERED FREEHOLD LAND

16. General procedure when taking a first legal or equitable mortgage. The bank should:

(*a*) *Obtain the title deeds and get a solicitor's report on title.*

(*b*) *Value the security.*

(*c*) *Search the local land charges register*(*s*).

(*d*) *Schedule the deeds on the security form.* This is then signed by the mortgagor either under seal (legal mortgage) or under hand (equitable mortgage).

(*e*) *Search the land charges register* at the Land Charges Department. (The search is usually made before the execution of the mortgage to see whether any undisclosed charges rank ahead of the bank. However, the protective fifteen day period which applies to a purchaser who searches cannot be relied on as protecting a mortgagee, and banks *always* search *concurrently with* or *after* the date of the mortgage: *see* **23** below.

(*f*) *Give notice to the insurers* of the bank's interest in the mortgaged property.

NOTE: (1) The advance should not be made until the result of the search on the land charges registry is known. (2) The procedure varies slightly if a *company* is creating the security.

17. Title to unregistered freehold land. Is evidenced by a bundle of title deeds, i.e. documents necessary to trace the title, e.g. conveyances, marriage certificates, discharged legal mortgages, assents, etc.

An *Abstract of title* is normally found with the deeds. This is a summary of documents and events tracing the chain of title to the present owner. The abstract should commence with a *good root of title*, i.e. a document which is at least fifteen years old (LPA 1969, s. 23) which deals with the entire legal and equitable estate. Such a document would be: (*a*) a conveyance, (*b*) an assent, (*c*) a discharged legal mortgage (on the presumption that the mortgagee checked the whole title).

18. Solicitor's report on title. To make certain of obtaining a *valid security* the bank usually requires a solicitor to report on title and to state: (*a*) the full names of the estate owner, (*b*) a full description of the property, (*c*) whether any restrictive covenants are likely to affect the security, (*d*) whether the bank will obtain a good marketable title, (*e*) whether the *Town & Country Planning*

Acts or any other statute affects the security. Where accommodation is required urgently, a branch official may be expected to check title.

19. Priority of mortgages. The procedure necessary to ensure priority against the security depends upon whether or not the deeds are deposited with the banker:

(*a*) *Mortgages protected by a deposit of deeds*. Priority is achieved merely by possession and not by registration. Consequently, when taking a legal or equitable mortgage a bank will gain first priority merely by taking the deeds, so long as at the time of deposit no prior incumbrance was registered on the land charges register, e.g. a puisne mortgage.

(*b*) *Mortgages unprotected by deposit of the deeds*. Priority is achieved by registration of the mortgage on the *land charges register*. Priority ranks from the date of registration and not from the date of creation of the mortgage: LPA 1925, s. 97.

A legal mortgagee without the deeds protects his position by registration of a C(*i*) entry, i.e. a *puisne mortgage*.

An *equitable mortgagee without the deeds* protects his position by registration of a C(*iii*) entry, i.e. *a general equitable charge*.

NOTE: (1) Legal mortgages gain no priority over equitable mortgages. (2) Non-production of the deeds to a prospective lender would suggest the existence of a prior legal or equitable mortgage. (3) A first mortgagee invariably takes the deeds in order to gain maximum protection, leaving subsequent mortgages to protect themselves by registration. It would be correct to say, therefore, that *most puisne mortgages are second legal mortgages*.

20. Bank releasing deeds on loan. Where a mortgagor wishes to inspect deeds charged to the bank, the bank will wish to protect itself fully against the likelihood of the mortgagor jeopardising its priority by creating a further charge while the deeds are in his possession.

To protect its priority the bank will usually:

(*a*) *Require the deeds to be forwarded to a solicitor* (for examination) against the solicitor's undertaking on the bank's own form to hold the deeds to the bank's order and return them upon demand intact. (The customer's written authority is required, and the solicitor's standing should be checked.)

Exceptionally in special circumstances the bank could

(*b*) *Deliver the deeds to the customer*, and—

(*i*) *If a legal mortgage exists.* Register a puisne mortgage (C(*i*) entry) on the land charges register,

(*ii*) *If an equitable mortgage exists.* Register a general equitable charge (C(*iii*) entry) on the land charges register. As a general equitable charge can in certain circumstances be overreached, even though registered, an alternative is to register the mortgagor's undertaking to create a legal mortgage as an estate contract (C(*iv*) entry).

Procedures (*b*)(*i*) and (*b*)(*ii*) are not desirable.

21. Searches at the land charges register. This register is a register of *names of owners* of land. Entries made on the register are regarded as being *notice to the whole world.* When a search of the register is made the *full names* of all existing owners should be quoted.

An application for an *official search* is made by completing form K15 and forwarding this to the Land Charges Department. The result of the search is forwarded to the bank and is *conclusive evidence* of the entries outstanding on the register at the end of the stated date. Usually the search form shows "no subsisting entries", but if this is not the case full details of any entry can be obtained by completing and forwarding form K19 (application for office copy).

22. What the search may reveal. *Five registers* are maintained at the Land Charges Department, and the 15p fee covers a search of all registers. The registers are of:

(*a*) *Pending actions*, e.g. a petition in bankruptcy.

(*b*) *Annuities.* Register closed since 1925.

(*c*) *Writs and orders*, e.g. appointment of a receiver; receiving order in bankruptcy.

(*d*) *Deeds of arrangement.*

(*e*) *Land charges:* subdivided into six classes, A–F:

A & B *Charges imposed by statute*, e.g. land improvement charges.

C(*i*) *Puisne mortgages*, i.e. legal mortgages unprotected by deposit of the deeds.

C(*ii*) *Limited owner's charge*, e.g. registration of an equitable interest by a life tenant using his own moneys to pay estate duty.

C(*iii*) *General equitable charges*, most commonly, equitable mortgages unprotected by deposit of the deeds. Also annuities created since 1925.

C(*iv*) *Estate contracts*, e.g. (*i*) contract for sale of land option to purchase a freehold or renew a lease.

D(*i*) *Death duties*, e.g. claims registered by Inland Revenue.

D(*ii*) *Restrictive covenants.*

D(*iii*) *Equitable easements.*

E *Annuities* created pre-1926 but registered post-1925.

F Charges by virtue to the Matrimonial Homes Act 1967, i.e. rights of occupation of spouse.

NOTE: Although D(*ii*) entries are most common, banks are mainly interested in C(*i*) and C(*iii*) entries. Sometimes C(*i*) and C(*iii*) entries turn out to be of no consequence, having been left on the register inadvertently.

23. When to search the land charges register.

(*a*) *If lending on loan account.* Obtain an official search prior to taking the mortgage. Thereafter, if the mortgage is completed within fourteen days of the date of the search the bank is not affected by any intervening entry except one arising pursuant to a "priority notice" on the register before the certificate was issued: LP(A)A 1926, s. 4 (as amended).

(*b*) *If lending on current account.* It appears that the fourteen days protection quoted in (*a*) above does not apply and that the bank should search on or after the date of its mortgage to acquire complete protection (*see* **25** below).

In practice, banks search concurrent with the mortgage date or afterwards in every case.

24. Tacking. S. 94(1), LPA 1925 stipulates three instances where a mortgagee can make further advances to rank in priority to a *subsequent mortgagee*:

(*a*) where his *mortgage deed* imposes upon him an *obligation* to make further advances; *or*

(*b*) where the subsequent mortgagee agrees; *or*

(*c*) where the mortgagee has no notice of the subsequent mortgage when he makes his further advance.

In relation to (*c*): *Registration* of a puisne mortgage or general equitable charge *on the land charges register* is deemed to be notice to the whole world: LPA 1925, s. 198.

25. Protection for a bank lending on current account. If the effect of s. 198 was not modified it would mean that a bank lending on current account would need to search the land charges register before each new advance, i.e. before payment of each cheque.

This impossible state of affairs *is remedied* by LPA 1925, s. 94(2), which provides: "... in respect of a current account a mortgagee shall not be deemed to have notice of a mortgage merely by reason that it was registered as a land charge or in a local deeds registry, if it was not so registered at the date of the original advance or *when the last search* (if any) by or on behalf of the mortgagee was made, *whichever last happened*."

The result of this section is that a bank *searching on or after the date of its mortgage* and continuing to advance without receiving *direct notice* of a subsequent mortgage which has been duly registered *is fully protected* as regards priority until either it does receive direct notice or it searches again. If the bank searched before completing its mortgage it would be similarly protected *from the latter date*, but a mortgage could have been registered during the interval between the search and the date of its mortgage.

26. Local land charges register. This is a register of *properties* maintained by each local authority. Various charges of importance to bankers are entered thereon, e.g. road charges, slum clearance plans, preservation orders, etc. Searches are made against the property by submitting form LLCI. For land in non-county boroughs, urban districts and rural districts a search on the county council register should also be made.

27. Change of use of property since 1948. If there has been development of or a material change in use of land since 1st July 1948, then planning permission should (usually) have been obtained, as otherwise the local authority can within four years of the change require the property to be restored to its original state: Town & Country Planning Act 1971. If a bank advance is to be used in changing a property, planning permission is usually required, and should be obtained before the advance is granted.

28. Receipt of notice of a subsequent mortgage. Where the bank as mortgagee receives *direct notice* of a subsequent mortgage it must stop its customer's account, as priority is not retained in respect of further advances, and the Rule in Clayton's Case will apply to its detriment: *see Deeley* v. *Lloyds Bank Ltd.* (1912). Note particularly that as the bank is unwilling to enter into an *obligation* to make further advances, it will *never* in practice have the right to "tack". On receipt of notice the bank must set off all available accounts in order to determine the amount of its priority in respect of the security. A *loan account*, however, cannot be set off: *see* I, **41**. The customer may be allowed to open a *new account* to be maintained in credit or secured to the bank's satisfaction.

If the subsequent mortgagee agrees in his mortgage that the bank can retain priority on fluctuating overdraft up to a fixed amount there is no need to stop the customer's account. Likewise, a letter or deed of postponement completed by the mortgagee would have the same effect. Unfortunately subsequent mortgagees are not always willing to co-operate in these matters.

Occasionally where the value of the security is such that both the bank and subsequent mortgagee are more than adequately secured, the bank may be willing to continue to lend on a new account relying on its original security. It would be necessary to ensure that the subsequent mortgagee had no right to "tack" or to "consolidate". The bank would have in effect a first and third mortgage.

29. Matrimonial Homes Act 1967. This Act enables a spouse who is not the *legal* owner or tenant to protect their right to *occupy* the matrimonial home by registering either a class F charge in respect of unregistered land or a notice or caution in respect of registered land.

(*a*) *Entry appearing on the register before execution of bank mortgage*. The registering spouse has priority; thus the bank would normally require the spouse's written notice of postponement of such priority before permitting an advance against the property.

(*b*) *Entry entered on the register subsequent to the bank's mortgage*. If either (*i*) the bank searches and discovers the entry or is given notice of the entry by the Land Registry, or (*ii*) the registering spouse gives direct notice of the entry to the bank, then the bank retains absolute priority only up to this time. Consequently the bank should act as it does when receiving notice of a second mortgage.

NOTE: In any application to the court by the bank for an order for vacant possession to effect a sale of mortgaged property it is advisable to join as defendant any spouse who remains in occupation and who has registered under the Act as they have the right to redeem the mortgage under s. 1(5) and *see Hastings & Thanet Building Society* v. *Goddard* (1970).

30. Clauses in a bank mortgage form. The following clauses are commonly inserted to give the bank the maximum possible protection:

(*a*) Continuing security clause.

(*b*) 'All moneys" clause.

(*c*) Mortgagor's undertaking to repair and insure and for the bank to do so on his default and to charge him with the cost.

(*d*) Money repayable "on demand".

(*e*) LPA 1925, s. 103, is excluded: *see* **11** above.

(*f*) LPA 1925, s. 93, is excluded; the bank retaining the right to consolidate. This has no practical effect where the mortgage covers *all sums owing on any account.*

(*g*) LPA 1925, s. 99, is excluded and the mortgagor undertakes not to grant or surrender leases without the bank's consent.

NOTE: Where a lease is given in breach of the terms in a mortgage it has been held that the tenant was not protected by the Rent Acts and could be evicted: *Dudley & District Benefit Building Society* v. *Emerson* (1949). If the lease was given on the same day or prior to the bank mortgage, then the tenant becomes a lawful occupant and is fully protected.

31. Discharge of a mortgage where the borrowing is repaid. The procedure for discharge depends upon whether the mortgage is legal or equitable:

(*a*) *Legal mortgage.* There are two alternative methods of discharge, either: (*i*) reconveyance under *seal* (this is the method most commonly used), or (*ii*) endorsed statutory receipt, which need *not be under seal*, although in practice most banks do seal the receipt when using this method.

NOTE: (1) *A discharged legal mortgage forms part of title* and must be handed over with the deeds. (2) If two properties have been charged on the one deed and only one is to be released an "express release" is necessary.

(*b*) *Equitable mortgage.* No formal reconveyance or receipt is needed, even if the mortgage was under seal. (A discharged equitable mortgage does not form part of title and may be filed with expired securities.)

NOTE: Where the bank has received *notice* of a subsequent

mortgage, it must hand the deeds and discharged mortgage to this mortgagee. In the absence of notice there is no need to search the land charges register to ascertain whether there is a subsequent mortgagee: LPA 1925, s. 96(2) (as amended); but *see* **32** below.

32. Surplus proceeds on sale. Where a bank *exercises its power of sale* and there are surplus proceeds a search *must* be made to ascertain whether there is a subsequent mortgagee who has a right to these proceeds. When selling the property the bank is only under a duty to take care and obtain a fair and reasonable price at the time of sale. There is no breach of duty if it is disclosed that it is a mortgagee sale and there is no obligation on the bank to wait for a possible upturn in the market or to keep a business, such as an hotel, running, pending sale: *Bank of Cyprus* (*London*) *Ltd.* v. *Gill* (1979). The bank usually either sells by public auction or by private treaty after having placed the sale in the hands of reputable estate agents, who will have recommended acceptance of the price offered, so as to avoid any likelihood of contention of sale at an unrealistic price.

33. Procedure for taking a second legal mortgage.

(*a*) *Value the property* and check that the difference between this and the amount outstanding on first mortgage (plus interest) is sufficient to provide a security figure substantially in excess of the amount to be advanced.

(*b*) *Arrange for an investigation of title.* (The deeds will be in the hands of the first mortgagee.)

(*c*) *Search the local land charges register*(*s*).

(*d*) *Get the depositor to execute a legal mortgage under seal* (this will refer specifically to the first mortgage).

(*e*) *Register the mortgage* as a C (*i*) charge on the land charges register.

(*f*) *Search the land charges register after registration.* (The bank's C (*i*) registration should be revealed.)

(*g*) *Serve notice of mortgage on the first mortgagee and ask* him to *acknowledge receipt and confirm:* (*i*) the amount of the first mortgage, (*ii*) the amount outstanding (principal and interest), (*iii*) whether payments are up to date, (*iv*) whether he has any obligation to make further advances which can be "tacked", (*v*) whether he has any powers of consolidation, (*vi*) whether he has notice of any prior mortgages, (*vii*) the amount of insurance cover existing on the property. (Satisfactory answers are required to these questions, and it is usual therefore to make similar initial enquiries *before* agreeing to take the second mortgage).

(*h*) Give notice of the bank's interest to the insurers, except where a private dwelling place is mortgaged and is insured for £70,000 or less with an insurance company which is a member of the British Insurance Association. A special arrangement exists with these companies and the Clearing Banks, whereby, provided the insurance policy is seen (or the prior mortgagee confirms that he holds it) and the last premium receipt is exhibited, it is not necessary to give notice or see subsequent premium receipts.

34. Remedies of a second legal mortgagee. These are similar to those of a first legal mortgagee. The bank will take one of two courses:

(*a*) *Sell the property*. In this case, provided the net sale proceeds after costs are sufficient to discharge any prior charge(s) and give a worthwhile return to the bank under its security, no special problems are encountered, although, of course, the solicitors acting will need the deeds or the Land Certificate.

(*b*) *Appoint a receiver*. In practice a receiver for rents will have to account to any prior mortgagee for net collections unless the prior mortgagees are content to see the moneys pass to the bank.

Very occasionally the bank may be willing to pay off the first mortgagee so that the property can be sold as if by the first mortgagee. In rare instances the first mortgagee may be willing to take over the bank debt. If the first mortgagee proves uncooperative application can be made to the Court, which *may* force him to be "paid off". LPA 1925, s. 50. This section is rarely evoked.

35. Procedure for taking a legal sub-mortgage.

(*a*) *Ensure that if full security cover is required the sum to be advanced is below* that still owing on the original mortgage, because once the original mortgagor repays his debt, his deeds and mortgage must be returned to him.

(*b*) *Value the property* to see that it adequately covers the sub-mortgage advance.

(*c*) *Obtain the deeds and original mortgage* for retention. Check the *mortgagor's title* and assess the covenants contained in the mortgage.

(*d*) *Get the depositor to execute the bank's sub-mortgage form.*

(*e*) *Give notice of the sub-mortgage* to the original mortgagor and direct him to make his repayments to the bank.

(*f*) Give notice of the bank's interest *to the insurers*.

NOTE: If the original mortgage is only equitable the bank can only obtain an equitable interest in the land.

36. Remedies of a legal sub-mortgagee.

(*a*) *Where the sub-mortgagor defaults*. The bank can sue him or sell the sub-mortgage.

(*b*) *Where both the original mortgagor and sub-mortgagor are in default*. The bank can exercise all of the sub-mortgagor's rights as contained in his mortgage. (These are unlikely to be as extensive as in a bank mortgage.)

LEASEHOLD LAND

37. Leasehold land as security. Leasehold land is only held for the period of years created by the lease subject to the payment of ground rent and the observance of any covenants. At the end of the term the *land reverts to the freeholder or sub-lessor*. (Subject, of course, to any existing legislation, e.g. Rent Acts and Leasehold Reform Act 1967). In practice, leaseholds are charged as security by way of mortgage. Banks draw up a suitable mortgage form which covers both leaseholds and freeholds.

38. Valuation for security purposes. The usual factors help determine the value of leasehold property: *see* **5** above. An important additional factor with leaseholds is the *unexpired term of the lease*.

(*a*) *Long-leases*. Where a lease has, say, sixty or more years to run and the ground rent is moderate the unexpired term is unlikely to affect valuation.

(*b*) *Short-leases*. Generally *diminish in value as the term reduces*. Such leases should be valued on a conservative basis, because if the agreed repayment programme falls behind, the security value may not cover the outstanding debt. (It is often prudent to suggest that the leaseholder should approach the freeholder to try to obtain a new lease giving greater security of tenure.)

(*c*) *With leases of intermediate length* (say fourteen to sixteen years) much will depend upon the type of property as to the effect of the term on valuation, e.g. an unexpired shop lease of fourteen years in a city centre may be more valuable than the long lease of a similar shop in the suburbs.

39. Disadvantages of leaseholds as security. Leases usually include:

(*a*) *Provision by the lessor restricting underleasing or assignment*, either: (*i*) completely, or (*ii*) except by permission or under licence, or (*iii*) unless the mortgagee gives notice.

(*b*) *Restrictive covenants or onerous provisions,* e.g. agreed periodic increases in rent. (Some covenants or provisions may be unacceptable to a bank as mortgagee.)

(*c*) *Forfeiture clauses*, i.e. provisions as to defaults or omissions leading to forfeiture, e.g. bankruptcy of lessee. Relief can be obtained from forfeiture by an application to the Court under the LPA 1925, s. 146. Usually the terms upon which relief is likely to be granted (e.g. payment of arrears of rent, and future rents) make this option unattractive to a mortgagee.

(*d*) *Tenant's liability clauses.* The lessee may agree to be liable for repairs, dilapidations, insurance, rates, taxes and assessments, etc. Liability should be assessed.

(*e*) Arrears of rent will have to be discharged out of any sale proceeds.

40. Procedure on taking unregistered leasehold land as security.

(*a*) *Obtain the title deeds from the lessee.* These should include the head lease (or copy lease) together with any assignments or other accompanying documents to form a complete chain of title. The current *ground rent* receipt must be produced (and annually thereafter).

(*b*) *Obtain a solicitor's report on title.*

(*c*) *Obtain a professional valuation* (usually).

(*d*) *Obtain from the freeholder any necessary permission* for creation of the mortgage.

(*e*) *Follow the procedure outlined in* **16** above for unregistered land.

(*f*) *Give notice of the mortgage* to the freeholder if required.

REGISTERED LAND

41. Object of registered land. The object of the system of registered land is to simplify transfer. The State *guarantees the title to land* by issuing a *land certificate* which takes the place of the title deeds. Thus the involved investigation of title deeds on transfer is eliminated. It is intended that all land in England and Wales will ultimately be converted into registered land.

Land registration is governed by the Land Registration Acts

of 1925 and 1936, which provide that areas should be periodically designated for compulsory registration. Several new compulsory land-registration areas have been designated in the 1960s. The machinery of land registration is not unlike that for registered stocks and shares. The name of the freeholder or leaseholder is entered on the land register, and he is then issued with a land certificate as evidence of his title. When he wishes to transfer his title he forwards a completed transfer and the land certificate to the Land Registry, who effect the transfer.

42. Meaning of compulsory registration. There are many areas throughout the country where registration is compulsory, e.g. Middlesex, Surrey, Kent, Berkshire, etc. Students must note that even in a *compulsory* registration area *not all the land is registered*, as registration only becomes *obligatory*: (*a*) on a sale of freehold, or (*b*) on grant or assignment of a lease with forty years or more to run, or (*c*) on grant of a lease for twenty-one years or more where the freehold has been registered with an absolute title. (Leases for under twenty-one years cannot be registered.)

NOTE: Bankers may come across land which is registered but which is *not* situated within a compulsory area. This position arises because voluntary registration could formerly be effected in *any* area. *Voluntary registration* has now, with, certain exceptions, been suspended: Land Registration Act 1966.

43. The land register. The Registry is divided into District Registries covering certain counties, metropolitan districts, and London boroughs. It is obviously important to address enquiries to the appropriate Registry. The land register is divided into *three* parts:

(*a*) *The property register.* Which records: (*i*) the title number, (*ii*) a short description of the land, (*iii*) the nature of the estate, i.e. freehold or leasehold, (*iv*) the land registry general map reference.

(*b*) *The proprietorship register.* Which records: (*i*) the class of title, e.g. absolute, good leasehold, etc., (*ii*) the name, address and description of the registered proprietor, (*iii*) the date of registration of title, (*iv*) matters affecting the proprietor's right to deal with the land, e.g. bankruptcy inhibitions, cautions, etc.

(*c*) *The charges register.* Which records: (*i*) legal mortgages by way of registered charge and equitable mortgages by way of Notice of Deposit, (*ii*) restrictive covenants, etc.

NOTE: (1) *A search of the register* can only be made by the registered proprietor, chargees or persons authorised by them. (2) The *land register* concerns registered land and the *land charges register* concerns unregistered land. Students must take care *not to confuse these registers*, as they are in no way connected.

44. The land certificate. This is issued by the Land Registry to the registered proprietor. The land certificate provides *conclusive evidence of the title of the proprietor* (*see* **45** below) and is a *facsimile* of the land register. It bears the date when it was last brought up to date with the register. (The registry will bring the land certificate up to date with the register at any time without fee.)

45. Types of title. The Land Registry enters one of four types of title on the proprietorship register. The bank's approach to registered land as security is determined to a large extent by the type of title which has been registered.

(*a*) *Absolute.* Usually a *freehold* title which has the *absolute guarantee of the State.* The only evidence required of title is the *land certificate.* A *leaseholder* will only be granted an absolute title where the freeholder has been registered with absolute title.

(*b*) *Good leasehold.* The State guarantees the title of the leaseholder, but gives no guarantee of the freeholder's right to grant the lease. The bank requires both the lease and land certificate when taking good leasehold property as security.

NOTE: *Absolute* and *good leasehold* titles are only subject to interests on the register and to minor interests and overriding interests. Overriding interests are not registrable, but bind the estate: LRA 1925, s. 70. Examples of overriding interests are easements and leases for under twenty-one years.

(*c*) *Possessory.* The State guarantees the proprietor's title only in respect of *dealings after registration.* A purchaser or mortgagee (e.g. the bank) has to investigate *prior title* from the *deeds.* The holder of a possessory title will acquire either: (*a*) a good leasehold title, after ten years (if a leaseholder), or (*b*) an absolute title, after fifteen years (if a freeholder).

(*d*) *Qualified.* Only issued where there are defects in title (rare in practice.) When dealing with such a title the bank proceeds as for unregistered land.

46. Mortgages. It is possible for a proprietor to create a legal or equitable mortgage over his land. Bankers usually require customers to complete either: (*a*) a registered legal mortgage, or (*b*) an equitable mortgage created by deposit of the land certificate and protected by notice of deposit, or (*c*) an unregistered legal mortgage protected by notice of deposit of the land certificate.

The usual bank security form can be used, as it will be drawn to cover both registered and unregistered land. Care must be taken to see that the title number is entered on the charge form.

47. Searches at the land registry. Searches can only be instituted with the written authority of the proprietor or his solicitor. (It will be recalled that any member of the general public can search the *land charges register*, i.e. for unregistered land. The latter register does not, of course, concern registered land.)

Official searches are issued, and a bank taking a *legal registered mortgage* is able to gain priority over intervening entries (other than those arising from a "priority notice"), if it has its charge registered within 20 working days of the date of the search certificate (or a further 15 working days if an extension is applied for and granted). (The 20 working day priority period covers lending on *current account*. You will recall that this is *not* the case with *unregistered land*: *see* **23** above.)

48. Priority of mortgages. Priority of *all* mortgages over registered land depends upon the date of registration at the Land Registry. As the bank's legal registered charge covers *further advances*, the registry will *notify it by post if any subsequent charge is entered on the register*, e.g. a second mortgage. Consequently, there is no need for protection similar to that given by LPA 1925, s. 94(2) for unregistered land: *see* **25** above. (A special fund provides indemnity for loss occasioned by absence or non-delivery of the notice.)

The decision in *Williams & Glyn's Bank Ltd.* v. *Boland* (1980) however, has thrown the mortgagee's position into some confusion. This ruling was based on LRA 1925, s. 70, which refers to the *overriding interests* of a person who has an equitable interest and who is in actual occupation of the property at the time it is mortgaged. These rights are superior to the mortgagee's unless they are postponed or the party concerned joins in the charge.

In the Boland case, the registered proprietor shown on the Land Certificate was Mr Boland and the bank took a mortgage from him. When it sought possession of the matrimonial home *Mrs*

Boland defended the action on the grounds that she had made money and other contributions to the purchase and upkeep over many years and had an overriding interest by way of actual occupation; she was successful in defeating the application for *possession* but the court decision did not state that her equitable interest in money terms ranked ahead of the bank.

Bankers and other lenders are still considering their practices in view of this case, which seems to extend not only to domestic and matrimonial situations, but all other registered titles. (Moreover, for practical purposes the position is the same in respect of unregistered land.)

Thus it is necessary for a lender to ascertain precisely who is in occupation and on what basis, when he takes his mortgage, and to obtain postponements/charges over any overriding interests. Even so, the position of occupants could change later, when the bank's rights *might* be affected, if it continued to lend, especially on a fluctuating current account. Students should therefore consult their own bank's practices in this field.

49. Completing a legal registered mortgage. The basic procedure is as follows:

(*a*) *Examine the land certificate* and, if satisfied as to the proprietor's title, proceed as in (*b*).

(*b*) *Make a search of the land register* by completing and forwarding Form 94 (proprietor's authority required). In the absence of adverse entries, proceed as in (*c*).

(*c*) *Require the proprietor to execute the bank's form of legal mortgage* under seal.

(*d*) *In order to gain priority over intervening entries* forward to the Land Registry, within 20 working days of the date of the search: (*i*) the official search certificate, (*ii*) the completed legal mortgage and a certified copy thereof, (*iii*) the land certificate, (*iv*) a registration fee.

(*e*) *The registry returns* the original charge, which is bound into a *charge certificate*, and this constitutes the bank's security.

NOTE: Local searches, insurance, etc., are dealt with as with unregistered land.

50. Unregistered legal mortgage protected by notice of deposit of the land certificate. The Land Registration Act 1925 provides that a *lien* may be created on registered land by deposit of the land certificate; being equivalent to deposit of deeds as security in the case of unregistered land (i.e. an *equitable* mortgage): s. 66. Once notice of the deposit of the land certificate is entered on the land register, any prospective *purchaser* or *mortgagee* is deemed to know that the land certificate has been deposited as security.

Being dissatisfied with the rights of an equitable mortgagee, the bank usually insists upon the completion of a *legal mortgage which is held unregistered. Notice of deposit of the land certificate is given to the registry.*

The procedure is basically as follows:

(*a*) *The proprietor executes the bank's form of legal mortgage* under seal.

(*b*) *The land certificate is forwarded to the registry* to be brought up to date. *Simultaneously* the bank gives notice of deposit by completing and forwarding Form 85A in duplicate.

(*c*) *The registry returns the duplicate of Form* 85*A* and the land certificate, which has the bank's interest endorsed thereon. The bank may then safely proceed to lend if satisfied as to the entries on the land certificate and having made the usual local searches and given notice to the insurers.

NOTE: The C of A decision in *Barclays Bank* v. *Taylor & Anor.* (1973) reversing the H C decision confirmed the effectiveness of this existing practice. Mr & Mrs D deposited their land certificate with B bank as security, the bank giving notice of deposit to the Registry. A year later the customers executed a legal mortgage (which the bank did not register) in replacement of a previously signed memorandum. Some years later, unknown to the bank, a sale was agreed to the defendants, who registered a caution giving them an equitable interest. HELD: The deposit of the land certificate with the bank gave them a *prior* equitable interest, enabling them to register their legal mortgage with priority.

However, since this case, several banks have been more cautious, and insist on registering their charge even though this incurs land registry fees for the mortgagor.

51. Notice of intended deposit. Where property is being *newly purchased with moneys to be advanced by the bank* the land certificate will not become immediately available. Consequently, the bank may require the purchaser's solicitor to lodge with the *Land Registry* "notice of intended deposit" on Form 85B or 85C as appropriate. The certificate will then be delivered direct to the bank when issued. No further notice of deposit is required.

The purchaser's authority would be obtained in writing, and he must sign Forms 85B or C prior to lodgment by the solicitor. Form 85B is used for *a first registration*; Form 85C is used where the property is *already registered land* but transfer is awaited.

52. Release of security.

(*a*) *Registered legal charge*. The bank seals Form 53 and forwards this and the charge certificate to the registry. The land certificate is then returned by the registry.

(*b*) *Withdrawal of notice of deposit*. The bank completes, under seal or hand, the back of Form 85A and forwards this and the land certificate to the registry. The land certificate is duly returned with notice of deposit deleted. The supporting bank form of legal or equitable mortgage does not form part of title.

53. Sale of registered land.

(*a*) *By bank as mortgagee*. As mortgagee a bank can exercise its power of sale in the same circumstances as with unregistered land (*see* **11** above). If the bank holds an *unregistered legal mortgage* it will usually register it and then proceed with sale. (Registration of a legal mortgage prior to sale may be unnecessary in view of the *obiter dicta* in *Re White Rose Cottage* (1965).) If an equitable mortgage under hand is held, the depositor's co-operation or the Court's authority is necessary before sale can be effected.

(*b*) *Sale by mortgagor*. If the mortgagor wishes to sell the mortgaged property over which the bank has a legal registered charge, then the bank's agreement is required and it will release its charge by sealing Form 53, although some banks have a special agreement with the Land Registry enabling them to act under hand, on a specially prepared form.

54. Procedure for completing a second legal registered mortgage. (Registration of the *second mortgage* is permissible only where the first mortgagee has *registered* his mortgage.)

(*a*) *The property is valued* and the amount outstanding on first mortgage ascertained: *see* **33** above.

(*b*) *The proprietor's title is checked* (with his permission) by obtaining an office copy of the land certificate (cost 20p), then:

(*c*) *Make a search of the land register* by completing and forwarding Form 94 (proprietor's authority required). In the absence of adverse entries then:

(*d*) *The second mortgage is completed*, and registered within 20 working days of the date of the search certificate (as in **49** above). The registry issues a *certificate of second charge*.

(*e*) *The usual enquiries are made to the first mortgagee, and notice of the second mortgage is given.*

(*f*) *Notice of the bank's interest* is given to the insurers.

55. Procedure for completing a legal registered sub-mortgage.

(*a*) Proceed as in **54**(*a*) above and *see also* **15** above.

(*b*) Obtain the *charge certificate* from the sub-mortgagor.

(*c*) *The sub-mortgage is completed* and forwarded with the charge certificate to the registry. The registry issue a *certificate of sub-charge*.

(*d*) *Notice of the sub-mortgage is given to the original mortgagor*, who is directed to make all his repayments to the bank.

(*e*) *Notice of the bank's interest* is given to the insurers.

MORTGAGES BY LIMITED COMPANIES

Companies are often required to execute legal mortgages to secure their banking accounts, and students must familiarise themselves with the necessary procedures.

56. Procedure common to all mortgages created by limited companies.

(*a*) *Examine the company's memorandum and articles* to ascertain the borrowing powers of the company and directors respectively.

(*b*) If the company has implied power to borrow it has implied power to charge its property as security, but *check whether any special procedures are necessary* and take a copy of the borrowing and charging resolution.

(*c*) *Search the Companies Registry* to ascertain whether any prior charge exists; search the local land charges register.

(*d*) *Register the charge at the Companies Registry within twenty-one days of creation* by completing and forwarding Form 47.

NOTE: Registration must be effected whether the security is by way of legal mortgage, equitable mortgage or mere deposit of the deeds or land certificate, and irrespective of whether the land is registered or unregistered.

57. Unregistered land: further registration on land charges registry necessary where a company creates a charge (other than under a floating charge) *without deposit of the deeds*, e.g. second equitable or second legal mortgage. Thus a further search of the register is also necessary to establish whether there is a land charge and also because writs, orders, etc., are not recorded at the Companies Registry.

58. Registered land: requirements as regards registration. All charges created by companies must be registered both at the Companies Registry and at the Land Registry. Speed and care are essential in view of the critical time elements applying to both registers.

59. Examination of Gazette. The *London Gazette* (or Stubbs, etc.) must be examined regularly, because entry of any subsequent charge constitutes notice to the whole world.

PROGRESS TEST 13

Unregistered land

1. State the advantages of a legal over an equitable mortgage. **(8, 11)**

2. Outline the procedure for taking a first legal mortgage from: (*a*) an individual, (*b*) a limited company. **(16, 56)**

3. What do you understand by "a bundle of title deeds"? **(17)**

4. Why does a bank search the *land charges register* after completion of its mortgage? **(23, 25)**

5. How does a mortgagee protect his priority? **(19)**

6. How can a bank protect itself when releasing deeds on loan? **(20)**

7. Distinguish between a C(*i*) and a C(*iii*) entry on the land charges register. **(22)**

8. What do you understand by "tacking"? **(24)** How can the right to "tack" affect the bank in practice? **(33(*g*))**

9. What action is necessary where direct notice of a second mortgage is received in respect of property charged to the bank? Would any different action be required if the customer had both a loan account and a credit current account? **(28)**

10. Outline the procedure for taking: (*a*) a second legal mortgage (*b*) a sub-mortgage. **(33, 35)**

Unregistered leasehold land

11. List the disadvantages attaching to leasehold land as security. **(39)**

12. How would you complete a legal mortgage over leasehold property? **(40)**

Registered land

13. Explain the meaning of "areas of compulsory registration". **(42)**

14. What do you understand by the "protection period" in respect of official searches at the Land Registry? **(47)**

15. How would you complete a legal registered mortgage? **(49)**

16. Outline the system of "notice of deposit" of the land certificate as security. **(50)**

17. Does a legal registered mortgage over registered land created by a *limited company* need to be registered at both the Land Registry *and* the Companies Registry? **(58)**

18. Do *all* charges over land created by a *limited company* need to be registered at the Companies Registry? **(56)**

CHAPTER XIV

Stocks and Shares

STOCKS AND SHARES

There are many *groups* of stocks and shares which may be offered to banks as security, e.g. British Government stocks (i.e. *Gilts*), Commonwealth and African Loans, Foreign Government Bonds, American and Canadian shares, Corporation stocks, Industrial and Commercial stocks and shares. Each of these groups may consist of several *types* of stocks and shares (now referred to as shares for convenience), e.g. *Preference, Ordinary* (i.e. *equities*), and by further *subdivision* may be either in *registered* or *bearer* form.

1. Acceptability as security. The acceptability of any of these shares as security depends mainly upon whether they are quoted on a Stock Exchange and have a ready market for sale. *Quoted shares* are usually very acceptable and are commonly deposited.

When advancing money against shares, an adequate margin should be allowed to cover any future depreciation in their value. This margin will vary, depending upon the period and amount of the advance and the nature of the shares offered as security, e.g. a greater margin will be required for mining shares than for Gilts. Periodical revaluations are essential.

2. Registered securities. Nearly all shares issued by United Kingdom companies (and the British Government) are in this form. The share owner's name is entered in the company's register of members, and he is then issued with a certificate, which is *prima facie* evidence of his title and shows the number/amount and type of shares which he owns.

The shares can only be transferred by the *registered owner* signing an *instrument of transfer* and having this delivered together with his share certificate to the issuing company, who will then register the *transferee* as the new owner, and issue him with a new certificate.

3. Bearer securities. These include share warrants and bonds to bearer. No records are maintained in the issuer's share or bond register of the name of the actual owner. Ownership is transferred by delivering the share warrants or bonds to another person, who, as bearer, becomes the new owner. Obviously the issuer cannot know the names of the owners of its bearer securities. Consequently, numbered *coupons* are attached to the share warrants or bonds so that dividends falling due may be claimed. Bearer securities are fully negotiable, but certain restrictions apply in the United Kingdom: *see* **21** below.

QUOTED SHARES

4. Quoted shares. These are the shares of *public* companies which are quoted on the London or provincial Stock Exchanges. Banks favour such shares as security, because most quoted shares are readily marketable, and thus valuation can easily be obtained from either the *Financial Times*, *The Stock Exchange Daily Official List* or from stockbrokers.

UNQUOTED SHARES

5. Unquoted shares. These are the shares of companies which are not quoted on any Stock Exchange, *being mainly shares in private companies*. But note that the shares of some public companies also have no quotation.

6. Disadvantages of unquoted shares. Unquoted shares suffer from several disadvantages, and are usually undesirable as security because:

(*a*) *Valuation is extremely difficult.* The bank will try to value such shares by using one or more of the following methods:

(*i*) Obtaining a valuation from the secretary of the company, who may be in a position to quote *recent prices* at which the shares: (1) changed hands, or (2) were valued for probate purposes.

(*ii*) Working out a price from: (1) the breakdown value of the company's assets from its balance sheet and accounts, or (2) the past dividends paid by the company.

(*b*) *Transfer will usually be restricted* by the company's articles. Consequently, the articles require careful study to ascertain:

(*i*) Whether there is any *restriction* on the shares being transferred to the bank's nominee company.

(*ii*) Whether *special formalities* are required when: (1) transferring the shares to the bank's nominee company, or (2) selling the shares. As an example of the difficulties with which a bank may be faced *see*: *Hunter* v. *Hunter* (1936). The shares often have first to be offered to existing holders. Further, the restricted market for the shares often means accepting a low price.

(*c*) *Waiver of notice of deposit* may be requested by a primary shareholder wishing to retain his business privacy.

Because of the above disadvantages, it rarely proves possible to take a *legal mortgage* over *private company* shares. However, in practice, the bank is usually willing to accept them under *equitable mortgage*, relying upon the depositor's integrity, the shares being mainly regarded as *evidence of means* but poor security.

LEGAL MORTGAGE OF REGISTERED SHARES

7. Method of creating a legal mortgage. To create a legal mortgage the shares *must be transferred into the bank's name*. To facilitate ease of control each bank has formed several *nominee companies*, the shares being transferred into the name of one of these companies. *Personal* nominees are still used by some banks.

8. Advantages of taking a legal mortgage.

(*a*) *A perfect title can be obtained.* Once the shares are transferred into the name of the bank's nominee company, it obtains a perfect title ahead of all prior equitable interests of which it was unaware at the time of transfer.

(*b*) *Ease of realisation.* Should the depositor default, the bank can realise its security without the need for co-operation.

9. Disadvantages of taking a legal mortgage.

(*a*) *Partly-paid shares.* If partly-paid shares are taken into the name of the bank's nominee company, then it remains liable for future calls.

(*b*) *Director's shareholding qualification.* A legal mortgage cannot be entertained where a *director* has only sufficient shares to comply with his company's articles regarding qualification holding.

(*c*) *Danger of liability for omissions regarding distribution of notices.* All notices sent by the issuing company will come direct to the bank, who must ensure that its customer is sent the relevant details without delay.

(*d*) *Rule in Sheffield Corporation* v. *Barclay* (1905). If the bank sends a transfer containing a *forged signature* to a company for registration, then even though it has acted in good faith, it is bound to indemnify the company for any loss.

EXAMPLE: Two trustees T and H were the registered holders of Sheffield Corporation stock. This stock was transferred by way of legal mortgage to Barclays Bank nominee. H's signature to the transfer was, however, forged by T. After the bank sold the stock H discovered the forgery, and the Corporation had to reinstate him as owner of £11,169 of stock. The Corporation claimed indemnity from the bank. HELD: By sending the forged transfer the bank had impliedly guaranteed its genuineness and must reimburse the Corporation.

NOTE: All depositors of shares as security should be required to complete the transfer in the presence of a banker who can verify their signature(s).

10. Completing the legal mortgage. The following procedure will be followed:

(*a*) *The certificate must be handed to the bank*, who will verify the holding and the name(s) of the registered owner(s).

(*b*) *The depositor(s) must execute a common form of transfer*, usually under hand (in the case of shares quoted on the Stock Exchange they must always be transferable in this manner), and the bank's nominee company is named as *transferee*.

(*c*) *As the shares are held as security for a loan*, the transfer, duly stamped, need only show a nominal consideration. (Transfers of British Government stocks are *exempt from stamp duty*.)

(*d*) *The transfer and share certificate is then forwarded to the company* for registration and issue of a new certificate in favour of the bank's nominee company. A registration fee may be payable.

(*e*) *The customer is required to sign a bank memorandum* when depositing his certificate and transfer. This is not absolutely vital for completing the security, but is *always* taken because the *memorandum outlines*: (1) the shares which have been charged, and (2) the bank's rights in relation to dividends, bonus issues and realisation etc.

11. Discharge of a legal mortgage. To discharge its mortgage the bank follows a procedure the reverse of that used when taking the security. Stamp duty and registration fee are as stated in **10** (*c*) and (*d*) above.

12. Shares charged by a company. The procedure is identical to **10** above, but the following additional steps are necessary for both *legal and equitable* mortgages:

(*a*) *Search the Companies Registry* to ensure that the shares are not already the subject of a charge, e.g. the shares may be covered in a floating charge in a debenture, in which case the bank would be unable to obtain priority if the creation of prior charges was prohibited.

(*b*) *Obtain a copy of the board of directors' resolution* authorising stated officials to sign the bank's memorandum and transfer form under *hand.* (The transfer may not always be taken if the mortgage is *equitable.*)

NOTE: The company's articles may require it to act under seal but this is extremely rare.

EQUITABLE MORTGAGE OF REGISTERED SHARES

Although an equitable mortgage is far inferior to a legal mortgage of shares, the former is more commonly accepted by banks. This is because with equitable mortgages: (*a*) the dangers are mainly *theoretical*, most depositors being persons of integrity, and (*b*) the work and cost involved are much reduced.

13. Advantages of an equitable mortgage.

(*a*) *From the depositor's viewpoint* the shares remain in his name and the costs are less than for a legal mortgage.

(*b*) *Little formality* is involved.

(*c*) *Particularly convenient* where large portfolios are involved or the customer continually changes his holdings. (An *omnibus equitable charge* is available whereby any shares of the depositor coming into the bank's hands are automatically covered as its security.)

14. Disadvantages of an equitable mortgage.

(*a*) *The bank's future priority cannot be safeguarded* by giving notice of its *equitable interest* to the company, as by the CA 1948, s. 117, the company is not bound to recognise *any trust*.

(*b*) *The bank's equitable title* is defeated by a *prior equitable title*, even if it has no notice of this title when taking its security. For example, the depositor may, unknown to the bank, be a trustee, in which case the beneficiary's *prior* equitable title prevails over the bank's equitable title. Consequently, care must be exercised when accepting shares in joint names, because the holders may be trustees. (The certificate will not, of course, indicate this fact.)

Unfortunately, this defect can only be overcome by taking a *legal mortgage before knowledge of the prior equitable title.*

EXAMPLE: C, the apparent owner of debentures, charged them to the bank under equitable mortgage. On discovering that C was not the owner but a trustee, the bank requested C to transfer the debentures into its name. C complied. HELD: The bank could not obtain priority over the earlier equitable interest, for it was *not* acting *bona fide*. It knew that the earlier interest existed: *Coleman* v. *London County & Westminster Bank* (1916).

(*c*) *If the customer defaults and refuses to comply with his undertaking contained in the memorandum* to complete a legal mortgage, then the bank will have to apply to the Court for an order for sale. (If a *blank transfer* is held this difficulty is overcome: *see* **16** below.)

(*d*) *Bonus shares* and other notices *are forwarded to the depositor* (*see* **17** below).

(*e*) *The depositor may obtain a duplicate certificate* and dispose of his shares (*see* **18** below).

(*f*) *The company may retain a lien* over its shares (*see* **20** below).

15. Completing an equitable mortgage. A simple deposit of the certificate as security constitutes an equitable mortgage. However, in addition to obtaining the certificate, the bank *always* requires the depositor to sign its memorandum of deposit. This sets out the security terms whereby the depositor undertakes, *inter alia*: (*a*) to complete a legal mortgage when called upon to do so, (*b*) to charge bonus issues in order to maintain the security value. Occasionally a *blank transfer* is also taken from the depositor to strengthen the bank's position: *see* **16** below.

METHODS OF STRENGTHENING THE BANK'S POSITION AS EQUITABLE MORTGAGEE

16. Holding a blank transfer. A blank transfer (often more appropriately referred to as an *undated unstamped transfer*) is a *partly completed transfer* which the depositor signs and lodges at the bank, with his share certificate and memorandum. The transfer is left *undated*, and sometimes the transferee's name is also left blank.

If the depositor defaults, the bank has an *implied* right to fill the blanks, stamp up the transfer and effect a sale of the shares. The bank's memorandum *expressly* confirms that this right is exercisable *at any time*. The holding of blank transfers without registration suffers from two defects:

(*a*) *Once the bank learns of a prior equitable interest*, e.g. of a beneficiary under a trust, *it cannot register a legal mortgage* and so defeat the earlier claims: *Coleman* v. *London County & Westminster Bank* (1916).

(*b*) If a transfer by *deed* is necessary (which can now apply *only* in respect of *partly-paid shares* and where the company's Articles require transfer by deed: Stock Transfer Act 1963) the holding of a *blank transfer* is of no avail, as a deed must be complete on delivery: *see Powell* v. *London & Provincial Bank* (1893). (If a *deed* is necessary, then it could be completed, dated and stamped and *held unregistered*.)

17. Memorandum covers bonus issues. If a company makes a bonus issue (sometimes called a *scrip* issue) it issues free shares to its existing shareholders. The certificate covering the bonus issue is duly forwarded to the *registered holder*. Where the bank has only an *equitable mortgage* over shares, then its security position is detrimentally affected when a bonus issue is made *unless* the new certificate is deposited as security. For example, if a company makes a *one* for *one* bonus issue, then the value of the bank's security over these shares will drop by approximately half.

A careful watch must be kept for notice of any bonus issues affecting the bank's security. The depositor is then called upon to honour his undertaking in the bank's memorandum to deposit the additional shares as security.

18. Protection against depositor fraudulently transferring his shares. Unknown to the bank, a depositor may inform the issuing company that he has lost his share certificate so that he can obtain a duplicate certificate and dispose of his shares, *see: Rainford* v. *James Keith & Blackman Co. Ltd.* (1905).

Before he can obtain a duplicate certificate the company will require an indemnity, and consequently fraud is rare. Nevertheless, if a successful fraud was perpetrated and the depositor disposed of his shares the bank would be left holding a worthless piece of paper. The bank can always prevent such fraud by serving a stop notice (formerly known as a notice in lieu of *distringas*) (*see* below) on the company after completing its equitable mortgage. This is rarely done in practice, because the process is cumbersome and the risk is remote.

19. Stop Notice—Notice in lieu of distringas. *In exceptional circumstances*, e.g. where the bank feels that a depositor of shares might fraudulently attempt to transfer them, a bank will serve a stop notice on the company. This has the effect that the company must give the bank eight days' notice of any attempted transfer of the shares, and enables the bank to obtain an injunction restraining transfer. A stop notice is obtained by filing at the Central Office of the Supreme Court a sworn affidavit of the bank's equitable interest. A copy of the affidavit and duplicate notice is then served on the company.

20. Effect of giving notice of deposit. When taking an equitable mortgage of *unquoted* or *partly-paid* shares some banks give notice to the company that the shares have been deposited as security. The company usually returns the notice, stating that by virtue of CA 1948, s. 117, it cannot enter notice of any *trust* in respect of its shares. However, the giving of such notice is useful *and serves three main purposes*:

(*a*) *If the company, by its articles, retains a lien on its shares for moneys owing from the shareholder*, then the sum becomes *fixed* on receipt of the bank's notice. *Future* amounts attaching under the company's lien rank *after* the bank's lien: *Bradford Banking Co.* v. *Briggs* (1886). (It is a rule of the Stock Exchange that a company *cannot* claim a lien over *fully paid* quoted shares.)

(*b*) A reply may be received *that the depositor is no longer a shareholder*, i.e. he may have obtained a duplicate certificate and sold his shares.

(*c*) The company may *unofficially* record equitable interests and inform the bank of any of which they know.

BEARER SECURITIES

These have already been briefly described: *see* **3** above. *Bearer securities include:* bearer bonds, bearer scrip, share warrants to bearer, debentures to bearer and also American and Canadian share warrants.

21. Former restrictions attaching to bearer securities. The Exchange Control Act 1947, no longer applies and there is now no need for *bearer securities* to remain only in the hands of an authorised depository.

22. Negotiable aspect of bearer securities. Bearer securities are *fully negotiable*, and thus provide an excellent security, because a bank taking the securities in good faith and for value obtains a *perfect title*, even though the pledgor has a defective one.

EXAMPLE: A stockbroker pledged to his bank foreign bearer bonds which were in fact the property of a client. The broker absconded, and the bank realised these securities. HELD: The client had no right to the value of the bonds, as these were clearly negotiable instruments, which the bank had taken in good faith and for value: *London Joint Stock Bank* v. *Simmons* (1892).

23. Bearer bonds as security. Foreign government *bearer bonds* are the commonest *bearer* securities deposited with banks as security. As with all types of bearer securities, a mere delivery of the bonds as security is sufficient, i.e. they are *pledged.*

NOTE: (1) No transfer form is necessary and no stamp duty is payable. (2) The usual bank memorandum is completed and signed by the pledgor. (3) The bonds must be undefaced, correctly stamped and have all unmatured coupons attached. (4) Under the terms of its memorandum the bank can sell the bonds immediately the pledgor defaults. (5) The bank obtains a perfect title to bonds taken in *good faith and for value.*

AMERICAN AND CANADIAN SECURITIES

These are the shares of American and Canadian industrial and commercial concerns.

24. Treated as bearer securities. Most of these shares are issued in favour of a *registered holder*, but the certificates have a *combined form of transfer and power of attorney* on the reverse. Once the form of transfer on the reverse *is endorsed in blank*, the shares are treated as *bearer securities*, being transferable by *mere delivery*. The *holder* is then enabled at any time to register his own name as the owner by lodging the certificate.

By *usage* shares in this form have become *quasi-negotiable.*

25. Not fully negotiable. It must be stressed that these shares are *not* fully negotiable, because unless the holder's name has been registered, he cannot sue in his own name. Consequently, the bank can only be 100 per cent certain of obtaining a perfect security *by taking a legal mortgage*, i.e. by registering its own bank nominees as the holder.

26. Shares in good marking names. To constitute a good delivery on the Stock Exchange the shares have to be in a "good marking name" and be regularly endorsed. A list of good marking names can be found in the *Stock Exchange Year Book*, and these include brokers, finance houses, banks and certain bank nominee companies. Most shares are in good marking names. The marking names receive the dividends and pay them over to the holders of the certificates upon application through authorised depositaries.

27. Taking the shares as security.

(*a*) *If the shares are in a good marking name and endorsed.* The depositor must sign the usual *equitable mortgage*. Being in a transferable state, the security is then readily saleable should the depositor default.

(*b*) *If the shares are not in a good marking name but in the depositor's own name and endorsed.* The bank is *usually* willing to accept an *equitable mortgage* as in (*a*) above. On the depositor's default it would register its own nominee and then proceed with sale.

(*c*) *If the shares are neither in a good marking name nor in the depositor's name.* The bank requires the shares to be transferred into its nominees' name, i.e. a *legal mortgage* is obtained. A memorandum is also taken.

NOTE: (1) The endorsement must be *exactly* as on the face of the certificate, *including titles*. (2) The endorsement of an *individual holder* should be *witnessed* and *guaranteed* by a bank or member of a stock exchange. (3) The endorsement of a limited company, corporation, society or institution must include its signed guarantee that all papers necessary to ensure transfer have been filed with the registrars or transfer agents. (4) The certificates should be in *denominations* which will be accepted on the London Stock Exchange. (5) *On transfer*, certificates in *marking names* must show that the latest dividend has been collected.

28. Bank's position in the event of a prior equitable claim. What is the bank's position if a depositor of security turns out to be a *trustee* and the bank are faced with the *prior equitable claims of a beneficiary*? Presuming the bank have obeyed Exchange Control regulations and also acted in good faith and for value, then:

(*a*) If the shares have been registered into the *bank's marking name* it has *an unassailable legal title*.

(*b*) *If the shares are in "good marking name"* (other than the bank's) *and endorsed*, then the bank *may* be able to retain the shares, as the Market regards them as *bearer* securities, *but this seems unlikely*, as the bank has *not got a legal title*. The position is not settled, however.

(*c*) *If the shares are in the depositor's name and endorsed* the bank must give up its security, because the beneficiary's prior equitable title defeats its own.

NOTE: If a *stockbroker* deposits certificates as security, being correctly endorsed by individuals or marking names, it appears that even if they actually belong to one of his clients the bank will obtain a good title when acting in good faith and for value. For, by depositing *blank endorsed shares* with the stockbroker the client is estopped from denying his authority to deal with them: *Fuller* v. *Glyn Mills, Currie & Co.* (1914).

MISCELLANEOUS SECURITIES

29. British Government stocks on the Post Office register. *Investors of small sums* are able to purchase Government stocks through the P.O. Savings Department at a reduced commission rate. Note that this is a *different register* from the Bank of England Government stock register. Stocks on the P.O. register may be mortgaged as follows:

(*a*) *Legal mortgage.* Completed by transferring the shares into the name of the bank's nominee company (special P.O. transfer form required).

(*b*) *Equitable mortgage.* The stock certificate is deposited, together with an amended memorandum of deposit and a *signed undated application form for sale*.

30. National Savings Certificates/Premium Bonds.

(*a*) *A legal mortgage cannot be taken* over either of these securities.

(*b*) *Equitable mortgage.* The *certificates* or *bonds* are deposited, together with an amended memorandum of deposit and a *signed undated application form for repayment.*

NOTE: In respect of equitable mortgages over the securities mentioned in **29** and **30** above the bank is dependent upon the *integrity* of the depositor. *The depositor could undermine the bank's position by:* (1) obtaining duplicate certificates, and disposing of his securities, or (2) nominating a person to receive his holdings on death. (In the case of Premium Bonds the personal representatives of the deceased may claim repayment.)

31. Unit trusts as security. Registered fixed and flexible unit trust sub-units provide a satisfactory security.

(*a*) *Legal mortgage.* The procedure is as outlined in **10** above.

(*b*) *Equitable mortgage.* (*i*) The depositor is required to sign (but leave *undated*) the form of *renunciation* on the reverse of the sub-unit certificate, (*ii*) the *certificate is lodged* at the bank with the usual memorandum of deposit, (*iii*) *notice of deposit* is given to the managers. Thereafter the bank can, at any time, date and forward the sub-unit certificate to the managers, who purchase them and remit the proceeds. An *alternative* method of creating an equitable mortgage is to hold the sub-unit certificate with a *signed undated transfer form* until registration is required.

32. Rights issues on shares in the name of the bank's nominees. The notice of rights is received by the bank, and instructions must be obtained from the customer as to whether he wishes the bank to take up or sell the rights. If the bank *failed to take any action*, e.g. because it could not contact its customer, then the customer would be able to claim the market value of the rights if these were forfeited. Nowadays many companies sell the rights on the holder's behalf if no action is taken.

NOTE: A rights issue is usually offered to existing shareholders to enable them to buy additional shares at a preferential price.

PROGRESS TEST 14

1. Distinguish between registered shares and bearer securities. **(2, 3)**

2. Why is a legal mortgage over shares superior to an equitable mortgage over shares? **(8, 14)** Why, then, is the latter more commonly accepted?

3. Outline the general procedure for completing a legal mortgage and an equitable mortgage over registered shares. **(10, 15)**

4. How would the bank's position be affected where a company whose shares are charged to the bank under equitable mortgage makes a bonus issue? **(17)**

5. What is a "blank transfer"? Why may such a transfer be taken with an equitable mortgage? **(16)**

6. Outline the decision in *London Joint Stock Bank* v. *Simmons*. **(22)**

7. What is an American share certificate? Describe any similarities to bearer securities. **(24, 25)**

8. What do you understand by a "good marking name"? **(26)**

9. How are American and Canadian shares taken as security? **(27)**

10. What is the bank's position where, after taking an American share certificate as security (in good marking name and endorsed), it finds out that there is a prior equitable title? Would your answer differ if the good marking name was the bank's own nominee company? **(28)**

CHAPTER XV

Other Securities and Facilities (Consumer Credit Act Considerations)

LIFE POLICIES

1. Advantages as security.

(*a*) *Assignment of a policy* can be effected simply and a *perfect title* easily obtained.

(*b*) Policies of the type accepted as security *have an increasing value* provided the premiums are duly paid.

(*c*) *The security can be realised immediately* the assignor defaults.

(*d*) The policy moneys fall due *immediately the assured dies* (or at earlier maturity).

NOTE: A policy is a particularly useful cover for advances made to sole traders or professional men where otherwise on death difficulty might occur in respect of repayment.

2. Disadvantages as security.

(*a*) *Insurance contracts are uberrimae fidei* (of the utmost good faith); therefore non-disclosure by the assured enables the insurer to avoid the contract: *London Assurance* v. *Mansel* (1879).

(*b*) *The proposer must have an insurable interest* in the life assured, otherwise the contract is void.

An insurable interest is:

(*i*) *Presumed:* On own life; husband on life of wife (and vice versa); creditor on life of debtor.

(*ii*) *Not presumed:* Between parents and children. (Unless a pecuniary interest exists.)

(*c*) The policy may be avoided *because of a breach of covenant* by the assured.

NOTE: In respect of (*a*), (*b*) and (*c*), once the company has arranged the policy and accepted notice of the bank's assignment, it will rarely attempt to avoid the contract.

(*d*) *The premiums may fall in arrears.* If so, they will usually be deducted from any surrender value payable. *Further*, by virtue of a clause in the assignment the bank may debit its customer's account to meet outstanding premiums. Usually the bank requires premiums to be paid by standing order *or* premium receipts produced.

3. Types of policy. Two main types of policy are acceptable as security:

(*a*) *Whole life policy*, i.e. effected to provide a capital sum, with or without profits, in the event of the assured's death.

(*b*) *Endowment policy*, i.e. effected to provide a capital sum, with or without profits, on a certain maturity date or on the assured's death, whichever occurs first.

4. Suicide. Suicide is no longer a crime in English law: Suicide Act 1961. *Nevertheless*, the bank should examine the policy to ascertain whether or not a "suicide clause" is included which would affect the value of its security. Normally because of the inclusion of a protective clause in the policy *assignees for value* (e.g. the bank) may recover the policy proceeds in full in the event of the assured's *sane or insane* suicide.

5. Legal assignment of life policies. The Policies of Assurance Act 1867, lays down the following procedure for completing a legal assignment:

(*a*) *A written assignment*, either: (*i*) *endorsed on the policy*, or (*ii*) *by separate instrument*; must be completed and delivered by the policy owner(s) as required in the Schedule.

(*b*) *Written notice of the assignment*, quoting the date and nature of the instrument *must be given to the insurer*, who must duly acknowledge receipt.

6. Equitable assignment. This is achieved, for example, (*a*) by depositing the policy informally as security with or without a memorandum, or (*b*) where notice of assignment is not given to the insurer.

7. Advantages of legal over equitable assignments. The advantages are such that *a bank will rarely entertain taking an equitable assignment.*

(*a*) *Legal assignment: advantages.* The assignee *can*: (*i*) sue on the policy in his own name; (*ii*) realise the security without the assignor's aid.

(*b*) *Equitable assignment: disadvantages.* The assignee *cannot*:

(*i*) sue on the policy unless joined by the assignor; (*ii*) realise the security without the assignor's or the Court's assistance.

8. Married Women's Property Act 1882. By virtue of the Act (s. 11), a policy taken out by: (*a*) a husband on his own life for the benefit of his wife and/or children, or (*b*) a wife on her own life for the benefit of her husband and/or children; *creates* a trust in favour of the beneficiaries. If the bank accepts such a policy as security, care must be exercised to see that *all parties join in the bank's form of assignment*. (A woman depositor may need to be independently advised.)

NOTE: (1) If: (*a*) the persons are not *positively named*, or (*b*) any present (or future) children *under the age of* eighteen, are named as beneficiaries; then the bank will not be willing to accept the policy (as it stands) as security. *This is because: under* (*a*) there is a danger that a different beneficiary will become entitled; *under* (*b*) the bank cannot obtain a valid assignment from a minor. (2) *Distinction must be made between:* (*a*) a policy in the form mentioned above, attaching under the Act, and (*b*) a policy taken out (for example) by a husband *on his wife's life for his own benefit*. In this latter instance only the husband's signature is necessary on the assignment.

9. Taking the security.

(*a*) *Preliminary enquiries, etc.* The bank should satisfy itself that:

(*i*) The insurance company is *reputable*.

(*ii*) The proceeds are payable in *sterling* in the United Kingdom.

(*iii*) The policy has attained a *surrender value*.

(*iv*) The policy contains *no onerous clauses* which are likely to prejudice the security, e.g. suicide, restrictive travel, etc.

(*v*) The *age of the assured has been admitted*.

(*b*) *The assignment of the policy is completed* by executing a legal mortgage under seal. The policy is retained with the mortgage.

(*c*) *Notice of assignment*. This is given to the insurance company and a registration fee may be payable (*see Bankers' Almanac*). The duplicate notice is returned, duly signed, as an acknowledgment. *Simultaneously* the company will be asked: (*i*) whether it has notice of any prior assignment over the policy, (*ii*) to confirm that the premiums are paid to date, (*iii*) to supply the current surrender value.

(*d*) *Effect of giving notice.*

(*i*) Enables bank to sue in own name.

(*ii*) Binds the company to pay the bank.

(*iii*) Ensures priority for the bank over subsequent assignees (from the date of registration).

(*iv*) Enables the bank to acquire priority over earlier assignees *who have not given notice* to the insurance company; *provided* that the bank are not under *actual or constructive notice* of the earlier assignment.

EXAMPLE: A lender (assignee) accepted without further enquiry that the borrower (assignor) had left his policy at home. HELD: Priority attached to a prior *equitable* assignment which had *not been registered*, because the later assignee was under *constructive notice* of the prior assignment: *Spencer* v. *Clarke* (1878).

10. Releasing the security to the assignor.

(*a*) *Legal assignment.* The bank reassigns the mortgage to the assignor under seal. The discharged mortgage forms part of title and *must* be retained by the assignor together with the policy. (Consequently, a separate mortgage form is usually executed initially for each policy.)

(*b*) *Equitable assignment.* No reassignment is necessary, and the memorandum need only be cancelled. The policy is returned to the assignor.

Notice is given to the insurance company that the bank's interest is terminated.

11. Enforcing or obtaining payment of the security. By virtue of the clauses contained in its form of assignment, the bank may, immediately the customer defaults, sell or surrender the policy or convert it into a paid-up one.

12. Procedure for enforcing or obtaining payment is as follows:

(*a*) *If a legal assignment exists, and:*

(*i*) *Life assured dies.* (1) The assured's death certificate must be produced to the insurance company. (2) The latter's receipt must be completed and submitted with the policy and assignment (undischarged), together with bonus notices and last premium receipt.

(*ii*) *Policy matures.* The company usually notifies the bank before the maturity date. The bank proceeds as in (*a*) (*i*) (2) above.

(*iii*) *Customer defaults.* The bank may then surrender the policy; sell the policy; convert the policy to a paid-up one (unlikely unless the maturity date is near); let the assignor borrow from the company on the policy in order to repay his overdraft. (The bank normally surrenders the policy if the customer defaults.)

(*b*) *If an equitable assignment exists, and:*

(*i*) *Life assured dies.* Evidence of death required (as above). The personal representatives must join with the bank on the insurance company's receipt.

(*ii*) *Policy matures.* The assured must join with the bank on the insurance company's receipt.

(*iii*) *Customer defaults and refuses to co-operate.* A difficult position arises; application would need to be made to the Court for an order for sale or foreclosure.

13. Notice of second mortgage over bank's security. Once the bank receives such notice it should proceed as it would in respect of a similar notice for unregistered land: *see* XIII, **28**.

SHIPS

The legal requirements relating to: (*a*) registration and other matters concerning ships, (*b*) creation of mortgages over ships; are laid down in the Merchant Shipping Act 1894.

14. Registration. Every British ship (with the exception of certain small vessels) *must be registered at a port of registry*: ss. 2–3. Before registration can be effected, certain information regarding the ship's construction, tonnage, ownership, etc., must be furnished to the registrar.

NOTE: (1) The registrar issues a *certificate of registry* which must always accompany the ship. (2) A ship cannot be registered *until construction is completed.* (3) The name of the *port of registry* must be painted on the ship's stern.

15. Ownership. The property of a ship is divided up into sixty-four *shares*. Each share may be held jointly by up to five persons. It is common for all sixty-four shares to be owned by one person or corporation. To effect a transfer of a ship a bill of sale must be drawn up in statutory form.

16. Valuation for security purposes. This is extremely difficult, as due allowance must be made for depreciation, changing market demand, etc. Frequent revaluations are necessary. As the bank usually allows a considerable margin between the *valuation* and the *amount advanced*, a costly professional valuation by a marine surveyor is rarely required.

Most ships are registered at Lloyd's Register of Shipping, and consequently the bank may obtain therefrom additional information regarding the ship. The Lloyd's *survey certificate* can be inspected. (Lloyd's may refuse to renew the classification of a ship unless the vessel is rendered fit as required by the periodical survey.)

17. Insurance of a ship. This is a complex matter calling for expert advice. Consequently, when a mortgage is contemplated the bank usually requires that the ship's policies be forwarded to its brokers, who will ensure that all known risks have been covered.

The bank requires the assured to endorse the policies in blank and lodge them as security. It will then, as assignees, give notice of its interest to the insurers. The latter will be asked to acknowledge the notice and confirm that there is no prior interest. (The bank should check that the various premiums are duly paid.)

18. Legal mortgage over a ship (or a share therein). The Act stipulates that a mortgage must be drawn up as detailed in the First Schedule. Two kinds of mortgage forms are available (obtainable through HM Stationery Office). The bank usually requires to use the one which *secures a running current account*, i.e. to be executed by *either*: (*a*) individuals or joint owners (Form 12), *or* (*b*) a corporate body (Form 12A).

NOTE: (1) Various details of the ship must be entered on the mortgage deed, and there is space to record general clauses, e.g. consideration, continuation, etc. (2) The mortgage deed does not incur stamp duty. (3) The mortgage is usually supported by a memorandum setting out additional clauses, e.g. agreement: (*a*) to retain the Lloyd's classification, (*b*) to repay the bank on demand, etc.

19. Registration of mortgage at port of registry.

(*a*) *Registration of mortgage.* To achieve priority over later mortgages created over the same ship it is necessary for the bank to *register their mortgage* at the port of registry immediately it is created.

Priority depends upon the *date of registration* and *not* on the *date of the mortgage*: s. 33.

(*b*) *Unregistered mortgage* remains valid, *but loses priority* in respect of any later mortgagee who registers (even where the latter registers after notice of the prior mortgage).

(*c*) *Memorandum of registration.* The registrar issues this upon registration. (A registration fee is payable: Merchant Shipping (Fees) Regulations 1971).

(*d*) *Searches at the port registry.* To ascertain that no outstanding charges are entered on the register an *official search* is obtained before the mortgage is executed and then a *personal inspection* made after registration.

20. Registration of mortgage at Companies Registry. Where a mortgage is executed by a *limited company*, it *must* be registered at the Companies Registry within twenty-one days: CA 1948, s. 95.

21. Lending on loan account. Registration of a *subsequent mortgage* at the port of registry is *probably* deemed notice to the whole world. Consequently, it is better for the bank as first mortgagee to lend on *loan account*, so that if it fails to stop the customer's account because the subsequent mortgagee does not give direct notice of his mortgage it will not be detrimentally affected by the application of the Rule in Clayton's Case.

In practice, the likelihood of a subsequent mortgagee failing to give direct notice is remote, and the bank may be prepared to lend on *fluctuating current account* for good customers, unless term lending with fixed repayments is contemplated.

22. Realisation of security by bank. If the customer defaults the bank has power to: (*a*) sell the ship or share therein, or (*b*) take possession in order to recoup itself out of profits. (This is rarely if ever resorted to.)

23. Discharge of mortgage. The mortgagee deed, duly receipted, must be produced to the port registry for cancellation of the entry.

24. Partly completed ship as security. A *legal* mortgage cannot be effected until a ship is *completed and registered.*

A limited company purchaser may conveniently charge the unfinished ship as security by executing a *floating charge*. This "equitable" charge will only attach over the completed stages *conveyed* to it by the builder. Consequently, if the builder retains the whole title until final completion the purchaser cannot effect a charge.

The charge must be registered at the Companies Registry within twenty-one days: CA 1948, s. 95.

NOTE: An agreement to execute a legal mortgage *when the ship is constructed* will be contained in the floating charge.

25. Disadvantages of ships as security.

(*a*) Difficult to value.
(*b*) Depreciate heavily.
(*c*) Often difficult to sell should the need arise.
(*d*) Mortgages are postponed to maritime liens, and it is often impossible to insure against all liens.

Nevertheless, it is well recognised that the shipping industry deserves special treatment, and banks endeavour to lend moneys in order to: (*i*) help supply *working capital* for day-to-day operations, (*ii*) help customers *replace* old or worn out ships (particularly small coastal vessels, e.g. trawlers). Normally repayment of loans for replacement purposes can be arranged over medium or long term.

AGRICULTURAL CHARGES

Under the Agricultural Credits Act 1928, a farmer (not being an incorporated company or society) may create an agricultural charge over *all or any of his farming stock and other agricultural assets*, the charge being either *fixed or floating, or both.*

26. Fixed charge. The property (i.e. farming stock or other agricultural assets) *must be specified in the charge*, but may include: (*a*) the progeny of livestock specified therein; (*b*) any agricultural plant substituted for that specified therein.

NOTE: "Farming stock" means: crops, horticultural produce, livestock (including poultry and bees) and their progeny and produce, seeds, manures, agricultural vehicles, machinery, other plant, agricultural tenant's fixtures (including those removable by law). "Other agricultural assets" means: A tenant's right to compensation under the Agricultural Holdings Act 1923.

27. Floating charge. The property affected is the farming stock and other agricultural assets *from time to time belonging to the farmer*, or such part thereof as is mentioned in the charge.

28. Effect of a fixed charge.

(*a*) *Farmer's obligations.*

(*i*) *Proceeds of sale.* Although the farmer has power to sell any property comprised under the fixed charge, he must pay the proceeds to the bank in discharge of his liabilities (unless the bank waives this requirement).

(*ii*) *Insurance proceeds* (as in (*i*) above). The farmer must pay to the bank any insurance or compensation moneys received in respect of the property.

(*b*) *Bank's rights.* By virtue of the Act (s. 6(1)), the bank's security clauses will empower it to demand repayment from the farmer and on default to appoint a receiver, who may be required to manage or sell the property in order to reduce the farmer's debt.

29. Effect of a floating charge.

(*a*) *Farmer's obligations.* These are similar to those under the fixed charge, *with the exception that* moneys which he receives under proceeds of sale, insurance or compensation may be expended in the purchase of farming stock, which on purchase *becomes subject to the charge.*

(*b*) *Floating charge becomes fixed.* This occurs:

(*i*) Upon the making of a receiving order against the farmer.

(*ii*) Upon the farmer's death.

(*iii*) Upon dissolution of partnership (where the property charged is partnership property).

(*iv*) Upon notice being given by the bank in conformity with the security clauses, e.g. (1) when the farmer: (*a*) enters into a composition, (*b*) breaks conditions or covenants, (*c*) fails to repay on demand; *or* (2) when execution is levied against the farmer's property.

NOTE: To protect its position where one of the above events occurs, the bank would need to act *immediately* by demanding repayment and on default *appointing a receiver.*

30. Bank's form of charge. All the obligations, etc., previously mentioned will be outlined in the charge form, together with covenants whereby the farmer agrees to:

(*a*) Keep the property in good *repair.*
(*b*) Keep the property fully *insured* and premiums paid.
(*c*) *Cultivate and manage* his farm in a good and proper manner.
(*d*) Allow the bank to *inspect* his property.

31. Procedure for taking the charge.

(*a*) *Searches.* The bank completes form AC6 (i.e. application for official search), and forwards this to the Land Charges Registry, who issue an official search that indicates thereon whether any prior charges are in existence.

(*b*) *Execution of charge.* The farmer must execute the bank's form of charge under seal. No stamp duty is payable.

(*c*) *Registration of charge.* The charge requires registration within seven days of execution. This is effected by the bank completing form AC1 (which requires the farmer's signature) and lodging it at the Land Charges Registry.

(*d*) *Priority in respect of charges.* Depends upon the date of registration; an unregistered charge is void except against the farmer.

(*e*) *Insurance.* The bank may require that its interest be notified to the Insurance Company(ies).

NOTE: After registration the bank institutes a further search which should only reveal its own charge; it is then protected for all future advances on current account until such time as it receives direct notice of a further charge or until it makes another search which reveals a further charge.

32. Advantages of agricultural charges.

(*a*) *Easy and cheap* to take.

(*b*) A *fixed* charge cannot be executed over property comprised in a *floating* charge.

(*c*) *Speedy action can be taken* if the farmer incurs losses.

33. Disadvantages of agricultural charges.

(*a*) A farmer's *credit could be curtailed* if he completes a charge.

(*b*) *Valuation* of a farmer's property may prove both *difficult* and *lengthy*.

(*c*) A farmer may *wrongfully dispose of property* covered by the charge.

(*d*) The security is invariably run-down and in poor condition by the time the receiver is appointed.

(*e*) Rent, rates or taxes normally *attach in priority to the charge*: s. 8(7).

(*f*) If a farmer becomes bankrupt within three months of executing a fixed and/or floating charge, then, unless he was solvent when creating it, the charge is only available *for advances made after it was executed*: s. 8(5). Therefore the Rule in Clayton's Case *cannot aid the bank*: compare XI, **48**.

(*g*) The receiver may need to run the farm for a while after his appointment and this brings onerous tasks and obligations.

Because of the particular disadvantage of **33**(a) few agricultural charges are in fact taken.

34. Release of charge. Form AC3 is completed and forwarded to the registry.

MILK MARKETING BOARD CHARGE

The Board buys all milk from the producers and then sells it to the distributors and manufacturers. As the producer is paid on or about the 20th of the month following delivery, he is thereby in a position to offer as security a charge over moneys due or to become due under his present or future contracts.

35. Procedure for completing the charge.

(*a*) *Producer's contract.* The producer's contract, which must be registered with and countersigned by the Board, should be examined by the bank and retained.

(*b*) *Bank charge.* The producer must execute the charge form which refers to present and future contracts.

(*c*) *Notice to the Board.* Notice of execution of the charge (which also contains the irrevocable authority of the producer authorising payment of moneys to the bank) is given to the Board by the bank. The Board are required to acknowledge receipt and thereafter to forward any contract moneys direct to the bank.

NOTE: (1) If the producer is a *limited company* the charge must also be *registered at the Companies Registry* within twenty-one days of creation pursuant to CA 1948, s. 95 (i.e. as a charge on book debts. (2) *The bank should institute a search* to ascertain that the producer has not executed an agricultural charge, as payments due under a milk contract would be attached thereunder. (3) *The value of the security* can never exceed the payments owing by the Board, i.e. for up to a maximum of seven weeks' deliveries. (4) *Farmer's bankruptcy.* If the farmer becomes bankrupt the *equitable* charge (outlined) becomes void as regards moneys due but not paid under *further contracts* (being *unspecified*) *which have been arranged*: *see* **40** below.

Consequently, where new contracts are arranged the bank should preserve its position by requiring execution of a *new charge*.

36. Release of security. The charge, being equitable, need only be cancelled. Notification is given to all parties that the bank's interest has ceased.

ASSIGNMENT OF DEBTS

37. Existing debt. An assignment of an existing debt may be either legal or equitable. The value of such an assignment depends upon: (*a*) the ability of the debtor to pay (status enquiry needed); (*b*) the right of set-off which the debtor has against the assignor.

38. Legal assignment. In order to create a legal assignment, the provisions of the LPA 1925, s. 136, must be fulfilled, i.e.

(*a*) The assignment must be in writing and signed by the assignor.

(*b*) Notice of the assignment in writing, must be given to the debtor.

(*c*) The assignment must be absolute and not by way of charge only.

39. Equitable assignment. An equitable assignment is not a suitable security for a bank, but would arise for instance, if (*a*) it was not in writing, or (*b*) notice was not given to the debtor.

40. Avoidance of registration as bill of sale. A banker will not wish to register an assignment as a *bill of sale*, and consequently will only accept as security assignments *not requiring registration* (*see* BA 1914, s. 43), i.e.:

(*a*) assignments of *existing debts* due from *specified* debtors, or

(*b*) assignments of debts *accruing due* under *specified contracts*.

A *general assignment* of debts would not be entertained because of the need for registration.

41. Procedure for executing a legal assignment.

(*a*) *The assignor is required to execute a form of assignment* (not purporting to be by way of charge only).

(*b*) *Notice of assignment is given to the debtor*, who is asked *to acknowledge its receipt* and confirm: (*i*) the *amount* of the debt; (*ii*) whether he as any right of *set-off* against the assignor; (*iii*) whether he has received *notice of any prior assignments*.

NOTE: By giving notice of the assignment to the debtor, the assignee ensures that: (1) *He retains priority* over any subsequent assignee giving notice. (2) He will only be affected by any right to set-off *existing when the debtor received notice.* (3) *The debt will not pass to the assignor's trustee in bankruptcy* under BA 1914, s. 38. ("order or disposition"). (4) *He can sue on the debt* in his own name. (5) *He must be paid* the sum owed by the debtor.

As previously mentioned, a banker would never be interested in a *general assignment* of debts. Likewise, he would only be interested in taking a *specific assignment of an existing debt* as a last resort when no tangible security was available. In such a case the above procedure is followed. The usual security clauses are inserted in the charge, e.g. covering all liabilities owed to the bank on a continuing basis.

42. Assignment of book debts by a limited company. In addition to the foregoing procedure, an assignment by a *limited company* must be registered at the Companies Registry within twenty-one days of its creation, *as a charge on book debts*: CA 1948, s. 95. Failure to register will avoid the assignment against the liquidator or any creditor of the company:

EXAMPLE: A limited company addressed a letter to the Ministry of Fuel and Power which: (1) referred to a specific contract between themselves, and authorised the Ministry to remit all moneys due thereunder to their bankers, whose receipt was to be sufficient discharge; (2) stipulated that the instruction was *irrevocable* unless the bank agreed to its cancellation in writing. The bank obtained acknowledgment, and the same procedure was followed when the contract was extended. The company went into liquidation when the amount owing under the contract was £30,000. The liquidator contended that the letter was void for want of registration at the Companies Registry, as a charge on book debts. The Court upheld his contention: *Re Kent & Sussex Sawmills Ltd.* (1947).

Before taking the assignment a search at the Companies Registry should be made to ensure there are no prior charges, e.g. debentures, in existence.

43. Assignment of a future debt growing due under a contract. Occasions may arise where a *company* customer requires an advance to finance a contract and the main security it can offer is an assignment over moneys to become periodically due under the contract.

Three legal points emerge prior to consideration of the proposition:

(*a*) *Only an equitable assignment is possible of a future debt.* Nevertheless, the bank would proceed as for a legal assignment of an existing debt; equity will enforce *specific performance* provided valuable consideration is present.

(*b*) *If a debenture incorporating a floating charge* has been (or is being) taken from the company an assignment would further strengthen the position, as, unlike a floating charge, it is not overruled by preferential creditors in the event of liquidation.

(*c*) Such an assignment *requires registration at the Companies Registry*.

NOTE: (1) The security will be wholly or partly worthless if the customer cannot complete the contract. (2) The debtor must prove good for his debt in the future. (*See also* VIII, **71–78**.)

DISCOUNTING BILLS

The branch banker will normally only be involved in discounting *inland trade* bills of exchange.

Discounting is a useful service to *customers* in providing them with *immediate funds* against trade bills which have been drawn in their favour or negotiated to them. The customers endorse the bills, and the banks then purchase them, becoming holders for value or holders in due course. Discounting is profitable for banks and provides them with a speedy self-liquidating "security".

Accommodation bills are not acceptable for discount, and banks will only be willing to discount bills arising from certain recognised *trading transactions*.

NOTE: Foreign bills for discount (negotiations) are channelled to one of the bank's foreign departments to be dealt with. This is specialist work and beyond the scope of this HANDBOOK.

44. Considerations concerning discounting. Before agreeing to discount his customer's bills a banker must consider several factors:

(*a*) *Are bills normally issued and discounted as regards the trade in which the customer is operating?* For instance, in the timber and furniture trades bills of exchange are used for payment, and discounting is common.

(*b*) *Are both the customer and acceptor financially sound?* As discounting is *in effect* an advance to the customer against security of the acceptor's bills, both parties must be financially sound. (A status report on the acceptor is vital.)

(*c*) *Before agreeing a discount limit* the bank should apply the principles of lending against the proposition, e.g. the customer must have business ability and be financially sound (past and up-to-date balance sheets and accounts will help verify this).

(*d*) *The term of the bills should be short* (usually three to six months).

(*e*) *The rate of interest* should be agreed.

45. Procedure when discounting.

(*a*) *As regards the bill:* it must be examined to ascertain that (*i*) it is correctly drawn up, and *bears the customer's endorsement*, (*ii*) it is fully negotiable and transferable, (*iii*) it is domiciled (i.e. accepted payable) at a bank.

(*b*) *As regards the acceptor:* the acceptance should be regular and the acceptor's signature verified.

(*c*) *As regards the customer: see* **44**(*b*) and (*c*) above. (The customer will usually be *both drawer and payee*.)

(*d*) *As regards the bank's records:*

(*i*) *It should be possible to ascertain at any moment* the total *value* of discounts outstanding against any *one* acceptor. (A good "spread" of acceptors is preferable.)

(*ii*) *Status reports on acceptors* should be kept up to date.

(*iii*) *All bills are marked with the due date*; given a reference number; recorded and book entries are passed.

(*iv*) *The due dates of bills should be diarised* (preferably in several diaries), so that presentation for payment is not overlooked.

46. Bills dishonoured. If a bill is dishonoured by non-payment, then:

(*a*) *If the customer's account is sufficiently in* credit; the amount of the bill should be debited thereto and the bill returned to him.

(*b*) *If the customer's account is not sufficiently in credit;* the bill should be retained and the amount debited to a suspense account. (The existing balance, if any, is retained as part cover.) Notice of dishonour should *immediately* be given to all parties liable on the bill and payment requested.

See also VI, **27**.

BRIDGE-OVER ADVANCES

47. Definition. An advance of the deposit or purchase price to the purchaser of a property which is to be repaid from the sale of his existing property and/or provision of long-term mortgage finance, e.g. from a Building Society.

48. Main steps in house purchase.

(*a*) The prospective purchaser accepts a "sale offer" subject to "contract and survey". Sometimes a *deposit* is payable *but there is no binding contract at this stage.*

(*b*) *If the purchase proceeds*, then after the purchaser's solicitor checks title, *contracts are signed and exchanged* by purchaser/vendor, *whereupon*: (*i*) a 10 per cent *deposit* will be paid to the stakeholder, i.e. solicitor or estate agent (less the original deposit, if any), (*ii*) the *completion date is fixed* in the contract, i.e. the date when principal moneys and ownership with vacant possession pass.

49. Importance to bank of exchange of sale contract. Before agreeing an advance the bank prefers a *binding contract for the sale* of the customer's property to exist, *because repayment is to come from the proceeds of that sale. Additionally*, if the purchase is to involve new mortgage facilities to be granted by a Building Society, then evidence that the mortgage has been agreed in principle must be produced or verified from the solicitors or society. The customer's solicitor will be in a position to verify other facts. e.g. agreed sale/purchase price.

50. Amount required. Where purchase completion is to *precede* sale completion, then the customer will usually require to borrow the *whole of the purchase price* (*see* example, **54** below). Where sale completion is to *precede* purchase completion, then only the 10 per cent *deposit* should be required. (Where no firm sale contract exists, the bank may be willing to finance the purchase under an open-ended bridge-over: *see* **56** below.)

51. Customer's solicitor. As the bank must deal closely with the customer's solicitor and rely on his undertakings, his integrity should be confirmed, by obtaining a satisfactory status reply from his bankers.

The customer's written permission is always required giving the bank irrevocable authority to act for him and to obtain the necessary solicitor's undertaking.

52. Bank's security. The usual security for this type of advance is a *solicitor's undertaking*. However, if the deeds/land certificate can pass through the bank's hands it will have an equitable charge over the security.

53. Types of solicitor's undertakings. All clearing banks now invariably use the following *standard* printed undertakings, which, by agreement between the Committee of London Clearing Bankers and the Law Society, if used and unamended, protect the bank in the rare event where the *solicitor* defaults. Undertakings on the solicitor's own paper are not so protected, and should be very carefully perused, if accepted and relied upon.

(*a*) *Undertaking to hold deeds on loan* and return them in the same condition as received.

(*b*) *Undertaking that on the bank providing purchase moneys* the deeds of the property purchased will be forwarded to the bank or held to its order.

(*c*) *Undertaking to forward the proceeds of sale* (less costs) to the bank, or alternatively, to return the deeds.

54. Example of typical transaction. The bank's customer is selling 4 Blank Street for £34,250, against which there is an outstanding mortgage of £12,150. He is buying 6 Ash Street for £46,500 and has arranged a mortgage of £30,000 (to be provided on repayment of his existing mortgage). Contracts have been signed and exchanged in respect of both properties, completion date of purchase being 21st March and of sale being 15th April. Evidence to support the customer's statements has been produced, and his solicitor is of known reliability.

The following authority and undertakings are required: The customer's authority (*i*) *to pay the purchase price* to the solicitor against his undertaking to hold the deeds of the new house to the order of the bank pending release to the building society, (*ii*) *to instruct the solicitor* to give his undertaking to account to the bank for both the net sale proceeds of the present house and the proceeds of the mortgage on the new house (less all costs).

Property Sale	£	*Property Purchase*	£
Sale price	34,250	Purchase price	46,500
Less outstanding Building Society mortgage	12,150	*Less* agreed Building Society mortgage	30,000
Equity	£22,100	Shortfall: to be met from equity in existing property	£16,500

Customer requires to borrow £46,500, i.e. £4,650 for 10 per cent deposit on (say) 1st March and £41,850 on completion date 21st March.

Bank will be repaid on 15th April, when it should receive from the solicitor approximately £48,100, i.e.

	£
Net sale proceeds of old property*	18,100
Plus new mortgage moneys	30,000
	£48,100

This is more than sufficient to repay the bank, debit interest and charges. The lending should, incidentally, be taken on loan account, so that a Bank Interest Certificate can be given to the customer for tax benefit purposes.

*NOTE: This figure is calculated (approx.) by allowing for legal charges on the sale and purchase transactions and deducting estate agents' costs (if they have been used) as well as the amount outstanding on the old Building Society mortgage. A completion statement may be exhibited to the bank showing these figures in detail.

55. Building advance linked with bridge-over. A customer who wishes to have a new house built on his own land may request a building advance to be repaid from the sale proceeds of his existing property and/or Building Society mortgage finance. Facilities of this nature will only be provided where the customer is of good standing and the bank are satisfied that:

(*a*) *The advance will be short term*, i.e. the existing property is readily saleable and new mortgage facilities have been agreed in principle.

(*b*) *Planning permission* has been granted.

(*c*) The *builders* are capable and financially sound.

(*d*) The *contract* will be for a *fixed* price. (Ascertain the position re extras.)

(*e*) The advance is to be made in stages against *production of architect's certificates.*

(*f*) The customer has a *good title.* (NOTE: (1) a legal or equitable mortgage will be required, (2) the security value will increase as building progresses.)

(*g*) *A solicitor's undertaking* in respect of sale proceeds of the old property and mortgage moneys will be taken in due course.

(*h*) An insurance policy has been taken out to cover the house being built.

56. Open-ended bridge-overs. This is similar to a normal bridge-over, except that *no firm sale contract exists as regards the customer's property.* Because the contemplated sale might never take place, the bank are in effect advancing money against the deeds of the property to be purchased, and consequently, such facilities should not be granted unless the customer has means to carry through the transaction or the existing property is very readily saleable. As contracts for the sale of the customer's existing property are not exchanged, the bank will be reluctant to become involved except for an undoubted customer, where it is certain that no unexpected difficulties in finding a buyer are likely to arise. The bank will look for a very adequate margin, in case it should be necessary for the customer to reduce the asking price to obtain a sale. Moreover, interest accruing on all borrowings should be carefully taken into account. If the facility is agreed the customer may be required to execute a legal or equitable mortgage over his new property. Where registered land is concerned "notice of intended deposit" might be given to the Land Registry, in respect of the new property, if no other mortgagee is involved.

REVERSIONARY INTERESTS

57. Definition. An interest is an estate falling into possession in the future on the contingency of an event mentioned in a will or trust instrument, e.g. on the death of a life tenant.

58. Lending against a reversionary interest. Banks may not be keen to lend against the security of a reversionary interest because: (*a*) if the remainderman cannot provide repayment from his income, then a long-term loan may result if the life tenant enjoys a long life; (*b*) even though the reversioner's interest has a market value, a sale is often difficult to arrange. Where a remainderman wishes to borrow: (*a*) *for personal spending* he will usually be referred to a company which deals in reversions or to an insurance company; (*b*) *for business purposes* the bank may be prepared to facilitate him provided his prospects are good and repayment can be expected from income.

59. Example of a feasible proposition. Your customer X, who has recently qualified as a solicitor, asks for a loan of £15,000 to enable him to purchase a share in a local solicitor's practice. You regard the proposition as completely satisfactory, but as X has no assets other than the reversion to his grandmother's estate upon the death of his aunt now aged fifty-five, who has a life interest in the estate, which is worth £35,000, a mortgage of his reversion is the only possible security.

The bank must ascertain:

(*a*) *The terms of the trust* (*or will*) to discover whether X's interest is *contingent* or *absolute*. If the former is the case, then as X's interest will completely disappear if he predeceases his aunt he will be required to assign a life policy as cover for the borrowing.

(*b*) *The nature of the estate*. Are the assets marketable?

(*c*) *The present market value of the reversion*. This will depend upon the value of the estate and the age of the life tenant. (The older the *life tenant*, the shorter will be his life expectancy, and the more valuable will be the reversion.)

An actuarial valuation will be necessary.

(*d*) *How the overdraft is to be repaid*. Is the remainderman in a position to make repayments out of income and so avoid a long-term advance?

(*e*) That the *trustees dealing with the estate assets are persons of integrity*.

60. Completing the security.

(*a*) The estate assets are verified and valued, and enquiries are made to see whether the trustees have power to vary these. If so, it may be necessary to renew enquiries from time to time.

(*b*) The remainderman must execute the bank's form of mortgage.

(*c*) Notice of the mortgage is given to the estate trustees, who are required to acknowledge it and confirm that no prior interest exists.

NOTE: On the customer's default the bank can either sell the reversionary interest or await the death of the life tenant. Until this latter event occurs there is no right to deal with estate assets.

61. Trustees borrowing to lend to a remainderman. The trustees of the estate may approach the bank, saying that they are willing to borrow in order to facilitate the remainderman. Borrowing by trustees involves different considerations, *see* VIII, **34**, but may prove acceptable, for instance, where the TA 1925, s. 16, applies and where the lending to the remainderman falls within s. 32 of the same Act. Legal advice is advisable. In practice, it is usually deemed better to lend to the person who is to receive the benefit and from whom repayment is to be expected, i.e. the remainderman.

62. Lending to a life tenant. The same procedure as in **60** above is adopted where a life tenant wishes to borrow against his life interest. A mortgage over a life policy on his life is always required, because his interest ceases on death. On his default the remedies outlined above are available, and the bank also has a right to his income from the estate assets.

ADVANCES AGAINST PRODUCE

63. Produce advances for imports. Advances to finance exports and imports are common, but the former is outside the scope of this HANDBOOK, being dealt with in *Finance of Foreign Trade*, by D. P. Whiting, M. & E. HANDBOOK Series. Advances against *imported* goods predominate for such produce as cotton, wool, wheat and other readily marketable goods. By granting produce advances, banks enable imports to be paid for at sight or usance under documentary collections or credits. The importer can then be financed for the period until he sells the goods and receives the sale proceeds. The bank looks to the goods as its security.

64. Advantages of goods as security.

(*a*) *A produce loan is self-liquidating*, i.e. the goods which form the bank's security are sold to effect repayment of the advance.

(*b*) By nature, a produce loan *provides for speedy repayment*.

(*c*) *The security is cheap to take* and little formality attaches.

(*d*) *A good title is virtually assured* when dealing with *undoubted* shippers and customers.

NOTE: (1) A *vital* aspect of produce lending is that *the integrity and business ability of the customer must be beyond question.* (2) *Status reports* are usually obtained on foreign shippers, buyers and warehousekeepers.

65. Disadvantages of goods as security.

(*a*) *Variations in market price may lower the value of the bank's security*, and so a good *margin* should be required.

(*b*) *Valuation of certain types of goods is difficult.*

(*c*) *Perishable goods deteriorate and become worthless* if a sale cannot be effected within the usual time. *Consequently*, a bank may insist on perishable goods being pre-sold before agreeing an advance.

(*d*) *Heavy insurance and storage charges* may accrue.

(*e*) *Comprehensive clerical records*, detailing the shipment quantities, marks, numbers, etc., *must be kept*, so that the current position *vis-à-vis* each customer and each shipment can be seen at a glance. A bank occasionally confirms with a warehousekeeper that he is holding goods as shown in the bank's records.

(*f*) *Trust releases provide opportunity for fraud* by the customer: *see* **73** below.

(*g*) *The warehousekeeper has a lien for any unpaid charges*, and the bank may suffer loss because of this unless it periodically confirms that all charges are paid or unless the lien is waived on all the goods which comprise the bank's security.

66. Pledge of goods as security. The bank obtains its security by way of *pledge*, i.e. by obtaining *actual* or *constructive* possession of the goods as security. In practice, *constructive possession* of the goods is common. This is done by securing the *documents of title* to the goods *or* arranging for the goods to be *warehoused in the bank's name.*

NOTE: A *mortgage* is not taken, because it would require registration under the Bills of Sale Acts, with all the resulting stigma which attaches.

67. Memorandum of pledge. The customer is required to execute a memorandum of pledge (or letter of hypothecation as it is often called). Note particularly that execution of this document does not create the pledge but only *evidences* the terms of the existing pledge.

If the document *created* the pledge, then unless the goods were "still at sea or in transit from quay to warehouse" registration under the Bills of Sale Acts would be necessary.

68. Terms of the pledge. The memorandum of pledge records the terms of the security. These include: (*a*) particulars of the goods and documents; (*b*) an express power of sale exercisable at any time; (*c*) the customer's undertaking that the goods are insured and that any insurance proceeds will be held for the bank.

69. Documents relating to imports. The bank will be particularly concerned with the *document of title*, i.e. the Bill(s) of Lading. The two other important documents are the Invoice and Insurance Policy: other documents may also be required under Exchange Control and import regulations.

The three main documents are briefly dealt with below.

70. Bill of Lading. Issued by the shipowner or his agent, this has three functions:

(*a*) *Evidences shipment of goods*, i.e. it is a receipt for the goods.

(*b*) *Confirms the contract of carriage.*

(*c*) *Is a document of title to goods* while they are at sea and until delivered to the consignee or his order or assigns.

NOTE: (1) Bills of Lading are usually drawn in *sets of three*, being mailed separately to prevent total loss. Delivery of the goods is made to the *first presenter of a valid bill*, whereupon the remaining bills become void. (2) When taking a pledge the bank requires: "a full set of clean, on-board bills of lading, drawn to order, blank endorsed and marked freight paid."

The bank may relax its requirements for "clean" bills and prepaid freight, in certain circumstances, and perhaps under indemnity.

71. Supplier's invoice. Issued and signed by the supplier and shows the nature and value of the goods, etc., the price basis is shown, e.g. CIF, FOB, etc.

72. Insurance policy. Issued in favour of the shipper by his insurers. The policy must be *endorsed* by the shipper *in blank*, so that the bank can have recourse to the insurance proceeds in the event of loss or damage to the goods while in transit. Particular attention will be paid to the terms of the policy and as to the cover provided.

NOTE: The bank may be willing to accept an Insurance Certificate instead of a Policy, even though the former does not give a right to the proceeds without production of the actual Policy.

73. Trust Letter. Where the bank releases documents of title to goods or the goods themselves to the customer, it is *essential* that the customer executes a *Trust Letter, as otherwise the pledge is extinguished*, and the goods would be regarded as being within the disposition of the bankrupt (BA 1914, s. 38) if the customer's bankruptcy ensued. When the customer has effected a sale he will be allowed to deal with the goods *as trustee for the bank* under a Trust Letter.

A Trust Letter incorporates:

(*a*) *The customer's acknowledgment* of the bank's security rights in the goods and sale proceeds.

(*b*) *The customer's undertaking:*

(*i*) To hold in trust for the bank: (1) the goods, (2) the sale proceeds, and to pay the latter to the bank, (3) any insurance proceeds.

(*ii*) To keep the goods adequately stored and insured.

(*iii*) To return unsold goods to the bank, on request.

(*iv*) To give the bank, on request, authority addressed to buyers requiring them to pay purchase moneys direct to the bank.

NOTE: When in *breach* of his trust undertaking a customer pledges the documents of title with another lender, the latter will usually obtain priority to the security: *Lloyds Bank* v. *Bank of America NT & SA* (1938).

74. Pledge and trust release over imported goods which are to be warehoused. Where an importer requires to warehouse goods prior to effecting sale, the undermentioned procedure is followed:

(*a*) *A separate produce loan account* is usually opened for each shipment.

(*b*) *A specific memorandum of pledge* is signed by the customer, the documents being listed on the schedule.

NOTE: (1) A *general* letter of pledge (or hypothecation) is completed where a customer requires regular produce facilities, and this will cover all advances and future lodgments of produce. (2) Where the customer (importer) has opened a documentary credit the application form incorporates a letter of hypothecation (but a further memorandum of pledge is usually taken).

(*c*) *The documents of title* are released to the customer against a *Trust Letter*, whereby the customer undertakes, *inter alia, to warehouse the goods in the bank's name* and deliver the warrant or receipt to the bank. Alternatively, the bank may attend to the warehousing itself.

(*d*) The customer undertakes *to insure the goods*. Sometimes the bank gives notice of its interest to the insurers.

(*e*) When the customer sells the goods (or part thereof) the bank issues a *Delivery Order* in his favour, addressed to the warehousekeeper. This enables the customer to obtain delivery of the goods. Where a Trust Letter has not been previously signed, the customer is required to complete one when requesting the issue of the Delivery Order. The buyer's name is noted and a status enquiry may be made as to his standing.

(*f*) The customer is required *to pay in the proceeds of sale* within the usual time.

75. Delivery orders. These are *not* usually issued in favour of *buyers*, because this extinguishes the pledge. Exceptions may, however, occur where the buyer's standing is good and he proffers his cheque in settlement.

76. Goods sold ex-ship or ex-quay. Where pledged goods are sold ex-ship or ex-quay, the documents of title are delivered either: (*a*) to the customer under a Trust Letter, or (*b*) to the buyer against payment.

77. Pledge over goods in an independent warehouse. If the bank is willing to make an advance against a pledge of goods *which are already warehoused in the customer's name*, then it is *essential* to get the ownership of the goods *changed into the bank's name* by forwarding the dock or warehouse warrant or receipt to the warehousekeeper with a transfer order. Once the bank receives from the warehousekeeper a new warrant or receipt in its name, it must then obtain from the customer a memorandum of pledge. The procedure from **74**(*e*) above is then followed.

NOTE: *Warehousekeeper's receipts* are *not transferable*. However, *some warrants* issued by dock or warehouse companies under special Acts of Parliament are *transferable when endorsed*. Consequently, a pledge over *transferable warrants* is achieved merely by obtaining their deposit. Nevertheless, transferable warrants are often exchanged for warrants in the bank's name.

78. Statutory protection for pledges. Various protections are given by the Factors Act 1889, and the Sale of Goods Act 1893, enabling pledgees to obtain, in certain circumstances, a perfect title to goods *even though the pledgor* has a defective title or acts beyond his authority. These technical aspects are extremely important, but are beyond the scope of this work.

SECURITIES GENERALLY AND CONSUMER CREDIT ACT CONSIDERATIONS

79. The Consumer Credit Act 1974. This Act has important considerations for the lending banker taking security. However the Act is not yet fully in force, and only certain sections are applicable, having been brought into operation by Statutory Instrument. Eventually the taking of *security* for *all debtor/creditor agreements* covered in the Act may well vary in many ways from that used for overdrafts, non-regulated loans, and commercial lendings. Students should ensure that they keep abreast of developments.

It is likely that the bank's present rights to *enforce* its *security* over *land* will be restricted, in respect of all lendings.

80. Total Charge for Credit. The "Truth in Lending" Regulations under the Consumer Credit Act are now in force. They apply to private and business borrowers, and partnerships, but not to limited companies. Only lendings up to and including £5,000 are controlled, except where a charge over deeds or registered title is concerned, where there is no limitation by amount. The Quotation and Advertisement Regulations cover regulated agreements: *see* **XVI**, 14. Advertising is classified into "simple, intermediate, or full" categories and any advertisement which falls between these constitutes an infringement, carrying potential fines or imprisonment for the individual involved.

Moreover, in all applicable cases the borrower can request a *quotation* and the lender must reply in writing. It is necessary to include all aspects of charges in the quotation, e.g. interest, arrangement fees for setting up the lending, *charges for taking the security including legal costs* and any other applicable charges directly related to the lending.

This enables the Total Charge for Credit and the Annual Percentage Rate to be quoted, albeit without any commitment to lend, unless the commitment is undertaken. The quoted Annual Percentage Rate enables the prospective borrower to compare the facilities of various lending institutions. Certain assumptions are allowed when projecting quotations or advertisements for certain categories of borrowing, e.g. the Bank's Base Rate can be projected at the current rate, with a note appended that it is subject to variation from time to time. Any inclusion of front end fees must state whether these are based on reasonable estimates, or are fixed and once quoted are not subject to variations. These "Truth in Lending" Regulations also extend to *any* amount in respect of Advertisements and Quotations for credit to Individuals secured by land. *See also* XVI, **14–19**, and Appendix III.

PROGRESS TEST 15

1. How would you complete a legal assignment over an endowment policy in your customer's name and favour? **(5, 9)**
2. What remedies are available to a legal assignee of a life policy should the assignor default? **(11)**
3. How is a legal mortgage over a ship effected? **(18)**
4. Why is it advisable to lend against a ship's mortgage on loan account? **(21)**
5. Can a legal mortgage be taken over a partly completed ship? **(24)**
6. Outline fully the nature of an Agricultural Charge. **(26, 27)**
7. What is the procedure for completing: (*a*) an Agricultural Charge; (*b*) a Milk Marketing Board charge? **(31, 35)**
8. How is a legal assignment over book debts affected? **(38, 41)** Are any additional steps necessary where the assignment is created by a limited company? **(42)**
9. Outline the usual considerations with regard to discounting bills of exchange. **(44)**
10. What is a bridge-over advance? **(47)** What security would be taken for this type of advance? **(52, 53)**
11. In what circumstances might a bank be willing to lend against the security of a reversionary interest? **(58)** How would the security be completed? **(59, 60)**
12. Outline the advantages and disadvantages of goods as security. Why is the integrity of the customer of vital importance? **(64, 65)**
13. How can a bank obtain a pledge over: (*a*) goods at sea; (*b*) goods in an independent warehouse? **(76, 77)**
14. Explain the nature and use of the following documents:

(*a*) Trust Letter **(73)**
(*b*) Delivery Order **(75)**
(*c*) Warehousekeeper's warrant **(77)**
(*d*) Warehousekeeper's receipt **(77)**
15. What is Total Charge for Credit? **(80)**
16. What is a Quotation, and why is it important? **(80)**

PART SIX

ADVANCES TO CUSTOMERS

CHAPTER XVI

Principles of Good Lending (Consumer Credit Act Considerations)

COMMERCIAL BANKS AS LENDERS

The practical lending problems which will be studied in the next chapter on Balance Sheets are those arising at branch level. These are everyday propositions which are brought by a variety of customers to their bankers. Decisions to all such propositions can usually be given in the course of a few days at the outside. (NOTE: Students should already be aware, from previous studies, of the role of commercial banks in the economic structure as a whole.)

1. Control over bank lending. This is exercised down through various levels.

(*a*) *Control by the Treasury and Bank of England* is exercised both directly and indirectly. These controls change from time to time. In the economic interest such customers as exporters and farmers usually receive favourable treatment.

(*b*) *Control by the commercial bank itself* has various graduations from the directors down to the branch manager. Generally speaking, the larger the amount required by the customer, the higher the authority to which the application will need to go within the bank for decision. A typical set-up would range from the Branch Manager up through the Area Superintendent, Area Board, Directors' Committees and finally to the Board of Directors.

(*c*) *Control by the branch* is exercised through the manager. The manager will have a sanctioning limit and will have complete control as regards advances under this figure. He will forward details of proposals for applications beyond his sanctioning limit to a higher authority for decision, while at the same time adding his own recommendation.

2. Functions of the bank as lender. A commercial bank used to be regarded as the provider of short-term funds to suitable borrowers, and this is still a primary function. However, in recent years medium-term and even appropriate longer-term propositions have been entered into, to assist the commercial sector. Banks are now helping with house-purchase although within narrower confines than a Building Society. In the personal sector the bank personal loan is based on instalment repayments and it competes with hire purchase. There are other budgeting schemes available, and no doubt further developments can be expected in the future.

ELEMENTS OF A GOOD BANKING ADVANCE

The main elements concerned in creating a good advance are:

(*a*) *The integrity and reliability* of the borrower.

(*b*) *The nature of the proposition:* its purpose, duration and amount.

(*c*) *The borrower's ability* to apply the advance: evidenced by past performance and future budgets.

(*d*) *The repayment* programme; including bank interest.

(*e*) *The security.*

(*f*) *The borrower's value* to the bank, bearing in mind his *connections* with other important customers.

3. Integrity and reliability of the borrower is a basic factor. The money which is being lent is that of the depositors and shareholders of the bank, and every endeavour should therefore be made to avoid bad debts.

Much of the information concerning the customer will usually be known to the manager already. Other information can be obtained from his account, record sheets, balance sheets, etc. The whole success of the lending will usually depend upon the true representation of the facts by the customer and upon his ability to carry through any scheme to a satisfactory conclusion.

(*a*) *Personal borrowers* should have been suitably introduced. Regard should be made to the customer's occupation, position and salary, as well as to the previous conduct of his account. Continuity of employment is important as regards capacity to repay. The salaried person who attempts to live permanently beyond his means should be discouraged from doing so.

The ability of a borrower to claim tax relief on interest paid varies from time to time following differing government approaches and legislation under the Finance Acts. Students should refer, therefore, to the current position in their own bank's internal rule books. Briefly, under current Finance Acts the following factors determine whether tax relief may be available.

(*i*) Date of advance and whether on overdraft or loan account.

(*ii*) Amount of Interest paid.

(*iii*) Purpose and Amount of the Advance (e.g. Interest on a Bridging *Loan* of up to £25,000 to facilitate the purchase of domestic property is available for tax relief.)

(*b*) *Sole traders* should have a thorough knowledge of their business and the capacity to apply any advance to the use intended. The financing of overtrading by traders (and others) must be avoided.

NOTE: Personal and professional customers and sole traders who are borrowing will often be required to lodge a life policy as security to cover the bank in the event of their death.

(*c*) *Partnership customers.* Before lending the bank must have confidence as to the harmonious working of the partnership. The firm's history should be known. The partners' business acumen should be good.

(*d*) *Limited companies.* The company's history and standing will usually be known, and its financial progress must be viewed from its balance sheets and accounts. The industriousness and business acumen of the directors is of prime importance.

4. The nature of the proposition is of paramount importance. Is it a banking proposition?

Short-term advances are favoured and desirable, applications arise for working capital, seasonal needs, end-of-year tax payments, bridge-over facilities, etc. However, medium-term and longer-term finance is not excluded now, especially as business needs and planning become more complex in the modern world. The exposure to risk could be greater in a longer-term advance, and usually security will be taken. Frequently such term facilities are on loan account repayable at fixed intervals by agreed instalments.

Where moneys are required for financing a new venture (i.e. outside the customer's usual sphere), extreme caution is necessary.

5. The amount. Often the customer will have an exact amount in mind. A separate calculation should be made to check whether this amount is correct. If the amount asked is insufficient the proposition will need reshaping and reconsidering. Conversely, the amount asked may be beyond that which the bank is willing to lend; however, it may be possible to agree a reduced advance if the customer will co-operate in expanding his business more slowly or (in an appropriate case) bring into his business some additional capital or long-term loans. It is a common mistake for the customer to ignore *major* factors, such as tax, overheads, wages, etc., and other *incidentals*, such as legal expenses, bank interest and charges, and agents' fees. These could all bring pressure on the account later if ignored now. Banks like their money to turn over, and loans for working capital purposes should liquidate itself over a reasonable period. Static overdrafts are to be avoided.

A vital question arises as to the total of the proprietors' stake in the business. Is this reasonable for the type of business and amount of turnover involved? *As a general rule*, the bank's stake in the business should not exceed that of the proprietors, but there are exceptions, e.g. produce loans, stockbrokers' loans and finance for building.

6. Ability to apply the advance to the stated purpose. Before agreeing an advance the bank must be confident that the customer has the *ability* to carry through the proposition. If the loan is not used for the stated purpose loss could result to the bank. The customer's personal integrity should be beyond question, and he must be hard-working and industrious.

7. The repayment programme. A clear and evidently possible repayment programme is normally required. The source must be obvious. In this respect self-liquidating advances, such as a bridge-over advance, are ideal.

Before agreeing to a medium-term advance the repayment programme should be seen to be *realistic*. For example, where a company is to purchase fixed assets with the bank advance the source of repayment may be dependent upon the business achieving a good increase in turnover and profits. But will the bank be happy to extend the repayment programme if repayment falls behind? Was the repayment programme so tightly scheduled that it was doomed to failure from the outset? Was a long-term advance really required from an institutional lender or could the bank's merchant banking or hire purchase/leasing arm help?

8. Security. Every good proposition should stand on its own, i.e. ignoring the security aspect. However, many propositions entail risk, and often this is such that the bank will only grant the advance if it is sufficiently secured so that loss will be avoided should the proposition or the customer fail.

Where a proposition is bad, no amount of security should warrant an advance being granted, e.g. an application to finance speculation, or pay off pressing creditors.

Security will almost certainly be required if after valuing a customer's Balance Sheet assets on a "gone-concern" basis the bank would be at risk as an unsecured creditor. When taken, security should be of adequate value and preferably be easily realisable.

9. The value of the customer and of his connections. Although a customer's proposition may not be ideal in principle, it may be agreed because of his connections. For example, a loan to a subsidiary company may need to be refused if it were not for the support given by its substantial parent company. A private individual may be instrumental in bringing *good* business to the branch from his own business connections, e.g. an accountant, solicitor or broker.

POSSIBLE DANGERS

10. Overtrading. Too much emphasis cannot be placed on the dangers of supporting permanent overtrading. Many a good small business has been ruined by the desire to expand too quickly without the necessary finance. Increased debtors, larger overheads, increased stocking and work-in-progress all lock up working capital. Consequently, as turnover expands more liquidity is required to help finance these items, and unless this is rectified by the introduction of further capital, this will remain so until any resulting increase in profit is realised and retained in the business.

A shortage of finance may bring disastrous consequences if creditors press for payment.

11. Liquidity. In the event of a lack of finance through overtrading, a business will often turn to the bank for help. The bank will have already seen from the customer's account any noticeable signs of lack of liquidity. For example, the overdraft may be forming a hard core at or above the account limit. Although a small degree of overtrading might be tolerated, overall consideration of the position is vital. The usual need is for an injection of new capital or in some instances loan capital or long-term mortgages. (Other signs of overtrading and lack of liquidity are noted in the next chapter.)

12. Over-optimism. Most customers will present a very rosy picture of their requirements and prospects. The banker must sift out and verify the *actual facts*. To do this, facts and figures produced must be up to date. Evidence of the customer's claims and statements may be required.

13. Perfect principles: imperfect proposition. Very few propositions measure up to all the ideals of the principles of lending. Nevertheless, the bank will often feel that an imperfect proposition is worth supporting as it stands, particularly if the bank can be adequately secured. At other times an advance will only be granted if a satisfactory compromise can be reached. Occasionally the risk to the bank is such that the proposition must be declined. The important thing for the banker is being able to ascertain where the risk lies and whether it is worth accepting in view of the small margin of profit on moneys advanced.

CONSUMER CREDIT ACT 1974

14. Regulated Agreements. S. 48 of the Consumer Credit Act 1974, only parts of which are currently in force, seeks to regulate personal credit and hire agreements up to £5,000, with certain exceptions. These are:

(*a*) Normal trade credit;

(*b*) Low cost credit;

(*c*) Finance of foreign trade;

(*d*) Land transactions repayable in less than four instalments; and

(*e*) Mortgage lending by Building Societies, local authorities and certain insurance companies.

Thus *Regulated Agreements* can apply to loans to individuals, whether on sole or joint account, in partnership, or in any trustee or executorship capacity, and also loans to non-corporate bodies or professions or traders. However, loans to corporate bodies, e.g. limited companies, are exempt.

Overdraft lending is caught by the Act, but it has been recognised that if overdrafts were subject to the *documentation* side (the written agreement Regulations are *yet to be introduced*) this could result in the demise of the system. Consequently by an amendment in the Banking Act 1979, the Director General of Fair Trading *will* be able to give a determination that overdraft agreements be excluded from this documentation part of the Act, *in due course*.

Penalties for default of Consumer Credit Act provisions are fines and/or imprisonment of the officer lending the money.

15. Canvassing. It is an offence to canvass a debtor-creditor agreement (Regulated Agreement) off trade premises (s. 49(i)), which are bank premises or the *business* premises of the customer, without a prior invitation. Canvassing is any attempt to induce by way of personal contact any person to enter into an agreement with the bank or any of its subsidiary finance companies. *General* discussion of financial matters off trade premises is permissible provided the discussion is started by the party other than the banker, and provided the banker is not attending the meeting with the object of canvassing. Communication by telephone or in writing is permissible in any event.

The canvassing of *overdrafts* for *existing customers* is *exempted* from the Canvassing Regulations.

16. Security. *See* XV, **79–80**.

17. Total Charge for Credit. *See* XV, **80**.

18. Licensing. The Regulations specify six categories of Consumer Credit activity, and consequently certain types of traders need to hold a licence, e.g. credit-reference agencies, debt-collectors, debt-counsellors and debt-adjusters, and the licence should be exhibited to the bank when such an account is opened, or when the customer wishes to borrow. The Public Register of Consumer Credit licences is open to public inspection or by way of search. A bank must therefore have its own licence, and must ensure that its customers in the credit industry are licensed—especially if it is lending unsecured, as the agreements of an unlicensed trader may be unenforceable, with dire results on the repayment of the bank's own moneys.

Bankruptcy, liquidation, mental incapacity or death revoke the licence.

19. Circulars to Minors. It is an offence to send a minor any document which invites him/her to borrow or seek information or advice on borrowing or obtaining credit for purchases or in respect of services.

20. Generally. *See* Appendix III.

PROGRESS TEST 16

1. Outline in detail the integral elements of a good banking advance. **(3–8)**
2. Of what importance is security to a banker? **(8)**
3. What do you understand by overtrading? **(10)**
4. What are Regulated Agreements? **(14)**
5. How does "canvassing" affect a banker? **(15)**
6. Why do certain customers need a Consumer Credit Act Licence, and why is the bank interested? **(18)**

CHAPTER XVII

Balance Sheets

GENERAL COMMENTS

1. Further study recommended. The Stage 2 Institute of Bankers rules require a candidate to pass Accountancy before entering for the Practice of Banking 2 examination paper.

As lending and the art of interpretation of balance sheets can sometimes be beyond the practical day-to-day experience of the student, he is strongly advised to supplement the use of the HANDBOOK by reading the books recommended by the Institute and by obtaining past examination question papers and studying the examiners' reports.

2. Interpretation of balance sheets. The preparation of balance sheets will not be dealt with, only the interpretation.

3. Examination questions. These are designed to test a candidate's ability to apply his knowledge of balance sheets and accounts to a practical lending proposition. A commonsense and realistic approach must be adopted.

A proposition will be outlined, usually showing the borrower's balance sheet(s), and the candidate may be asked:

(*a*) whether he would grant the advance;
(*b*) what advice he might give to the customer;
(*c*) what he can elicit from the information given;
(*d*) what further information he would need in order to reach a decision.

NOTE: Candidates sometimes give decisions to propositions when not asked to do so, usually based on completely inadequate information. Care must be exercised not to fall into this trap.

BALANCE SHEET AS AN AID TO LENDING

4. Lending against the balance sheet. A banker never lends against his customer's balance sheet. A banker lends on the strength of the proposition after bearing in mind the "Principles of Lending".

The balance sheet is an *aid* to the banker and helps him to *assess* the proposition. In particular, several past balance sheets and accounts provide him with: (*a*) information which he requires to establish the progress of the customer's business; (*b*) a basis for background questions concerning business activity.

5. Single balance sheet shows a static position. Because a single balance sheet only shows a *static* financial picture of a business concern *as at a given date*, it is usually essential to obtain at least the last three years' copies together with accounts so that the *dynamic* progress of the business can be measured. Obviously where only the latest balance sheet and accounts is produced to the banker but these *show clearly that the proposition is not viable* it is pointless to call for past accounts. Attention is now tending, however, to focus more on future budgets and cash flows, and these, if well prepared and if actual performance is measured against them, can be helpful.

6. Sole trader's balance sheet.

(*a*) *Information contained therein.*

(*i*) Assets and liabilities of the business.

(*ii*) Trader's capital account and drawings. (The Trading and Profit and Loss Accounts give a useful guide as to the scale of business operations.)

(*b*) *Information not contained therein.*

(*i*) To what extent a conservative valuation of assets has been adopted. (A conservative valuation is often adopted for tax purposes.)

(*ii*) The nature and amount of the trader's personal assets and liabilities. (These may, of course, be known from other sources, e.g. the safe-custody register.)

There is an *added safeguard* where lending to a sole trader in that both his business and personal assets are available should he default. A bank may be prepared therefore, relying upon the trader's ability and personal assets, to lend more than is warranted by the balance sheet figures.

7. Partnership balance sheet. Similar to **6** above. The capital account of *each* partner is shown. As the partners will have admitted J & S liability, the bank will retain a concurrent right to recover from both the business assets and each partner's personal estate should the partnership become bankrupt.

NOTE: It is important to establish whether the balance sheets of the sole trader or partnership have been audited by qualified persons.

8. Limited company balance sheet. As a limited company is a separate entity, the bank can only look to its assets for recovery, unless of course collateral security has been provided.

NOTE: (1) *By virtue of the* Companies Acts 1948 and 1967, substantial information concerning the company's affairs and financial position must be shown in or appended to the balance sheet and revenue accounts. (2) *Qualified Auditors must verify the accuracy of the balance sheet and account figures.* These do not, of course, necessarily represent the true value of the assets concerned, e.g. fixed assets, stock, etc. The bank will be particularly concerned to see whether the *Auditor's Certificate* contains any qualifications regarding the Accounts. (3) *If the customer will not produce his balance sheet* (highly unlikely) a search at Companies House will reveal the required figures, although these are often out of date. (4) As an added safeguard the directors may be required to guarantee the company's account and perhaps additionally lodge their own supporting security, e.g. deeds of house. Apart from the actual security aspect, guarantees are often required from the directors in order to impress upon them that in controlling the company's affairs they are under a primary responsibility to see any proposition through.

BALANCE SHEET STRUCTURE

9. Basic structure of company balance sheets. It is only proposed to deal with the basic structure of limited company balance sheets and accounts. Nevertheless, most of the information which follows in this chapter applies equally to other types of business accounts.

10. Modern trend. There is an increasing tendency to produce balance sheets in vertical form. This method is more commonly adopted by public companies. The heading of "Liabilities" and "Assets" are dispensed with in the vertical-form balance sheet. A variety of sub-headings may be found endeavouring to show, without need of calculation, such items as capital employed, working capital, current liabilities, current assets, etc.

11. Bankers' comparative record form. Because customers' balance sheets take a variety of forms, most banks retain a comparative balance sheet record form on which they enter the figures from the customer's own balance sheet. This enables a standardised approach to be adopted, and provides for continuity and ease of comparison with past years' figures.

12. Grouping of balance sheet items. The bank is particularly concerned with ascertaining totals for the following groups of liabilities and assets so that the company's liquid position and other important features can easily be seen:

LIABILITIES SIDE	ASSETS SIDE
(A) Proprietors' Stake	(C) Fixed Assets
(B) Long-term Liabilities	(D) Intangible/Fictitious Assets
(E) Current Liabilities	(F) Current Assets

The make-up of these groups is discussed below. At this stage it may be mentioned that the bank is vitally interested in the company's *working-capital* figure, which can be easily ascertained from the above. Viz.:

Current Assets *less* Current Liabilities = Working Capital i.e. F − E (often called *liquid surplus*). A + B *less* C + D gives the same result.

NOTE: (1) *Current Liabilities* are those liabilities falling due for repayment within the next year from the balance sheet date. (2) *Current Assets* are those assets which are circulating (e.g. stock, work-in-progress, debtors, cash) together with those which can easily be turned into cash (e.g. quoted investments).

13. Exam balance sheet.
(Adapted)

Capital Employed	£
Capital (Authorised (£25,000))	20,000
Reserves	7,500
Profit and Loss A/c	3,000
	£30,500

Fixed Assets			£
Land and buildings			20,000
Plant and machinery			7,500
Motors, etc.			2,000
			29,500
Goodwill			3,000
Current Assets	£	£	
Stocks:			
Raw materials	4,000		
Finished products	6,000		
Debtors	17,500		
Cash at bank	1,500		
		29,000	
Current Liabilities			
Creditors	12,000		
Tax	2,500		
Dividend	1,500		
		16,000	
Liquid surplus			13,000
			45,500
Less Other liabilities: debenture			15,000
			£30,500

Additional information often disclosed in examination:

	£
Sales	110,000
Purchases	70,000
Gross profit	42,000
Overhead expenses	26,000
Depreciation	1,200
Directors' remuneration	6,700
Dividend	2,100
Tax	2,800
Net profit	3,200

14. Vertical form converted to side by side. Students who have not had the practical experience of dealing with vertical form balance sheets will usually find it easier to adopt the banking comparative-form approach. Once the position of the groups have been memorised and the student has learnt the group into which the various balance sheet items belong, it becomes a simple matter to convert any examination balance sheet into this form. (NOTE: It is not suggested that students do this as part of their answer but purely in rough form, so that the salient features immediately emerge.)

The reconstruction of the balance sheet in **13** is now shown:

Liabilities	£	£	*Assets*	£	£
Proprietors' Stake			*Fixed Assets*		
Capital	20,000		Land and buildings	20,000	
Reserves	7,500		Plant and machinery	7,500	
Profit and Loss A/c	3,000		Motors, etc.	2,000	
		30,500 (A)			29,500 (C)
Debenture		15,000 (B)	*Intangible Assets*		
			Goodwill		3,000 (D)
Current Liabilities			*Current Assets*		
Creditors	12,000		Stocks		
Tax	2,500		Raw materials	4,000	
Dividend	1,500		Finished products	6,000	
		16,000 (E)	Debtors	17,500	
			Cash at bank	1,500	
					29,000 (F)
		£61,500			£61,500

LIABILITY ITEMS

15. Capital resources (proprietors' stake). These are the accumulated resources of the business to date (£30,500 in our example) and include share capital, capital reserves, revenue reserves and profits.

If losses have accumulated these are shown as a deduction from capital or as a fictitious item on the asset side of the balance sheet.

If the capital resources are sizeable as against the other liabilities this is a good sign. The bank will also be concerned that a *reasonable proportion* of annual profit is "ploughed back", i.e. retained in the business and not distributed as dividends, etc.

NOTE: (1) *Revenue reserves.* These are appropriations to reserve from trading profit. (2) *Capital reserves.* These arise, for example, where assets are sold or revalued in excess of their book values.

If there is any excess of fixed and intangible assets over proprietors' capital and finance for these assets must have been provided from outside the business, i.e. from *long-term sources*, such as debentures, loans, mortgages, or from *short-term sources*, such as creditors, tax not yet due, etc. If there is a *liquid deficit*, then as short-term sources (i.e. current liabilities) are providing too much of the finance, *the business could prove vulnerable should creditors press for payment*.

16. Long-term loans and mortgages.

(*a*) *Debentures*. The terms of issue, interest rate, repayment and details of any charge over the assets must be ascertained. Care must be exercised if the repayment date is nearing, as this could undermine the company's liquid position. Redeemed uncancelled debentures pose further problems (*see* XI, **53**).

(*b*) *Mortgages*. Proceed as in (*a*) above. Note that this item may be shown as a liability in the balance sheet *or* as a deduction from the mortgaged asset(s).

(*c*) *Loans*. Are they in fact long-term or repayable by yearly instalments or on demand? Who are the lenders? Are the loans secured? If the loans are from *directors* the bank may require that they be *postponed* or *capitalised*, especially where: (*i*) withdrawal would deplete the company's effective resources, i.e. capital and/or liquid, or (*ii*) the proprietors' stake is insubstantial unless the loans remain added thereto.

17. Hire-purchase creditors. Details of the assets on which hire purchase is owing should be established and the amount and frequency of repayments ascertained.

18. Tax. The tax for the year is often shown in examination questions beneath the balance sheet. If profits are being made a tax provision will almost certainly be found to have been made in the balance sheet of a company. Current tax *due but unpaid* should be distinguished from a provision for future tax to *become payable*. Although the company retains the use of tax moneys until the tax is due, the point arises as to whether sufficient cash resources will be available to pay the tax on the due date.

19. Creditors. The amount and make-up requires examination, viz.:

(*a*) Are the creditors well spread so that there is not too much reliance on credit from one source?

(*b*) Are any creditors pressing?

If the amount of creditors is larger than seen previously the reason should be established. It might be that the increase is proportionate to increased purchases. Alternatively, longer credit might now be given or perhaps a non-liquid position makes it impossible to pay creditors.

The current ratio of creditors/purchases compared with previous years' ratios would help draw attention to whether average credit taken is reducing or increasing;

RATIO

$$\frac{\text{Creditors} \times 52}{\text{Purchases}} = \text{Number of weeks credit taken}$$

20. Bills payable. Usually only found in the balance sheets of certain trades, e.g. timber trade. If it appears as a new item this could imply that the creditors are getting restless and wish to fix their date of payment.

21. Dividend. Has a dividend been declared/proposed? Is the amount reasonable? Does it remain unpaid at the balance sheet date (look at B/S)? Has it been paid since?

22. Bank overdraft. Is a limit in existence? If so, is it fully utilised?—exceeded? How has the overdraft moved since the balance sheet date? What are the monthly maximum/minimum figures for the account?

EXAMPLE: *X Ltd.*

	1979		1980	
	Max.DR –	Min.DR/Max.CR	Max.DR –	Min.DR/Max.CR
Jan.	13,100 –	8,300	12,600 –	9,100
Feb.	13,500 –	9,200	13,900 –	9,900
Mar.	11,000 –	7,100	15,800 –	10,200
Apr.	7,100 –	5,000	17,100 –	11,100
May	5,000 –	2,700	14,000 –	9,300
June	2,700 –	3,000 CR	8,000 –	5,200
July	2,900 –	1,700 CR	8,900 –	6,300
Aug.	4,000 –	2,100	10,200 –	8,300
Sep.	5,300 –	3,900	11,300 –	8,900
Oct.	6,100 –	4,100	13,800 –	10,200
Nov.	8,500 –	6,300	15,200 –	13,800
Dec.	10,800 –	8,500	17,100 –	15,200
Limit £14,000 to 31.12.79			Limit £14,000 to 31.12.80	
Turnover ½yr to June	130,000		110,000	
½yr to Dec.	90,000		70,000	

NOTES: The following may be deduced from these figures, and possible reasons are considered. Discussions with the directors should confirm or answer the banker's fears.

(1) In 1979 the account worked well within the agreed overdraft facility throughout. (2) In 1979 there was a good "swing" each month in the range of balances and in June/July the account swung into credit. (3) In 1979 the borrowing was least in the spring/summer months—seasonal sales? (4) In 1979 most of the annual turnover (sales) was effected in the first six months of the year. (5) In 1980 this was true again, but the amount was reduced (despite inflation?) considerably. (6) In 1980 the overdraft reduced at a much slower rate in the spring than in 1979 (less sales/profits?). (7) In 1980 the overdraft exceeded the agreed limit in Mar./Apr. and at the year end, and the trend is disturbing. (8) In Nov./Dec. 1980 there is little "swing" between Max/Min figures—disturbing. (9) In those consecutive months where the Max.DR figure for the first month is the same as the Min.DR figure for the next, it is a fair assumption that there has been a continuous rising trend over the two or more months.

ASSET ITEMS

23. Fixed assets. Stated briefly, these are the assets retained permanently in the business in order to help earn profits. The nature of what constitutes fixed assets varies from business to business, but the following are commonly fixed assets in most businesses:

(*a*) *Land and buildings.* The cost, date of purchase, age, area, description and general maintenance are all important. If leasehold, the length of the unexpired lease is important. Has an annual amortisation charge been made? Does the amortisation charge shown indicate that the lease has almost expired? (Usually the *cost price* of the land and buildings is shown, but be watchful for additions and revaluations.)

(*b*) *Plant and machinery.* The exact nature and condition of these items should be established. Are they modern and well maintained? Are reasonable depreciation amounts allowed?

(*c*) *Fixtures, fittings, motors, loose tools, etc.* As in (*b*) above.

24. Intangible/fictitious assets. These include, goodwill, patents, trademarks, copyrights and preliminary expenses. While these may have considerable value when the business is a going concern, little or no value will attach if the business winds up. Consequently, they are usually ignored (or regarded as a deduction from capital resources) by a banker in his assessment of the balance sheet. Also a debit Profit and Loss Account (i.e. accumulated losses) is usually shown under fictitious assets.

25. Quoted investments. Must be distinguished in the balance sheet from trade and non-quoted investments. Consequently, an accurate valuation of these assets is usually obtainable.

> NOTE: Trade, non-quoted investments, investments in subsidiaries and loans to directors will for convenience be regarded by the bank as fixed assets when assessing the balance sheet.

26. Debtors. The amount and make-up requires examination, viz.:

(*a*) Are all the debtors good?

(*b*) What is the bad debts record like? Is there an adequate bad-debt provision in existence?

(*c*) Are the debtors well spread? If so the failure of one will be unlikely to jeopardise the company's position.

(*d*) Are debtors insured? (This would provide added security.)

If the amount of debtors is larger than seen previously, the reason should be established. It might be that the increase is proportionate to increased sales. Alternatively, longer credit might now be allowed. If the latter has been done to maintain sales, is the credit control adequate?

A comparison with previous debtors/sales ratios would help draw attention to alterations in the period of credit allowed.

RATIO

$$\frac{\text{Debtors} \times 52}{\text{Sales}} = \text{Number of weeks credit allowed}$$

> NOTE: The ratios in **19** and **26** will additionally be effected by any change in the proportion of cash to credit purchase or sales.

Factoring of debtors can assist the cash flow of a business considerably. The factoring company "buys" the debtors each month (usually for an agreed percentage amount (e.g. 90 per cent) of the sales ledger) and collects them on its own behalf. Thus debts are assigned, usually by a single omnibus factoring agreement between the company and the factor. Naturally a charge is made. The company is protected from risk of non-payment by its customers and is saved the expense and trouble of collecting moneys due. The factor will maintain the sales ledger and issue the invoices. A banker lending against a debenture will include a clause in his security precluding the company from factoring debtors without his prior agreement; nevertheless factoring can occur or be attempted without permission to ease difficulties in liquidity, and the lending banker must be alert. If the debenture holder is ready to agree to factoring, a priority agreement will be entered into between the three parties.

27. Stock. This is valued by competent persons, e.g. the company's directors. The figure shown in the balance sheet is usually the cost or market value, whichever is lower. The bank must be watchful for any change in the basis of valuation from year to year, as this may alter the gross profit figure considerably, as well as distorting the ratio of stock to cost of goods sold. This is an area where an unscrupulous person can "doctor" a balance sheet easily.

Raw materials, work-in-progress and finished goods will usually be valued separately, and any changes in the usual ratios require investigation. For example, (*a*) an increase in the work-in-progress figure may indicate bottlenecks in production, (*b*) an increase in finished goods may indicate either unsaleable stock or stockpiling. The directors must be asked to account for any appreciable changes in ratios.

RATIO

$$\frac{\text{Stock} \times 52}{\text{Cost of goods sold}} = \text{Number of weeks taken to turn over stock.}$$

NOTE: The figure for Sales may have to be used in place of Cost of Goods Sold (i.e. sales less gross profit), in the examination, as the latter will not normally be shown or ascertainable.

28. Work-in-progress. Only to be found in the balance sheets of manufacturing or contracting businesses. The total will include costs of raw materials, labour and administrative charges expended on the work to date.

29. Bills receivable. These will usually be bills accepted by trade debtors. The payment date is fixed, and discounting may take place where the acceptor is undoubted.

30. Credit bank balance. If the balance sheet shows a credit bank balance, has it been utilised since that date to pay off, for example, tax, dividends or creditors? Alternatively if a credit balance remains (*a*) how much can be made available towards any scheme for which the customer has asked for bank finance *and/or* (*b*) how much is available to help finance an increase in working capital? What is the total cash flow as seen from the account? What are the monthly maximum/minimum figures for the account?

REVENUE ACCOUNTS

31. Revenue accounts provide beneficial information to bankers. Bankers are particularly interested in their customers' revenue accounts, from which they can establish totals for the accounting period for purchases, sales, gross profit, administrative costs, net profit, etc. Revenue Accounts take the following form:

(*a*) *Manufacturing Account*. This account shows direct costs of production, which are then debited to:

(*b*) *Trading Account*. From which can be seen the total cost of goods sold and the gross profit made thereon. Gross profit is then credited to:

(*c*) *Profit and Loss Account*. From which can be seen overheads and expenses, e.g. administration, establishment, finance, bad debts, depreciation, etc. The resulting net profit or loss is transferred to:

(*d*) *Profit and Loss Appropriation Account*. Net profit is brought down on the credit side, and any undistributed profit from the *previous year* is added thereto.

The *whole* of this profit is then appropriated as regards tax, reserves, proposed dividends (gross), writing off goodwill, etc. The remaining *credit* balance is carried forward to the balance sheet as the new *undistributed profit figure to date*. (A *debit balance* would be shown among the fictitious assets as a *loss*.)

32. Profit trends. These are particularly important in assessing the progress of the company.

(*a*) *Profit and Loss Account*. The following must be noted for examination purposes:

(*i*) If the figure is shown as a deduction from capital or under fictitious assets this indicates accumulated losses. But even so, there may have been a profit made during the accounting year, so examine this year's profit and loss account together with previous years.

(*ii*) If the net profit figure *for the year* is greater than the accumulated profit figure seen in the balance sheet this indicates past losses.

(*iii*) A provision for taxation in the balance sheet is indicative of a profit for the year.

(*b*) *Ratio: Gross Profit to Sales.* This should be constant or rising. Any adverse movement calls for investigation from the trading account.

$$\frac{\text{Gross Profit} \times 100}{\text{Sales}}$$

(*c*) *Ratio: Net profit to Gross profit.* This should be constant or rising. Any adverse movement calls for investigation from the profit and loss account.

$$\frac{\text{Net Profit} \times 100}{\text{Gross profit}}$$

NOTE: When calculating the above ratio it is advantageous to add back tax to the net profit in order to get a comparable trend.

33. No set ratios exist. It should be noted that the ratios outlined in **32** above will differ materially with the type of business. Banks collate details of ratios for varying types of business. Nevertheless, for various reasons it is unlikely that the ratios of any one particular business will agree with average ratios for the trade. What is more important is that having satisfied oneself that the ratios of a particular business are reasonably satisfactory, any adverse changes should then be discussed with the company.

LIQUIDITY

34. Working-capital surplus. One of the primary concerns of a banker is that the balance sheet of the company requiring to borrow shows a satisfactory liquid surplus, i.e. its current assets exceed its current liabilities. Ideally the bank will always be looking for this liquid surplus, although, if liquidity is becoming stretched, this may be the very reason why overdraft facilities are sought. Nevertheless, a surplus does not necessarily imply that the company has sufficient cash assets to pay its debts as and when they fall due. Consider the following:

	A Ltd.	B Ltd.	C Ltd.
Current Assets	£	£	£
Bank	25,000	20,000	15,000
Stock/Work-in-progress	15,000	15,000	25,000
Debtors	20,000	25,000	20,000
	60,000	60,000	60,000
Less *Current Liabilities*			
Creditors	30,000	30,000	30,000
Working capital surplus	£30,000	£30,000	£30,000
Ratio	2.0	2.0	2.0

Although the ratio is 2.0 in each instance (i.e. 60,000 ÷ 30,000), it is obvious that the actual "liquid" position of Company A is better than that of Company C because less is tied up in stocks and work-in-progress and more cash is available to meet the demands of creditors.

35. Working-capital deficit. It must not be thought that wherever a company has a working-capital deficit that the bank will be unwilling to lend. Everything depends upon the surrounding circumstances as to whether support will be given during periods of non-liquidity. Such factors as: (*a*) the weight of capital resources in relation to total liabilities and to the sales turnover; (*b*) the estimated true value of the assets; (*c*) the ability, attitude and co-operation of the directors; (*d*) the prospects in the particular trade; will influence the bank in its decision. Security will normally be required where accommodation is granted in such circumstances.

36. Overtrading. This has been touched on in XVI, **10–11**. Put simply, overtrading amounts to a position where the scale of business operations outstrips available financial resources.

37. Overtrading seen from the banking account. The following features indicate overtrading:

(*a*) The development of a "hard core" in borrowing which previously fully fluctuated. (Good periodical fluctuations in an account balance indicate continuing business activity and payment by debtors.)

(*b*) "Hard pressed" account dealings, e.g. customer continually: (*i*) drawing cheques before paying in covering funds, (*ii*) issuing post-dated cheques.

(*c*) The need for weekly excesses for wage payments.

(*d*) Payment of creditors: (*i*) "on account" in round sums, (*ii*) "in advance" to obtain deliveries which would not otherwise be forthcoming.

NOTE: Although (*a*) above is usually associated with *increasing turnover*, it must be remembered that other actions by the customer can also bring about "hard-core" borrowing, e.g. purchase of fixed assets, loans to other companies, etc.

38. Overtrading seen from the balance sheet and accounts. The following features indicate overtrading:

(*a*) Current liabilities substantially in excess of capital resources.

(*b*) Small capital resources in relation to sales turnover.

(*c*) A declining debtors/creditors ratio.

(*d*) The taking of longer credit and/or giving of shorter credit: (*i*) than is usual in the trade, (*ii*) than previously.

(*e*) The appearance of bills payable.

(*f*) Increased overheads coupled with diminishing cash resources.

(*g*) Increased borrowing from all available outside sources at high interest rates.

NOTE: The indicators listed in **37** and **38** *cannot* be taken as conclusive evidence of *excessive overtrading*. A slight degree of overtrading can exist without danger. Nevertheless, a close watch of the situation is required.

39. Example of envisaged overtrading. A customer produces the following balance sheet and states that as he is about to *double his turnover* he wishes to increase his existing borrowing limit from £3,000 to £6,000.

	£	£	£
Fixed assets			2,000
Current assets			
Stocks:			
Raw materials	4,000		
Finished goods	5,000		
Debtors	5,000		
	——	14,000	

	£	£	£
Current liabilities			
Creditors	7,000		
Tax	1,600		
Bank	2,900		
		11,500	
Liquid surplus			2,500
			£4,500
Capital			3,000
Profit and Loss A/c			1,500
			£4,500

40. Examination of the request. Let us exaine the request in relation to the amount asked, basing our calculations *solely* on the balance sheet figures. We will assume *that current assets will double if turnover is to double*. This *unconfirmed* assumption is based upon the fact that a *doubling of sales* will necessitate the customer having twice as much tied up in stocks and debtors. Thus an additional £14,000 of current assets must be financed from some source. But from where?

If puchases double it is reasonable to assume that the creditors figure will do likewise. This will provide £7,000 towards the £14,000, leaving a shortfall of £7,000, which would be partly covered by the additional £3,000 bank lending, if agreed. However, a further £4,000 would need to be borrowed in order to leave the liquid surplus as before at £2,500. (In any case, this surplus may be regarded as insufficient margin for the new increased turnover.)

41. Pointers concerning the request. It appears that the customer would really need (at least) an extra £7,000, not £3,000, in order to finance a doubling of turnover. Consequently:

(*a*) The customer would soon find that his working capital was insufficient to finance the increased volume of trade which he had undertaken.

(*b*) An overtrading position would arise, and the customer would need to rely more and more on his creditors.

(*c*) If the bank agreed the £6,000 limit asked the customer would almost certainly need to return later for a larger limit. In any case, the bank's stake would be greater than that of the proprietor(s).

NOTE: (*i*) If the proprietor(s) put in an additional £4,000 as capital or long-term loans, then the proposition would be feasible. (*ii*) If short-term lenders provided the £4,000, then although with the bank limit of £6,000 the liquid position would be restored, the capital resources would remain low at £4,500.

42. Conclusion concerning the request. In practice, the customer would be asked to produce his financial budget and cash-flow figures. These figures, together with what the bank can derive from the cash flow seen from the customer's current-account ledger, may prove that the position will not be as bad as first envisaged. For example, it may prove possible to save on future overheads or production costs, to hold less stocks to take longer credit and to speed up collection of debtors.

In our example it seems unlikely that the bank would agree to lend, unless the necessary capital or long-term loans were put into the business or unless the customer agreed to proceed more slowly against a smaller bank advance.

43. Undertrading. The indication for this will be a fall in sales. Initially the bank account may look healthier as past sales proceeds come in (if stocks are not replenished), but ultimately the effect of continued overheads will reverse this position.

The situation is more difficult to remedy than overtrading, because such factors as increased costs, changes of taste, bad or indifferent management, fall in production, etc., bring about the position. More usually a reappraisal and perhaps drastic reorganisation of the whole business is required.

IMPACT OF THE ADVANCE ON LIQUIDITY

44. Utilisation of the advance. In the above example the impact of overtrading on financial resources has been shown. It is now proposed to outline the impact of a bank advance on liquidity generally. Borrowing from the bank will be utilised within three groups:

(*a*) To add to *fixed assets*, e.g. premises.
(*b*) To add to *current assets*, e.g. stock.
(*c*) To discharge *current liabilities*, e.g. tax.

The effect on liquidity is dependent upon which group the lending falls under.

In **45–47** below brief consideration is given to the position where a company wishes to borrow £30,000 for these three different uses. The following balance sheet is common to each proposition:

	£		£
Capital resources	64,000	Fixed assets	46,000
Current liabilities	36,000	Current assets	54,000
	£100,000		£100,000

NOTE: The working capital £18,000 gives a 1.5 ratio.

45. Bank lending for purchase of fixed assets. Unless on medium- or long-term loan, this will *always* deplete the working capital, because the borrowing on overdraft, being repayable "on demand", must be regarded by the borrower as a current liability. Thus the lending of £30,000 turns the liquid surplus of £18,000 into a deficit of £12,000 (*ratio* 0.818). As the repayment programme for this type of lending would be geared to annual repayments, e.g. over five years, it may be that the bank (*albeit in its own eyes*) will be willing to regard a proportion of the advance as being appropriate to long-term liability when viewing the effect on working capital.

Several questions must be satisfactorily resolved before agreement can be reached for lending for purchase of fixed assets. For instance, full details will be required showing the exact nature of the proposed expenditure and outlining the expected increase in profits resulting therefrom. No doubt the company will be optimistic as regards expansion of turnover, but it must be remembered that additional working capital will be needed to finance the expansion. Have the company budgeted for this? Figures must be produced showing from where the additional finance will come.

In our example it may be that the company will be advised to borrow on mortgage from a long-term institutional lender, e.g. an insurance company or subsidiary banking company, and the bank may be willing to stand in and lend purely for the additional working-capital needs which are bound to arise. Here again *the position is flexible*, and a good customer may be helped here if the bank can be satisfied both as to the soundness of the proposition and the prospects for repayment over medium term, covering principal and interest.

The point is that the working-capital position must be closely examined to see that *every factor* has been considered. Also the company must not have too much of its resources tied up in fixed assets. As security, the bank would require a charge over the fixed assets and perhaps a floating charge over the company's remaining assets.

46. Bank lending for additions to current assets. Both current liabilities and current assets will increase by £30,000, so that the working capital remains as before. However, the ratio worsens from 1.5 to 1.27. This implies that the £18,000 liquid surplus is now financing a smaller proportion of the current assets. Whether this margin will remain sufficient will depend upon the total of current assets to be financed and the cash flow.

47. Bank lending for payment of current liabilities. This brings no change in the liquid-surplus or working-capital ratio, because the bank advance is substituted for the liability paid off.

The bank will be wary in that it will not wish to take over the creditors' position where the working capital is not adequate or where stocks or work-in-progress are over-valued. Lending to enable a company to pay its tax is commonly agreed where a definite source of repayment can be seen.

BORROWING REQUIREMENT AND REPAYMENT

48. The amount. *See* XVI, **5**.

49. Repayment programme. Short-term programmes are attractive, although there is an increasing willingness to accommodate medium and long-term loans especially in connection with purchase or additions to fixed assets. More often, in respect of medium- and long-term lending the banks are requiring the customer to take the borrowing on loan account and make agreed fixed monthly/annual reductions. *See also* XVI, **7**.

50. Borrowing repayable over short-term. Where short-term advances are to be repaid from a known and certain source, e.g. outstanding undoubted debtors, undoubted bills of exchange, proceeds of life policy, proceeds of asset sold, etc., then it is usually unnecessary for the bank to require the customer to furnish projected budgets concerning his business. However, where the repayment is not from a guaranteed source or where a customer requires an annual limit it is usually desirable to call for projected budgets of the type mentioned in **51** below.

51. Customer's budget as aid to determining the borrowing requirement and repayment period. Where necessary (particularly in the case of applications for term loans) the bank should require the customer to furnish projected budgets showing fully the use to be made of the bank advance and outlining the expected receipts/expenditure and net profit (before depreciation) over the term of the advance.

The bank's records concerning the customer's past forecasts, past performance and past profits (as seen from the bank accounts and B/S and accounts) will be used by the manager as an aid to help check that the contents of the budgets appear correct. Adjustments must be made if the manager finds that the figures appear over optimistic.

With these budgets available the manager is able to confirm the maximum borrowing requirement and also whether repayment is likely to be achieved within the term indicated by the customer or within such longer term as the bank considers acceptable.

Budgeting has become more important for the lending banker in recent years, and whilst very small businesses are not usually required to produce budgets in any degree of sophistication, the principle of "knowing where we are going" and of making forecasts, and then checking against actual performance, can still be a most useful business and financial discipline.

For the larger concern budgets are prepared for capital expenditure (long-term and short-term), for operating purposes (e.g. annual trading performance) and cash use (cash flow, in and out). The cash flow is, of course, of particular significance and help to the bank. In addition to helping the making of a lending decision at the outset the importance of a budget can lie in the deviations which subsequently arise in practice, enabling the borrower and lender to review the overall position in the light of changed circumstances. Revised forecasts may then be necessary, and/or steps taken to correct matters.

In practice it is the trend in cumulative figures which is more helpful than any strict adherence to budget figures in any one month.

52. Repayments from increased profits: allowance for tax. Where repayment prospects are to be dependent in whole or in part upon

EXAMPLE OF CASH FLOW FORECAST JAN/JUNE

	Jan.	*Feb.*	*Mar.*	*Apr.*	*May*	*June*	**Total**
RECEIPTS							
Debtors	50,000	50,000	53,000	55,000	58,000	60,000	326,000
Other cash items			1,000				1,000
(A) Total receipts	50,000	50,000	54,000	55,000	58,000	60,000	327,000
PAYMENTS							
Creditors	37,000	40,000	39,000	41,000	40,000	38,000	235,000
Rent			5,000		5,000		10,000
Wages etc.	9,000	8,000	8,000	7,000	7,000	7,000	46,000
Capital expenditure		10,000					10,000
Sundries	1,000	1,000	4,000	1,000	1,000	4,000	12,000
(B) Total payments	47,000	59,000	56,000	49,000	48,000	54,000	313,000
Net cash movement (A) – (B) = IN	3,000			6,000	10,000	6,000	25,000 IN
(B) – (A) = OUT		9,000	2,000				11,000 OUT
Bank borrowing *b/f* at beginning of month	DR30,000	DR27,000	DR36,000	DR38,000	DR32,000	DR22,000	DR30,000
Forecast bank borrowing *c/f* at end of month	DR27,000	DR36,000	DR38,000	DR32,000	DR22,000	DR16,000	DR16,000

a future *increase* in the customer's profits then verifying the budget figures becomes even more important. Also, the manager must check that a figure for tax has been allowed therein to cover the *whole* of the expected profit.

53. Repayment of advance: importance of future net profit + depreciation; but interference of other factors. The customer's *projected net profit* (i.e. profit after allowing deductions for tax, directors' fees or proprietors' drawings, dividends or other appropriations but before charging depreciation) *expected to be earned over the period of the advance* can be regarded as the total amount which can become available to repay the advance unless (*a*) repayment is to be forthcoming from sources other than profits, e.g. sale of a fixed asset or funding of bank advance, etc., or (*b*) repayment of creditors is postponed, or (*c*) repayment of certain creditors will not fall due in the period, e.g. tax.

Students should take particular note that *net profit*, i.e. *with depreciation added back*, will not necessarily be represented by *actual cash* which will become available to pay off the customer's overdraft within the agreed lending period, as part or all of the *profit* which is required to pay off the overdraft *may find its way into* (*a*) an increase in current assets, e.g. stock, work-in-progress, debtors, (*b*) an increase in fixed assets, e.g. premises, plant or machinery, (*c*) a reduction in current liabilities, e.g. creditors, repayment of directors' loan moneys. It can be seen, therefore, that these profits may in certain instances be diverted from the banking account for a short or indefinite period or possibly forever, e.g. if spent (contrary to agreement) on a fixed asset which fails to help generate earnings.

Despite these obvious dangers the net profit calculation provides *a useful starting point* in helping an examination candidate, who has been given *limited* information in a question, to arrive at *a provisional conclusion* as to whether repayment of an amount requested by the customer appears feasible within a reasonable period.

EXAMPLE: The customer requests to borrow £20,000 to be repaid over five years and produces his latest accounts showing: (annual) net profit £1,000—after charging—depreciation £4,000, tax £500, directors' fees £6,000. At first sight it would appear that repayment could not be achieved within five years on annual net profits of £1,000, but the depreciation figure is merely a bookkeeping entry and does not affect the net cash inflow which is therefore £1,000 + £4,000 = £5,000. If the same net cash inflow is maintained in subsequent years it would be possible to repay the loan in four years (ignoring bank interest) if these profits *were only to be used to repay the overdraft.*

In practice the bank would also be using the customer's projected budgets mentioned in **51** above to establish the likely *net cash* to become available to pay off the overdraft within the period agreed, after making due allowance for sums to be used by the customer out of future profits, e.g. expenditure on additional plant.

NOTE: Although depreciation is a bookkeeping entry which does not concern *cash flow* it must not be forgotten that the life of the depreciated asset is shortening and will ultimately usually need to be replaced.

BREAK-UP OF A BALANCE SHEET

54. Reasons for undertaking a break-up valuation. It is only after examining a company's "going-concern" position (i.e. current dynamic position) that a banker would in practice wish to examine the "gone-concern" position (i.e. the envisaged financial position should liquidation occur).

Where both the company's capital resources and working capital surplus are substantial, there is little point in more than a cursory appraisal of the gone-concern position. It is only where one of these positions does not exist, or where there are prior secured creditors, or the bank lending is exceptionally large, that a banker would do a detailed break-up valuation of the balance sheet assets *in order to see better the extent of the possible risk*. The banker may be trying to decide whether he needs to take security to safeguard his position, or whether in a situation where he is already deeply lent he can safely lend more or give further time before perhaps calling in his advance.

It must be stressed that accuracy in estimates is difficult, and should liquidation occur the company's liability and asset structure would usually prove different at that time. Also the actual realisation figures may be completely different from those contemplated.

Where the bank takes a debenture incorporating a floating charge, it will carry out a periodical revaluation of its security to cover changes in the company's liabilities and assets, and break-up valuations of assets may be estimated on written down percentages, as e.g. plant and machinery 50 per cent, debtors 50 per cent, stock 60 per cent of book values. These figures are not "sacrosanct", and merely serve to show the very different picture which usually results when a business is closed down in liquidation or receivership and unattractive assets have to be sold.

55. Example of break-up valuation. The following simplified example shows the banker's basic approach to break-up valuation.

It has been assumed that the bank is to lend the company £52,000, mainly for purchase of fixed assets. The envisaged borrowing and increase in assets have been allowed for in the table.

Liabilities		*Assets*		*Estimated realisation value at liquidation*
	£		£	£
Capital	30,000	Land and buildings	30,000	22,500
Reserves	15,000	Plant and machinery	20,000	8,000
Profit and Loss A/c	13,000	Fixtures and fittings	4,000	Nil
		Motors	12,000	6,000
	£58,000	Stock	42,000	21,000
		Debtors	15,000	7,500
Bank advance	52,000	Goodwill	14,000	Nil
Unsecured creditors	20,000			
Tax (preferential)	7,000			
	£79,000		137,000	65,000

	£
Available Cash to pay off creditors	65,000
Less Preferential: Tax	7,000
Leaving	£58,000 to cover £72,000 unsecured creditors.

Thus a bank lending of £52,000 would entail risk. In this instance in view of the total bank commitment, the working-capital deficit and the estimated break-up risk, the bank would certainly require a charge over the fixed assets and possibly a debenture incorporating a fixed and floating charge as its security.

NOTE: (1) No fixed ratios for break-up valuation exist, because everything depends upon the type of business and other varying factors involved, e.g. the premises might be specialised and of little use for other purposes. (2) Due allowance would need to be made in respect of any creditors secured on the assets of the company. (3) The break-up approach is by no means the only factor which determines whether security will be required.

COMMON INTERPRETATION MISCONCEPTIONS

56. Students' misconceptions. Certain misconceptions appear so frequently in answers to interpretation questions that a short list of the more obvious ones has been made in **57–71** below. Students are advised to give these careful study.

57. Reserves always imply cash. Incorrect. Profits which are retained in the business in the form of reserves are normally invested in additional stock, fixed capital, etc. Consequently, reserves are rarely represented by cash. The true factor is that if all the assets were realised at book values, then after deducting intangibles and paying off all other liabilities the proprietors would obtain a return of capital, and share any resulting surplus formerly represented by reserves and profit and loss account.

58. Large cash balance at bank implies: (*a*) that no borrowing is really required, or (*b*) that the company's liquid position is satisfactory. These factors would not usually be true where current liabilities exceed current assets, or where, say, an excess of current assets over current liabilities was comprised of unsaleable stock. In these circumstances the cash would be required to help pay off outstanding creditors, tax, dividends due, etc.

59. A build-up of reserves is better than a build-up of profits. Incorrect. As revenue reserves are appropriations of profit, there is no practical difference between the two.

60. The debtors figure in the balance sheet should always exceed the creditors figure. This would only be expected if the length of credit given and taken was the same. Obviously where a retailer buys on credit and sells for cash his creditors figure would be higher.

61. An excess of current assets over current liabilities implies true liquidity. This is not always so. For instance, if a stock figure appears higher than average for the type of business, it may be found that old or unsaleable stock has been included in the total.

62. A liquid surplus indicates that no borrowing is needed. Often the case, but consider the following:

	£		£
Creditors	10,000	Debtors	14,000
Bank	Nil	Stock	9,000

Working capital surplus = £13,000. But where is the cash to pay wages?

63. Any agreed reductions in borrowing will automatically occur so long as covering profits are made. Incorrect. What if the realised increased profits are channelled to purchase more fixed assets or to pay the directors additional remuneration? The bank could find itself last in the list of benefactors unless watchful.

64. Small past net profits are indicative that a bank advance cannot be repaid. Often true, but remember to (*a*) see if the charge to *depreciation* is large as this is a bookkeeping entry which does not affect cash flow; (*b*) ascertain whether any *exceptional* charge has depleted profits; (*c*) allow for future increases in profits.

65. Losses shown in the balance sheet indicate loss for the year. Incorrect. The figure indicates accumulated losses to date. It may be that a profit has been made over the year; check the profit and loss appropriation account for details.

66. Periodical repayment of bank borrowing as arranged means that business progress must have been good. It is to be hoped that this is true. However, it may be that reductions have not come from trading profit but from, say, postponement of payment of creditors. The balance sheet requires examination to verify the true position.

67. A company lacking fixed assets to charge as security will be unable to charge tangible security where borrowing is taken to purchase land and buildings. Incorrect. The assets to be purchased can ultimately be charged.

68. Building Societies provide long-term loans for purchase of factory or business premises. Incorrect. Only house purchasers are usually helped, and occasionally farmers. Insurance companies, subsidiary banking companies, and other specialist lenders, e.g. Agricultural Mortgage Corporation, provide long-term loans. Additionally stocking finance can be provided by Finance Houses.

69. The directors will introduce £5,000 .... This does not mean from the company's own resources but from the directors' private resources or from other outside sources.

(*a*) If the *directors* are introducing the moneys themselves the effect on any outstanding guarantee liability of the directors concerned should be noted.

(*b*) If *outsiders* are introducing loans the effect on the company's ability to service bank borrowing should be noted.

(*c*) It is important for the lender to know that the source and timing of the funds to be introduced are entirely certain, since otherwise, if the bank has already lent, it may have to go in further than it wishes by advancing this sum too.

70. Advances should not be granted to recently formed companies accumulating losses. Perhaps in general correct, but balance sheets and accounts should be seen, since incorporation and the facts behind the figures should be examined. Much will depend upon the actual progress and the reason for the losses. It may be that the bank has every confidence both as regards the directors and the prospects in the industry concerned.

Obviously formation expenses and overheads will curtail or eliminate profits in initial years. (This occurs, for example, where a new branch bank is opened until adequate new business is forthcoming.) Nevertheless, the need to conserve funds and plough back profits may in the light of an advance proposal mean that a longer-term loan from an outside source would be more suitable.

71. The balance sheet of an existing business provides a complete guide for any future proposition. Untrue. For instance, if the customer wishes to purchase an additional business, production of balance sheets and accounts for his existing business will only show the state and progress of that business. *It will tell us nothing about the business being bought*.

Consequently, the balance sheet(s) and account(s) of the new business to be purchased should also be required, so that the results can be examined, particularly with a view to estimating what profits can be expected and whether any bank advance granted towards the purchase could be satisfactorily repaid *from the profits of the existing and new business*. The physical factors, such as staffing, location, etc., should not be overlooked, and if the business is run down, the likelihood of improvement under new management should be borne in mind.

APPROACH TO BALANCE SHEET QUESTIONS

72. Use all the information given. It is most important *to read the question carefully*, noting all pertinent facts before trying to interpret the balance sheet. The balance sheet *must* be interpreted in the light of the business to which it refers. It is of no use merely outlining ratios and break-up values unless conclusions are drawn or questions raised regarding the proposition or business.

The candidate is deliberately placed in the position of having to delve behind the figures in order to reach any possible conclusions from the limited information given. Care should be taken not to arrive at a decision where the information given is inadequate. It is intended that the candidate should ask the prospective borrower to furnish any further information which is required.

73. General points to look for. Always be on the look-out for the following:

(*a*) The business of the borrowing concern not being stated. How, therefore, can the stock turnover be seen to be reasonable?

(*b*) Balance sheet already well out of date—request interim figures.

(*c*) No trading figures given for purchases, sales, etc. Consequently, no comparison can be made as regards credit given and taken. Also stock turnover cannot be ascertained.

(*d*) No comparative figures given for previous years. How can the progress of the business be measured? In respect of (*c*) and (*d*) call for appropriate figures.

(*e*) Directors taking excessive drawings and/or the payment of excessive dividends, from small profits. If this has been the policy when the profits are small, what will be the policy if profits increase?

(*f*) Change of premises necessitated. What effect will this have on production? Will the new premises be conveniently situated as regards labour, transport, amenities, etc.?

(*g*) Prospective borrower operating from premises held on short lease. What plans have been made regarding termination? How will the plans affect the liquid position?

74. Examination approach. There can be no fixed approach, because everything depends upon the nature of the proposition and business involved and the exact wording of the question.

However, candidates will invariably be expected to *mention or discuss*:

(*a*) The *acceptability of the proposition*, bearing in mind the principles of lending.

(*b*) The *amount asked*, bearing in mind; (*i*) whether this can be seen to be insufficient or too much for the envisaged project, (*ii*) whether the bank's stake will be too great.

(*c*) The *borrowing powers of the company and its directors* where lending to a company. Noting particularly from the figures given whether the directors' limit would be exceeded and the manner in which this could be resolved if the bank advance was agreed.

(*d*) The *customer's record*. As seen from past balance sheets and accounts and perhaps up-to-date figures.

(*e*) The *factors which have been presented* in the examination question. Making a note of any further information which is required.

(*f*) The effect of the bank lending or envisaged expansion *on liquid resources*.

(*g*) The evidence required to show that the existing profits and increased profits after allowing for tax *will be sufficient to pay off the bank borrowing, including interest, within a reasonable period.*

(*h*) The situation of *overtrading* (where appropriate).

(*i*) The necessity of *giving advice or suggesting alternative solutions* where an advance must be declined.

(*j*) The *physical factors* of the proposition, such as staffing, location, available market for the product, expanding or declining industry, etc.

(*k*) The *security required.*

NOTE: Where there is a *prior charge by way of debenture*, the bank may require that the debenture *be postponed* so that suitable security can be obtained, e.g. to enable the bank to complete a legal mortgage over new property purchased with the bank advance.)

CURRENT COST ACCOUNTING

75. Current Cost Accounting. This modern and increasingly important concept must be known by students, and they should ensure that they have studied it for their Accountancy Paper and are now entirely up-to-date for the Practice of Banking examination.

The approach taken to audited accounts changes progressively as the subject is studied by the accountancy profession, but overall Current Cost Accounting attempts to take into the accounts the effects of changed price levels (inflation) at which assets (e.g. stock), fall due for replacement (e.g. upon being sold). Depreciation of assets is based on historic values but may be charged and based on revalued figures.

Current Cost Accounting also attempts to provide for an additional charge against profits in respect of any extra funds required simply to maintain trading at the same level in a different price environment.

It is mandatory for certain sized companies now to provide accounts prepared under the latest Current Cost Accounting rules, although historic accounts are still exhibited.

Early evidence emerging from Current Cost Accounting indicates that in most cases "true" profits are reduced. As with any balance sheet appraisal, however, the *trend* over a period of accounts produced on this basis will be one of the most helpful lending aids to a banker.

PROGRESS TEST 17

1. Why do bankers require several years' balance sheets and accounts when examining a borrowing proposition? **(4, 5)**

2. Into what groupings does a banker usually split up balance sheet items on his comparative form? **(12)**

3. What do you understand by working capital? How is the balance sheet figure for working capital arrived at? **(12)**

4. What information would you require regarding the item "debenture(s)" appearing in a company balance sheet? **(16)**

5. What do you understand by comparative ratios? Show how the usual ratios are determined by respect of creditors, debtors, stock. Examine the possible reasons for changes in any of these ratios. **(19, 26, 27)**

6. Give examples of indicators of overtrading as seen from: (*a*)

the customer's banking account; (*b*) the customer's business accounts. **(37, 38)**

7. Show simply how an increase in turnover brings a need for increased finance. **(39–42)**

8. What questions must be resolved where a banker is asked to lend to a customer for the purchase of fixed assets? **(45, 51–53)**

9. How important is a "break-up valuation" of a company's assets to a banker who is about to lend unsecured? **(54, 55)**

10. List several common errors which many students make when interpreting balance sheets. **(57–71)**

11. What general points would you look for in a borrowing proposition, and how would you approach examination questions concerning borrowing? **(73, 74)**

12. What is a Cash Flow Forecast? **(51)**

13. What help is Current Cost Accounting to the lending banker? **(75)**

CHAPTER XVIII

Group Borrowing

THE NATURE OF GROUPS AND THEIR ACCOUNTS

1. The nature of a group. A group comes into existence when two or more companies enter the relationship of holding company and subsidiary.

A company is a subsidiary of another if that other:

(*a*) is a *member* of it and *controls* the composition of its board of directors; or

(*b*) holds more than *half* in nominal value of its *equity* share capital.

Additionally a subsidiary of a subsidiary is regarded as a subsidiary of the holding company: CA 1948, s. 154.

2. Consolidated accounts. Where the relationship of holding company and subsidiary exists, a consolidated balance sheet will need to be produced at the end of each financial year. This balance sheet is an *amalgamation* of all the separate balance sheets of the companies which form the group. It will in effect show the position of the group as against the outside world, but note that *the group is not a separate entity*. (A consolidated profit and loss account must also be produced.)

The *holding* company will also produce its own balance sheet which will show, *inter alia*, an item "shares in subsidiaries". *Each subsidiary* company will also produce a balance sheet for the *benefit of its own members*.

3. The consolidated balance sheet. This balance sheet is prepared for the benefit of the holding company's shareholders, and although it assists bankers in showing the group's strength, it can *without further information* prove misleading in that, unknown to the bank, borrowing may be required by the weakest member.

Note the following points regarding the consolidated balance sheet:

(*a*) The *capital* shown is that of the *holding company*.

(*b*) The *accumulated reserves and Profit and Loss Account balance* is that of the *whole group* after excluding inter-company profits and minority interests.

(*c*) The *interests of outside shareholders* in subsidiaries (i.e. the minority interests, if any) are shown on the liabilities side.

(*d*) The *assets* shown are those of the *whole group*.

(*e*) All *inter-company debts* are cancelled out.

(*f*) *Either*: the liabilities side will show "Capital Reserve", being book profit on purchase of shares in subsidiaries; *or* the assets side will show "Goodwill", i.e. excess cost of control of shares in subsidiaries.

4. The holding company's balance sheet. Shows the position of the *holding company* as a separate entity. The balance sheet discloses, *inter alia*: (*a*) shareholdings in subsidiaries; (*b*) loans and dividends owing from subsidiaries; (*c*) loans to subsidiaries.

5. The Balance Sheet of a subsidiary shows the position of the subsidiary as a separate entity, and therefore the total of its capital resources can be seen. Also all inter-company loans, etc., will be shown.

LENDING TO COMPANIES WITHIN A GROUP

6. The banker's approach to group borrowing. The following should be noted:

(*a*) The principles of lending should not readily be departed from.

(*b*) The consolidated balance sheet shows the group's strength, *but each company is a separate entity* and must be dealt with as such.

(*c*) *Unsecured* lending to one group member can be jeopardised by a transfer of its assets to another member. Consequently, one of the secured positions mentioned below should be aimed at:

(*d*) The *integrity and reliability* of the controlling directors must be beyond doubt.

(*e*) The balance sheets and profit and loss accounts of *each* member of the group should be studied to ascertain the *progress* of both the group and its individual members.

(*f*) The group dealings may be interwoven and complicated, but lending should not be contemplated until the *overall position* can be clearly seen.

(*g*) The consolidated balance sheet will reveal whether accounts are maintained with other banks.

(*h*) Searches should be made at the Companies Registry on each company to ascertain if there are any *outstanding charges*.

(*i*) Where security is to be taken from one company for the liabilities of another, the bank must be satisfied that "commercial justification" exists for the giving of the security. In other words there must be a positive answer to the question, "Is the borrowing for the benefit of and to promote the prosperity of the giver of the security?" In most cases in a holding/subsidiary company group structure and relationship few difficulties are likely to be met—but see *Charterbridge Corporation* v. *Lloyds Bank Ltd.* (1969) for further discussion on this problem area.

7. Lending to a holding company.

(*a*) *Where it trades and wishes to borrow on its own behalf.* The usual considerations apply, and if its working capital and assets are ample apart from investments in, and loans to, subsidiaries the bank may be willing to lend unsecured.

(*b*) *Where it trades and wishes to borrow to finance group members.* The considerations in (*a*) apply. But if its own assets are insufficient to support the borrowing, guarantees may also be required from the subsidiaries supported by legal mortgages or debentures. The subsidiaries' balance sheets should be required.

(*c*) *Where it does not trade but wishes to borrow to finance group members.* If it has no tangible assets the strength of the subsidiaries must be seen from their balance sheets. They will usually be required to give guarantees supported by legal mortgages or debentures. In addition, a floating charge from the holding company is often required.

8. Possible alternatives when lending to a holding company.

(*a*) Lending *unsecured*. (If liquidation occurs the consolidated surplus would need to be lost before the bank advance is at risk.)

(*b*) Lending against *directors' guarantees*.

(*c*) Lending against the security of the *holding company's assets*, with or without guarantees from the subsidiaries, supported by mortgages or debentures.

9. Lending to a subsidiary. Unless its balance sheet is exceptionally strong, *one* of the following securities may be required:

(*a*) *A guarantee by the holding company*. (This effectively puts the consolidated surplus of the group behind the guarantee.)

(*b*) *A guarantee by each of the other group members*. (Here the bank would rank as an unsecured creditor against each guaranteeing company.)

(*c*) *A legal mortgage over the subsidiary's own fixed assets*.

10. Lending to the group. Where each company requires a borrowing limit, the bank will usually require one or other of the following guarantees:

(*a*) *Cross-guarantees*, i.e. guarantees from each company to secure the overdraft of each of the other companies in the group. (This position approximates to being an *unsecured* creditor of each company for the *aggregate* group borrowing.)

(*b*) *Cross-guarantees supported by debentures*. (This position approximates to being *secured* on all the group's assets for the *aggregate* group borrowing.) The best security position.

11. Additional notes.

(*a*) In all the above instances, the memorandum and articles of the borrowing and securing companies must be carefully examined and altered where necessary to enable borrowing and security to be perfected.

(*b*) When taking guarantees from group members supported by mortgages or debentures, it is better if the guarantees are *unlimited*, as this avoids any restriction on the amount recoverable under the supporting security.

(*c*) When lending *unsecured* to one company, the total group resources will *not* be supporting the borrowing unless the lending happens to be concentrated on the holding company's own account.

BANKING DIPLOMA EXAMINATION QUESTION

G.P. Ltd. is a holding company with four manufacturing subsidiaries. Its balance sheet is as follows:

Liabilities	£	*Assets*	£
Capital	300,000	Cash at bank	5,000
Reserves	100,000	Investments in subsidiaries	355,000
Profit and Loss A/c	23,000	Owing by subsidiaries	184,000
	423,000		
Creditors	2,000		
Owing to subsidiaries	85,000		
Tax provision	23,000		
Dividend provision	11,000		
	£544,000		£544,000

Two of the subsidiary companies own their freehold factories, two of them occupy rented premises and all of them own plant and machinery in their premises, being operated as separate units. All finance is provided by G.P. Ltd. G.P. Ltd. asks you for a limit of £250,000 to finance its subsidiaries, £150,000 to be used for building and machinery and the balance for general trading. You are offered a floating charge by G.P. Ltd. Say how you would deal with the proposition, and how you might strengthen the bank's security.

BRIEF ANSWER

THE PROPOSITION

(*a*) As only the *holding company's balance sheet* has been produced, the proposition cannot be dealt with unless further information is provided.

(*b*) The *capital resources* show a very healthy position, always assuming that the assets are worth their true face value, and the bank's stake would be reasonable.

(*c*) *Funds* will obviously need to be made available from amounts owing by subsidiaries to help meet the tax and dividend. But are the subsidiaries in a liquid position?

(*d*) *The balance sheets of the subsidiaries will need to be produced* to verify (*c*) and to value the "investments in subsidiaries" on a "break-up" basis after allowing for payment of all creditors.

(*e*) *The last three years' balance sheets and profit and loss accounts* of the holding company and its subsidiaries are needed to assess the progress. Also past and present consolidated balance sheets to assess the group's progress.

(*f*) *Are the directors* regarded as men of integrity and ability?

(*g*) In the light of (*e*) above and on the figures produced by the directors showing the *exact* use to be made of the borrowing and showing the increased profit expected therefrom, it will be seen whether repayments can be achieved within a satisfactory period.

THE SECURITY

(*h*) *The borrowing and charging powers* of G.P. Ltd. must be checked.

(*i*) While the security of a floating charge from G.P. Ltd. would give the bank the power to control G.P. Ltd. by appointing a receiver, it provides no tangible or readily realisable security. *Additionally*, guarantees should be required from the subsidiaries (preferably for £250,000 each) supported by legal mortgages and floating charges.

(*j*) *The subsidiaries' memoranda* must be examined to see whether the guarantees and debentures can be given.

PROGRESS TEST 18

1. What do you understand by: (*a*) a holding company; (*b*) a subsidiary? **(1)**
2. What are consolidated accounts? **(2, 3)**
3. What attitude would you adopt when approached for borrowing by a group of companies? **(6)**
4. What factors should be particularly examined when lending to a holding company so that it can provide finance for the group? What security might you require? **(7, 8)**
5. What is the best security position when lending to each company within a group? **(10)**

APPENDIX I

Cheques Act 1957

5 & 6 ELIZ. 2 CH. 36

1. (1) Where a banker in good faith and in the ordinary course of business pays a cheque drawn on him which is not indorsed or is irregularly indorsed, he does not, in doing so, incur any liability by reason only of the absence of, or irregularity in, indorsement, and he is deemed to have paid it in due course.

(2) Where a banker in good faith and in the ordinary course of business pays any such instrument as the following, namely—

(*a*) a document issued by a customer of his which, though not a bill of exchange, is intended to enable a person to obtain payment from him of the sum mentioned in the document;

(*b*) a draft payable on demand drawn by him upon himself, whether payable at the head office or some other office of his bank;

he does not, in doing so, incur any liability by reason only of the absence of, or irregularity in, indorsement, and the payment discharges the instrument.

2. A banker who gives value for, or has a lien on, a cheque payable to order which the holder delivers to him for collection without indorsing it, has such (if any) rights as he would have had if, upon delivery, the holder had indorsed it in blank.

3. An unindorsed cheque which appears to have been paid by the banker on whom it is drawn is evidence of the receipt by the payee of the sum payable by the cheque.

4. (1) Where a banker, in good faith and without negligence—

(*a*) receives payment for a customer of an instrument to which this section applies; or

(*b*) having credited a customer's account with the amount of such an instrument, receives payment thereof for himself;

and the customer has no title, or a defective title, to the instrument, the banker does not incur any liability to the true owner of the instrument by reason only of having received payment thereof.

(2) This section applies to the following instruments, namely—

(*a*) cheques;

(*b*) any document issued by a customer of a banker which, though not a bill of exchange, is intended to enable a person to obtain payment from that banker of the sum mentioned in the document;

(*c*) any document issued by a public officer which is intended to enable a person to obtain payment from the Paymaster General or the Queen's and Lord Treasurer's Remembrancer of the sum mentioned in the document but is not a bill of exchange;

(*d*) any draft payable on demand drawn by a banker upon himself, whether payable at the head office or some other office of his bank.

(3) A banker is not to be treated for the purposes of this section as having been negligent by reason only of his failure to concern himself with absence of, or irregularity in, indorsement of an instrument.

5. The provisions of the *Bills of Exchange Act* 1882, relating to crossed cheques shall, so far as applicable, have effect in relation to instruments (other than cheques) to which the last foregoing section applies as they have effect in relation to cheques.

6. (1) This Act shall be construed as one with the *Bills of Exchange Act* 1882.

(2) The foregoing provisions of this Act do not make negotiable any instrument which, apart from them, is not negotiable.

(3) The enactments mentioned in the first and second columns of the Schedule to this Act are hereby repealed to the extent specified in the third column of that Schedule.

7. This Act extends to Northern Ireland, but, for the purposes of section six of the Government of Ireland Act, 1920, so much of the provisions of this Act as relates to, or affects, instruments other than negotiable instruments shall be deemed to be provisions of an Act passed before the appointed day within the meaning of that section.

8. (1) This Act may be cited as the *Cheques Act* 1957.

(2) This Act shall come into operation at the expiration of a period of three months beginning with the day on which it is passed.

APPENDIX II

European Communities Act 1972

This Act came into effect on 1st January 1973. Section 9 which has nine sub-sections, is of importance to bankers. The section was enacted to:

(*a*) bring UK law into line with EEC law by affording protection to persons transacting in *good faith* with a company and its directors where unbeknown an *ultra vires* position arises (in this respect persons are no longer deemed to know or are bound to examine a company's memorandum or articles); (*b*) provide for publicity of important information regarding a company in a manner easily accessible throughout the EEC.

The main provision of the section concerning bankers is as follows:

> **9.** (1) In favour of a person dealing with a company in *good faith*, any *transaction* decided on by the *directors* shall be deemed to be one which it is within the capacity of the company to enter into, and the power of the directors to bind the company shall be deemed to be free of any *limitation* under the memorandum or articles of association; and a party to a transaction so decided on shall not be bound to enquire as to the capacity of the company to enter into it or as to any such limitation on the powers of the directors, and shall be presumed to have acted in good faith unless the contrary is proved.

1. General benefits of sub-section 1. *The* ultra vires *doctrine is restricted but not abolished.* Some ambiguity remains as to the courts' possible interpretation of the words in italics in s. 9 above. Nevertheless, it is clear that a bank which *has not seen the memorandum and articles of association* of its company customer but relies upon the resolution or assurances of the directors and deals in *good faith* in connection with transactions such as *borrowing*, accepting *security*, accepting *signing instructions*, etc., will be fully protected even where such transactions are *ultra vires* (either because they exceed the company's capacity and/or the directors' limitations); thus the directors' actions bind the company.

However, the banks have been unwilling to alter their existing practice of requiring up-to-date copies of memorandum and articles which they check as a prerequisite to opening an account, taking signing instructions, borrowing, etc., and existing statute and case law will remain relevant. In any case the *Rule in Turquand's Case* may well still have an important part to play where, for example, directors contravene the articles in respect of internal matters.

2. Legal benefits to banks although existing practices have remained unchanged.

(*a*) *Where the bank retain the memorandum and articles but do not examine them* for "limitations" prior to entering a transaction, then possibly the courts would still regard them as having acted in *good faith* (i.e. honestly), even though they were departing from normal banking practice.

(*b*) *Where the bank have read the memorandum and articles but misinterpret the legal meaning or scope* of these (as, for instance, in *Re Introductions Ltd.* (1969)), then the bank could still be said to have acted in *good faith.*

NOTE: In practice if there appears to be any doubt or ambiguity, then the passing of a special resolution will, as formerly, place the legality of the transaction beyond doubt.

3. Bank having actual knowledge of ultra vires position. Where the bank know that an *ultra vires* position occurs in relation to a transaction, e.g. where the memorandum and articles have been examined and it is known the directors are exceeding their borrowing powers under Table A, Art. 79, then obviously they will not have acted in *good faith*, and thus the company will not be bound.

NOTE: *Good faith* is to be presumed until the contrary is proved.

4. London Gazette—official notification. The Registrar of Companies must now publish in the *London Gazette* (*Edinburgh Gazette* for Scottish companies) "official notification" of the fact that he has received or issued certain documents (ECA 1972, s. **9**(3)), namely:

(*a*) certificates of incorporation;

(*b*) documents bringing about an alteration in the memorandum or articles;

(*c*) returns of directors or changes in directors;
(*d*) a company's annual return;
(*e*) a notice of the situation (or change) of a company's registered office;
(*f*) a copy of a winding-up order;
(*g*) an order for the dissolution of a company on a winding up;
(*h*) a return by a liquidator of a company's final meeting on a winding up.

5. Protection for persons dealing with a company in respect of certain events. A company *cannot rely against other persons* (e.g. the bank) *on the happening of any of the following events*: (*a*) the making of a winding-up order; (*b*) the appointment of a liquidator in a voluntary winding up; (*c*) any alteration of the company's memorandum or articles; (*d*) any change of directors; (*e*) (as regards service of any document on the company) any change in the situation of the company's registered office, *unless the event in question* has been published in the *London Gazette* or was known to the person concerned at the relevant time, *but* if the matter had been published less than fifteen days before the relevant time the person concerned may treat it as ineffective against him if he can show that he was unavoidably prevented from knowing it (ECA 1972, s. **9**(4)).

NOTE: There is always the possibility of loss if the bank ignores notices (under **4** and **5** above) affecting their relationship with their customers, consequently the *London Gazette* should continue to be examined carefully by the bank.

APPENDIX III

Consumer Credit Act 1974

PART II
CREDIT AGREEMENTS, HIRE AGREEMENTS AND LINKED TRANSACTIONS

8. (1) A personal credit agreement is an agreement between an individual ("the debtor") and any other person ("the creditor") by which the creditor provides the debtor with credit of any amount.

(2) A consumer credit agreement is a personal credit agreement by which the creditor provides the debtor with credit not exceeding £5,000.

(3) A consumer credit agreement is a regulated agreement within the meaning of this Act if it is not an agreement (an "exempt agreement") specified in or under section 16.

9. (1) In this Act "credit" includes a cash loan, and any other form of financial accommodation.

(2) Where credit is provided otherwise than in sterling it shall be treated for the purposes of this Act as provided in sterling of an equivalent amount.

(3) Without prejudice to the generality of subsection (1), the person by whom goods are bailed or (in Scotland) hired to an individual under a hire-purchase agreement shall be taken to provide him with fixed-sum credit to finance the transaction of an amount equal to the total price of the goods less the aggregate of the deposit (if any) and the total charge for credit.

(4) For the purposes of this Act, an item entering into the total charge for credit shall not be treated as credit even though time is allowed for its payment.

10. (1) For the purposes of this Act—

(*a*) running-account credit is a facility under a personal credit agreement whereby the debtor is enabled to receive from time to time (whether in his own person, or by another person) from the creditor or a third party cash, goods and services (or any of them) to an amount or value such that, taking into account payments made by or to the credit of the debtor, the credit limit (if any) is not at any time exceeded; and (*b*) fixed-sum credit is any other facility under a personal credit agreement whereby the debtor is enabled to receive (whether in one amount or by instalments).

(2) In relation to running-account credit, "credit limit" means, as respects any period, the maximum debit balance which, under the credit agreement, is allowed to stand on the account during that period, disregarding any term of the agreement allowing that maximum to be exceeded merely temporarily.

(3) For the purposes of section 8(2), running-account credit shall be taken not to exceed the amount specified in that subsection ("the specified amount") if—

(*a*) the credit limit does not exceed the specified amount; or

(*b*) whether or not there is a credit limit, and if there is, notwithstanding that it exceeds the specified amount—

(*i*) the debtor is not enabled to draw at any one time an amount which, so far as (having regard to section 9(4)) it represents credit, exceeds the specified amount, or

(*ii*) the agreement provides that, if the debit balance rises above a given amount (not exceeding the specified amount), the rate of the total charge for credit increases or any other condition favouring the creditor or his associate comes into operation, or

(*iii*) at the time the agreement is made it is probable, having regard to the terms of the agreement and any other relevant considerations, that the debit balance will not at any time rise above the specified amount.

Part III
Licensing of Credit and Hire Businesses
Licensing principles

21. (1) Subject to this action, a licence is required to carry on a consumer credit business or consumer hire business.

(2) A local authority does not need a licence to carry on a business.

(3) A body corporate empowered by a public general Act naming it to carry on a business does not need a licence to do so.

22. (1) A licence may be—

(*a*) a standard licence, that is a licence, issued by the Director to a person named in the licence on an application made by him, which, during the prescribed period, covers such activities as are described in the licence, or

(*b*) a group licence, that is a licence, issued by the Director (whether on the application of any person or of his own motion), which, during such period as the Director thinks fit or, if he thinks fit, indefinitely, covers such persons and activities as are described in the licence.

(2) A licence is not assignable or, subject to section 37, transmissible on death or in any other way.

(3) Except in the case of a partnership or an unincorporated body of persons, a standard licence shall not be issued to more than one person.

(4) A standard licence issued to a partnership or an unincorporated body of persons shall be issued in the name of the partnership or body.

(5) The Director may issue a group licence only if it appears to him that the public interest is better served by doing so than by obliging the persons concerned to apply separately for standard licences.

(6) The persons covered by a group licence may be described by general words, whether or not coupled with the exclusion of named persons, or in any other way the Director thinks fit.

(7) The fact that a person is covered by a group licence in respect of certain activities does not prevent a standard licence being issued to him in respect of those activities or any of them.

(8) A group licence issued on the application of any person shall be issued to that person, and general notice shall be given of the issue of any group licence (whether on application or not).

23. (1) Subject to this section, a licence to carry on a business covers all lawful activities done in the course of that business, whether by the licensee or other persons on his behalf.

(2) A licence may limit the activities it covers, whether by authorising the licensee to enter into certain types of agreement only, or in any other way.

(3) A licence covers the canvassing off trade premises of debtor-creditor-supplier agreements or regulated consumer hire agreements only if, and to the extent that, the licence specifically so provides; and such provision shall not be included in a group licence.

(4) Regulations may be made specifying other activities which, if engaged in by or on behalf of the person carrying on a

business, require to be covered by an express term in his licence.

24. A standard licence authorises the licensee to carry on a business under the name or names specified in the licence, but not under any other name.

37. (1) A licence held by one individual terminates if he—

(*a*) dies, or

(*b*) is adjudged bankrupt, or

(*c*) becomes a patient within the meaning of Part VIII of the Mental Health Act 1959.

(2) In relation to a licence held by one individual, or a partnership or other unincorporated body of persons, or a body corporate, regulations may specify other events relating to the licensee on the occurrence of which the licence is to terminate.

(3) Regulations may—

(*a*) provide for the termination of a licence by subsection (1), or under subsection (2), to be deferred for a period not exceeding 12 months, and

(*b*) authorise the business of the licensee to be carried on under the licence by some other person during the period of deferment, subject to such conditions as may be prescribed.

(4) This section does not apply to group licences.

PART IV
Canvassing etc.

48. (1) An individual (the "canvasser") canvasses a regulated agreement off trade premises if he solicits the entry (as debtor or hirer) of another individual (the "consumer") into the agreement by making oral representations to the consumer, or any other individual, during a visit by the canvasser to any place (not excluded by subsection (2)) where the consumer, or that other individual, as the case may be, is, being a visit—

(*a*) carried out for the purpose of making such oral representations to individuals who are at that place, but

(*b*) not carried out in response to a request made on a previous occasion.

(2) A place is excluded from subsection (1) if it is a place where a business is carried on (whether on a permanent or temporary basis) by—

(*a*) the creditor or owner, or

(*b*) a supplier, or

(*c*) the canvasser, or the person whose employee or agent the canvasser is, or

(*d*) the consumer.

49. (1) It is an offence to canvass debtor-creditor agreements off trade premises.

(2) It is also an offence to solicit the entry of an individual (as debtor) into a debtor-creditor agreement during a visit carried out in response to a request made on a previous occasion, where—

(*a*) the request was not in writing signed by or on behalf of the person making it, and

(*b*) if no request for the visit had been made, the soliciting would have constituted the canvassing of a debtor-creditor agreement off trade premises.

(3) Subsections (1) and (2) do not apply to any soliciting for an agreement enabling the debtor to overdraw on a current account of any description kept with the creditor, where—

(*a*) the Director has determined that current accounts of that description kept with the creditor are excluded from subsections (1) and (2), and

(*b*) the debtor already keeps an account with the creditor (whether a current account or not).

(4) A determination under subsection (3)(*a*)—

(*a*) may be made subject to such conditions as the Director thinks fit, and

(*b*) shall be made only where the Director is of opinion that it is not against the interests of debtors.

(5) If soliciting is done in breach of a condition imposed under subsection (4)(*a*), the determination under subsection (3)(*a*) does not apply to it.

50. (1) A person commits an offence who, with a view to financial gain, sends to a minor any document inviting him to—

(*a*) borrow money, or

(*b*) obtain goods on credit or hire, or

(*c*) obtain services on credit, or

(*d*) apply for information or advice on borrowing money or otherwise obtaining credit, or hiring goods.

(2) In proceedings under subsection (1) in respect of the sending of a document to a minor, it is a defence for the person charged

to prove that he did not know, and had no reasonable cause to suspect, that he was a minor.

(3) Where a document is received by a minor at any school or other educational establishment for minors, a person sending it to him at that establishment knowing or suspecting it to be such an establishment shall be taken to have reasonable cause to suspect that he is a minor.

51. (1) It is an offence to give a person a credit-token if he has not asked for it.

(2) To comply with subsection (1) a request must be contained in a document signed by the person making the request, unless the credit-token is a small debtor-creditor-supplier agreement.

(3) Subsection (1) does not apply to the giving of a credit-token to a person—

(*a*) for use under a credit-token agreement already made, or

(*b*) in renewal or replacement of a credit-token previously accepted by him under a credit-token agreement which continues in force, whether or not varied.

52. (1) Regulations may be made—

(*a*) as to the form and content of any document (a "quotation") by which a person who carries on a consumer credit business or consumer hire business, or a business in the course of which he provides credit to individuals secured on land, gives prospective customers information about the terms on which he is prepared to do business;

(*b*) requiring a person carrying on such a business to provide quotations to such persons and in such circumstances as are prescribed.

(2) Regulations under subsection (1)(*a*) may in particular contain provisions relating to quotations such as are set out in relation to advertisements in section 44.

Part V
Entry into Credit or Hire Agreements
Preliminary matters

55. (1) Regulations may require specified information to be disclosed in the prescribed manner to the debtor or hirer before a regulated agreement is made.

(2) A regulated agreement is not properly executed unless regulations under subsection (1) were complied with before the making of the agreement.

APPENDIX IV

Examination Technique

The best way to make certain of success for this examination subject is to plan your examination campaign well in advance and allow yourself plenty of time to cover the course adequately. If through unforeseen circumstances you fall behind in your timetable you must be prepared to spend additional time as soon as possible in order to get back on schedule.

The examination syllabus. The Practice of Banking syllabus is extensive, and a mass of information must be assimilated for use in the examination.

Students must refer to the syllabus which can be obtained from the Institute of Bankers.

PREPARATION

The preparation necessary prior to taking the examination can conveniently be outlined under three main headings:

(*a*) Immediate preparation.
(*b*) Preparation at the bank.
(*c*) Preparation during the study year.

These are discussed below, and students should pay particular attention to these factors, as by their very nature they form the platform for successful examination study.

Immediate preparation. A student cannot expect to pass his examinations unless he obtains the equipment necessary to ensure success. *Prior* to commencing studies, the student should obtain:

(*a*) *A copy of the syllabus for the examination.* This should be studied carefully and a note made of any changes.

(*b*) *Past Examination Papers and Examiners' Reports.* Get as many past years' papers and reports as possible.

On reading the examination papers you should note:

(*i*) The type of question set.
(*ii*) The limited choice of questions available for answering.

(*iii*) That while some questions are repeated (in reasonably similar form) within four to five years, some questions may not be repeated for up to twenty years, some questions are never repeated again.

It is hoped that by seeing how diverse the questions are the student will realise the amount of study which will be necessary.

On reading the examiners' reports you should note:

(*i*) The type of answer required by the examiner.

(*ii*) The type of mistakes most commonly occurring in the examination.

(*c*) *Textbooks for supplementary reading.* While the HANDBOOK is comprehensive, it always pays to read as many books as possible on an examination subject. Consequently, in order to add to basic knowledge, students are advised to obtain several of the books recommended by the Institute.

NOTE: It is strongly suggested that students should spend time in writing answers to old examination questions, working back from the most recent examination paper. These answers should then be checked against both the HANDBOOK and the Examiners' Reports.

Preparation at the bank. Students should make sure of using to the full any facilities which are available at their own branch which will prove helpful for the examination.

Obviously the student who is dealing with securities taken in by the branch is in the most advantageous position for learning. However, even if the student is not based in a securities department, it should still be possible for him to:

(*a*) Examine the account files which are maintained in respect of each borrowing customer.

(*b*) Examine the balance sheets of various types of business concern which maintain accounts at the branch, noting particularly the manager's comments relating thereto.

(*c*) Obtain a copy of every available type of security form for his own records. Study the contents of these forms and examine the reason for the inclusion of every clause.

(*d*) Read his own bank's instructions regarding banking operations and securities.

No student should hesitate to ask his more experienced colleagues to explain or advise on practical points which he cannot understand.

Preparation during the study year. The student should draw up a study plan, taking particular care to allow a substantial amount of time for revision and memorisation purposes during the six weeks prior to the examination. The aim throughout the year should be to study regularly. By *study* is meant:

(*a*) Reading the HANDBOOK and other textbooks with a view to understanding the subject matter.

(*b*) Reading the *Institute Journal* and other professional publications in order to keep up to date with case law, new statute law affecting bankers, changes concerning current practice.

(*c*) Writing answers to past questions under examination conditions, allowing twenty-five minutes per question.

Remember that it is of no use memorising the important sections of law at too early a stage in your study. With the examination in March/April it is far better, until, say, the end of January, to have continual regard to the *understanding of the subject matter* rather than to be concerned with memorisation.

Having thoroughly mastered the subject, memorisation and revision should be attempted over the last one or two months, depending upon the student.

Last-minute learning should not be attempted, but last-minute *memorising of facts* is extremely useful. For instance:

(*a*) In relation to securities: Agricultural mortgages will not be seen at many branches, consequently students may find it difficult to memorise the information and procedure relating thereto for more than a few days. But provided the student has previously read and understood the nature of an Agricultural Mortgage, he can memorise the procedure just prior to the examination.

(*b*) Case-names and details can be more easily remembered over the short period. If the student makes a list of the main cases, with brief details, for each main subject, then with the aid of a partner he can learn names, dates and details within the last fortnight before the examination. (The partner can give the case name and the student recount the details, and then vice versa.)

AT THE EXAMINATION

If the student has mastered and learnt his subject matter and follows the basic rules common to all examinations he should have no difficulty in producing a first-class paper.

The examination approach should be as follows:

(*a*) Read the instructions concerning the examination carefully so that the exact number of questions to be attempted from each section of the paper is known.

(*b*) Read carefully through the whole of the paper, marking the questions which you are going to attempt. Check that you have marked the correct number of questions in that section.

(*c*) Attempt one question from each section first. It is essential to do this because you *may* run out of time and the examination can only be passed if you reach a sufficient standard in each section of the paper.

In relation to each question which you decide to answer:

(*d*) Read the question carefully, bearing in mind the points which you feel deserve special attention.

(*e*) Make a rough note of all the points you wish to bring out in your answer together with the name of any relevant case.

(*f*) Place the points in logical sequence.

Planning. The planning of your answer is most important, and it may be written in essay form or tabulated where you are specifically asked to write in note or letter form. When quoting case details underline the case-name in order to draw the examiner's attention. If you cannot remember the case name quote any details if known.

Reasons should always be given for any statements or decisions given. Where a position is marginal, points for and against a certain course of action should be stated. Remember that nothing annoys an examiner more than a poorly constructed and badly written paper full of crossings-out, spelling mistakes and careless errors.

APPENDIX V

Examination Questions

These are taken from past Part II Practice of Banking examinations and grouped into the usual examination form.

Allow three hours for each test, and answer two questions from each section. Correct Sections A and B against the text and Section C (Balance Sheet questions) against the specimen answers at the end of this appendix.

Sections A and B questions are similar to those now encountered in the Practice of Banking 1 Examination, and Section C questions are similar to some of the questions in Practice of Banking 2 on lending. No questions appear here in connection with that part of the Practice of Banking 2 Examination which is concerned with Banking Services and Marketing.

TEST 1

SECTION A

1. Ambler has two accounts at your branch. No 1 account is overdrawn £2700 against the deposit of shares in a public company; No. 2 account is £800 in credit. There is no letter of set-off. You learn today that dealings in the shares held as security have been suspended. In your clearing are cheques for £700 drawn on the No. 2 account. Ambler has no other security and to your knowledge he has no other assets of any material value.

Discuss whether you would be justified in amalgamating the accounts and returning the cheques unpaid. Give reasons for your conclusions.

2. As manager of your branch you are faced with the situations described below. State how you would deal with them and give your reasons.

(*a*) You receive a telephone call from a firm of jewellers to the effect that someone purporting to be your customer, John Smith, is in the shop and wishes them to accept his cheque for

£200 in payment for a ring. They ask you to confirm that his cheque for this amount would be met on presentation. John Smith is a valued customer, well known to you personally and quite good for the amount.

(*b*) Owing to lack of funds on the account of your customer, John Hay, you have not made payments under his monthly standing orders for the last two months. The owners of the flat in which he lives write to ask you why Hay's rent, normally paid by you under a monthly standing order, has not been received by them for two months. They ask you specifically whether payment has been held up for lack of funds.

(*c*) A wealthy and important customer calls and tells you that he is very concerned about his son, who also has an account with you. He suspects that the young man has fallen into bad company and asks you whether there is any evidence from the son's banking account of overspending and frittering away of capital.

3. Your wealthy customer, Russell, has died in a mental home, which he entered four years ago as a voluntary patient. About two years ago his condition deteriorated and you were advised that he had been certified incapable of managing his own affairs.

For the past five years his son has operated his account under the bank's usual form of authority given by his father. After Russell was certified the account became overdrawn, on the understanding that repayment of the overdraft would be made in due course by realisation of part of Russell's assets.

(*a*) What is the bank's position *vis-à-vis* Russell's executors in respect of drawings made by the son:

(*i*) before Russell was certified;
(*ii*) afterwards?

(*b*) What is the bank's position regarding repayment of the overdraft and the charges accrued thereon?

(*c*) Would you have recommended any other way of handling the account at any stage?

SECTION B

4. A valued customer of long standing, Admiral B, is taking up an appointment in the tropics, and deposits in safe custody with you a locked tin trunk. The trunk is placed in your safe. Two years later he returns, and on opening the trunk he shows you the remains of his wife's fur coats which have disintegrated owing to damage by moth. Discuss the bank's position in the event of a

claim against them by the Admiral.

5. You receive a garnishee order against your customer, Brown, in respect of an unpaid judgment debt of £100. How should you proceed on the assumption that Brown's account was:

(*i*) a current account overdrawn £25;
(*ii*) a current account with a credit balance of £75;
(*iii*) a current account with a credit balance of £350;
(*iv*) a deposit account with a balance of £1500;
(*v*) two current accounts, one £200 in credit and the other overdrawn £240?

6. The name of your customer, Jackson, appears in the accounts of your branch as follows:

Account	*Balance*	*Security*
(*a*) Jackson and Mrs Jackson (his wife) (Joint a/c, either to sign)	Dr £250	Shares value £300, in the name of Jackson
(*b*) Jackson & Jones (grocers) (Partners: Jackson, Jones)	Cr £52	Nil
(*c*) Jackson, Smith & Rolls, trustees of the estate of Smith, deceased	Cr £1,200	Nil
(*d*) Bettatuck Ltd. (confectioners) (Directors: Jackson, Wallace, George)	Dr £2,500	Joint & several guarantee by directors — £3,000; Mortgage, company's premises — £4,500

You receive notice that the partnership of Jackson and Jones has been adjudged bankrupt.

State, with reasons, what action you should take in respect of each account.

SECTION C

7. A. Howard, an employee of a public company banking with you, calls to say that he wishes to transfer his account to you as he feels that it is more sensible to bank with his employer's bankers and he is finding the new manager at his present bank unsympathetic towards his requirements. Over the past two years his promotion within the company has involved him in a wider social life, with

the result that his expenses have overtaken his increases in salary. He has charged a life policy for a nominal sum of £2,500 and a surrender value of £600 to the bank. The original borrowing arrangement two years ago was for an overdraft of £100 but this has risen to £500. He now wishes to buy a new car, and is approaching you rather than his present bankers for the reason mentioned above.

His salary is £2,250 a year, he has two children about to go to private schools and, as well as an outstanding hire purchase commitment on his present car, he has other hire purchase commitments in respect of furniture, a refrigerator, a washing machine and a central heating installation. He tells you that he would prefer to consolidate all his commitments at your branch and wishes to borrow £1,500 from you to clear his present bank borrowing and hire purchase commitments and cover the net cost of the exchange of cars. He is confident that he can repay over three years since this will involve him in an outlay of only £10 a month more than his present commitment for hire purchase repayments. In addition to the life policy, he offers as security a second mortgage over his house, which is valued at £6,500 and is subject to a mortgage of £3,500.

How would you answer his request? Give your reasons and state what advice, if any, you would give to Howard.

8. Beta Products Ltd. manufactures high quality leather products on which there is a good margin of profit.

The company has banked with you since its formation in 1952. With regard to borrowing powers, Table A of the Companies Act, 1948, applies in full.

The balance sheet of the company as at December 31st, 1969, was as under:

	£		£
Capital	20,000	Cash at bank	17,000
Reserves	30,000	Debtors	50,000
Profit and Loss Account	36,500	Stocks	25,000
Creditors	30,000	Land and buildings	15,000
Current taxation	6,000	Plant and machinery	18,500
Future taxation	8,000	Motors	6,500
Proposed dividend	3,000	Furniture and fittings	1,500
	133,500		133,500

You also have the following figures for the year 1969:

	£	
Sales	225,000	(including exports £80,000)
Net profit	10,000	
(after:		
(*a*) depreciation	4,000	
(*b*) tax	8,000	
(*c*) dividends	3,000	
(*d*) directors' remuneration)	8,000	

The company entered the export field two years ago and is confident that it can increase exports by a further £100,000 over the next two years. It is necessary, however, that the factory should be extended within the land area already owned. Planning permission has been obtained for an additional 10,000 square feet of factory floor space.

The directors request you to provide overdraft facilities of £35,000 to finance this extension.

What considerations would you have in mind in dealing with this proposition?

(You are not required to detail the *procedure* for charging any security that you consider it necessary to take.)

9. Mr Badger and Mr Bean have a small business in building paddle boats and similar types of small craft used in children's boating pools, holiday camps, etc. Their partnership's account, which they have had with you for three or four years, has never carried balances of more than a few hundred pounds, but has worked quite smoothly, and you have had no occasion to discuss their affairs with them.

They now call to tell you that they have received a very substantial order from a group of holiday camps. This would mean purchasing materials to the value of £5,000 and they seek facilities from you, to be repaid on payment by the holiday camps. They state that the total order should yield them £10,000, which will be paid on delivery in four months' time. They have only £2,000 in cash available, and seek an overdraft of £3,000.

They are very keen to arrange matters quickly as they think that this order, which is very much higher than any they have had before, is the first step towards bigger things.

Set out the additional information you will require to enable you to consider their request.

TEST 2

SECTION A

1. The Southtown Insurance Co. Ltd., a well-known public company, keeps a substantial account at your branch.

It is the practice of the company to pay all their staff by cheque, and many of the staff have opened accounts with you.

Three years ago the company employed a claims clerk, who opened a banking account with you and has been paying into it his monthly net salary of £84.

In the past 18 months, this clerk has been dealing with claims under lapsed policies that have acquired a surrender value. After completion of the usual formalities, the company issued cheques payable to policy-holders in respect of their surrendered policies, but it now appears that, in eight cases, the original claims had been fraudulently prepared by the clerk, who kept the cheques and then paid them in for the credit of his account at your branch.

The insurance company is claiming from the bank restitution of the amount involved—£1,500.

You ascertain that, in four instances, involving £900, the cheques were paid in at your branch: in three instances, involving £400, they were paid in by credit transfer at a neighbouring branch, and in one instance a cheque for £200 was paid in at another bank for the credit of the account with you. The balance on the clerk's account is *debit* £5.

Discuss the bank's position, with regard to this claim.

2. You have a joint account at your branch, in the name of John Brown and Mary Jones, with a mandate for either to sign.

The balance on the account is in credit (£240) when you receive notice that a receiving order in bankruptcy has been made against Mary Jones.

A cheque for £120, drawn on the joint account, is in the clearing that day, signed by John Brown.

Brown subsequently calls to see you. He wishes to withdraw the balance on the account which, he claims, all belongs to him.

He also wishes to take away a locked deed box which you are holding in the joint names. He tells you that it contains all his personal and private papers.

State, with reasons, how you would deal with:

(*a*) the cheque for £120, in the clearing;
(*b*) the two requests by Brown.

3. (*a*) You learn that Eric Jones, one of the two directors of a small private limited company which banks with you, has been adjudicated bankrupt.

Does this affect the conduct of the company's account with you?

(*b*) Adam Fair is introduced to you by a well-known customer who informs you that Fair, who is an undischarged bankrupt, has been known to him for many years and has now taken up a salaried appointment and wishes to open a banking account with you.

What would be your response to this request?

SECTION B

4. (*a*) Your customer, James Albert, sends his secretary to your bank with a note authorising her to have access to his deed box for the purpose of listing the contents. She extracts certain pieces of jewellery and takes them away. Subsequently Albert, on examining the box, finds these items missing. His secretary has left him and he holds the bank responsible for the missing items.

What is the bank's position?

(*b*) Your customer, Alan James, died last week. You receive a visit from a young man who tells you that he is Richard James your late customer's son, and produces his father's will in which he is named as executor. He asks that a valuable diamond ring which his father left with you in safe custody be given up to him so that he can take it away for probate valuation.

What is your reply?

5. (*a*) Mrs Brixton has kept a modest account at your branch for the past three years. Some 18 months ago she went into business on her own and opened a boutique. She gave the bank, as security for an overdraft, an equitable charge, by way of a memorandum of deposit, over various shares. These were registered in her name, and were valued at £1,500. Blank transfers were signed but not completed.

The venture has failed and the present bank overdraft is £850.

The bank has made formal demand for repayment of the debt and seeks to enforce its security. It now emerges that the shares are held by Mrs Brixton as trustee for her children.

What is the bank's position?

(*b*) You have agreed to an advance to a private customer which is to be secured by a legal charge over freehold property in Stanmore, Middlesex, purchased by the customer in 1960. Set out the procedure for taking the charge and protecting the bank's position.

6. (*a*) You receive notice that a receiving order in bankruptcy has been made against your customer, Micawber, whose account is overdrawn £5,200 against security legally charged by Micawber as follows:

(1) deeds, the value of which you estimate at £4,000;

(2) a life policy, nominal value £5,000 with a surrender value of £600.

What courses of action are available to you?

(*b*) In similar circumstances, you hold as security only a guarantee by Copperfield for £4,500. What action would you take?

SECTION C

7. Engineering Limited was incorporated eight years ago when the account was opened at your branch. The company later ran into trading difficulties and there were substantial losses.

Four years ago, two new directors took over management of the company and since then it has progressed. To assist the company at that time, a limit of £15,000 was made available against the guarantee of the new directors, supported by freehold deeds valued at £10,000.

The following is a summary of balance sheets for the last three years:

	31.12.67	*31.12.68*	*31.12.69*		*31.12.67*	*31.12.68*	*31.12.69*
	£	£	£		£	£	£
Creditors	22,828	21,559	23,276	Debtors	22,853	23,318	36,715
Loans from directors	17,143	15,103	12,153	Stock	3,755	6,376	10,502
Bank	11,480	11,367	16,946	Work-in-Progress	16,185	15,843	15,133
Capital	36,350	36,350	36,350	Plant and machinery	15,109	19,226	20,786
				Profit and loss ac.	29,899	19,616	5,589
	87,801	84,379	88,725		87,801	84,379	88,725

Net Profit	6,150	10,283	14,027
After (*a*) depreciation	3,020	3,370	3,236
(*b*) Directors' remuneration	4,000	5,500	2,900
Sales	84,000	100,000	120,000

The 1970/71 order book is satisfactory and the company now has an order for £80,000. It requires, for twelve months, additional facilities of £15,000 to assist with this contract.

This order is for the supply of components to a first-class company to enable it to complete an export order of £350,000.

Submit this proposal to your control, dealing with all the aspects that you think relevant. With regard to borrowing powers, Table A of the Companies Act 1948, applies in full.

8. Alpha Limited, a manufacturing company, has banked with you for a number of years, during which time it has borrowed, without security, on a temporary basis.

Eighteen months ago it changed over to a new product that has not been successful. In September last, in order to improve the bank's position, a debenture was taken over the assets of the company—the overdraft being then £10,000. Clause 7 of the debenture states:

> "The charge so created is a fixed charge by way of legal mortage on the Company's freehold and leasehold property and fixed plant and machinery. As regards all other premises hereby charged it shall be a floating security."

A Receiver was appointed under the bank's debenture on 2nd April 1970.

Since the debenture was taken, the entries put through the account are summarised as follows:

Dr	*Cr*	*Present Balance*
£8,000	£6,000	£12,000 dr.

The following details regarding the value of assets and the financial position have been sent to you by the Receiver and are to be taken as true values:

	£
Leasehold factory	1,500
Plant and machinery	750
Fixtures and fittings	250
Stock	2,250
Debtors	8,750
Bills receivable	1,150

The creditors are:

	£
Tax, 1966/67	2,250
1967/68	750
1968/69	500
Salaries—office staff for one month	300
Directors' fees not paid	1,000
Directors' loans	4,000
Rates since Oct. last	550
Creditors	13,000

When the debenture was taken, a brother of a director mortgaged a cottage to the bank as additional security. This should realise £1,500 after payment of expenses.

Prepare a statement to show what amount the bank can expect towards repayment of the company's indebtedness.

9. Mr and Mrs Gold are directors of a private limited company operating a newsagents, tobacco and confectionery shop, which they run between them with the aid of one assistant. They purchased the shop some five years ago at an overall cost of £9,000, towards which they contributed £5,000, borrowing £4,000 from your branch against a mortgage over the leasehold shop premises, which include a flat for their own occupation, and against their personal joint and several guarantee. The borrowing has been reduced steadily as arranged at the rate of £800 per annum, and they now have the opportunity to purchase an additional, very similar, business in a neighbouring suburb about two miles away. They seek your help in providing £4,000 towards the purchase price of £9,000 inclusive of stock, fixtures, etc. They assure you that they can clear this borrowing at the rate of £1,000 per annum over four years.

Extracts from the accounts of their existing business are set out below. How would you deal with their request?

	October 1964			October 1965			October 1966		
	£	£	£	£	£	£	£	£	£
Fixed assets									
Lease and goodwill at cost			6,530			6,530			6,530
Fixtures and fittings at cost less depreciation			677			721			681
			7,207			7,251			7,211
Current Assets									
Stock	2,025			1,690			1,528		
Debtors	423			312			388		
Cash	331			10			146		
		2,779			2,012			2,062	
Current Liabilities									
Creditors	1,582			1,598			1,902		
Bank overdraft	—			34			—		
Taxation	310			180			175		
Bank loan	2,400			1,600			800		
		4,292			3,412			2,877	
Liquid deficiency			1,513			1,400			815
Surplus resources			5,694			5,851			6,396
Less Loan by directors			5,405			5,505			6,025
			289			346			371
Capital (authorised £1,000)			100			100			100
Profit and Loss A/c			189			246			271
			289			346			371
Purchases			21,185			20,046			23,896
Sales			24,515			24,021			28,336
Profit (before directors fees, depreciation and taxation)			719			675			1,252
Directors' fees			402			402			1,002

TEST 3

SECTION A

1. George Brown and Arthur Harris, well dressed and well spoken men of around thirty-five years of age, whom you do not know, call to say that they are proposing to open a business in your district, and will be trading as partners in XYZ Enterprises. They produce £200 in cash, which they tell you is the initial capital of £100 each, and ask you to open an account in the name of the partnership, issuing them with a cheque book so that they can make some of the initial payments in connection with the business. They each wish to open private accounts also and produce a further £100 each, which they ask you to credit to these individual accounts. As the setting up of the partnership will involve them in a certain amount of travel in the United Kingdom, they ask you to let them have a bank cheque guarantee card each, so that, should they be held up anywhere in their travels, they will be able to obtain cash without any difficulty.

How would you handle their request? Give reasons for any

actions you may take.

2. Cranshaw Ltd., a private limited company banking with you, is currently the subject of a petition for an order for compulsory winding up. The lease of the premises from which the company operates is in the personal name of Crankshaw, who holds 80 per cent of the shares in the company, the remaining 20 per cent being held by his wife. Crankshaw has only a small personal account with you through which pass modest payments for normal day-to-day outgoings, and to your knowledge he has no material assets.

In an effort to stave off the liquidation of Crankshaw Ltd., Crankshaw is in course of arranging a five-year loan of £6,000 against the security of the lease in his name. He has not disclosed the position of the company to the proposed mortgagees and asks you to reply to an enquiry through their bankers as to his sufficiency for £6,000 over five years. He particularly asks you not to refer to the position of Crankshaw Ltd. in your reply.

State, with reasons, how you would reply to the enquiry.

3. Your customer, Mrs Simpson, a widow, runs a confectioner and tobacconist business and keeps an average balance of £200 credit. On Friday, there are two cheques in the clearing for £200 and £250, payable to cigarette suppliers. If both cheques were paid, the account would be overdrawn by £190.

The cheque for £250 is returned "Refer to drawer—please re-present".

Some seven days later your customer, very annoyed, contacts you regarding the non-payment of the cheque, which has again been returned. It now transpires that, three weeks previously, she paid in a credit for £300 at another branch of your bank in the next town. In reply to your enquiry at that branch, it is confirmed that, although the credit was marked for Mrs Simpson's account at your branch, it had been wrongly posted to an account with them. You see from your ledger, however, that ten days ago a statement had been sent by post to the customer.

Mrs Simpson states that the return of the cheque has damaged her credit and that she will claim damages.

What is the bank's position and what action should it take to deal with these problems?

SECTION B

4. Your customer, the Beta Company Ltd., has an overdraft limit of £8,000 against which you hold the joint and several guaran-

tee of the company's three directors. No security is held in support of the guarantee, and you rely mainly on the standing of one director.

The board has now requested you to increase the overdraft limit to £15,000 so that the company can complete a valuable export order. The directors are prepared to give you additional security by way of a debenture on the terms set out in the bank's usual form of charge.

The company owns no property but operates from premises held, on a short lease, on a trading estate.

What considerations would you have in mind when dealing with this request?

5. Your customer, John Brown, died just over two and a half years ago. The account is now in the names of his executors, who are his son and a married daughter. The mandate is for "either to sign" on the account but, as the daughter has been living abroad since May 1970, all your dealings have been with the son, who has signed all cheques for some considerable time.

Your bank's inspectors recently visited the branch and have indicated that they are not satisfied with the mandate.

What do the inspectors have in mind and what are the different ways in which the position could be brought within their requirements?

6. (*a*) You have granted overdraft facilities to a customer against a guarantee covering all sums due to the bank from time to time up to a limit of £750, the guarantee being drawn subject to one month's notice of determination. Today, with the balance of the account £500 overdrawn, the guarantor advises you that he wishes his liability under the guarantee to cease as from next month. What is your reply?

(*b*) You receive notice of the death of Jones, who guarantees the account of your customer, Robinson. You are relying fully upon the guarantee, which is drawn on the bank's usual form requiring one month's notice of determination from the guarantor or his personal representatives in the event of his death. What action should you take?

SECTION C

7. Your customers, Cannon Electronics Ltd., have been expanding rapidly, having started manufacturing specialised components for the electronic industry some three years ago in a small way, approach you to assist them in purchasing small factory premises

and installing certain items of additional tooling equipment. The cost of the factory will be £10,000 and of the equipment £1,500. The directors can introduce £5,000 themselves and seek the balance of £6,500 from you, offering reductions of £1,500 per annum. The company's balance sheet as at 30th September, 1963, is as set out below:

	£		£
Capital	15,000	Debtors	14,000
Creditors	10,600	Stock	9,000
Bank overdraft	500	Tools, etc.	1,500
		Furniture	100
		Profit and Loss a/c	1,500
	£26,100		£26,100

The directors are calling on you tomorrow to discuss the proposition. What points will you wish to cover at the interview? You are not required to decide whether or not to grant the facilities.

8. Your customers, Speciality Merchants Ltd., who are retailers of domestic durable goods of all kinds, have an overdraft limit of £10,000, which is secured by a mortgage over the freehold warehouse shown in the balance sheet at £5,000, but currently valued at £7,000, and a joint and several guarantee by the two directors for £10,000. The guarantee is supported by life policies with a total surrender value of £6,000. The directors have no other assets apart from their stake in the business and their houses, which are mortgaged elsewhere, and in which there are only modest equities.

Comparative figures extracted from the latest series of balance sheets and accounts are set out opposite, and it will be noted that sales have been falling steadily. In an effort to offset this trend the directors have decided that they must adopt a more vigorous selling policy and sell slightly more expensive goods, at the same time offering credit terms to their customers. This policy will necessitate carrying higher stocks, and, claiming that the figures for the past six months, during which they have been pushing their new policy forward, have shown an increase in sales of approximately 50 per cent, they seek your agreement to an increased overdraft limit of £15,000.

They produce their own draft figures for the past six months—sales £50,000, purchases £35,000 and gross profit £10,500.

How would you deal with their request? Give your reasons, setting out what you can learn from the figures.

SPECIALITY MERCHANTS LTD.
FIGURES AT 28th FEBRUARY 1967, 1968 AND 1969

	1967			1968			1969		
	£	£	£	£	£	£	£	£	£
Fixed Assets									
Fixtures, motors etc.			3,725			3,660			3,635
Freehold warehouse			5,000			5,000			5,000
Leasehold property			2,000			1,600			1,200
			10,725			10,260			9,835
Current Assets									
Stock	18,000			18,500			22,000		
Debtors	700			400			4,000		
Loan to director	—			—			1,800		
		18,700			18,900			27,800	
Current Liabilities									
Creditors	8,000			7,600			14,000		
Bank	6,500			7,000			9,800		
		14,500			14,600			23,800	
Liquid surplus			4,200			4,300			4,000
			14,925			14,560			13,835
Capital			10,000			10,000			10,000
Loan by director			2,725			2,000			1,700
Reserve for tax			100			150			—
Profit and loss account			2,100			2,410			2,135
			14,925			14,560			13,835
Sales			80,000			72,000			65,000
Purchases			54,000			49,000			45,000
Gross profit			16,000			15,500			14,000
Overheads			9,000			8,500			7,795
Depreciation			600			540			480
Directors' remuneration			6,000			6,000			6,000
Net profit			400			460			—
Net loss			—			—			275

9. Your customer, Jupp, runs a small private limited company which assembles electrical control units in rented premises on an annual lease. The business has been built up with generous support from your branch, backed more by your faith in your customer's ability than by any tangible security. Several times recently he has exceeded his overdraft limit of £1,500, but you have allowed this on his assurance that receipts due from debtors would shortly remedy the situation.

Since he appears to be finding it increasingly difficult to keep within his overdraft limit, you ask him to discuss his problems with you. He is convinced that the difficulty is only temporary: his turnover in the past three months was 50 per cent higher than it was in the corresponding period last year, and his order book indicates that his turnover for the next six months will be double that in the corresponding period last year. He expects this trend to continue.

As a result of this expansion he has had to increase his purchases and recruit more staff, but is satisfied that the increased turnover will enable him to improve his position. He asks you to raise his overdraft limit to £3,000 during the next month so that he can satisfy his more pressing creditors, many of whom are small suppliers who cannot give him long credit. He is confident that he will be able to reduce his limit to the original £1,500 after this period.

As security you have a life policy with a nominal value of £2,000 and surrender value of £200, and Jupp's personal guarantee for £1,500. He owns a house valued at £5,000 with an outstanding building society mortgage of £1,500. The latest balance sheet of his company is set out below.

Balance sheet as at 31st December 1965

	£	£	£
Fixed Assets			
Plant, loose tools, etc. (after depreciation)			500
Vehicles (after depreciation)			500
		1,000	
Current Assets			
Stocks			
Raw materials	2,000		
Finished products	2,500		
Debtors	2,500		
		7,000	
Current Liabilities			
Creditors	4,000		
Tax	250		
Bank	1,490		
		5,740	
Liquid surplus			1,260
			£2,260
Capital			1,500
Profit and loss account			760
			£2,260

Examine his request in the light of the facts and figures quoted, setting out any advice you consider he should be given, and giving your answer to his request.

SPECIMEN ANSWERS TO SECTION "C" TEST PAPERS

TEST 1 HOWARD

Howard's request for you to take over his account and provide him with £1,500 to repay his existing commitments must, in this instance, be firmly declined giving the reasons and offering such advice as he is willing to accept. He is obviously living beyond his means and while this may be acceptable in moderation prior to receipts of back-pay, imminent salary increase or expected future funds, e.g. maturing life policy, etc., it is obvious here that he would need a substantial increase in *net salary* in order to repay £1,500 plus interest over three years let alone maintain his children in private schools. The fact that the advance would be fully secured (although a second mortgage is not attractive) does not alter the fact that the proposition is unsatisfactory.

I would ask Howard to substantiate his figure concerning the extra £10 outlay a month. Has he taken into account bank interest? In any case his existing overdraft has risen to £500 over two years; thus he has not made repayments to his present bankers! I would then point out that with a current net salary of somewhere around £150 per month he would have fixed monthly outgoings of about £50/55 on the bank loan, £25/30 (gross on a twenty-five years' Building Society mortgage). What about his life policy premium, rates, food, clothing, social life, upkeep of car and domestic equipment, childrens' schooling, etc.?

I would advise Howard to think seriously before taking on extra commitments. However, if he considered his immediate prospects good and the purchase of another car was essential then it would be more advisable to spread repayments over a longer period by taking a loan on his policy or borrowing on second mortgage, but he would still need to exercise stringent economies in the short-term if his financial position was not to get completely out of hand.

TEST 1 BETA PRODUCTS LTD.

The progress of the company can only be seen by referring to the last few years balance sheets and accounts (probably already in the bank's possession) and also from the present bank balance and monthly max/min figures (which should have usually shown continued improvement if the company is having a profitable year since the last balance sheet date). The amount asked (£35,000) is reasonable in relation to the proprietors' resources (£86,500). The B/S shows that the company is very sound and has traded profitably last year (£10,000 N.P.) and ploughed back profits in the past. Consequently, because of this and also the long-standing connection the bank will wish to grant the facility if satisfactory answers are provided to the following questions:

(1) Has the company traded profitably since the B/S date? We would require up-to-date figures for debtors, creditors, stock. Are the debtors well spread?

(2) Have the directors prepared a capital budget detailing fully the expenditure on the extension? Has a fixed price contract been arranged with a reputable and financially sound builder?

(3) Is any disruption to business likely and has due allowance been made for this? Is the plant and machinery modern and currently under utilised or will additional plant and machinery be required?

(4) The present liquid surplus is healthy at £53,000, but this will be affected by the bank lending and increased turnover. Has a cash flow chart been prepared showing how the extra stock and debtors will be financed? Is it realistic or does it become obvious that additional money is required for working capital purposes?—in which case the bank could lend the latter leaving the company to borrow the £35,000 from an institutional lender and thus deferring repayments over a much longer term.

(5) What increase in profits is expected and what repayment terms are offered? The bank will not wish to lend on too long a term for the purchase of fixed assets. 4/5 years repayment terms to include bank interest would seem reasonable here as in 1969 the cash flow was £14,000 (i.e. net profit + depreciation) and this will increase further as profits increase.

(6) What security is offered? A L/M over the land and buildings, if showing satisfactory value on a gone-concern basis, would be adequate security.

(7) As a substantial proportion of the company's turnover is exported have they obtained E.C.G.D. cover? Where are the markets and what are the usual payment terms? A short term E.C.G.D. bankers guarantee would enable the bank to provide immediate and cheap finance against the exports.

(8) The directors' borrowing powers under Table A are only £20,000, thus to regularise the position, either the proviso in Art.

79 should be deleted, or the reserves capitalised, or a general meeting held to authorise the excess.

TEST 1 BADGER AND BEAN

Little is known of the financial position of B. and B., and therefore, to assess their proposition the bank will require:

(1) Three years' balance sheets and accounts and up-to-date figures to see the progress made, assets employed, proprietors' capital, current liabilities and turnover. (It can then be established whether the bank's stake would be too great and also whether the firm owns its own premises, and if so, the value thereof and suitability as security.)

(2) Details of the contract and estimated profit thereon; extent of penalty for late delivery; other contracts on hand and the likely effect thereon.

(3) A cash budget showing how the £3,000 borrowing figure is arrived at. (Particular note should be taken of whether finance for wages and overheads is mentioned as the £5,000 figure only appears to cover materials!)

(4) To know whether additional staff/machines will be required to facilitate the order and if so whether they are available. Are suitable storage facilities available?

(5) To establish the security available (partnership or personal) as the stock of boats is obviously not suitable. (Remember that the partners are liable to the full extent of their private resources and consequently an enquiry should be made into their personal means.)

(6) To determine whether it would be possible for the boats to be delivered in batches against payment rather than for payment to be delayed until all the boats are completed.

Before the bank would finally commit themselves it would also be necessary to confirm that the holiday camp group is good for payment.

TEST 2 ENGINEERING LTD.

I have been asked by the directors to raise the limit by £15,000 for twelve months making the overall limit £30,000.

The company made substantial losses several years ago. The present directors took over management four years ago and at that time we granted a limit of £15,000 against the guarantee of the directors supported by freehold deeds valued at £10,000. Since then the company has returned to increasing profitability (net profit

£14,027 this year, £6,150 in 1967) although a small overall loss is still shown in the balance sheet. When this is eliminated this year tax will once again become payable. The company's working capital position has improved considerably but the limit has remained to finance the expansion of turnover.

The 1970/1 order book is satisfactory and this additional £15,000 is required to assist with an order for £80,000 for the supply of components to a first-class company to enable it to complete a large export order of £350,000. I have seen the contract terms, which requires delivery in stages against payment, and which I am assured can be met. The directors have produced a cash flow showing estimated monthly receipts/expenditure and I have checked this and agreed their requirement figure.

From the balance sheet date the company has continued to progress and reliable figures have been produced for current assets, liabilities and turnover. The debtors are well spread and reduced from the B/S figure. The bank limit has not been exceeded (only in the company's own books: £16,946). The stock will need to be increased but this has been allowed for. The plant and machinery is modern and there is unutilised capacity. As regards liabilities, no creditors are pressing and the directors have agreed to postpone further repayment of their loans—which were in any case only withdrawn last year against a corresponding reduction in directors' fees.

I suggest that in view of our increased commitment a debenture incorporating a fixed and floating charge should be required to give us adequate margin.

I strongly support this application and should it be sanctioned will (in view of our policy of not relying on the "temporary borrowing" protection in Art. 79) require the company to remove the proviso of Art. 79 Table A so that the £36,350 directors' borrowing limit is removed. NOTE: Premises are leased from the managing director and security of tenure is assured.

TEST 2 ALPHA LTD.

In preparing the statement the application of the following rules is necessary. On the winding-up of a limited company the order of priority against the assets is as follows:

(1) Secured creditors—recoup from their security.
(2) Preferential creditors.
(3) Floating charge security, which may be wholly or partly

avoided under CA 1948, s. 322 if winding up occurs within one year of the charge.

(4) Unsecured creditors.

Thus the bank's *fixed charge* is *fully valid* but as the company is *winding up* within a year the bank's *floating charge is valid either*:

(*i*) *fully,* if the company was *solvent* when the charge was created, *or*

(*ii*) *for moneys advanced at the time of or subsequent to the creation of the charge* and in consideration for it if the company was *insolvent* when the charge was created—i.e. £8,000 being the new debits (the favourable application of Clayton's Case and decisions in re Thomas Mortimer Ltd. (1925) & Re Yeovil Glove Co. Ltd. (1964) have been applied here).

Thus the bank's position depends upon whether the company was solvent (i.e. could meet its current liabilities as they fell due) or insolvent when the floating charge was executed. Unless it was obviously not so the bank would usually prepare its statement on the basis of the company's prior solvency, i.e. as in Statement 1 below.

			STATEMENT 1 *Bank's position presuming floating charge fully valid*		STATEMENT 2 *Bank's position presuming floating charge valid for £8,000*
		£	£		£
Assets available for distribution		14,650	12,000	Amount owing to bank	12,000
Less Bank's fixed charge		*2,250*	*2,250*		*2,250*
Available for pref. crs.		12,400	9,750	amount owing after deducting fixed charge	9,750
Less Pref. crs. Requirements:					
Tax (any 1 year)	2250				
Salaries	300				
Rates	550	*3,100*			
Available for floating charge holder		*9,300*	*9,300*		*8,000*
Bank's shortfall against company			450		1,750
Third party security (available quite separately)			*1,500*		*1,500*
Re 1: Position covered					
Re 2: Dividend on bank's unsecured claim unlikely: final shortfall					250

TEST 2 GOLD (LTD. CO.)

Firstly it must be ascertained from the figures in our possession whether Mr and Mrs Gold are running their present business successfully as otherwise it would be imprudent to lend to finance a similar additional enterprise.

The bank loan has been reduced as agreed but not from trading profits the funds having been diverted from creditors (up by £300) while the stock has been reduced. It may have been deliberate policy as part of astute management to take longer credit (which is still just under one month) and to reduce unsaleable lines of stock, but the customers must be questioned very closely on these points.

It is noted that although profits have been very small they have almost doubled this year on increased turnover of only 16 per cent. Perhaps the customers might be able to convince us and interim figures confirm that we can at last expect better progress. Have the customers now eliminated the most unprofitable lines?

A disturbing point is that the lease valuation includes goodwill. What is the true value of the lease, how long has it to run, and why has it not been depreciated?

The liquid position of the company is still unsatisfactory and the directors have had to put in further loans this year. Would they now be willing to capitalise these or execute a letter of postponement to show that there is no immediate intention to withdraw them immediately the cash flow is improved?

If the bank are convinced in all the above matters then the latest proposition can be examined. The balance sheets and accounts of the business to be purchased should be required to see that a fair price is being paid and to ascertain its profitability. The following questions should be posed to the Golds:

> Are they being professionally advised as to valuation? Is the business run down but with potential? Is the stock of value? Are the premises freehold or leasehold and what is their value? Who will take control and how will this impair the running of their existing business?
>
> Have they allowed for the greater difficulty of control and the increased working capital to be required to cover both businesses? From what source are they contributing the £5,000 (if from their own resources how will this affect both their need to draw more from the company for living purposes and also any future guarantee liability; if from an outside source then what would be the arrangement for servicing?)

Can they produce calculations to support the fact that the two businesses will produce sufficient profits to repay the bank loan + interest in the time suggested?

What security is offered—leasehold premises and new premises and guarantee?

Only after having received the answers to the above questions can the bank reach a reasoned decision.

TEST 3 CANNON ELECTRONICS LTD.

In order to formulate all the necessary questions concerning the business the bank manager will require balance sheets and accounts since the company's inception and also interim figures. A frank discussion must follow concerning the company's prospects and the amount and type of finance required for its expansion. It is presumed that the directors can be regarded as men having good business and technical ability. The following points require elucidation at the interview:

(1) How "specialised" is the product? In an industry showing such rapid change can the company keep abreast and adapt their products accordingly?

(2) Is there a widespread market for their products? What is the turnover? Presumably much of the work is done under contract? Is the expansion in anticipation of demand or is the demand already there? Who are the debtors and are they all good? What length of credit is taken?

(3) Is the company making profits? The B/S figure represents the accumulated loss to date since incorporation. If profits are not yet being made what is the reason?

(4) What is the stock comprised of? It seems high in relation to total assets but how often does it turn over?

(5) What length of credit is taken? Are any creditors pressing? Has the bank overdraft been repaid or is there a limit?

(6) Is the factory to be purchased freehold or leasehold and is it nearby? Is there a firm contract for purchase? What disruption to production will be caused by movement of labour/machinery? How much rent will be saved on the existing premises?

(7) Will the directors introduce the £5,000 as capital or loan money? The latter would be unacceptable to the bank unless repayment was postponed.

(8) Have the directors budgeted for the extra working capital which will be needed to cover stock, work in progress and debtors once the increased production gets under way? The expenditure

on fixed assets will of course reduce the liquid surplus (£11,900 at B/S date) but only by, say, £1,500 + i.e. the amount of the first year's repayment, because in their own eyes the bank will be prepared to regard the remaining loan as a long-term liability.

(9) Have the directors considered taking out a long-term mortgage on the property to be purchased? Would not this seem more sensible in the light of the need to conserve cash in order to aid the rapid expansion of the company? The bank could then lend the working capital required.

(10) If, however, the directors are still adamant that they require this loan then it must be ascertained from the accounts and projected budget whether the company is likely to be able to repay £1,500 p.a. + interest of, say, £600 in the first year or whether it would be better to allow smaller repayments initially. Do the premises provide adequate security and will the directors give a J & S guarantee? Finally are the borrowing powers of the company and directors in order?

TEST 3 SPECIALITY MERCHANTS LTD.

A study of the past accounts reveals several disturbing features which require explanation by the directors.

The company are losing ground and are making insufficient profits to service the existing overdraft let alone an increased one. The sales have fallen by almost 20 per cent over the past three years.

Over the same period the stock has risen against falling purchases. In fact stock now turns over only once every 6 months as compared with once every four months in 1967. It could be that the 1969 year end stock figure was inflated by the initial build up of the more expensive new lines. Likewise the sudden appearance of a large debtors figure could have been connected with the commencement of the new credit selling policy. Confirmation must be obtained on these points.

In view of the company's serious cash shortage the loan of £1,800 to a director (which would appear to contravene the Companies Acts) was untimely. Has this loan now been repaid? Likewise the progressive withdrawal of loan moneys by the director and continued drawing of substantial annual fees makes one wonder whether the directors have the true interests of the company at heart.

The draft figures for the past six months show vast improvement (if correct) in sales and gross profit which if maintained for the year would produce figures of £100,000 and £21,000 respectively. If the overheads and directors' fees remain the same as in 1969 this would leave a net profit of some £7,000 before tax. However, the directors have produced no figures for interim overheads and these are likely to increase with turnover (as they did in 1967) particularly as advertising and credit control expenses are incurred.

The question of the current stock position must be raised as it may include old unsaleable stock which will need to be written off. The lease appears to expire within three years. Can it be renewed on reasonable terms or will a move of premises be necessary bringing extra cost and disruption to business?

The directors must now be asked to produce their cash budget covering expected receipts and expenditure for the next six months and to show how they arrive at the borrowing requirement of £15,000 (which would give the bank a greater stake than the proprietors). This figure looks extremely suspect as the £10,000 limit has hardly proved adequate in that the length of credit taken has increased in the 1969 accounts to 4 months and stood at £14,000. The current position regarding creditors must be sought. Are any pressing for payment?

The additional £5,000 has been requested for buying stock but surely further finance will be required to help pay off creditors and to cover credit sales. When the directors produce interim figures for stock, debtors and creditors and inform us of the credit terms we will be able to calculate the true requirement by checking against the projected cash budget.

As the company has had no experience in selling on credit the directors must be questioned as to their methods of control and the cost to the company. Have the company insured against bad debts?

Finally it must be borne in mind that the bank is owed about £10,000 by the company and will be looking to future trading profits rather than security realisation to recover its money. Only after the meeting with the directors will it be possible to decide on the best course of action which at this stage may well be to advise the directors to continually assess the financial position and to alleviate their current cash difficulties by approaching a finance company to seek stocking finance to be tied up with hire purchase finance for their customers.

TEST 3 JUPP (LTD. CO.)

Although we have backed Mr Jupp in the past because of faith in his ability it is obvious that he has embarked on a programme of rapid expansion without sufficient working capital, i.e. he is overtrading.

The B/S produced shows the position three months ago and by Jupp's own admission turnover is already up 50 per cent and over the next six months will double that for the same period last year. Any increase in turnover requires financing from the company's existing working capital (unless further credit can be taken or debtors pay up faster) until such time as profits through sales are realised in cash. Consequently Jupp's scheme to borrow an additional £1,500 to pay off pressing creditors and to repay this *in one month*, while at the same time continuing to expand his business on insufficient working capital, would appear over-optimistic. He should be asked to produce interim figures for both current liabilities and assets and calculations to show how repayment can be achieved in one month. With these figures in our possession (which may, no doubt, show a worsening liquid position) it will be easy to demonstrate to Jupp that he requires more permanent capital.

When turnover doubles then a corresponding doubling of both current assets and liabilities is likely, and allowing for the fact that the present liquid surplus is completely inadequate due to the fact that it is comprised of stock then the true permanent borrowing figure required from the bank is likely to be £6,000/7,000. This is a figure far beyond that which the bank would agree to as the proprietors' stake is only £2,260.

The question of the annual lease must also be taken up with Jupp. Can a longer lease be obtained at a reasonable price to give greater security of tenure? In any case are the premises suitable and large enough to allow for expansion of business?

Thus Jupp cannot be helped to pay off his pressing creditors unless EITHER he also obtains an additional £4,500/5,500 capital or long-term loan from outside sources to enable him to expand his business at the present rate, or ALTERNATIVELY, he is willing to expand his business far more slowly and within the confines of his limited working capital resources and as agreed with the bank. (Here, the bank may require an embargo for the time being on further expansion before they would increase the limit to a maximum of, say, £2,500.) In either event the bank would need to establish the continuing profitability of the business, agree the repayment term and also take from Jupp a new increased guarantee for £2,500 supported by a second legal mortgage over his house. It should be made quite clear that if he does not adhere to the arrangement the bank will not continue to support him.

Index